T0265924

Wars of Ambition

Wars of Ambition

The United States, Iran, and the Struggle for the Middle East

AFSHON OSTOVAR

OXFORD
UNIVERSITY PRESS

Oxford University Press is a department of the University of Oxford. It furthers
the University's objective of excellence in research, scholarship, and education
by publishing worldwide. Oxford is a registered trade mark of Oxford University
Press in the UK and certain other countries.

Published in the United States of America by Oxford University Press
198 Madison Avenue, New York, NY 10016, United States of America.

© Oxford University Press 2024

CIP data is on file at the Library of Congress

ISBN 978–0–19–094098–0

DOI: 10.1093/oso/9780190940980.001.0001

Printed by Sheridan Books, Inc., United States of America

For my mother—for everything

CONTENTS

PART I

ACKNOWLEDGMENTS

This project has gained from the advice and support of numerous individuals. Over the many years I wrestled with the ideas for this book, as well as when I was writing them down, I benefited from countless conversations with friends, colleagues, and students, as well as from discussions with interlocutors in the Middle East during my travels to the region. Here I would like to list some of those who have either indirectly or directly assisted in this effort. First and foremost, this book would not have happened without the support of David McBride, whose patience, understanding, humor, and encouragement made undertaking it imaginable and completing it possible. Likewise, Mary Funchion and all of the those at Oxford University Press who have helped in the book's development and production are the real unsung heroes in publishing. Beyond that, I would like to thank the anonymous reviewers who provided critical feedback on both the proposal and an initial draft of the book—their thoughtful and constructive criticism vastly improved the final product. Numerous colleagues both at the Naval Postgraduate School and elsewhere across the academy and beyond also provided invaluable insights at various points and encouragement when it was most needed. Listing everyone would kill too many trees, but I'd at least like to thank: Clay Moltz, Maria Rasmussen, Mohammed Hafez, Carter Malkasian, Daniel Byman, Bernard Haykel, Marc Lynch, Frederic Wehrey, Ryan Evans, Aaron Stein, Aaron Rawnsely, Inna Rudolf, Hassan I. Hassan, Fabian Hinz, Sanam Vakil, Assaf Moghadam, Paul Kapur, Feisal Istrabadi, Jamsheed Choksy, Sumit Ganguly, Hussein Banai, Ryan Gingeras, Naazneen Barma, Mike Malley, Chris Darnton, Emily Meierding, Jessica Piombo, Covell Meyskens, Alex Motavski, and Alexandra Sukalo.

I'd be remiss if I did not also express my sincere gratitude to my family—parents, in-laws, siblings, aunts, uncles, and cousins. My aunt Goly, in particular, has been a foundation of loving support my whole life, and to whom I am forever grateful. Finally, I'd like to thank Danny and Michele—my housemates and my world. Writing is a lonely venture and they have made it much less so. Michele also played a direct role in the book's fruition. She produced the maps and index, developed the cover design, and her peerless skills and expertise greatly improved the manuscript. Tsunami, our cat, has just reminded me that she too should not be left out. To her credit, her constant need for attention was an abiding reminder to get out my chair and disengage from the computer. Thank you, Tsusu.

Monterey Peninsula, October 31, 2023

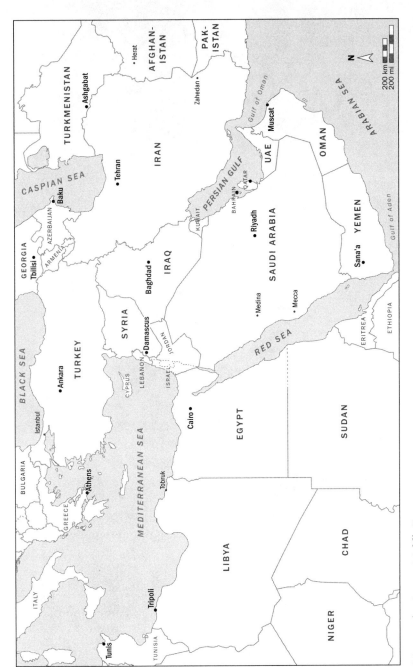

Map 1 The Greater Middle East

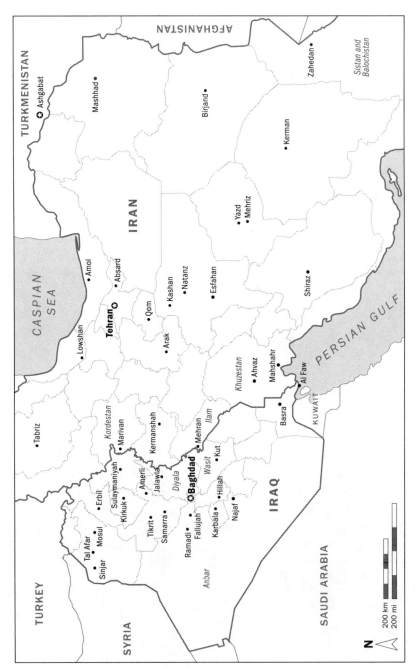

Map 2 Iran and Iraq

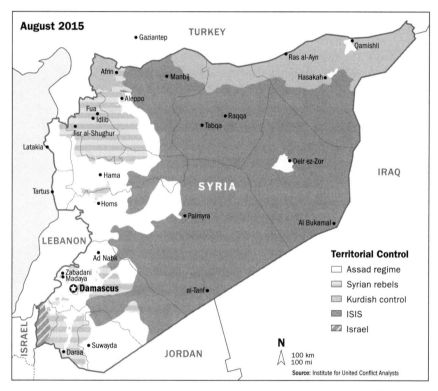

Map 3 The Syrian War in 2015

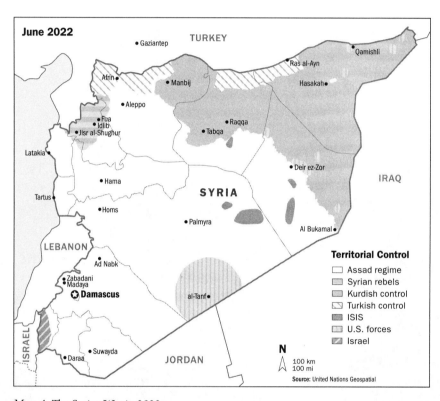

Map 4 The Syrian War in 2022

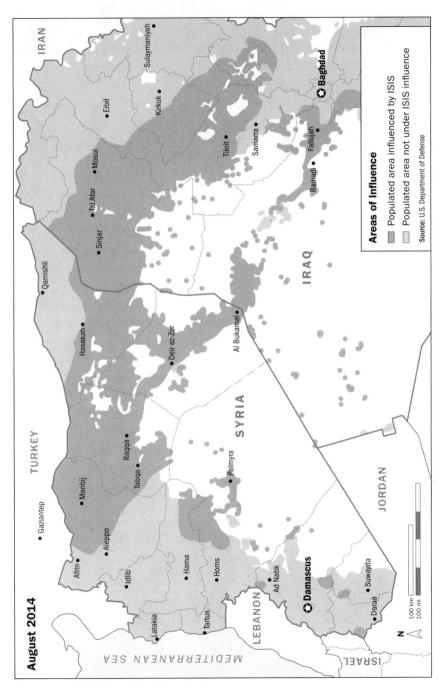

Map 5 ISIS's Territorial Expansion

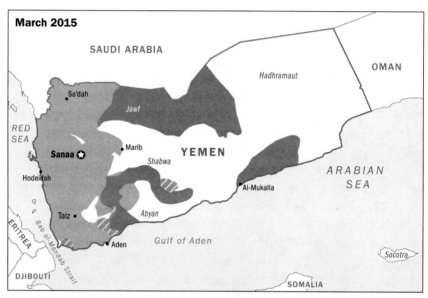

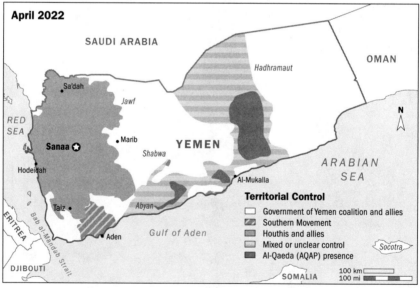

Map 6 The Yemen War

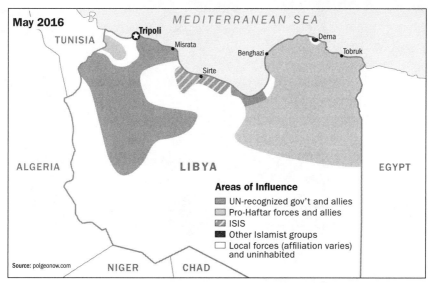

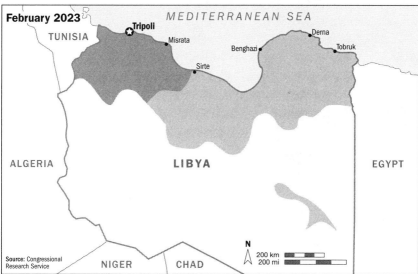

Map 7 Libya's Second Civil War

Introduction

In early September 2022, as Ukrainian troops pressed forward through Russian lines near the eastern city of Kharkiv, they encountered a new weapon deployed by the Russian military. The low-flying object was shot down by Ukrainian forces as it headed toward their position. In the wreckage, they discovered something they had been anticipating for months: an Iranian Shahed-136 drone. American officials had warned that Iran had been delivering loitering munitions to Russia since the summer, and the weapons were finally being used on the battlefield.[1] Within weeks, hundreds of Iranian drones swarmed across Ukrainian skies, overwhelming air defenses and striking critical civilian infrastructure with destructive precision. A dispatch of military specialists from the Islamic Revolutionary Guards Corps (IRGC), Iran's preeminent military force, deployed to occupied Crimea to aid Russian counterparts in drone operations, which also included the use of Shahed-131 and Mohajer-6 variants.[2] With Iran's assistance, Russia concentrated drone attacks against Ukraine's electrical grid, destroying a third of the county's power stations by late October, and dooming millions of Ukrainian civilians to darkness and cold as the freezing temperatures of late fall and winter set in.[3] Iranian officials initially denied supplying weapons to Russia, but Western intelligence services assessed that their provision was part of a deepening strategic pact between Tehran and Moscow. The agreement promised growing trade and military cooperation, and would include Russian transfers of advanced weapons systems and components to Iran in exchange for access to drones, missiles, and knowhow.[4]

The significance of Iran's involvement in Ukraine transcended simply selling arms to a willing buyer: it enunciated Tehran's resolute commitment to challenging Western hegemony when and where it could, and solidified its alignment in the global competition of great powers. Ukraine in this sense was not a country that Iran considered deeply—if it did, Iran's leaders would have found more in common with a small country fighting Russian expansionism than the reverse—rather, Iran viewed Ukraine as another battlefield in the struggle between the American-led global order and those who oppose it. Such a move was unsurprising given Iran's anti-West trajectory since 1979, and a predictable evolution of its relationship with Russia, with which it had partnered in Syria's civil war. Perhaps more than any other state, the Islamic Republic of Iran has been dedicated to countering Western influence and uprooting the United States as the principal outside power in the Middle East. By becoming a combatant in the war on Ukraine, Iran reiterated that position, and expanded its involvement to the battlefields of Eastern Europe. Tehran sought to be a player in the wider struggle between the West and the Eurasian powers of Russia and China, and was willing to risk further alienation by extending a lifeline to the Russian military through its provision of weapons that were being used to amplify the death and suffering of the Ukrainian people. Iran had joined a revanchist state's war of conquest, becoming party to the same type of imperialism its 1979 revolution had rallied against.

Those steps invited deeper levels of scrutiny by Iran's critics in the West, for whom Russia's aggression was considered a grave, if not existential, threat to European security. It also provoked the ire of the beleaguered Ukrainian people and those who supported them. In his December 22 address to a joint session of the U.S. Congress, Ukrainian President Volodymyr Zelenskyy spoke of how Iran's assistance had invigorated Russia's campaign and exacerbated the dire humanitarian situation in his country: "When Russia cannot reach our cities by its artillery, it tries to destroy them with missile attacks. More than that, Russia found an ally in its genocidal policy: Iran. Iranian deadly drones, sent to Russia in hundreds, became a threat to our critical infrastructure. That is how one terrorist has found the other."[5] The United Kingdom's foreign ministry issued a statement that "condemned Iran's decision to supply drones and training to Russia," calling such behavior "further evidence of the role Iran plays in undermining global security." The spokesperson for France's foreign ministry, Anne-Claire Legendre, noted that Iran's drones had been used "in bombardments that were aimed at civilian targets [which] likely constitute war crimes."[6] A joint UK-French statement further labeled Iran's actions a contravention of its obligations under the 2015 nuclear deal.[7] In the eyes of Western officials across Europe and North America, the threat of Iran was no longer limited to the Middle East, or expressed through terrorism abroad. The regime's military power, drones and missiles in particular, had become as worrisome as its nuclear program and support to militant proxies.[8]

That Iran was even able to become a party to the war in Ukraine was revealing of something else: the West's failure to contain Iran as a strategic threat. No country outside of North Korea had been subject to more scrutiny, sanctions, and political pressure by the United States and its allies than the Islamic Republic. Yet, despite decades of efforts to isolate and weaken the Iranian regime, its ambitions never ceased and its resolve never wavered. Instead, Iran looked for ways to do more with less, focusing its investments in areas that would best exploit its enemies' vulnerabilities while navigating the constraints imposed upon it by the West. Through the first quarter of the 21st century, by prioritizing the development of missiles and drones, expanding its proxy network, and distracting the West with its nuclear enrichment program, which served as a lightning rod that insulated its other activities, Iran's approach enabled it to make significant strides in military strength and regional influence. Beyond its persistence, a key to Iran's success has been its leaders' willingness to sacrifice the well-being of their people at home for the empowerment of the regime's aspirations abroad. When it came to the guns versus butter debate, Iran's leadership chose the former at nearly every turn.

Iran's entry into the Russo-Ukrainian war was thus significant for several reasons. However, more than its singular involvement, Iran's support to Russia also marked a consequential step for Middle East powers and highlighted the region's evolving geopolitical orientation. Thinly-veiled partisanship in the conflict set Iran apart, but its desire to oppose the Western consensus on Russia did not. All of the Middle East's leading states, including those considered allies and partners of Washington, hesitated to meaningfully hold Russia accountable or participate in the U.S.-led sanctions regime against it, preferring instead to walk the fine line of neutrality. Their refusal to join the pressure campaign against Moscow was as symptomatic of America's decreasing influence as it was of their desire to exercise independence and move toward nonalignment in global affairs. That desire led regional powers to seek balance in their relations with the United States, China, and Russia, while also adopting more assertive policies closer to home, including through military involvement in third-party conflicts. The region had long been vital to geopolitics because of its location, oil, and wealth, but the potential for Middle East powers to impact extraregional affairs through military means was also growing.

Providing support to Russia was a culmination of Iran's growing power and confidence, both of which had been honed through decades of militarized policies aimed at overturning the Middle East's political order. The U.S. invasion of Iraq in 2003 was a catalyst in that regard. Saddam Hussein's ouster eliminated Iran's main regional counterweight, and made Iraq accessible to Iranian covert and overt influence campaigns. Iraqi expatriate militant groups, who had been living in Iran since the 1980s, returned to their homeland and became Tehran's conduits inside the country. The IRGC also cultivated a cadre of new Iraqi clients and formed lethal militias willing to fight the U.S.-led occupation on Iran's behalf. By the time U.S. forces departed Iraq in 2011, the militants and politicians on Iran's payroll, or susceptible to its coercion, controlled much of the Iraqi state.

The Arab Spring created more instability which Iran steered to its benefit. Iran intervened early in Syria to aid the regime of Bashar al-Assad against the popular revolution swelling against him—a role that expanded considerably with the outbreak of war. The IRGC became a leading element in the fight against the rebellion, and facilitated the involvement of its Lebanese and Iraqi proxies in the war. Qassem Soleimani, the IRGC's mythologized field commander and chief strategist, was also instrumental in encouraging Russia's intervention into Syria in 2015. As the reverberations of the Syrian war began to envelop Iraq through the rise of the Islamic State of Iraq and al-Sham (ISIS), Iran intervened again, this time by the invitation of Baghdad. The IRGC and its Iraqi clients fought ISIS in a campaign that paralleled the U.S.-led intervention in support of the Iraqi government, and expanded their reach into the Iraqi state as a result. The outbreak of civil war in Yemen provided Iran another opportunity to gain from regional strife. Iran provided military aid to the Houthis in their war against the government of Yemen and its backers: Saudi Arabia and the United Arab Emirates (UAE). Iran transferred advanced weapons to the Houthis, giving them the ability to strike Saudi and Emirati territory with drones and missiles, and a coercive edge in the conflict.

Iran pursued those policies as part of its larger objective to remake the Middle East into a bastion of resistance to Western hegemony. However, it was not alone in using intervention and proxies to advance its aims. The region's other leading states exploited conflicts with similar means and for similarly ambitious ends, using the tools at their disposal to push for a political order more in line with their aspirations. Turkey adopted an assertive and militaristic posture toward certain conflicts, directly occupying parts of northern Syria, intervening in Libya and Iraq, and backing Azerbaijan in its battles with Armenia over the Nagorno-Karabakh (Artsakh) region. Ankara's military industry also became a major exporter of drones and other weaponry inside and outside of the region, with over two dozen states having imported Turkish unmanned aerial systems. That list has included Ethiopia, which used the weapons in its devastating conflict in Tigray, as well as Ukraine, Kyrgyzstan, Somalia, and Morocco, with many more interested.[9] Qatar was the leading financial backer of the rebellion in Syria and, alongside Turkey, supported Libya's internationally recognized government in that county's civil war. Saudi Arabia supported rebel militias in Syria, and in 2015 led a military invasion of Yemen in support of the United Nations-backed government's campaign against the Houthis. The UAE oversaw the southern portion of the Saudi-led war in Yemen, where it also developed proxy militias, and intervened in Libya alongside Egypt and Russia in backing Khalifa Haftar's forces against the government in Tripoli. The UAE also established military bases in Somaliland, Libya, and the Yemeni island of Socotra as part of its expanding strategic maritime footprint. For its part, beyond interventions in Syria, Iraq, and Yemen, Iran provided weapons and assistance to the Taliban in Afghanistan, supplied advanced weaponry to Hezbollah in Lebanon and militant factions in Gaza, exported its drones to Russia, Ethiopia, Venezuela, and Sudan, and developed a joint-production drone facility in Tajikistan.[10]

In many ways, this book is about Iran's emergence as a regional power with global ambitions. That rise has come through Iran's aggressive posture toward the United States and its allies and partners in the Middle East, especially Israel—a stance that has mired Iran in conflict. When conceptualizing this project early on, I intended to focus narrowly on the opposing agendas of Iran and the United States. However, the more I pondered and wrote about those dynamics, the more it became clear that their clash could not be discussed adequately in isolation. Iran's quest to upend American supremacy in the Middle East has been inseparable from its campaign against Israel, its rivalry with Saudi Arabia, and the ebb and flow of regional politics writ large. Those adversarial relationships are interwoven into the larger tapestry of social upheaval and strategic competition involving both regional and external powers. Although some actors have been more consistent and dogged in their pursuits than others, all belligerents in the region's conflicts have striven to reshape the political landscape through force. In order to consider Iran's involvement in that competition, I needed to also engage with the broader environment in which the decisions of Iran, its partners, adversaries, and other influential players were made. That expanded the aperture considerably, ultimately encompassing the region's major conflicts in the post– 9/11 era and the sociopolitical convulsions that molded them.

To give the present inquiry some binding, the Middle East—an area of West Asia stretching roughly from Iran to the Mediterranean, and from Turkey to Yemen—is the focus. Sitting at the nexus of Europe, Asia, and Africa, the Middle East's political geography touches numerous regions, is home to primary maritime chokepoints (i.e., the Suez Canal, Bab al-Mandab, and Strait of Hormuz), and possesses vast hydrocarbon deposits. Those characteristics have made the region a significant player in the global economy and a locus of converging foreign interests. When examining issues emanating from the Middle East, it is not always simple to delineate the boundaries of their impact. Yet, because this book can be only so long, certain parameters must be imposed. For that reason, our discussion does not incorporate some important cases that have occurred at the outer confines of the region. The war in Afghanistan is not discussed in any depth because that conflict's center of gravity was more closely linked to rivalries in South Asia. Similarly, other nearby conflicts, such as in Sudan or Nagorno-Karabakh, are not discussed. The latter, despite Turkey's military support to Azerbaijan, and Iran's political backing of Armenia, is more firmly rooted in the legacy of the former Soviet Union than to Middle East affairs. An exception is made for Libya. Libya's post-Qaddafi experience was heavily influenced by the involvement of Middle East powers, Turkey and the UAE in particular, and intersected with their interventions in Syria and Yemen. In that respect, Libya demonstrates how the struggle to remake the wider region transcends the U.S.-Iranian feud. It is therefore an instructive case, and is considered alongside conflicts in Iraq, Syria, Yemen, Lebanon, Israel, and Gaza. The simmering conflict between Iran and Israel, which is driven by the Islamic Republic's aim of destroying Israel as a Jewish entity, fuels the Palestinian crisis, and reverberates across the region and beyond, also features heavily and is the focus of the book's latter section.

Through the ensuing chapters, this book explores the interaction between America's involvement in the Middle East following 9/11, Iran's counter to it, the reverberations that the actions of both generated, and how the U.S.-Iranian showdown became entwined in a much broader, more complicated struggle. That discussion is constructed as a narrative in order to capture the tumult of this period as it unfolded. The complex political environment and its, at times, dizzying pace fashioned the policies of ambitious states, and drove their approaches to strategic competition. The United States and Iran receive the most attention in this story because their opposing campaigns to transform the Middle East have been the most prominent and have fueled the most instability. It is incontrovertible that America's war in Iraq initiated a cycle of destabilization in the Middle East. It is equally inconvertible that Iran's counter-crusade has fueled war and insecurity across the region. Yet, to focus solely on the United States and Iran would be to minimize the impact of the region's other main players: Turkey, Saudi Arabia, Israel, the UAE, and Qatar. The major involvements of those states in regional conflict are an important part of the story and feature herein.

The Arguments

At its core, this book is about the opposing campaigns fought by the United States and Iran to reconfigure the Middle East. More broadly, it is about conflicting visions of the future that both reside in, and transcend, the region's politics. The George W. Bush administration's effort to remake the region served as an opportunity for Iran to advance its own revisionist ambitions. Washington's and Tehran's imaginations for a new regional order could not have been more divergent. Bush hoped to bring liberal democracy to Iraq, and for a democratic Iraq to become a springboard for the spread of democracy to neighboring authoritarian states. The hope was not only to build a region more stable, prosperous, and amenable to Western values, but also more friendly and accepting toward Israel. Iran sought to achieve the opposite—an end to America's dominance and to Israel's existence as a Jewish state. Those had been Iran's goals since the 1979 revolution, and even though it had steadfastly pursued them over the subsequent decades, its progress in the region had largely plateaued by the onset of the 21st century. The Iraq War changed that. Iran exploited that conflict, along with other crises, such as those that followed the Arab Spring, in pursuit of its agenda. The ensuing clashes with the United States, Gulf Arab powers, and Israel disrupted the region and its politics.

The resonances of that fight have been global. What Iran has worked to achieve has run parallel to, and acted in concert with, the much broader revisionist campaigns of Russia and China. In that way, the struggle for the Middle East has been a microcosm of the larger geopolitical battle between those aiming to preserve the American-led global order and those seeking to overturn it—and thus reflective of the politics and dividing lines of an emergent multipolar world.

Beyond that, this book puts forward seven additional, interrelated arguments. First, the rivalry between the United States and Iran both inspired and intersected with a larger struggle for power and influence in the Middle East, and drew in other leading states (Turkey, Saudi Arabia, the UAE, Qatar, and Israel) that pursued their own agendas. How that broad collection of state actors individually and collectively responded to the changing political environment, the policies they enacted outside their borders, and where and how they chose to challenge opponents was integral to the growth, development, and persistence of the region's instability, especially following the Arab Spring.

Second, America's involvement in the Middle East since 9/11 precipitated a decline in its regional influence. The war in Iraq, and the seismism of its post-Baathist politics, led to lasting resentment against the United States from many of its regional partners and allies. Likewise, inconsistent policies toward the Arab Spring and its resulting conflicts further engrained Arab and Turkish dissatisfaction with Washington. Iran's rising power was another significant factor that dragged down America's regional relations. Washington's inability to contain Iran's upward trajectory, and perceived unwillingness to use sufficient force to curb Iran's reach, respond to its attacks, and end its nuclear enrichment and strategic weapons programs made Arab states lose confidence in America and reassess the security benefits of their partnership. Through its evolving defense posture, which progressively prioritized countering China in the Indo-Pacific and Russia in Europe, Washington also contributed to a perception within the region that it was no longer as committed to defending its partners as perhaps it once was.

Third, as American influence slackened, regional powers became more assertive in using military power as an extension of their foreign policies, particularly in reaction to the wars spawned by the Arab Spring. This was, in part, an unintended consequence of Washington's desire for regional partners to take on more of the burden of their security, but also a natural outcome of the growing development of these states and their decades of military investment, which the United States and Europe, as well as Russia and China, fostered through defense sales and cooperation. The net result of regional states becoming more involved in fighting their own battles was an era of intensifying strategic competition. That competition, however, was indecisive, and instead of ending conflicts in the region, it prolonged them.

Fourth, through its aggressive posture aimed at challenging the United States, encircling Israel, and prevailing over its Arab neighbors, Iran's behavior has been more destabilizing than that of other regional states. Iran has played a larger role in more conflicts than any other Middle East power, and its promotion of militant proxies has both fueled turmoil and inhibited political development in several states. Iran has proliferated advanced rockets, missiles, and drones to its proxies, who have in turn used them against neighboring countries. Those weapons have been launched against Israel from Lebanon, Syria, Gaza, Iraq, and Yemen; from Yemen and Iraq against Saudi Arabia and the UAE; and from Iraq and Syria against U.S. and partner forces stationed in both countries. Iran has also used missiles and drones in direct attacks against Saudi Arabia, Iraq, and Syria, as well as against U.S. forces in Iraq. More destabilizing, however, has been Iran's political interference in those foreign countries. The primary mechanisms of Iran's influence are its militant clients. Those armed groups thrive in weak states, and as such, have become impediments to progress and stability in their countries. The Iran-backed Shia militias in Iraq are perhaps the best example of that. They have prospered on insecurity and corruption, and have worked against the advancement of democracy and the routinization of government authority in Iraq whenever it has threatened their autonomy. Hezbollah has acted similarly in Lebanon, as have the Houthis in Yemen and Islamist factions in Gaza.

Fifth, the Islamic Republic of Iran's campaign against Israel is the single most destabilizing conflict in the Middle East, and the one with the greatest potential to cause a broader regional war. The goal of constructing an existential challenge to the State of Israel is the driving motivation behind Iran's involvement in Lebanon, Syria, Gaza, and the West Bank, and also figures prominently in its support to clients in Iraq and Yemen. Iran has aimed to slowly strangle Israel by keeping it mired in a series of increasingly destructive, unwinnable wars through funneling advanced weaponry and financial backing to groups such as Hezbollah, Hamas, and Palestinian Islamic Jihad. That aggression has compelled Israel to pursue a retaliatory campaign. Because of the wide geography where the Iranian-Israeli conflict has played out, and because of the United States' deep commitments to Israel and correspondingly hostile relations with Iran, an outbreak of open war between Iran and Israel could encompass much of the region and draw in U.S. involvement.

Sixth, Iran has outcompeted its rivals in the wars in Syria, Iraq, and Yemen. That has enabled Iran to push the region and its politics closer to its desired ends. However, routinizing those achievements will be difficult. More so than erecting an alternative order, Iran has been most successful at sowing disorder. As such, Iran's advances have been built on unstable ground. The leading threat to Iran's regional influence is not that posed by the militaries of its adversaries, but rather the political development of the countries wherein it is most involved and the constancy of its ruling regime at home. As protest movements in Iraq, Lebanon, and the rebellion in Syria have shown, Iran has failed to cultivate any sort of popular support for either itself or its clients in the countries where it has the strongest footholds. That failure is echoed in Iran, where cascading waves of popular tumult have repeatedly underscored how little the country's citizens, its younger generations in particular, identify with the project of the Islamic Republic and its ideology. Young Iranians increasingly reject the religious bases of the country's ruling system and its revolutionary foreign policy. The needs and will of Iran's citizens are entirely divorced from the regime's foreign policy objectives, which make the continuation of those policies dependent on the survival of the Islamic Republic as a system ruled by the unchecked authority of the supreme leader and the coercive power of the IRGC, whose mutual fixation on Israel and the United States drives Iranian strategic decision-making. The future of Iran's revisionist regional influence is therefore as dependent on the continuation of its ruling regime at home as on the enduring weakness of the states wherein its forces and proxies operate.

Finally, a new order is emerging in the Middle East; but it is neither settled, nor does it neatly conform to the American or Iranian projects. Rather, more than the forging of new loyalties, it has been characterized by a broad shift toward greater independence and nonalignment in geopolitics. In zero-sum terms, this can be viewed as a success for Iran. Even if it is by a relative measure, America's influence has declined with its regional partners and allies, and their foreign policies have become increasingly detached from U.S. interests. That has benefited Iran and suits its objectives. Yet, while the Middle East is moving toward what might be called a post-American era, it is not necessarily moving toward an Iran-centric one. Iran's geographic sway is primarily contingent on its use of non-state clients—armed groups who are strongest when acting as coercive elements and spoilers. It is unlikely that those groups will be able to transform their fractured countries into strong, stable states, much less present a credible alternative bloc attractive to Iran's current competitors. Furthermore, even if their interests are less aligned, retaining strong relations with Washington is likely to remain important for most regional states. America is too powerful and integral to the region's security architecture for regional states to easily abandon it. Even were the United States, in a desire to focus on competition with

China in the Indo-Pacific, to seek a reduction in its commitments in the Middle East, it cannot simply walk away.

As tensions between the United States and Eurasian powers rise, and inch closer toward cold war or confrontation, the Middle East will continue to be a zone of mutual interest, albeit one without firm loyalties. The Middle East's ability to affect global conditions will maintain its attractiveness to both the United States and competing foreign powers. The region's wealth and hydrocarbons alone guarantee it a measure of lasting significance. And the evolving military capacity of Middle East states, most defined by the progressing weapons industries of Iran and Turkey, combined with their willingness to pursue bold strategic policies, has boosted the region's potential for impact. Whether through direct action or indirect support, the region's leaders understand how to influence global affairs, and will seek to make themselves indispensable to external powers to maximize the benefit of those relationships without compromising their sense of independence. At the very least, this suggests that regional states will continue to seek greater balance in their relations with outside powers, and deepen engagement with Russia and China, even if the cost is reduced trust in Washington.

China's outward neutrality in regional affairs and productive relations with rival camps distinguishes it from the United States, and has enabled it to appear as a potential peace-broker. Backed by its extensive economic and political leverage, China's ability to work with all sides could help encourage states, and perhaps even their proxies, to reduce acts of aggression, at least in those circumstances or during such times when the belligerents are acquiescent to Chinese brokerage and incentives. However, maintaining that neutrality will not be easy and could limit the extent of its relationships. In contrast to the United States, China cannot easily take a partisan stance in disputes, or give one side an obvious advantage over the other, without jeopardizing its broader regional aims. China is unlikely to hold regional partners accountable for issues that do not concern its core interests. Moreover, China's laissez-faire approach, which emboldens authoritarians, stifles political development, and turns a blind eye to, if not serves to enable, political oppression and human rights curtailment, could just as easily reinforce the underlying social conditions that have fueled regional unrest, or worsen them. Instead of bringing peace, China might instead preserve an environment in which insecurity, injustice, and unaccountability prevail. Iran's quest to remake the region and the ambitions of other states, such as Turkey, are unlikely to change regardless of China's level of engagement, and could face fewer impediments were China to eventually supplant the United States as the dominant foreign presence in the Middle East.

The Middle East's Elusive Stability

This book is primarily concerned with the actions of states, their leaders, and their non-state proxies. To that extent it is mainly about geopolitics and, to a lesser degree, the sociopolitical movements that shape them. The first quarter of the 21st century has been a turbulent period for the Middle East, and gave rise to many conflicts. Although there is no doubt that the region has been a hotbed of instability, it is important to acknowledge that there is disagreement on why that has been the case, or if the region is even unique in that regard.[11] Geopolitics certainly has been a factor, but other factors, such as the legacy of European imperialism and foreign involvement, the weakness and lack of capacity of its states, and its abundant hydrocarbons, have also contributed to the region's volatility. Further, because the region is composed of middle-tier powers and lacks a natural hegemon who can dominate the neighborhood, its political topography may be conducive to competition.[12] Additional issues, such as reliance on foreign powers, extremism, ethnic and ideational politics, sectarianism, geography, and climate change, can also play a role in how conflicts originate and are fought.[13] All of those factors underlie, to differing extents, the politics of the Middle East and the turmoil they birth. Therefore, even though it is not the purpose of this book to identify primary or root causes, it is worthwhile to briefly note some of the leading explanations for the sources of insecurity in the region.

Perhaps the most familiar explanation, at least in terms of its hold within popular consciousness both in the West and in the Middle East, including among officials and elites, is the lasting imprint of European imperialism and American involvement in the region, especially post–9/11.[14] The case for this often stresses the end of World War I, when European powers carved up the region following the collapse of the Ottoman Empire and, through agreements such as Sykes-Picot and the mandate system, were instrumental in the formation of the modern Middle East. Western involvement continued through the Cold War, wherein the battle between the West and the Soviet Union treated the Global South like a chessboard.[15] As Rashid Khalidi writes: "The Cold War provoked a high degree of polarization, as states and political parties aligned themselves with the two superpowers in virtually every region of the world, exacerbating and aggravating pre-existing local conflicts or producing new ones, and envenoming the political atmosphere in numerous countries."[16] With the end of the Cold War emerged a period in which the United States' regional sway was no longer contested by a peer rival. This opened the doors to assertive American-led interventions, such as the liberation of Kuwait in the first Gulf War and the subsequent sanctions regime and non-fly zone imposed on Iraq. With 9/11, and the invasions of both

Afghanistan and Iraq as part of the broader "Global War on Terror," America's influence became chiefly associated with military conquest and the crises it elicited. The Obama administration's inconsistent response to the Arab Spring, such as its decision to intervene in Libya and hesitance to do so in Syria, has been viewed as similarly problematic. In this line of thinking, America's actions and inactions are often given equal weight—both in their own way responsible for conflict in the region.[17]

A second factor, commonly called the "resource curse," corresponds to the region's abundance of hydrocarbons and how that has influenced its political development. The Middle East is a leading oil-producing region, and possesses 48 percent of the world's proven oil reserves.[18] Those natural resources have endowed the region with great wealth, economic disparities, and challenges. As Michael Ross argues, "petroleum wealth is at the root of many of the Middle East's economic, social, and political ailments—and presents formidable challenges for the region's democratic reforms. . . . These countries suffer from authoritarian rule, violent conflict, and economic disarray *because* they produce oil—and because consumers in oil-importing states buy it from them."[19] The links between oil, instability, and conflict are not always clear-cut, but their interconnectedness has shaped the region's modern history. The reliance on oil has allowed many states to avoid political and industrial development, thereby hindering democratic and economic progress, prolonging kleptocratic authoritarian rule, and tying their economies to the ups and downs of commodities markets.[20] Oil has also made the region critical to the global economy and to the interests of foreign powers. The need to keep oil prices steady and shipments flowing and the capital generated from oil exports have insulated regional states from outside pressure or enabled them to withstand it.[21] Despite this, and contrary to popular imagination, interstate wars for oil are not common.[22] However, the presence of valuable natural resources can increase the risk of interstate conflicts and civil wars, as well as prolong them.[23] This is particularly true in less affluent states with declining economies, wherein fluctuations in the price of oil, or in its domestic production, can have an outsized impact on the economy and spark social upheaval.[24]

An outgrowth of both the resource curse and the legacy of foreign involvement is the prevalence of weak or fragile states, which are terms used to describe states with low levels of capacity, such as in low economic development or in the inability to maintain internal security. Such states can breed unrest, attract and be susceptible to external involvement, become the incubators for conflicts both within and beyond their borders, and lead to massive internal displacement and refugee flows.[25] The perception of weak states as sources of international security threats has at times been overblown and used to drive interventionist policies, but the issue has nonetheless loomed large in the Middle East.[26] Although the region has experienced periods of stability, state weakness featured prominently in the Arab Spring and helped propel the conflicts that followed. As F. Gregory Gause argues:

> There is no question that the Middle East is a mess. The usual explanations for the disarray, however, fail to capture the root cause. Sectarianism, popular discontent with unrepresentative governments, economic failure, and foreign interference are the usual suspects in most analyses, but they are symptoms of the regional crisis, not causes. The weakness, and in some cases collapse, of central authority in so many of the region's states is the real source of its current disorder.[27]

For Gause, the implication of this is the need for the West to encourage strong rulers and functioning governments over more idealistic aims of promoting democracy and human rights in the region. Marc Lynch acknowledges the impact of state weakness in kindling discontent and unrest, but comes to a different conclusion, arguing instead that "[a]utocratic regimes, in their single-minded pursuit of survival, are the root cause of the instability and have fueled the region's extremism and conflicts. The region's autocrats, from Damascus to Riyadh, are the problem and not the solution."[28] There is a tension, then, between the perception of stronger states as inherently stabilizing, particularly within their own borders, and the policies of those states, which can be destabilizing both inside and outside of them.

All of the above are sources of insecurity in the contemporary Middle East. To that extent, they help explain some reasons why peace and stability have seemed unattainable. However, they can only determine so much. What they do not do well is account for the agency of the rulers and military commanders whose decisions create and enact policy. What those in charge do with the hand they are dealt and how they respond to the crises they encounter are important. The Middle East is not a collection of bystanders, nor inescapably bound by geology and history. Rather, the region is dynamic, its states, as well as its non-state actors, possess agency and independence, and their choices have mattered.[29] This is not to absolve the United States, or other outside powers, of the region's morass; they have played a clear part. Nor is it to deny that geology and history influence the region's politics; they certainly have and will. It is to make the case that the collective actions of the region's many parties, in combination with outside forces, have contributed heavily to its fate. The region's states have immense power, and their actions at home and abroad have been a driving force in the region's turbulence.

Competition and Conflict

Competition is a natural part of the Middle East's ecosystem. With none of its leading states having an insurmountable advantage in terms of size or might, they have relied on various formal and informal means, such as diplomacy, investment, trade, client networks, and financial inducements, to influence matters outside their borders.[30] Some of those methods might incentivize the corruption of officials and inhibit political development, but they are not necessarily destabilizing. However, when influence is expressed through coercive means such as funding terrorism, proliferating weapons to non-state militants, spreading extremism, stoking political unrest, and using military force, it is destabilizing.

The prevalence of disruptive policies by regional powers has been underpinned by their strong military spending. Although that spending has fluctuated from year to year, due to factors such as the ups and downs of energy markets, or during global economic downturns, its growth has roughly corresponded with the rise in conflicts and competition in the contemporary Middle East. Simply spending a lot on weapons does not equate to effective military power.[31] For example, while Saudi Arabia has spent far more than any other regional state on its capabilities, its military effectiveness has struggled in Yemen. Similarly, while many Middle East states concentrated on developing air power capabilities through the procurement of advanced American and European aircraft, the utility of air power is limited, and it can be unproductive, if still devastating to civilians, if not paired with well-coordinated operations on the ground. Military spending is therefore not a perfect indicator of effectiveness, or of actual or potential policy. It is, however, useful as a general barometer for a state's relative prioritization of security over time.

To that end, according to data assembled by the Stockholm International Peace Research Institute (SIPRI), and using constant 2021 U.S. dollars, Iran's military expenditure from 2000 through 2010 averaged $18.4 billion annually, with a low of $9.8 billion in 2000 and a high of just over $25 billion in 2006, which came as Iran was escalating its involvement in Iraq and its standoff with the United States. During that time, Israel's annual expenditures averaged $14.7 billion, Saudi Arabia averaged $41.7 billion, and Turkey averaged $10 billion. Through the next decade, as the Arab Spring emerged and regional competition heated up, defense spending increased. From 2011 through 2021, Israel's average annual military expenditures rose to $19.4 billion (with a high of $22.5 billion in 2021), Saudi Arabia's average jumped to $70 billion (with a high of $91.5 billion in 2015), and Turkey's average increased to $13.6 billion (with a high of $18.5 billion in 2019). Iran's spending increase was relatively modest, rising to

$18.9 billion (with a high of $23.4 billion in 2017), and likely was constrained by the impact of economic sanctions. The annual data for both Qatar and the UAE are incomplete, and thus provide a less accurate picture, but given the years reported, Qatar averaged $2.7 billion (with a high of $11.2 billion in 2021) and the UAE averaged $15.2 billion (with a high of $26 billion in 2013) in annual military expenditures across both periods. The above numbers are based on official budgets and other publicly accessible data, and do not account for unreported military spending and related security programs. This is particularly relevant to Iran, whose support to proxies is not reflected in government figures but is a core strategic investment.[32] Clandestine activities are likewise unlikely to be captured in these figures. Nonetheless, the Middle East saw a general growth in military spending through the first two decades of this century.[33]

Robust military spending not only buttresses the region's strategic competition, its imbalance has shaped how states compete. Another angle to the spending figures above is the disparity they reveal between Iran and its chief adversaries: Israel, Saudi Arabia, and to a lesser extent the UAE. Relative to its main competitors, and especially so if you include the United States, Iran can afford to spend much less on defense. That has factored into Iran's approach to grand strategy, and reinforces the regime's reliance on foreign proxies as the basis of its security architecture. Although supporting armed groups abroad is not cheap, it costs Iran less, and perhaps far less, than purchasing expensive military platforms and systems from outside providers. Iran's military development has also been stymied by its foreign policy behavior and the sanctions that it has elicited from the West. Sanctions have undercut Iran's ability to procure advanced foreign-made armaments, leaving Iran's military unbalanced and outdated compared to most of its neighbors. Iran's air fleet, for example, is a legacy of the Cold War, with F-14 Tomcats purchased in the 1970s its most advanced fighter. That might change with the eventual importation of Su-35s or other more advanced aircraft from Russia, but having a refurbished air fleet will not fundamentally alter Iran's approach.[34] Iran has made allowances for its shortcomings, and instead of pursuing parity with its neighbors in terms of air power, has instead invested in ways to circumvent its adversaries' advantages and exploit their weaknesses. Militant proxies have been crucial in that regard; however, of similar and related importance has been Iran's domestic production of missiles and drones. Those industries have allowed Iran to develop and refine its own weapons systems and expertise, and be untethered from foreign suppliers, while spending a fraction of the cost it would take to import such weapons. Along with its proxies, and the top cover afforded by its nuclear program, missiles and drones have become cornerstones of Iran's deterrence framework, its most potent coercive tools, and their proliferation the most problematic aspect of its influence.[35]

Whereas defense spending might provide states with the means to use military power and military-backed coercion in regional competition, they still require reasons and opportunities to do so. The Middle East's long-standing, unsettled imbroglios have been common areas for exploitation. Of these, three significantly intersect with the conflicts and wars considered herein and deserve brief attention: the Palestinian-Israeli conflict, the Kurdish dilemma, and the Iranian nuclear issue. The former is the best known, and continues to churn without much hope for peace. The focal point of the conflict is Israel, the West Bank, and Gaza, but it extends to the Palestinian refugee communities in Lebanon and Syria, has encompassed Jordan and Egypt, and reverberates much more widely.[36] Although the Palestinian cause was at the heart of regional politics for decades following Israel's establishment, it gradually declined as a priority for many states. Arab powers, once the vanguard of opposition to Israel, ceded that position to Iran and its allied proxies—the self-styled "Axis of Resistance." Through its support to rejectionist militant groups—Hamas, Palestinian Islamic Jihad, and Hezbollah in particular—Iran increased the capacity of those groups to inflict carnage, and raised the stakes of Israel's security predicament. Iran's role in the Israeli-Palestinian conflict not only challenged the primacy of Arab states on the issue, it prompted change in their relations with Israel, leading to Israel's de facto rapprochements with Saudi Arabia, Qatar, and Oman, and the normalization of ties with the UAE, Bahrain, Sudan, and Morocco under the Abraham Accords. However, Israel's response to the attacks of October 7, 2023, and its war in Gaza have resurrected sympathies and passions for the Palestinian cause. The issue has always resonated strongly in Muslim societies, and could compel regional states to recalibrate their policies toward both Israel and the Palestinians. As such, the issue remains a delicate one, and a flashpoint for contentious politics and regional unrest.[37]

The Kurdish dilemma is another enduring problem that similarly straddles borders and attracts external involvement. It is an integral security concern for the states in which Kurds reside, has factored prominently in the wars in Iraq and Syria, is a main driver in Turkey's policies toward those conflicts, and is important to Iran's policies as well. The Kurds are the largest stateless ethnic group in the world, and the fourth largest ethnic community in the Middle East. An estimated 30 million Kurds live in a largely contiguous zone spread across four countries in the region: Turkey, Syria, Iraq, and Iran. In each state, they comprise between 10 and 20 percent of the population, as ethnic and, in Iran, religious minorities, primarily residing in geographically peripheral Kurdish-majority regions. Since the fall of the Ottoman Empire, that minority status has fueled Kurdish political movements seeking equal rights and autonomy within their domains. Reactionary political oppression by state governments, who fear losing territory to Kurdish separatists, has fueled armed insurgencies led by Kurdish political organizations and their Peshmerga armed wings. The lines of conflict are not always clear or consistent; and, because of the fractured landscape of Kurdish politics, which is divided by rival factions as well as national borders, Kurdish groups have been primary conduits in the interventionist activities of regional and external powers.[38] Turkey and Iran, for example, have both fought intermittent Kurdish insurgencies within and outside their borders, even as they have backed the Kurdistan Democratic Party (KDP) and the Patriotic Union of Kurdistan (PUK) in Iraq—groups that also have strong relations with the United States, Europe, and Israel. Those seemingly contradictory relationships underlie the complexity of Kurdish transnational politics, and have helped mold conflict in Kurdish zones.[39]

Finally, since its secret enrichment program was revealed in 2002, Iran's nuclear activities have cast a pall over regional politics. Iran has maintained that its nuclear program is intended for civilian purposes, but its past pursuit of nuclear weapons research and other secretive military efforts have caused lingering doubts about its aims.[40] Beginning with the Bush administration, the United States adopted a clear policy toward Iran: it would not be allowed to develop a nuclear weapons capacity. In order to prevent such a scenario, the United States led a sanctions campaign to compel Iran to compromise on its program, and threatened the possibility of military action were Iran to cross an unspecified threshold toward developing a nuclear weapon. The issue was briefly addressed in the 2015 nuclear deal, known as the Joint Coalition Plan of Action (JCPOA); however, that deal was broadly derided by Israel and Arab states, who saw it as a capitulation to Iran and the preservation of an unsustainable status quo. The Trump administration withdrew America's involvement from the JCPOA in 2018, which spurred Iran to advance its enrichment program further, reigniting crisis.

Iran's nuclear program has thus factored into regional politics in two key ways: first, it has been the basis of American foreign policy toward Iran, and has figured prominently in U.S. relations across the region. Second, the issue is a paramount concern for Israel and Arab states, and a factor in the conflict between Israel and Iran. Iran's adversaries see the nuclear program as an intensifier of the Iranian threat, not the cause, and want it to be dealt with in concert with Iran's other forms of aggression, regional activity, and weapons programs. To that end, they have pushed for economic sanctions to remain on Iran, and for the United States to take a more direct military approach toward the issue to either end Iran's enrichment capacity by force or compel a change in Tehran's strategic and regional policies—two things successive administrations in Washington have proved unwilling or unable to do.[41]

Interlaced with those simmering issues have been the clashing agendas of the region's major players. The most active fault line is between Iran and Israel.

The goal of destroying Israel as a Jewish entity is a cornerstone of the Islamic Republic of Iran's regional strategy. That goal is intertwined with its larger pursuit to overturn the regional order, and in service to both ends, Iran has built an extensive network of militant proxies across the region to threaten Israel's security. Israel—the region's only nuclear-armed power—has pursued a wide-ranging counter-effort, which has included military action against Iran's proxies, regular airstrikes against Iranian weapons shipments and military bases in Syria, and a campaign of covert sabotage and assassinations within Iran's borders aimed at degrading its nuclear, missile, and drone industries. The net result has been an undeclared war with no apparent terminus. The October 7 attacks against Israel were, at least in part, a product of Iran's campaign, and pushed the conflict into another, more dangerous stage. Whereas most of the region's conflicts have conceivable end points, the Iranian-Israeli conflict can only end with a reversal of Iran's policies toward Israel, the latter's surrender to Iran, or a definitive defeat of either side in war. A solution to the Palestinian-Israeli crisis agreed upon by all major Palestinian groups could also seemingly lead to an eventual end in hostilities. None of those is a foreseeable eventuality, which suggests that the Iranian-Israeli conflict will be a lasting one, and more likely to lead to episodes of direct military escalation and a furtherance of regional conflagration than not.

Iran has pursued a parallel campaign against Saudi Arabia and the UAE. Iran and its Arab neighbors have differing political systems, ideologies, and aspirations for the region, and have backed opposing sides in a number of crises. But Iran's efforts to overcome its rivals, both through direct force, and through proxies in Syria and Yemen, have proved more effective. Iran's ability to threaten its neighbors' security, and willingness to escalate, prompted a shift in both the Saudi and Emirati approaches toward Iran. Instead of challenging Iran's supremacy, they have turned to contain it by inviting the Chinese to play a larger role in regional diplomacy, and serve as a credible arbiter between both sides. China might succeed in redirecting Iran's attention away from its neighbors, but it is unlikely to change Iran's ambitions. Iran's Arab neighbors are thus stuck in a difficult position. To maintain peace with Iran, they must abide its behavior elsewhere, accept its advancing nuclear program, and tolerate its penchant for coercion. Arab states might choose to go down that path, and if they do, they will redraw the regional order to be one centered on alignment with Iran. Yet, if acceding to Iranian hegemony should remain unattractive, the conditions for recurrent tensions are likely to remain.

Even if their approaches diverge, Arab states and Israel both view Iran as a long-term problem. That shared concern helped push Persian Gulf monarchies and Israel closer together, including through strategic and military cooperation.[42] But as October 7 and the resulting Gaza war evinced, the Arab-Israeli convergence faces serious obstacles. The increasing power of Israel's ultra-conservative far right threatens to complicate its foreign relations. The Palestinian issue resonates strongly in the Arab world and has the potential to interrupt Arab-Israeli interactions. The individual motivations of Israel, Saudi Arabia, and the UAE, as well as their differing appetites for confrontation with Iran, are also unaligned. And while Saudi Arabia and the UAE have been strong allies in the past, Mohammed bin Salman's ambition to make Saudi Arabia the region's foreign business hub, which undermines the position of the UAE, as well as the two states' diverging goals in Yemen, and in foreign policy more broadly, presage an uncertain future.[43] Collectively, those factors are likely to make effective multilateral security cooperation, even regarding Iran, difficult to develop and harder to sustain.

Turkey's forcefulness has at times provoked nearly as much consternation among Arab states and Israel as Iran. Similar to Iran, Turkey seeks a shift in the status quo, one that returns it to the forefront of power in the region. Ankara is also keen to strengthen its energy security, which has motivated assertive behavior in the eastern Mediterranean and Aegean seas. To those ends, Turkey has expanded its military footprint when and where it can, intervening in Syria, Iraq, and Libya, and gaining a presence in the Persian Gulf through basing in Qatar. Ankara's behavior has emphasized independence in foreign policy and a resolute pursuit of core security interests, particularly in countering Kurdish militias associated with the PUK in Syria and Iraq. That approach has strained its relations with the United States, Europe, and much of the region, yet Turkey's utility within the North Atlantic Treaty Organization (NATO) and its willingness to use direct military force to advance its interests have made it impossible to ignore and difficult to restrain. Turkey has also mended fences when it has been expedient to do so, making it appear both erratic and pragmatic in equal measure.

Qatar has pursued a similarly independent agenda, one that straddles the line between neutral party and enabler of the region's extremists. Unlike other Middle East powers, whose competitive efforts are backed by varying degrees of military strength, Qatar's influence is run primarily through diplomacy, media, and above all money. Qatar strives for what could be called a middle path in the region, maintaining strong ties with the United States, Iran, and Islamist groups, while rejecting the more confrontational strategies of its Persian Gulf neighbors. Qatar has been able to exploit regional crises by partnering with groups shunned by its rivals, such as Al-Qaeda-associated jihadists in Syria, and Islamists in Egypt and Libya, and by providing a safe haven for the leaders of groups such as Hamas. That approach increased tensions with Saudi Arabia and the UAE, who led a failed four-year blockade of Qatar between 2017 and 2021 aimed at isolating it and coercing it into abandoning its regional line. Yet, it was that independence, and its diverse relationships, that enabled Qatar to outlast its neighbors and survive the embargo without significant compromise.

Through all of this has been the stewardship of the Middle East's leaders, who have played a definitive role in regional competition. States are not necessarily driven by any intrinsic interests that they might or should have. Rather, a state's policies are at times the fruit of the whims, anxieties, and ambitions of the individuals and cliques who govern them.[44] Such is true for democracies and more so for authoritarian governments, especially in the Middle East, where parliamentary systems and autocracies of various flavors preponderate. Perhaps uncoincidentally, since the war in Iraq began in 2003 and through 2023, the core period under consideration in this book, the region's instability has paralleled the continuity of those in charge. During that span, Iran has had one "supreme" leader, Ali Khamenei; Turkey has had one leader, President Recep Tayyip Erdoğan; and Israel has been led by successive conservative coalitions, with one prime minister, Benjamin Netanyahu, leading government for more than half that time. Similarly, Gulf Arab monarchies have been ruled by the same royal families. Saudi Arabia has had two primary rulers, King Abdullah and King Salman, with the latter's son Mohammed bin Salman (more commonly known as MBS) serving as the de facto head of state since 2015—a role he more formally inherited with his ascension to crown prince in 2017. The UAE has had two rulers during this period, Sheikh Khalifa bin Zayed Al Nahyan, whose presidential duties were reduced in 2014 after suffering a stroke, and his half-brother, Sheikh Mohamed bin Zayed, who assumed day-to-day leadership in 2014 and took formal control of the hereditary presidency in 2022. Qatar has also had two ruling emirs, Sheikh Hamad bin Khalifa Al Thani and his son, Sheikh Tamim, with the latter serving as the country's leader since 2013. With entrenched leaders, parties, and ruling families at the helm, policies have flowed from in-grained interests and perspectives. As Mehran Kamrava puts it, the region's policymakers "pursue security-producing programs that ultimately perpetuate their own insecurity."[45] Put another way, through their aspirations, desire for power, and in response to both actual and perceived threats, the region's leaders have helped fuel the Middle East's instability.

Setting the Scene: The Turbulent Late 20th Century

The conceit about writing history is that, no matter where one begins, it is never the beginning of the story. Something will have come before. This book begins in the wake of 9/11 because that was a pivotal point for the United States, the Middle East, and the world. Most importantly, it led to the invasion and occupation of Iraq, which became the arena of Iran's rise. However, in order to understand why 9/11 and America's war in Iraq were so disruptive, some preceding context is necessary. Here again, an arbitrary point will need to be chosen, and the tumultuous 1970s is a good place to start. In many ways, the turmoil of that period set the fault lines of the region's political seismology for succeeding decades. The major conflicts and political transitions of the latter 20th century continue to reverberate in the 21st century, and a partial overview of those decades can serve as something of a scene-setter for the remainder of the book. To that end, below is a synopsis of some of the major events and conflicts that set the stage for the post–9/11 era. As with any summary, it is a simplified and incomplete picture, but shall provide some necessary context for the reader and give the non-specialist a better sense of how the competitive landscape of the start of the 21st century was formed.

The Lebanese Civil War

Much like the Syrian conflict that erupted during the Arab Spring, Lebanon's 15-year civil war, which stretched from 1975 to 1990, attracted extensive external involvement and had an outsized impact on the Middle East. The country's fractured sectarian system, along with the separation of ruling elites from the underclasses, were dividing lines in the conflict. Lebanon's government divvied up parliamentary seats proportionally among major religious communities based on the state's foundational 1932 census. Even though the country had undergone a dramatic demographic shift over succeeding decades, 51 percent of the parliament remained reserved for Christians, who were no longer a majority, with Sunnis, Shia, and Druze communities sharing respectively smaller proportions of the other half. Wealthy Maronite Christian and Sunni Muslim elites controlled the country, with the government's presidency reserved for a Christian and its prime ministership for a Sunni.

That power-sharing relationship was upset by the introduction of the Palestinian Liberation Organization (PLO), which fled to Lebanon following its failed coup d'état against the Hashemite Kingdom of Jordan and subsequent expulsion from that country in 1971. The PLO brought its war with Israel to Lebanon, which was already home to a sizable and marginalized Palestinian refugee community. The strain broke the country's shaky political scaffolding. Maronite factions sought to purge the PLO from Lebanon to avoid being pulled into a conflict with Israel, whereas their Sunni counterparts backed the Palestinians. By mid-1976, as the country descended into disorder, Syria sent military forces across the border to assist Maronite factions against the PLO. The Syrian regime, led by President Hafez al-Assad, had common cause with the Palestinians against Israel, but backed rival Palestinian factions to that end. The Palestinians were a point of leverage in Syria's enduring conflict with Israel, and particularly in its effort to regain control of the Golan Heights, which had been seized by Israel in the 1967 war. Part of that area, known as Shebaa Farms, was also claimed by Lebanon.

Added to those fracture lines was brewing hostility between the PLO and Shia militants in southern Lebanon. During the 1970s, the Shia community of southern Lebanon had undergone a political awakening. The Shia were the most impoverished religious community in the country, and poorly represented by their absentee landholding elites who resided in Beirut or Paris. That weakness was exploited by the PLO, whose armed factions used southern Lebanon as a base of operations against Israel, and routinely appropriated Shia land for that purpose. The Shia were caught in the middle of the PLO-Israeli conflict, and, as Fouad Ajami explains, the combination of PLO aggression and cross-border fighting led to a "virtual exodus" of Shia "from the south into the ghettoes of Beirut."[46] Under the leadership of the Iranian cleric Musa al-Sadr, who served as something of a community organizer, the Shia began to fight back. In 1975, al-Sadr established the Amal militia to help the southern Shia community defend its territory from the PLO. Al-Sadr appointed Mostafa Chamran, a fellow Iranian activist and American-educated academic, to be Amal's commander. The rivalry between Amal and the PLO became another fissure as the civil war erupted in 1975. Musa al-Sadr's challenge to the PLO was unpopular among the region's supporters of the Palestinian movement, and earned him powerful enemies. After the Iranian cleric traveled to Libya in 1978 at the official invitation of that country's autocratic ruler, Muammar Qaddafi, he was never seen again. The Shia leader's disappearance and probable murder by Libyan authorities further hardened the divide between Amal and Palestinian factions in the war.[47]

Qaddafi was a fierce champion of the PLO and is believed to have ordered al-Sadr's assassination; however, pro-Palestinian Iranian radicals might have also played a role. Revolutionaries from across the globe traveled to Lebanon to join the PLO's struggle. This included Islamist activists from Iran, who had fled political repression at home. While some Iranian activists, such as Mustafa Chamran, linked up with al-Sadr and Amal, others joined ranks with the PLO. Al-Sadr's tensions with the PLO, and potential ambitions, created adversaries among competing Iranian revolutionary camps, particularly with activists associated with the exiled opposition leader Ayatollah Ruhollah Khomeini.[48] Unlike al-Sadr, the Khomeinist faction was invested in backing the PLO. They sought a defeat of Israel and the liberation of Jerusalem, but their immediate sights were set on overthrowing the Iranian monarchy.

Revolution in Iran and the Crises of 1979

Iran's 1979 revolution reconfigured regional dynamics more than any other event. It overturned decades of Western influence in Iran, and thrust the country into a contentious path. Prior to the revolution, Iran was closely allied with the United States, and strongly supported the West in the Cold War. Iran's ruling monarch, Mohammad Reza Shah, had been put on the throne at age 21 after the British and Soviets had deposed his father, Reza Shah, through military force in 1941 due to the elder's neutrality in World War II. The young monarch, who became commonly known as simply "the shah," lacked a constituency and the confidence of his father, who rose to power as a military commander in the Russian-trained Cossack Brigade.

In 1951, the shah was sidelined by the election of an ambitious prime minister, Mohammad Mossadegh, who devoted his office to nationalizing Iran's oil industry, then monopolized by the British under the Anglo-Iranian Oil Company (which later became British Petroleum, or BP). By 1953, Mossadegh's face-off with Britain, who refused to renegotiate terms, raised concerns in Washington under the newly elected government of President Dwight D. Eisenhower. The Eisenhower administration viewed the issue through the prism of the Cold War, and fearing that Mossadegh, a secular nationalist, might turn to the Soviets for help, worked with British intelligence and anti-Mossadegh elites in Iran to engineer the shah's return. The 1953 coup d'état that toppled Mossadegh's government, and placed the prime minister under house arrest for the rest of his life, reversed Iran's political development. It also marked America's entrance into Middle East affairs, where its influence began to eclipse that of Western European imperial powers.

Owing his place on the throne to foreign hands, the shah never felt secure as Iran's monarch. That insecurity grew into fear and paranoia, and drove his repression of critics and political opposition.[49] As Iran's secret police, known as SAVAK, jailed and disappeared suspected dissenters, the shah strove to modernize his country and make it the region's foremost military power. His heavy investments in defense were combined with an assertive regional posture throughout the 1970s. When the British departed the Persian Gulf in 1971, Iran seized control of the strategically located Abu Musa and Tunbs Islands—lands also claimed by the newly established state of the United Arab Emirates (UAE). Iran aided the Kurdish insurgency in Iraq, using that support to compel the Baathist regime in Baghdad to compromise on a border dispute between the two countries, which led to the 1976 Algiers Accord. Iran also sent troops to Oman to help the young Sultan Qaboos bin Said Al Said defeat Soviet-backed rebels in Dhofar. Muscular foreign policy and a rising middle class could not mask over the shah's many failures. Severe political repression had galvanized a diverse opposition movement, which encompassed liberals, leftists, and Islamists, who were united against the Pahlavi throne. Poverty also persisted across the country, and while urban Tehran benefited from Iran's bustling economy, much of the rest of the country suffered from mismanagement and neglect.

Spiraling discontent fueled Iran's revolutionary movement. Across 1978, a cycle of protests, boycotts, and violence grew into revolution. Under President Jimmy Carter, Washington pressured the shah to make concessions to the protestors, including the release of political prisoners. The shah complied, and with the influx of the opposition's most dedicated and radicalized jailed activists, the revolution became unstoppable. The shah left Iran in January 1979, and less than a month later, the revolution's charismatic leader, Ayatollah Ruhollah Khomeini, returned to the country from exile in France. Khomeini held the loyalty of the revolution's most powerful faction—the Islamists—and by the end of the year, they had wrested control of the country from their rivals and established the Islamic Republic of Iran—a Shia theocracy that put Khomeini at the helm as the country's ruling theocrat and "supreme leader."

With the Islamic revolution, Iran transformed from a secular, pro-Western ally in the Cold War to an anti-American crusader. Iran's foreign policy reversed. Unlike Arab states, Iran held positive relations with Israel under the shah. It now became Israel's leading nemesis, and the dream of liberating Jerusalem became the emotional heart of the ruling regime's regional foreign policy. More ambitiously, Khomeini and his acolytes sought to upend the region's pro-Western status quo, which meant purging American political influence from neighboring countries and seeking the destruction of Israel as a Jewish state. When pro-Khomeini students occupied the U.S. embassy in November 1979, taking 52 Americans hostage, the United States broke ties with Iran. Iran had adopted the United States as its archenemy, a stance that would shape its policies and define its place in the world thereafter.

The Iranian revolution was one of several events that made 1979 a turning point in the Middle East. Iran's shift from Western ally to adversary was in part balanced by the end of war between Egypt and Israel. Even as Israel gained an enemy in Iran, it lost one in Egypt with the signing of a peace treaty brokered by President Carter in March. Under the leadership of President Anwar Sadat, Egypt became the first Arab state to recognize Israel. Sadat's historic step toward peaceful coexistence was as brave as it was controversial among other Arab states and within Arab society. It became another source contributing to the rise of Islamist extremism, and led to Sadat's death two years later, when an extremist Egyptian army officer assassinated the Egyptian leader during a military parade.

A strand of that extremism had been incubating in Saudi Arabia, and exploded on the scene in November 1979 when a fringe group within the country's Salafi-Wahhabi community seized the Grand Mosque in Mecca in an armed takeover. The event was unconscionable to the Saudi ruling family, whose control of the country rested on its alliance with puritanical Wahhabi clergy and the enforcement of strict Islamic law. The Grand Mosque takeover exposed the throne's vulnerability to its right flank—opposition to its rule from

Islamists who viewed the Saudis as insufficiently pious and illegitimate, largely due to their engagement with the West. Added to this was the Soviet invasion of Afghanistan, which opened a new zone of competition in the Cold War. Western powers and their partners, particularly Saudi Arabia and Pakistan, rushed to aid anti-communist forces in the resulting conflict. Those forces, known as the Mojahedin, were dominated by Islamist factions whose zeal against the atheistic Soviets would eventually be aimed elsewhere. Saudi Arabia was suddenly presented with three major challenges: the Islamic revolution in Iran, which created an anti-monarchical theocracy that presented itself as a rival leader of the Islamic world; the enduring threat of the Soviet Union and global communism; and Islamic radicalism. The House of Saud's response to those threats focused on spreading its version of intolerant Salafi puritanism across the Muslim world in order to inoculate Muslim communities against both radical religious and secular populisms.[50] Saudi Arabia's rulers also reinstituted austere policies at home, hoping that such a stance would dry up any lingering doubts about their commitment to piety among the country's religious hardliners.

The Iran-Iraq War and Israel's Occupation of Lebanon

All of that receded into the background as Iraq and Iran went to war. Iraq was alarmed by the revolution in neighboring Iran and saw it as a threat to its delicate political geography, wherein members of the Sunni Arab minority, who dominated the governing Baath Party, ruled over a Shia Arab majority perceived as susceptible to Iran's theocratic revolutionism. Khomeini and his inner circle had spent part of their exile in Najaf, and retained close ties to outlawed Shia Islamist groups, such as the Dawa Party, and Shia religious authorities in Iraq. That Iran's new leaders routinely promised to "export" their revolution across the region reinforced Baghdad's concerns. Iraq's president, Saddam Hussein, took aggressive steps to prevent revolution from spreading in his country. He oversaw a crackdown on Shia activists, leading to the arrests, deportations, and murders of civilians, including that of the prominent Shia religious authority Ayatollah Muhammad Baqir al-Sadr, an outspoken supporter of Khomeini and Iran's revolution, and his sister, Amina.

Sensing a growing threat, Saddam sought to hit the fledgling theocracy as it was distracted with post-revolutionary turmoil, and in September 1980 ordered a large-scale military invasion of Iran concentrated on the country's oil-rich southwestern province of Khuzestan. Iranian forces were caught off guard, and their response struggled in the early months. Yet, through tenacity and creative tactics by the regime's newly established military, the IRGC, Iranian forces managed to gradually reverse Iraq's gains and push Iraqi troops across the border by June 1982. Instead of settling for the defeat of Iraqi forces in Iran, Khomeini opted to push into Iraq and seek an end to Saddam's rule, leading to six more years of war.

Iran's counter-invasion of Iraq coincided with Israel's intervention into Lebanon's civil war and its military occupation of the country's south. For Iran's leaders, the two conflicts were part of a larger historical process that promised the inevitable downfall of Israel. Iranian forces were filled with confidence and hubris, believing their fight to be righteous and in line with God's will. Iran's leaders described the war with Iraq as a fight between Islam and evil, between the dispossessed and imperialist elites. The IRGC adopted slogans such as "the road to Jerusalem runs through Karbala," which situated the struggle against Iraq as the first step in the revolution's inexorable diffusion. In this imagining, after the defeat of Saddam would come the ultimate destruction of Israel and the liberation of the Palestinians.[51] To that end, Iran also exploited the situation in Lebanon.

Israel's 1982 invasion was aimed at destroying the PLO's ability to launch cross-border attacks, expelling PLO leadership and militants from the country, and installing a pro-Israel government under President Bachir Gemayel and his Maronite Phalange Party. Given their own struggles with the PLO, Israel's war planners viewed the Shia of the south as natural allies, and for a short period, they were. However, Israel's military effort was undermined by a series of missteps and unconscionable decisions by its minister of defense, Ariel Sharon—the architect of the invasion and future prime minister. Foremost among them was turning over the Sabra and Shatila refugee camps of West Beirut, home to mostly displaced Palestinian and Shia civilians, to the Phalangist militia two days after its leader was assassinated. The Phalangists wanted to exterminate the Palestinian presence in Lebanon, and blamed the Palestinians for Gemayel's murder. The militia was out for revenge, and once inside the camps, they seized the opportunity afforded them by the Israeli military and massacred hundreds, perhaps thousands, of unarmed innocents.[52]

The event helped galvanize resistance to the Israeli military occupation among Lebanese Shia. Building on the shifting political winds, Iran brought together anti-Israel Shia factions from breakaway elements of Amal and those associated with the PLO to create a new Islamist organization: Hezbollah. Trained by the IRGC, and indoctrinated by Iranian revolutionary clergy, Hezbollah became a new front in the war, and a proxy for Iran. When the United States and France sent military forces to Beirut under United Nations peacekeeping auspices to facilitate the departure of the PLO, pro-Iranian militants viewed them as occupiers. Backed by Iranian assistance, Lebanese militants targeted Western forces in a series of operations, including the April 1983 bombing of the U.S. embassy in Beirut, which killed 62 people, and the simultaneous suicide bombings of two military barracks in October, which killed 241 U.S. Marines and 58 French paratroopers, respectively.[53] Hezbollah emerged formally in 1985 as an Islamist organization fully devoted to Iran's revolution and its supreme leader. It became the first foreign client of the IRGC, and established Tehran's foothold in Lebanon.

More so than its actions in Lebanon, Iran's push into Iraq sparked regional anxiety. Neighboring Arab monarchies—Saudi Arabia, Kuwait, the UAE, Qatar, Bahrain, and Oman—already feared the ripple effects of Iran's revolution, and in 1981, had banded together to form the Gulf Cooperation Council (GCC) as a united front against it. With Iran's invasion of Iraq, the revolution appeared to be spreading through brute force, and regional states moved to ensure that Iraq could buffer the threat. Saudi Arabia and Kuwait bankrolled Iraq's war, enabling Baghdad to strengthen its military through the course of the conflict with fresh infusions of advanced French and Soviet weaponry. Through their zeal and naivete, Iran's revolutionary leaders had alienated their country from all major powers and all neighboring states. No state aside from Syria backed Iran in the war, whereas almost all regional and foreign powers supported Iraq. That damaged Iran's war effort in a number of ways, and most crucially, undermined its ability to resupply and improve its military capabilities as the war dragged on. Iran's military had been built on American platforms and systems, which eventually compelled it to make a covert deal with the United States for resupplies. The Reagan administration still hoped to coax Iran's leaders back into more favorable relations, and agreed to provide spare parts to Iran already purchased by the shah through Israeli stockpiles—a convoluted and controversial scheme that was later exposed as the Iran-Contra affair. The gambit did not pay off politically for either side, and ended Washington's short-lived attempt at rapprochement with Tehran.[54]

Unlike the first stage of the war, Iranian forces failed to make meaningful forward progress into Iraq. The IRGC's main tactic was mass infantry assaults, or human wave attacks, a crude maneuver meant to overwhelm Iraqi lines through sheer numbers. That approach turned the tide against Iraqi forces in 1982, but provided diminishing returns thereafter, and resulted in the deaths of hundreds of thousands of Iranian soldiers across the war. By 1984, stalled on the frontlines, the belligerents turned to economic pressure. Iraq targeted Iranian oil installations, and Iran began targeting Iraq's main supporters in the Gulf, primarily through attacks on maritime shipping linked to Kuwait and Saudi Arabia. The United States already backed Iraq politically, and the attacks on oil shipments drew it deeper into the conflict. Even though the pro-Soviet Saddam was not liked or trusted by the Reagan administration, he was viewed as a more palatable alternative to Khomeini. By 1986, the U.S. Navy intervened to protect Kuwaiti shipping during a portion of the conflict known as the Tanker War, which involved both Iraqi and Iranian attacks on oil installations and shipping.

America's naval intervention amplified the pressure on Iran. It also culminated in catastrophe, when the USS *Vincennes* mistakenly shot down Iran Air Flight 655 over the Persian Gulf in July 1988, believing the aircraft to be an incoming Iranian F-14 despite the ship's tracking system indicating otherwise.[55] The tragic accident, which killed 290 Iranian civilians, was viewed in Tehran as a deliberate act meant to message Washington's full commitment to Iraq. Through resupply funded by Saudi Arabia and Kuwait, Iraq's military gained the upper hand toward the end of the war, and by that time, had reversed all of Iran's minor gains. Iran's leaders understood that they had no chance of winning in such a lopsided contest, and in August, agreed to a UN-brokered ceasefire. Khomeini likened the decision to drinking poison, and died a broken man the following June.

End of the Cold War, Dual Containment, and the Rise of Iran's Hardliners

The conclusion of the Iran-Iraq War coincided with the end of the region's other major conflicts. Soviet forces began departing Afghanistan in May 1988 and completed the withdrawal by February 1989, ending almost a decade of fighting. In November of that year, the Lebanese parliament ratified the Taif Accord, which ended the country's 15-year civil war. The agreement gave Muslims equal representation to Christians in Lebanon's denominational system of parliament, and major belligerents agreed to disarm and disband their militias. An exception was made for those militias active in the southern part of the country that continued to resist Israel's military occupation. Hezbollah was among those allowed to keep its heavy weapons. Syria, however, through its own military occupation, maintained dominion over the remainder of the country and managed its politics through clientage and coercion.

Finally, in Yemen, a long-standing divide between the northern and southern parts of the country was coming to an end. The split between north and south Yemen, which resulted in two separate states, had followed the withdrawal of the British from southern enclaves in 1967. The British retreat opened the door for the leaders of the south's Soviet-backed insurgency to establish their own sovereign country, the People's Democratic Republic of Yemen, the Middle East's first and only communist state. North Yemen was governed by the Arab nationalist Yemen Arab Republic (YAR), but competing factions backed by Egypt, Saudi Arabia, and Jordan continued to fight for dominance. By 1978, the north stabilized under the rule of Ali Abdallah Saleh, a colonel in the Yemeni army, who became president of the YAR. Through the 1980s the north and south explored potential reunification, and in May 1990, the two sides agreed to a power-sharing agreement and the establishment of a single government, giving birth to the Republic of Yemen. The honeymoon was short-lived, and southern politicians soon felt that they had lost more through unification than the north had gained. Acrimony led to the outbreak of violence, full secession of the south, and civil war in 1994. The more powerful north won a decisive victory in the fighting, and after seizing the port city of Aden, the southern capital, re-established the Republic of Yemen with Ali Abdallah Saleh as its sole leader.

The Yemeni civil war and the defeat of the south was in part a byproduct of the collapse of the Soviet Union in 1991 and an end of the Cold War. The precipitous decline of the Soviet Union, which followed the end of the failed campaign in Afghanistan, severely weakened pro-Soviet states. That included South Yemen, as well as Iraq, which, after eight years of conflict with Iran, was left with massive debt and a strong, mobilized military. Saddam Hussein expected his neighboring benefactors, who had bankrolled Iraq's war effort, to forgive the loans incurred. From the perspective of Saddam and his inner circle, Iraq had defended Gulf Arab states from Iran's Shia revolution. They contended that had it not been for the sacrifice of Iraqi troops, who died on the frontlines in the tens of thousands, the revolution would have steamrolled across the region. Saudi Arabia forgave Baghdad's debt. Kuwait, however, expected to be repaid the over $14 billion owed, and Saddam would brook no such ingratitude. Instead, Iraqi forces invaded Kuwait in August 1990 and quickly gained control of the small, oil-rich emirate. Were it not for the United States, the Iraqi victory would have led to the full annexation of Kuwait and the absorption of its vast oil resources into a territorially expanded Iraq. However, by mid-January, the United States led a coalition military intervention to liberate Kuwait from occupation. The full weight of the U.S. military was brought against Iraqi forces, who were thoroughly routed within weeks.

The victory was the high-water mark of American military power. After driving Iraqi forces out of Kuwait, President George H. W. Bush had a choice to make: settle for victory or seek an end of Saddam's ruinous reign. Bush chose the former, but also encouraged the Iraqi people to take matters into their own hands and rise up against the dictator who had led their county into two disastrous wars. With the perceived backing of Washington, Shia activists in the south, including Iranian-backed groups, and Kurdish Peshmerga in the north turned against the Baathist state in an uncoordinated, furious, and unsuccessful uprising that lasted into April. Without American military support, however, the Iraqi military was able to put down the unrest. Under United Nations Resolution 688, the United States, France, and Britain established no-fly zones over southern and northern Iraq to prevent further atrocities by the Iraqi military, but it proved insufficient cover for the cultivation of any serious threat against Saddam's rule. The Iraqi opposition, particularly in the south, was crushed by resurgent Baathist forces and embittered by a sense of abandonment by America.[56]

With its defeat in Kuwait, Iraq became a spent force. The United States pursued a strategy of dual containment in the region, seeking to keep both Iran and Iraq from advancing interests beyond their borders. Under heavy sanctions by the United States, and with its military power severely weakened, Iraq slid into economic decline through the 1990s. Iran was also suffering from the destructive war with Iraq, and from its estrangement from the West. Iran's focus turned inward as religious hardliners, who were fiercely loyal to the country's new supreme leader, Ali Khamenei, wanted to enforce more severe Islamic restrictions on society. They contended with reformists who aspired to loosen the constraints on the Iranian people and strike a more pragmatic relationship with the West. Iran was torn by its opposing factions, and its behavior showed the potential of both. The hardliners wanted to continue the revolution's war against Israel and the United States, which meant both policing piety at home, and funding foreign militant groups abroad.

Much of this effort fell under the purview of the IRGC, which, under the rule of Khamenei, was emerging as a pillar of the regime, and gaining an outsized voice in its foreign policy and national security. The IRGC looked for opportunities to expand Iran's influence through supporting militant groups that shared some aspect of their Islamist, anti-American, and anti-Israel ideology. Their greatest success was in Lebanon, where they continued the effort to develop Hezbollah into a powerful military force. The IRGC pursued similar efforts targeting Shia militants in Afghanistan and in the Persian Gulf, albeit with less lasting success.[57] Working with these militant groups, Iran was linked to deadly terrorist attacks, most infamously the 1994 bombing of the Argentine Israelite Mutual Association in Buenos Aires, which killed 88 civilians and injured hundreds more, and the bombing of the Khobar Towers in Dhahran, Saudi Arabia, which killed 19 U.S. Air Force servicemembers and injured nearly 500 civilians. As those attacks evinced, the IRGC's proxy network had extended Iran's ability to strike soft targets of its foes well outside its borders. The IRGC also sought to shape foreign conflicts through direct involvement, notably through its campaign of delivering weapons and providing ground advisors to the Bosnian Muslim Army during the Balkans war. American pressure led to the expulsion of IRGC advisors from Bosnia after 1995 as part of the Dayton Accords, but Iran's involvement in a multinational conflict in Europe presaged its global ambitions.

Those events paired uncomfortably with the election of reformist President Mohammad Khatami in 1997. Khatami was a hopeful figure, who spoke to both the desire for Iran's young people to live in a more open and free society, and for Iran to have better relations with the West. Those same aspirations were deemed as inimical to the revolution by hardliners, who undermined Khatami's attempted reforms at every turn. Khatami was re-elected to a second term in June 2001, but his ability to moderate Iran's foreign and domestic policies was severely curtailed by the regime's unelected centers of power, principally the supreme leader and the IRGC.

Failure of the Oslo Accords, a New Leader in Syria, and Turkey in Transition

The end of the Cold War and regional conflicts also loosened the politics surrounding Israel. Through a series of secret meetings in Oslo, Norway, Israel and the PLO struck historic agreements in 1993 and 1994. The Oslo Accords, as the agreements became known, resulted in the PLO's recognition of Israel and Israel's assent to the right to Palestinian self-determination as a separate state. Also established was the Palestinian Authority, which was given partial administrative governance over Palestinian areas in the West Bank and Gaza. A number of Palestinian militant groups rejected the Oslo Accords, including Gaza-based factions Hamas and Palestinian Islamic Jihad, as did Israel's right-wing Likud Party and extremists within the settler movement. The agreements between the PLO and Israel paved the way for peace between Israel and Jordan, which had been in a formal state of war since Israel's establishment in 1948. The peace deal, signed in October 1994 on the White House lawn by Israeli prime minister Yitzhak Rabin and Jordan's King Hussein, established full diplomatic ties between the two neighbors, with Jordan becoming only the second Arab state after Egypt, and only third Middle East state after Turkey, to recognize and have official ties with Israel.

The peace initiatives exacerbated Israel's political divide, leading to the assassination of Rabin in November 1995 by a Jewish religious extremist, and intensified the competition between the PLO and its rivals. Rabin's murder did not discourage the Clinton administration from moving forward with its ambitious Middle East peace agenda. In July 2000, President Bill Clinton hosted Israeli prime minister Ehud Barak and Palestinian Authority chairman Yasser Arafat at Camp David for talks aimed at achieving a two-state agreement. Despite encouraging signs, including a public handshake between Barak and Arafat, disagreements over the future of Jerusalem, the right of return for Palestinian refugees, and the viability of territory offered to the Palestinians remained insoluble. The talks ended without a deal—a significant setback in the effort toward a two-state solution. With hopes dashed, Israeli-Palestinian tensions heated up, sparking widespread protests in the Palestinian territories and waves of communal and factional violence that triggered a period of unrest known as the Second Intifada.

The intifada awakened a new wave of terrorism in Israel, and ended the sanguine enthusiasm that had followed the Oslo Accords and Israeli-Jordanian peace. Yet, as a new phase of heated violence began, Israel's war in Lebanon was ending. The Israeli occupation of southern Lebanon, which had lasted since its 1982 invasion, abruptly ended in May 2000 with the unilateral withdrawal of Israeli forces. Israel's ally in that occupation had been the Maronite-led Southern Lebanese Army (SLA), which quickly disbanded in the absence of Israeli military support. Syria and Hezbollah were poised to benefit the most from the Israeli retreat. Hezbollah had been a leading opponent of the occupation, and Syria, whose military occupation persisted, remained the de facto authority in the country. Lebanon was still part-and-parcel of Syria's decades-long conflict with Israel, and with negotiations concerning the Golan Heights deadlocked, that cold conflict showed no sign of resolution.[58] The June 2000 death of Syria's longtime leader, Hafez al-Assad, who had ruled the country since 1971, added more uncertainty to the political environment. Bashar al-Assad succeeded his father in July, and many within and outside of Syria viewed the 34-year-old British-trained ophthalmologist as a potential reformer. Bashar was indeed inclined to make some changes to the country's economic policies, and helped thaw relations with neighboring Turkey and Jordan, but his stance regarding Israel echoed that of his father.[59]

By the end of the 1990s, Turkey was also emerging from a tumultuous period. Turkey's government remained dominated by the military, which limited its political development and led to a series of nine short-lived coalition governments during the decade. The country was further hampered by a counterinsurgency campaign against the PKK in southeast Anatolia. The bloody 15-year conflict, which killed over 30,000 people, strained Turkey's economy and foreign relations. Syria supported the PKK through 1998 and the group was able to secure relative safe havens in the Kurdish regions of northern Iraq and northwestern Iran.[60] More significant was how the conflict dragged down Turkey's bid to join the European Union, which despite lobbying by Washington, continued to face obstacles in Brussels. While Ankara considered the PKK a terrorist group, and its military campaign justified to maintain territorial sovereignty, Europe viewed the Kurds as a marginalized ethnic minority, and the conflict an act of oppression by a military-controlled authoritarian government. Turkey's prospects rapidly shifted with Syria's abandonment of the Kurds and the capture of PKK leader Abdullah Öcalan in 1999, which prompted the group to declare a ceasefire. With the insurgency over, perceptions in Europe changed, and Turkey's candidacy to join the EU was accepted months later.[61] Politics were changing in Turkey too. The military's preference for secular Kemalism, which had relegated religion to state control and limited its influence, was gradually losing its hold in Turkish society and was giving way to resurgent forms of religious populism. With the establishment of the Justice and Development Party (AKP) in August 2001, whose religiously imbued platform focused on economic and political reform, Islamist populism was on the verge of eclipsing the secular politics of Turkey's founders.

Dawn of the 21st Century

As the 21st century began, the Middle East was rife with contradictions. Although some long-standing disputes remained unresolved, other signs of reform and change were unfolding. The major belligerents of the 1970s and 1980s had faded by the 1990s. Iraq was exhausted as a regional player and had been severely weakened by a decade of sanctions. Iran was gradually arising from its postwar malaise, but also was stunted by sanctions, isolation, and factionalism. Hezbollah and Hamas had replaced the PLO as the face of resistance to Israel, and of terrorism, even as Al-Qaeda's emergence in East Africa, through the 1998 suicide bombing attacks on U.S. embassies in Tanzania and Kenya, portended something worse. Islamic populism was growing as a social movement, while Islamist extremism was intensifying as a political one. Syria's new president, Bashar al-Assad, brought a modicum of hope to the region, as local and Western leaders sought to encourage the young ruler to adopt a different path than his father. The rest of the region was more firmly committed to partnership with the United States and the West. Pro-Western Arab states, with the slight exception of Yemen, were perceived to be broadly stable and secure. And with its bid to join the European Union, Turkey, already a member of NATO, was advancing toward closer integration with the West. When President George W. Bush took office in January 2001, the Middle East was largely friendly ground, and anti-American states were mostly marginalized and contained. With the Cold War in the rear view, and with no peer competitors, America's influence was strong.

The events of 9/11 altered that seemingly inexorable course. This book explores how that change began and evolved across a span of over two decades. Through the following 16 chapters, divided into four parts, the discussion will examine how the American-led war in Iraq became a springboard for the seismic shifts that followed. Part I focuses on the Bush administration's ambitious policies in the Middle East, to include the war in Iraq and the promotion of democracy in Lebanon and the Palestinian territories. The impact of the war, the contentious politics it inspired, and the opening it presented Iran, which sought to counter America's regional ambitions in pursuit of its own, set the stage for an evolving strategic competition between the Middle East's most powerful players. Part II looks at the wave of populism known as the Arab Spring, which gave birth to wars in Syria, Yemen, and Libya, and with the rise of ISIS, reignited conflict in Iraq. Those wars became the loci of a competition contested by local states, their proxies, and foreign powers. Those conflicts carry into Part III, which highlights how the erratic policies and, at times, isolationist inclinations of the Trump administration led to a further retreat of American influence in the region. That political climate encouraged more assertive and entrepreneurial adventurism by Middle East states, who sought to secure their interests directly, and establish strategic postures untethered from Washington. The fourth and final part, to include the Epilogue, focuses on the conflict between Iran and Israel, how Iran's growing strength invigorated cooperation between Israel and Gulf Arab states, how the slackening of America's influence opened the doors to an expansion of that of China and Russia, and how the attacks of October 7 could reignite another cycle of volatility. This period reveals two divergent paths—one leading toward greater collaboration and interconnectedness, and the other leading to confrontation and war. The concluding chapter returns focus to Iran, reconsiders how Iran's strategy has helped shape the region's emergent new order, and discusses prospects for what might lie ahead.

PART I

2

When the Levee Breaks

For most who remember it, September 11, 2001, began like any other day. I was living in Tucson, a third-year student in Near Eastern Studies at the University of Arizona. When I got to campus that Tuesday morning, I headed straight for the Center of Middle Eastern Studies, which during those days was something like a student lounge for those of us studying the region and its languages. It also had a computer lab with an ethernet connection—a cherished luxury for those such as me still reliant on dodgy dial-up at home. As I walked into the center, I saw a friend from Arabic class having an agitated conversation with the person behind the front desk. I asked what was going on. He turned to me and replied: "It's gone." "What's gone?" I asked. "The World Trade Center!"

The rest of the day is mostly a blur. I must have gone to work at some point, because several months later, I discovered a paycheck in a jacket pocket dated September 11—an experience that stands out because I had been a typical broke undergrad and yet the money evidently had meant nothing in the moment. My clearest memories are of rushing back to my studio apartment and turning on the news. I sat for hours watching the same cycle of images of destruction, death, and heartbreak as everyone else, trying to process what had just happened and failing. At some point I got a call from my mom. She was flying back to the West Coast that morning from a professional conference in Bermuda, but in the day's commotion, I had forgotten all about it. It turned out she had been on a flight from Boston to New York when American Airlines Flight 11—en route from Boston to Los Angeles—had struck the North Tower of the World Trade Center. When her flight touched down in New York, she, like countless others, was thrust into a confusing scene. She saw smoke in the sky but it was unclear what was causing it. While in the airport, and trying to figure out what had happened, she saw televised images of United Airlines Flight 175—also flying from Boston to Los Angeles—striking the South Tower. Nearly 3,000 innocent civilians, including 157 fellow travelers whom my mother may have passed in the corridors of Logan International hours earlier, had been killed that morning in the deadliest terrorist attack in history. She had been fortunate and was merely inconvenienced. It took her a week to get home, linking up with tense, anxious strangers to share rental cars and hotel rooms, all in a desperate effort to get back to loved ones and regain a sense of safety.

The events of 9/11 were a shock to America's system. As it had been for my family, and for millions of others, the event was overwhelming, and had burst a sense of security we had not appreciated, nor generally considered, in our daily lives. As much as the event upset America's psychic and social equilibrium, it portended a much broader geopolitical consequence, and served as a decisive end to the relative optimism that had defined the 1990s. The United States could have responded in any number of ways. Some responses could have resulted in limited actions with limited impact on the nation's trajectory. However, the decisions made by the Bush administration were far more ambitious and consequential to the future of American politics and foreign relations. The attacks radically changed perspectives on the danger of terrorism and its potential to cause mass harm. It was incumbent that the Bush administration take the threat posed by terrorist groups more seriously than its predecessors, and commit America's resources to prevent anything like 9/11 from happening again. The challenge was not in identifying the threat, but how to destroy it. In that regard, the Bush administration deviated from what many at the time, and many more in hindsight, considered a sensible path. That is to say, that while the war in Afghanistan was in keeping with holding those behind 9/11 accountable for the carnage and suffering they had inflicted, the war in Iraq was not. Yet, it was the latter that usurped the administration's focus and irrevocably altered America's course in the Middle East. The buildup to the war, how it forced partners and allies into difficult positions, the acrimony it provoked, and how it disrupted an already fraught region, set the stage for the tumultuous beginning of a new century, and a period defined as much by the American occupation as by how regional states and non-state actors responded to it.

The New Enemy

President George W. Bush learned of an airplane crash at the World Trade Center just prior to joining a second-grade classroom at Emma E. Booker Elementary School in Sarasota, Florida. As he was meeting with the class, Bush was informed by his chief of staff, Andy Card, of another crash, and was told: "America is under attack." As Bush recalls:

> My first reaction was outrage. Someone had dared attack America.
> They were going to pay. Then I looked at the faces of the children in

front of me. I thought about the contrast between the brutality of the attackers and the innocence of the children. Millions like them would soon be counting on me to protect them. I was determined not to let them down.[1]

The attacks were a massive test for Bush, who, still only nine months into his first term, was the first president since Franklin D. Roosevelt to deal with an assault of such magnitude by a foreign enemy on American soil. The American public needed to be reassured, and Bush rose to the occasion, communicating resolve in his speeches while promising action against the culprits and their supporters. Al-Qaeda was responsible for the attacks in New York and Washington, and the Taliban in Afghanistan protected them. The Taliban were international pariahs, infamous for their medieval barbarism and ultra-puritanical rule, which subjugated women and persecuted minorities. By providing Al-Qaeda a safe haven, the Taliban became a target. On September 20, President Bush gave the group an ultimatum: "Deliver to United States authorities all of the leaders of Al Qaeda who hide in your land [or] share their fate."[2] The Taliban refused, and on October 7, the United States went to war in Afghanistan, seeking to destroy Al-Qaeda and remove their protectors from power. The United States was backed by United Nations Security Council resolutions and NATO, with a coalition of Western allies—Britain, Canada, France, Australia, and Germany—directly aiding the military campaign. Forty other countries also participated in the war, most by allowing the U.S. military to use their airspace or airbases for the transportation of troops and materiel into the theater. The Taliban had no outside support. Only Pakistan, Saudi Arabia, and the United Arab Emirates recognized the Islamist group as the legitimate government of Afghanistan, and none would defend it from America.

When Bush announced the launch of military action in Afghanistan, code-named "Operation Enduring Freedom," he also signaled the start of a broader campaign:

> Today we focus on Afghanistan, but the battle is broader. Every nation has a choice to make. In this conflict, there is no neutral ground. If any government sponsors the outlaws and killers of innocents, they have become outlaws and murderers themselves. And they will take that lonely path at their own peril.[3]

Such was an early indication that America's response to 9/11 would not end with Al-Qaeda or the Taliban. The Bush administration took the attacks as the opening salvo in a renewed struggle between the forces of democracy and the enemies of freedom. With the Cold War barely a decade past, the West had a new nemesis. Any country that stood in the way, or was perceived to be in league with terrorists, could be in America's crosshairs. The Bush doctrine, as it was soon called, rested on a simple maxim: "If you're not with us, you're against us."[4]

Iran's Predicament

Leaders in the Middle East, and across the globe, took notice. The Islamic Republic of Iran, in particular, was in a delicate position. Iran was already listed as a state supporter of terrorism due to its connection to mass casualty attacks, such as the 1983 bombings of the U.S. embassy and Marine Corps barracks in Beirut and the 1996 Khobar Towers bombing in Saudi Arabia. Those incidents, and Iran's continued support for organizations such as the Lebanese Hezbollah, had made Iran's ruling regime synonymous with terrorism, especially in the minds of Washington lawmakers. Since taking office in 1997, Iran's reformist president, Mohammad Khatami, had tried to steer Iran's reputation in the opposite direction, and improve relations with the West by fostering a number of bilateral exchanges with the United States involving sports, cinema, and academia. Yet, despite a relative decline in tensions, Iran's ruling theocrat and supreme leader, Ali Khamenei, who set the parameters for Iranian policy, maintained a hostile line toward America.

The war in Afghanistan occurred in that context, and was as much a threat to Iran as an opportunity. The Taliban and Iran were adversaries. Iran had extensive links to the Afghan opposition, and the Taliban's brand of puritanical Sunnism, which was imbued with sectarian bigotry, clashed with Iran's governing system of Shia theocracy. The two sides had almost gone to war in 1998 after the Taliban seized Iran's consulate in Mazar-e Sharif and executed its diplomats. Iran's support for the Northern Alliance—the coalition of anti-Taliban forces that retained a hold in parts of Afghanistan's north—put it nominally on the same side as the United States. The Taliban were no friend of Iran, but neither was the United States, which had remained the Islamic Republic's foremost adversary. The prospect of a U.S. military buildup in neighboring Afghanistan was a potential threat to Iran's ruling regime, and was a pressing concern for its leaders.

Washington and Tehran had coalescing interests in Afghanistan as well. They both sought an end to the Taliban's rule, backed the same opposition forces that were likely to succeed it, and wanted to bring a measure of stability to the country. Iranian authorities pursued ways to ameliorate the situation, and an already ongoing, low-level diplomatic effort under the auspices of the United Nations, and organized by Germany and Italy, emerged as the forum where Iran was able to bring its concerns to American officials. That engagement led to a series of low-profile meetings between Iranian and U.S. diplomats. Washington was represented by Ryan Crocker, a veteran foreign service officer with extensive experience in the Middle East, and the newly appointed deputy assistant secretary for Near Eastern Affairs at the Department of State. Iran's delegation included its ambassador to Tajikistan, who had close ties to the IRGC and served as the regime's point man with the Northern Alliance. Through multilateral exchanges involving the Germans and Italians, and informal bilateral conversations, Crocker and his Iranian counterparts discussed a broad range of issues, including mutual concerns in Afghanistan and its possible post-Taliban future. Early on, the Iranians conveyed to Crocker that attitudes among regime leadership in Tehran regarding the United States were evolving beyond hostility and toward a more pragmatic stance, one that was open to a thaw in relations. They also expressed a willingness to support the Bush administration's effort to oust the Taliban. To that end, about a week before the war began, the Iranians provided Crocker with maps detailing their intelligence on Taliban positions, advice on where to strike them, and how they might respond.[5] Iran also offered the use of Iranian airbases, and pledged to support air-and-rescue operations for American pilots who might have to bail out over Iranian airspace.[6]

Iran was hedging its bets. Given the tenor of the Bush administration's rhetoric following 9/11, and the dramatic impact those attacks were likely to have on American foreign policy and decision-making in the Middle East, Iran was seeking ways to mollify its main foe and stay out the crosshairs. By offering assistance in the war in Afghanistan, Iran was also seeking to make the most out of a difficult situation. The United States was certain to invade Afghanistan, and Iran could either impede that effort, which would favor the Taliban, or it could offer to assist in America's primary objectives—overthrowing the Taliban and empowering the Northern Alliance—perhaps with the hope that a swift American victory would shorten the length of a subsequent military occupation. The reformists in the Khatami government were also keen to find pathways toward improving bilateral relations with Washington, and the mutual concerns in Afghanistan were a natural opportunity. The optimism was not shared by Iran's unelected authorities, with both the supreme leader and the IRGC's top brass hesitant to make any significant policy changes to placate the Americans. Power in the regime rested with those unelected institutions, and neither trusted the United States.[7]

Washington's engagement with Iran was cordial, but the Bush administration rebuffed Iran's major proposals. White House officials did not trust Iran's intentions, and the latter's offers of limited assistance were also deemed unnecessary for the war. The start of Operation Enduring Freedom was relatively quick and succeeded in most areas. The bombing campaign began on October

7, and by mid-December, the Taliban had been thoroughly defeated across the country. Where the campaign had failed was in capturing Osama Bin Laden and Al-Qaeda's leadership, most of whom had escaped across the country's eastern mountainous border to Pakistan. With the Taliban's fall all but complete, the United Nations sponsored a conference in Bonn, Germany, in early December, which brought together all major non-Taliban factions of Afghanistan and participating states to hash out a new caretaker government for the country. The United States pushed for the prominent Afghan expatriate Hamid Karzai to lead the post-Taliban government. The Iranian delegation, headed by Tehran's envoy to the United Nations, Mohammad Javad Zarif, agreed with the Americans, and helped persuade hesitant Northern Alliance factions to assent to Karzai's appointment.[8]

The Khatami government had hoped that the diplomatic alignment between it and Washington during the Bonn Conference could have been the starting point for a shift in bilateral relations. However, tensions remained, and were laid bare weeks later in President Bush's State of the Union address in late January 2002. In the speech, Bush stated that his administration would prevent terrorist-supporting regimes from developing weapons of mass destruction (WMD). "Some of these regimes have been pretty quiet since September 11, but we know their true nature," he said. Bush then identified North Korea, Iran, and Iraq as such actors, adding:

> States like these, and their terrorist allies, constitute an axis of evil, arming to threaten the peace of the world. By seeking weapons of mass destruction, these regimes pose a grave and growing danger. They could provide these arms to terrorists, giving them the means to match their hatred. They could attack our allies or attempt to blackmail the United States. In any of these cases, the price of indifference would be catastrophic.[9]

The Iranians were incensed by their inclusion in the "axis of evil," a literary flourish added by speechwriter David Frum, the implications of which neither Bush nor his national security staff had thought through.[10] Bush seemed to presage further targets for America's global war on terrorism, and Iran was on the list. The Iranian government officials who had spent months pursing quiet back-channel diplomacy with the Americans felt betrayed. Hossein Mousavian, who headed the foreign policy committee of Iran's Supreme National Security Council at the time, recalls President Khatami telling him after the speech: "I am confident that Bush put the final nail in the coffin of Iran-US relations." Iran pulled back from its engagement with the United States in response, and reverted to an adversarial position.[11]

The Allure of Iraq

Bush's speech actually had little to do with Iran. The true focus of the "axis of evil" had been Iraq, which soon became the administration's priority. In building its case for intervention in Iraq, the Bush administration focused on two primary accusations against Saddam Hussein's Baathist regime: that it possessed a secret WMD program, and that it had had high-level contacts with Al-Qaeda operatives prior to 9/11. There was debate within the intelligence community regarding Iraq's WMD capabilities, particularly regarding its nuclear program. Although the regime was thought to possess chemical and biological weapons, the state of its nuclear program was less clear. According to George Tenet, then the director of the Central Intelligence Agency (CIA), the intelligence community did not consider Iraq's nuclear program a pressing danger, but assessed "that left unchecked," Iraq could develop nuclear weapons by "the end of the decade."[12] As for Iraq and 9/11, Tenet was blunt: "CIA found absolutely no linkage between Saddam and 9/11."[13]

Even though the justifications for targeting Iraq were thin, it did not matter. There was broad support within the administration to make Iraq happen. Neoconservatives in and around the administration had long advocated for regime change.[14] Iraq would have probably figured heavily in the administration's Middle East policy even had 9/11 not occurred.[15] But the attacks had provided an opening for folks such as Paul Wolfowitz, the deputy secretary of defense, and Douglas Feith, the undersecretary of defense for policy, to push for a larger campaign to protect America's national security by uprooting the bad actors who threatened it. Iraq was central to that narrative. In the immediate wake of 9/11, as senior cabinet members and defense officials met with the president to discuss contingency plans for Afghanistan, Wolfowitz suggested they should go to war with Iraq as well, in part due to the regime's past support for Palestinian militants and missile strikes on Israel. Secretary of Defense Donald Rumsfeld agreed, arguing: "Dealing with Iraq would show a major commitment to antiterrorism." Colin Powell, the secretary of state, and a retired four-star general in the U.S. Army, counseled against expanding any response to Iraq, reasoning that it would look like a "bait and switch," which would lose the administration support from the United Nations and Middle East partners. Instead, Powell suggested to the president: "If we want to do Iraq, we should do it at a time of our choosing. But we should not do it now, because we don't have linkage to this event."[16] Bush decided to wait, but was eventually convinced by those around him that pursuing regime change in Iraq was just the type of bold action their pivotal moment in history required. They contended that by removing Saddam, and replacing his brutal dictatorship with a liberal democracy, the region would transform in the same way Europe and Asia had through the democratizations of Germany and Japan after World War II.

As he pushed for congressional support for military action against Iraq in October 2002, one year from the start of the war in Afghanistan, Bush offered a glimpse into the ambitious plan: "Freed from the weight of oppression, Iraq's people will be able to share in the progress and prosperity of our time. If military action is necessary, the United States and our allies will help the Iraqi people rebuild their economy, and create the institutions of liberty in a unified Iraq at peace with its neighbors."[17] That line was echoed by commentators in the media and prominent voices in the Washington, D.C., orbit, who sympathized with the idea of ridding Iraq of its ruthless dictator. Thomas Friedman, the *New York Times* columnist, who had covered the Middle East for much of his career, was a conspicuous cheerleader. As he wrote in a January 2003 essay aimed at the detractors of the administration's push for war: "What liberals fail to recognize is that regime change in Iraq is not some distraction from the war on Al Qaeda. That is a bogus argument. And simply because oil is also at stake in Iraq doesn't make it illegitimate either. Some things are right to do, even if Big Oil benefits." As with Bush, Friedman believed that regime change was not only necessary for America's national security, it was crucial for the Middle East's political development. He reasoned:

> If we don't help transform these Arab states—which are also experiencing population explosions—to create better governance, to build more open and productive economies, to empower their women and to develop responsible media that won't blame all their ills on others, we will never begin to see the political, educational and religious reformations they need to shrink their output of undeterrables. . . . This is something liberals should care about—because liberating the captive peoples of the Mideast is a virtue in itself and because in today's globalized world, if you don't visit a bad neighborhood, it will visit you.[18]

Across 2002, Bush administration officials made the case for war. Drawing on the emotional impact of 9/11, and the American public's fear of another terrorist attack, White House officials described Saddam Hussein as a ticking time bomb. As National Security Advisor Condoleezza Rice told *CNN*'s Wolf Blitzer in a September 8 interview:

> There is no doubt that Saddam Hussein's regime is a danger to the United States and to its allies, to our interests. It is also a danger that is gathering momentum, and it simply makes no sense to wait any longer to do something about the threat that is posed here. As the president has said,

"The one option that we do not have is to do nothing." . . . We've waited a very long time. It has been, after all, 11 years, more than a decade now, of defiance of U.N. resolutions by Saddam Hussein. Every obligation that he signed onto after the Gulf War, so that he would not be a threat to peace and security, he has ignored and flaunted. We know that in the last four years there have been no weapons inspectors in Iraq to monitor what he is doing, and we have evidence, increasing evidence, that he continues his march toward weapons of mass destruction. No one can give you an exact time line as to when he is going to have this or that weapon, but given what we have experienced in history and given what we have experienced on September 11, I don't think anyone wants to wait for the 100 percent surety that he has a weapon of mass destruction that can reach the United States, because the only time we may be 100 percent sure is when something lands on our territory. We can't afford to wait that way.[19]

When Blitzer pressed Rice on when Iraq might reach a nuclear weapons capability, she responded: "The problem here is that there will always be some uncertainty about how quickly he can acquire nuclear weapons. But we don't want the smoking gun to be a mushroom cloud."[20] Such statements were common from administration officials, and they were working to win domestic support for their cause. Public polling repeatedly showed that a majority of Americans believed that military action against Iraq was justified as part of the war on terrorism. As the Pew Research Center writes of its own polling during this period: "In the months leading up to the war, majorities of between 55% and 68% said they favored taking military action to end Hussein's rule in Iraq. No more than about a third opposed military action."[21] That support was reflected in Congress, which authorized the use of force against Iraq on October 11, with a number of Democrats joining with Republicans to give President Bush a stronger mandate for war against Saddam Hussein than the former's father had received a decade earlier for the liberation of Kuwait.[22]

An Unwelcome Crisis

Although a majority of Americans backed military action to topple Saddam, a sizable minority did not. Internationally, the looming invasion was even more unpopular. In the lead-up to the invasion, anger against the prospect of war erupted, as millions of people demonstrated across the United States, Europe, and the Middle East on February 15, 2003. From New York City to Rome to Damascus, protestors took to the streets to rally against a war they saw as unjust and unnecessary.[23] Yet, as disliked as the notion was in foreign publics, the Bush administration was in a singular position to force the issue. America was the world's superpower. It had the most extensive network of partners and allies around the globe, which was held together by a complex of interwoven economic, security, and political linkages. Those factors alone made it difficult to oppose, and 9/11 made disagreement even more arduous. The continental United States had never experienced such an attack, and the Bush administration rightfully sought to prevent it from happening again. The invasion of Afghanistan received wide international support because it was justified, and because the war on the Taliban made sense. For many, especially to those outside the United States, the Iraq War did not.

As Washington's gaze shifted to Iraq, America's allies and partners were forced to confront an uncomfortable reality: the Bush administration had a grand foreign policy vision and 9/11 would be the pretext to justify it. Allied and partner states had a difficult choice to make. They could either oppose a wounded America or go along with a war that had no clear connection to the war on terrorism. Unlike in Afghanistan, most of America's allies wanted no part of the war with Iraq. French president Jacques Chirac was outspoken in opposition, as was German chancellor Gerhard Schroder.[24] Canadian prime minister Jean Chrétien, who had committed troops to Afghanistan, also refused to join the coalition.[25] Prime Minister Tony Blair, who firmly believed in the righteousness of the cause of democracy, made Britain the leading exception. Australia, Spain, and Poland also agreed to join the U.S.-led effort.

America's Middle East partners were in a more precarious position. The war would impact their region directly, but it also targeted a regime that none trusted and a leader whom most reviled. Saddam Hussein's invasions of Iran and Kuwait had alienated his country from its neighbors. Saddam had no friends, and none of the surrounding states was willing to back him against the United States. Yet, as problematic as Saddam was, he was the devil they knew, and he still served a purpose. Iraq remained a bulwark against Iran and its regional ambitions. Syria and Jordan, meanwhile, had been profiting from U.S.-imposed sanctions on Iraq, and served as middle-men in the illicit trade of Iraqi oil. Access to cheap oil had benefited their economies, and black-market trade with Iraq had enriched numerous elites and tribal networks who controlled cross-border smuggling routes.[26] Jordan received all of its oil from Iraq, half of it for free and part of it subsidized. And the kingdom's total commerce with Iraq amounted to a fifth of its overall foreign trade, slightly more than its dealings with the United States.[27]

Beyond that, the region's leaders feared the insecurity that war would bring. As Turkey's prime minister, Abdullah Gül, said in an address to the Turkish parliament in January 2003: "Everybody has deep concerns about the situation that

will emerge after a war. . . . Once [Pandora's] box is opened, it will be very difficult to restore stability and everybody fears that there will be bloodshed and
this will continue after the war."[28] Those concerns were shared by Iraq's other
neighbors, who worried about the potential for refugee flows and uncertainty
on their borders. Turkey, Iran, and Syria were anxious that war would empower
the Kurds in northern Iraq, who had already benefited from the U.S.-imposed
no-fly zone and seemed poised to gain greater autonomy from an invasion.
More troubling for Syria and Iran, both enemies of Iraq's Baathist regime *and* the
United States, was that a war in Iraq would give America a military footprint in
a neighboring state—a presence that could one day be used against them. With
American forces occupying two of its neighbors, Iran would be in a perilous po-
sition. Of the surrounding states, only Kuwait, which had been subjugated by
Iraq 12 years earlier, openly supported the Bush administration's quest to end
Saddam's reign.

Despite such trepidation, the close ties that most Arab states shared with
Washington tempered their outward objections to the war. Neither Egypt nor
Saudi Arabia, the region's two most influential pro-American states, had the res-
olution or wherewithal to lead a regional front either in support of or against the
war. That impotence opened the door for more aspiring leaders to make a mark.
Turkey, whose government was controlled by the newly elected Justice and
Development Party (or AKP)—a party with Islamist roots brought to power
on a populist platform centered on reviving the economy—led the charge by
attempting to forge a regional consensus against the conflict. In February 2003,
Ankara hosted the foreign ministers of Syria, Iraq, Saudi Arabia, and Jordan to
discuss the issue. Prime Minister Gül also traveled to Saudi Arabia and met with
Crown Prince Abdullah to encourage Riyadh to advocate for a regional solution
that could forestall American military action.[29]

That effort motivated an emergency meeting of the Arab League on March 1
in Sharm al-Sheikh, Egypt. The Arab League—a deliberative body composed of
22 majority-Arab governments—was scheduled to hold their annual summit in
Bahrain at the end of the month, but Egyptian president Hosni Mubarak pushed
for the meeting to be held earlier in the hopes of establishing a unified Arab position against the war.[30] By taking up the mantle of organizing an Arab response to
America's pursuit of conflict, Mubarak was attempting to reassert Egypt's fading
leadership role in the region. He was also responding to surging anti-war sentiment in his own country, which had culminated days earlier in a demonstration
of an estimated 100,000 people in Cairo. The crowd chanted a variety of anti-
war and anti-American slogans, including "Vive la France! Arab leaders can go
to hell!" which praised the strong anti-war stance of the French president, and
juxtaposed it with the indecision of Arab rulers. Reaffirming that perception,
Mubarak discussed the reason for holding the hasty summit, stating: "While

other countries rallied to take action, the Arabs stood still, as if the Iraqi crisis
was of no concern to them. . . . We could not remain silent any longer."[31]

Mubarak's effort proved inefficacious. Far from unifying Arab states, the
summit accomplished little, save exposing their strident divisions. Jordan's King
Abdullah set the tone for the proceedings' opening session, cautioning: "We face
today a case that warns of an imminent war on Iraq. . . . Our Iraqi brethren will
not suffer alone the effects and destruction of any such war. The whole region
will."[32] At the center of the meeting was a bid by the UAE for Saddam Hussein
to go into exile and for a new government to be formed in Baghdad—an idea
the Emiratis claimed they had secretly proposed to the Iraqi leader two months
earlier.[33] UAE president Sheikh Zayed bin Sultan Al Nahyan summed up the
proposal's aims: "The Iraqi leadership should decide to give up power in Iraq and
to leave Iraq," in order to provide "a way out of this complicated and dangerous
crisis."[34] That idea—which seemed to echo a similar one floated in the American
press by Secretary of State Colin Powell a couple of days earlier—touched off
a storm of acrimony.[35] The plan intended to avoid war by allowing Iraq to willingly and proactively adopt new leadership to placate Washington's demands.
But many regional leaders saw it as regime change by another name—if not by
war, then by the threat of war. Perhaps seeing their own future in Iraq's fate, the
leaders of Syria and Libya argued that America was serving Israel's interests by
targeting Saddam. Bashar al-Assad warned that a war on Iraq would be only the
beginning of a larger campaign to upend states opposed to Israel, which would
include Syria, as well as Libya and Iran. "We are all targeted. . . . We are all in
danger," he said to the assembly.[36]

Muammar Qaddafi went on the attack and accused Saudi Arabia of being an
American lackey. In a long, meandering speech, the Libyan leader said that Riyadh
had struck a "deal with the devil" when it invited American troops to defend it
after the Iraqi invasion of Kuwait in 1990, implying that the kingdom's stance
against the war betrayed its true inclinations, which were to collaborate with the
United States when it suited its interests. Crown Prince Abdullah interjected at
that point, shouting: "Saudi Arabia has never worked for U.S. interests. You are a
liar and your grave awaits you."[37] The exchange was so jarring that the live television broadcast of the summit was quickly cut, and Abdullah reportedly "stormed
out of the meeting" only to be later "coaxed" to return by the leaders of Egypt,
Syria, and Lebanon.[38]

Personal acrimony scuttled any attempt to build consensus around the UAE's
initiative. It became evident that no states besides the UAE and Kuwait were
willing to openly entertain regime change or encourage Saddam to relinquish
power to spare his country the destruction of war. Arab League secretary Amr
Mousa refused to take up the plan for debate. And the Saudi delegation, despite tacitly supporting the UAE's proposal, along with Qatar and Kuwait, did

not endorse it at the summit.[39] Rather, speaking at a news conference, the Saudi foreign minister Saud al-Faisal gave only tepid recognition to the plan, saying "We're still discussing it. . . . I call it an idea. It's not an initiative."[40] The Arab League's indecisiveness and refusal to engage with the UAE's proposal was dismaying to the latter's representatives. Speaking to reporters, Abdullah bin Zayed, the up-and-coming son of the Emirati leader, said of the summit's lack of progress: "War is imminent. . . . And there is no way we can push the Americans and the British away from it. Unfortunately, the Arabs did not have the courage of talking about it."[41]

Other regional leaders and commentators similarly saw the summit as a squandered opportunity, and one that put Arab disunity on full display. Qatar's foreign minister Hamad bin Jassim Jabr Al Thani told reporters, "I think the Arab and Islamic world is divided because we do not know what we want to do," adding: "We do not speak with a single voice."[42] Ahmad Bishara, a veteran Kuwaiti official and the first secretary general of the Gulf Cooperation Council (GCC), called the idea of establishing Arab unity a "fleeting dream," remarking: "You cannot group people together just because they speak the same language. It is a contrived effort to put on a united face. Everyone is vying for their own interests. These are diverse regions, and if you try to put them all into one pot, it doesn't work."[43] Beirut's *al-Safir* newspaper described the summit as a testament to the reluctance of Arab states to proactively respond to regional crises, leaving it to Turkey and the Europeans to fill the void in leadership, concluding: "European countries . . . have more Arab national feeling than we Arabs ourselves."[44]

As the summit was ongoing, the Turkish parliament voted down a measure that would have allowed the United States to position forces within the country. Despite the outward backing of Prime Minister Gül and Recep Tayyip Erdoğan, the head of the AKP, and at least $26 billion in financial and military aid promised by the United States, the measure failed to get enough votes to pass, thereby eliminating Turkish soil as a launching pad for the impending invasion.[45] Gül and Erdoğan had been critical of the Bush administration, but had also lobbied parliament to pass the bill, hedging their bets in favor of retaining close ties with Washington and putting Turkey in the position to shape both the war and its outcome by participating in it. The Turkish public, however, was strongly opposed to the war, as were most of the country's elected politicians. Önder Sav, a parliamentarian from the center-left Republican People's Party, denounced the motion, stating: "We are calling on you not to be involved with this disgusting war. Turn back when you still have the chance, otherwise the whole Turkish public will suffer." Given the anti-war sentiment in the country, the vote against the bill was unsurprising. As Erdoğan told reporters: "What more do you want? . . . It was a completely democratic result. May it be for the best."[46] The vote also afforded Erdoğan, who succeeded Gul as prime minister less than two weeks later, the opportunity to pursue a more regionally focused Turkish foreign policy less constrained by Washington's preferences.

The news out of Ankara was not well-received in Washington. "I was frustrated and disappointed," President Bush recalled. "On one of the most important requests we had ever made, Turkey, our NATO ally, had let America down."[47] The absence of Turkish participation was an inconvenience but not much more, as the United States was still able to secure limited support from most of its Arab partners in the region. Beyond Kuwait, where the invasion was launched, Jordan and Saudi Arabia both allowed for limited access to key airbases, with Jordan also permitting smaller, more discrete basing for American special forces and rescue operations. Qatar and Bahrain played important supporting roles as well, with U.S. Central Command (CENTCOM)'s forward-operations center headquartered in Al Udeid Air Base outside of Doha and the U.S. Navy's Fifth Fleet based in Manama. Whether reluctant or enthusiastic, most of America's partners in the region played a part in the invasion.

Transient Victory

The start of Operation Iraqi Freedom (OIF) was highly successful. The first stage of the war began on March 20, 2003, and culminated in the fall of Baghdad and the collapse of the Baathist government on April 9. Coalition forces—which included nearly 250,000 troops, 45,000 from the United Kingdom, 2,000 from Australia, and almost 200 from Poland—overwhelmed Iraqi defenses from the ground, air, and sea in a thorough display of Western military supremacy. Outside of some persistent armed resistance by Baath Party loyalists, such as the fedayeen units, Coalition forces routed the Iraqi army and ended Saddam's 24-year rule in short order. President Bush's famous "mission accomplished" speech on board the USS *Abraham Lincoln* on May 1 was a near-theatrical enunciation of what appeared to be a complete and definitive victory for his administration. There was little doubt that America's power was unmatched and unstoppable.

Breaking the Baathist state was easy; putting it back together was not. The invasion had been expertly planned and executed. Less thought had been devoted to what would come next, and much of what had been considered rested on faulty assumptions.[48] Images of chaos quickly followed the collapse of the Iraqi government, with criminals and opportunists looting offices and museums, and episodic violence erupting across the country. State security forces had imploded along with the regime, and U.S.-led troops were too few, spread too thin, and ill-prepared to act as law enforcement. Restoring governance became the Bush administration's priority, and by late April, the Coalition Provisional Authority

(CPA) was established to serve as a caretaker government. Bush tapped L. Paul "Jerry" Bremer, a former State Department official who had served as ambassador to the Netherlands in the mid-1980s, to lead the CPA. Under Bremer, the CPA took over all the day-to-day responsibilities of state, was charged with the writing of a new democratic constitution for the country, and undertook the most controversial and consequential steps in the occupation. The CPA's first two orders initiated a process of "de-Baathification," aimed at purging all vestiges of the ancien régime from Iraq's officialdom, and disbanded the military. Prominent Iraqi exiles had pushed Washington to adopt those policies, and Bremer appointed one of them, Ahmad Chalabi, a Shia expatriate and former CIA asset, to implement them under the CPA.[49]

On the face of it, de-Baathification was meant to prevent the officials who had been responsible for the countless abuses of the Baathist state from ever again being in positions of authority. As Defense Secretary Rumsfeld later explained: "The goal [had been] to target those at the top of the party, the ones who were so closely linked with the former regime that they could not be trusted to serve in the post-Saddam government." Even though some in the administration cautioned that such a decree could inflame tensions, especially among Sunni Arabs, Rumsfeld contends that the idea "had broad support among the relevant cabinet departments and agencies."[50] Washington might have had the best of intensions, but in practice, the orders amounted to a wholesale blacklisting of Iraq's civil servants. All former government officials and public-sector employees, such as doctors and engineers, were permanently barred from joining the country's new civil sector. It was the exclusion of anyone who had worked for the Iraqi government—the country's largest employer—and affected an estimated 85,000 to 100,000 individuals, including 40,000 teachers and professors. Abolishing the military created an even greater displacement. The policy fired, and barred from future employment in the security forces, almost 750,000 people, including an estimated 385,000 from the military, 285,000 from the Interior Ministry and police, and 50,000 from presidential security services.[51]

De-Baathification alienated a large swath of Iraqis—people who now had little hope of recovering what they had lost—the majority of whom were trained soldiers and officers. Unsurprisingly, many of those former soldiers found common cause with the underground armed networks that began to proliferate across the country. Sunni Arabs had benefited the most from Baathist rule and were the group hardest hit by the CPA's policies. They comprised the second largest ethno-sectarian community in Iraq, which at the time was estimated at some 5.4 million people, or about 20 percent of the country's total population of 27 million.[52] An estimated 10 percent of the Arab Sunni population was directly impacted by the blacklist.[53] Correspondingly, it was in Sunni Arab-majority provinces and neighborhoods where the insurgency against the occupation grew the quickest and strongest.

Attacks against U.S. and Coalition forces steadily increased between May and December 2003. Former soldiers, police, and other reactionaries joined up with Islamist groups, hoping to mobilize the newly marginalized Sunni Arab population against the U.S.-led invasion that had displaced them from the top of Iraq's power structure. The most extreme of the new insurgent leaders was Abu Musab al-Zarqawi, a Jordanian jihadist of Palestinian descent, who cut his teeth in Soviet-occupied Afghanistan in the late 1980s. Zarqawi was an associate of Al-Qaeda, but had not been invited to join the organization by Osama Bin Laden. Instead, Bin Laden encouraged the aspiring militant to start his own organization near Herat in western Afghanistan, on the opposite side of the country from Al-Qaeda's bases in the east, and to focus on drawing recruits from the Levant, Jordan, Iraq, and Palestinian communities. Bin Laden was unsure about the zealous Jordanian and sought to keep him at a distance. Among the concerns that gave Bin Laden pause was Zarqawi's extreme hatred for Shia Muslims— a community the Jordanian considered an irredeemable enemy of true Islam. Although such a view infused the same brand of Sunni puritanical thought that both he and Bin Laden subscribed to, the latter considered Zarqawi's sectarian priorities misplaced and counterproductive.[54]

Following the invasion of Afghanistan in 2001, Zarqawi fled to Iran, along with dozens of other Al-Qaeda members and their families. Uncertain of where to go next, he eventually set his focus on developing a network of jihadists in Iraq in anticipation of another possible war. There he linked up with Abu Ayyub al-Masri, a veteran Egyptian jihadist and Al-Qaeda member, who had begun recruiting militants in Baghdad sometime prior to the U.S.-led invasion. Their effort led to the establishment of Jama'at al-Tawhid wa'l Jihad (the Monotheism and Jihad Group), the precursor to both Al-Qaeda in Iraq and to the Islamic State in Iraq and al-Sham (ISIS). By March 2003, Zarqawi's network was well situated to exploit the ensuing security vacuum. In the early days of the insurgency, Zarqawi's network was responsible for some of the largest and deadliest attacks against Coalition forces and Shia civilians.[55] Their plan, above all, was to galvanize Sunni Arabs into a single bloc by instigating a sectarian conflict with the Shia. To that end, they focused much of their effort on advancing the narrative that the Shia were part-and-parcel of the occupation, and on attacking Shia civilians and holy sites. Zarqawi strategized that were such attacks to trigger Shia reprisals against Sunnis, it would engender a cycle of violence that would lead to a sectarian civil war.[56]

By late 2003 and through 2004, Sunni insurgents routinely targeted individuals and groups perceived to be collaborating with the occupation. In addition to attacks against Coalition forces, suicide bombings of crowded marketplaces and Shia religious buildings became commonplace, as did targeted kidnappings and murders. The insurgency was highly fractured, with numerous groups and networks vying for recruits and seeking vengeance.[57] Over time these groups coalesced into a core of insurgent organizations, with Zarqawi's Al-Qaeda affiliate emerging as the most violent and ambitious. Estimates pegged the number of Sunni Arab insurgents active around this time as between a few thousand and 20,000.[58] The scale of the violence attributed to the insurgency worsened from week to week through 2004, with at times hundreds of civilians killed in terrorist attacks per day.[59]

The Mahdi Army Uprising

Intensifying violence across the country soon inspired insurgent activity from among the Shia population as well. Muqtada al-Sadr, the 30-year-old scion of the prominent al-Sadr family, and son of the martyred senior religious authority Grand Ayatollah Sadiq al-Sadr, led the most prominent group. Sanctions placed upon Iraq following its 1990 invasion of Kuwait had crippled the Iraqi economy, and impoverished millions of the country's most vulnerable. Sadiq al-Sadr utilized his vast network of followers to provide general services to the poor, who were among the hardest hit by the economic duress. Sadr's network afforded the marginalized and often overlooked Shia community services the state did not, including soup kitchens and health clinics. By 2003, the Sadrists had become the most important Shia bloc in Iraq and held the loyalty of millions.

For much of his career, Sadiq al-Sadr was able to retain his position by remaining outside of politics. His quietism made him a target of expatriate rivals, and he was at times accused of collaborating with the Baathist state. However, by the late 1990s, he became increasingly critical of the ruling regime. That criticism led to his assassination in 1999, after which he became even more revered by his millions of followers. With no unifying successor, the movement splintered into competing factions. Most followers looked to the Qom-based Grand Ayatollah Kazem al-Haeri for guidance, but al-Haeri did not openly advance a claim to lead the movement as a religious authority. That left space for other enterprising clerics, such as Ayatollah Muhammad Yaqubi, who headed the Basra-based Fadhila Party and its militant wing, to emerge as challengers. The most determined was Sadiq al-Sadr's son, Muqtada, who, as a junior seminarian in his late 20s, was also an unlikely candidate due to the primacy placed on seniority and scholarly production in the Shia clerical community. Despite his junior standing, Muqtada carried the legitimacy of the family's name and inherited much of its wealth. More decisively, he possessed an unpretentious charisma that connected with the Shia urban poor. With fiery rhetoric aimed at both American troops and the returning Shia expatriates who had backed the invasion, Muqtada inspired droves of young men to resist the foreign occupation. Although he lacked the credentials of a religious authority, he spoke the language of the street, and used that advantage to galvanize his followers into the largest and most formidable Sadrist faction.

Muqtada utilized his father's network of mosques, charities, and social welfare organizations to agitate against the occupation.[60] By the summer of 2003, he had organized his most zealous supporters into an armed militia called the Mahdi Army, a name designed to evoke the messianic expectations of his Shia base.[61] In early April 2004, the Mahdi Army made an audacious push for power across Shia urban centers in Baghdad and southern Iraq, seizing government buildings, police stations, and transportation nodes from Coalition forces. Muqtada's stronghold was the urban slums of Baghdad's Al-Thawra district, home to around one million residents—an area originally named Saddam City that later became known as Sadr City in honor of his father. The Mahdi Army took complete control of Sadr City during the uprising, and made major gains in the southern Shia cities of Karbala, Kut, and Kufa.[62] The militia's push peaked in Najaf, where an attempt to take the city led to nearly three weeks of fierce fighting. The initial spark was an attack on a local police station in the early hours of August 5. U.S. Marines were dispatched to help police forces repel the attack. The ensuing fighting encompassed much of the old city, eventually migrating to the sprawling Wadi al-Salam cemetery, where Sadrist fighters positioned themselves throughout the seven-square-mile complex of catacombs, tunnels, and tombs.[63] Local knowledge of the hallowed grounds gave the militia an advantage, but not enough of one to overcome the superior firepower and training of the Americans.[64] After days of fighting, Sadrist fighters retreated to the Imam Ali shrine and its surrounding buildings—a sacred place of worship and pilgrimage for the world's Shia. They took up points in adjacent pilgrimage hotels, using elevated positions to strike Coalition forces with rocket-propelled grenades (RPGs) and machine-gun fire. U.S. Army forces surrounded the area, but avoided an attempt to expel fighters from inside the holy shrine, understanding that to do so would incite Shia sentiments even further.

Finally, on August 25, in response to a series of artillery and machine-gun attacks from hotel positions, U.S. Marines called in airstrikes, which destroyed several of the buildings used by the militants.[65] Combat continued the next day, but with their strategic positions lost, the militants sought a negotiated end to the fighting. On August 27, the Iraqi government helped broker a deal between the militants and Grand Ayatollah Ali Sistani, the foremost Shia religious authority in the country. In exchange for a cessation of hostilities, Muqtada al-Sadr and his fighters were disarmed and given safe passage out of the city.[66]

The Mahdi Army continued fighting intermittently in Sadr City and other parts of southern Iraq for months, but ultimately, Muqtada signed a ceasefire agreement in September and the Mahdi Army's attacks gradually declined. The episode, however, put Muqtada al-Sadr and his militant network on the map. The U.S.-led occupation would now have to contend with both Sunni and Shia insurgencies.[67]

Enter Iran

The war in Iraq coincided with rising tensions between Washington and Tehran. Diplomacy on Afghanistan did not forestall Washington's concern for Iran's links to terrorism; and the war on terror focused the Bush administration's attention on Iranian activities in the Middle East. A number of issues kept tensions taut, and an event at sea threatened to set the tone for the administration's view of Iran. In early January 2002, Israeli Navy commandos intercepted the *Karine A* roughly 500 kilometers off the Israeli coast in the Red Sea. The vessel was owned by the Palestinian Authority, and was carrying 50 tons of weaponry, including rifles, Katyusha rockets, anti-tank missiles, and mortars.[1] The shipment was believed to be headed to Palestinian factions in Gaza, who were heavily involved in the wave of protests and terrorism, known as the Second Intifada, that had rippled across Israel and the Occupied Territories since September 2000. American and Israeli intelligence had both determined that the weapons had come from Iranian stockpiles and had been organized by the Iranian regime as part of a larger effort to aid Palestinian factions in their conflict with Israel. That effort was the fruit of an agreement made months earlier, in May 2001, between Iranian officials and two aides to Yasser Arafat, the chairman of the Palestinian Authority (PA), while the latter was meeting with Russian president Vladimir Putin in Moscow.[2] The incident prompted an immediate shift in the Bush administration's approach toward the Israel-Palestinian peace process, but figured less acutely in its dealings with Iran. Bush took the PA's clandestine smuggling effort during the ongoing intifada as a personal affront, something that had gone against assurances made to him by the Palestinian leader. "Arafat lied to me," Bush concluded. "I never trusted him again. In fact, I never spoke with him again. By the spring of 2002, I had concluded that peace would not be possible with Arafat in power."[3] As for Iran, the National Security staff saw it as a continuation of what they already believed: Iran was an active supporter of terrorism.[4]

Another problem in U.S.-Iranian relations was the issue of Al-Qaeda. The War in Afghanistan had led to a wave of jihadists and their families flooding across the border to Iran, including some of Al-Qaeda's inner circle. Some, such as Abu Musab al-Zarqawi, were able to transit across Iran and leave for other countries; but others had been detained by Iranian authorities, and were being held in various forms of house arrest. Washington pressed Tehran for answers on those incarcerated, leading to unproductive bilateral talks in late 2002 and early 2003. Iran refused to provide the type of information requested by the United States, and also refused to deport Al-Qaeda members to their home countries.[5] Iran saw the militants as assets that could be used as leverage with America or with their home countries. To that end, Iran dawdled in its discussions with the United States, providing some information, but holding key details back. As the Bush administration saw it, Iran was not coming clean about the Al-Qaeda members in the country, or its intentions with them. Further, there was concern that Iran had allowed some of the group's key members to continue operating.[6] Iran denied working with Al-Qaeda, but acknowledged holding around 200 of its fighters and their families in detention.[7]

More troubling than links to Al-Qaeda was the revelation in August 2002 that Iran had been secretly advancing its nuclear program. At issue were two buildings under construction: a nuclear enrichment site at Natanz and a heavy-water plant near Arak. Those facilities greatly expanded Iran's known nuclear activities, which were thought to have been confined to a nuclear power plant being built by Russia in Bushehr that was still under construction. Iran's concealment of its other efforts contravened its safeguard responsibilities under the Non-Proliferation Treaty (NPT). The Bush administration saw the revelation as an allusion to Iran's true intentions, which looked to go well beyond simply developing a nuclear energy program for civilian use. As Condoleezza Rice explains, the administration "quickly and clearly" set the stark policy line that "*any* nuclear program in Iran was unacceptable." That position created distance between the United States and most of the international community, including its close allies. Iran was an important oil producer, was integrated in the global economy, and held strong trade relations with Europe and Asia. Russia was also invested in Iran's nuclear program, and assured the United States that the Bushehr plant, which was intended to receive its nuclear fuel from Russia, as well as send spent fuel back, would be "proliferation-resistant." Consequently, as Rice saw it, Washington was "pretty lonely in calling out the growing dangers of the Iranian nuclear threat."[8]

Even in that solitude, the pressure that the Bush administration could exert was considerable. With the axis of evil and invasion of the Iraq as backdrops, the Khatami government temporarily suspended Iran's enrichment program in late 2003 in a deal coordinated with Britain, France, and Germany. Hardliners in the regime balked at the move, and pushed for the program's resumption a year later, setting off a showdown with the West. Through its behavior, Iran helped increase suspicions about the nature of its nuclear program. In truth, those suspicions were well founded: Iran had pursued a covert nuclear weaponization program until at least 2003, and its enrichment program became a strategic tool it would use against the West.[9]

Iran's support to terrorist groups, its harboring of Al-Qaeda members, and its secret nuclear program all made it a potential target in the war on terror. Iran had two choices: either change its behavior, or find a way to deter potential American aggression. With the war in Iraq, Iran found its best opportunity to pursue the latter. Iran's actions in Iraq also transcended its tensions with Washington. Iran and Iraq had fought a grinding war during the 1980s that ended in stalemate. Until its demise, the Baathist regime had been Iran's primary enemy, and Iran wanted to prevent Saddam's clique from ever returning to power. Iran thus pursued a two-pronged strategy in Iraq, which sought to maximize its influence in the country while undermining that of the United States.

Laying the Groundwork

Even though Iran had a clear motive to get involved in Iraq, the fact that it did seemed to take the Bush administration by surprise. Many within the administration perceived Iran and Iraq as implacable foes, and that replacing Saddam would not change that. Yet, Iran maintained strong ties to many of the Iraqi dissidents that Washington worked with before and during the war. That included Kurdish leaders, such as Jalal Talabani, and Iran's own clients, the Supreme Council for the Islamic Revolution in Iraq (SCIRI) and the Badr Corps militia. Members of both had lived in Iran since the early 1980s, where they had married, raised families, learned to speak Persian fluently, and developed close relations with Iranian officials. Those relationships were disregarded by the war planners in Washington. As Chairman of the Joint Chiefs of Staff, General Richard Bowman, the top uniformed officer in the U.S. armed services in 2003, recalls thinking during the planning process: "The Iraqis were not the Persians. . . . They are nationalistic, and I did not think they would come under Iran's sway."[10] Such a simplistic mindset echoed throughout the administration, which relegated the Iran question to an afterthought. As Department of Defense historian David Crist explains: "In all the back-and-forth deliberations about the impact on Iran of an American invasion of Iraq, no one bothered to test the theories." He continues:

> For an American military that prides itself on its planning prowess, surprisingly little had been done beyond the initial drive up to Baghdad. The opening gambit, as the Marines called the march to Baghdad, was rehearsed for nearly a year; what happened after reaching Baghdad

received little more attention than a massive CENTCOM PowerPoint presentation and two small staffs hastily assembled just before kickoff. But even that cursory swag had not been done regarding Iran. No Red Team was established to explore the ramifications of the removal of Iran's archrival. CENTCOM never war-gamed how Iran would react to another American invasion on its borders. The U.S. Navy's Fifth Fleet in Bahrain examined how to avoid an unintended skirmish with the Iranian navy in the northern Gulf, but beyond that senior officials merely opined and looked to peripheral issues.[11]

Iran played that myopia to its benefit. Even if Iran feared having American troops next door, toppling the Baathist regime would help it more than any regional state. Iran held deep ties with Iraqi expatriate organizations, and had established SCIRI and Badr (in 1982 and 1983, respectively) to be the core of a future liberated Iraq. During the Iran-Iraq War, both groups adopted the Islamic Republic's theocratic ideology and advocated for an Islamic government in their own country. SCIRI's leaders gradually toned down those positions during the 1990s, and particularly in the lead-up to the U.S. invasion; however, it was an unavoidable fact that both SCIRI and Badr were intimately linked to Iran and its leadership. Both groups returned to Iraq with extensive connections to Iranian officialdom, intelligence, and the IRGC—the driving force behind the regime's grand strategy. With Saddam removed, they returned to their home with Iran's encouragement and backing. Shaping Iraq's post-Baathist future became their mission.

The United States needed allies among the Shia, and both SCIRI and Badr, along with other Shia expatriate organizations, such as the Islamist Dawa Party, and veteran anti-Saddam activists, sought roles in the new Iraqi democracy. Through those contacts, Iran gained access to key parts of the Iraqi government. SCIRI, which was led by the senior cleric Ayatollah Abd al-Aziz al-Hakim and his family, entered the fray as a political party, whereas Badr integrated as a security force. Both organizations, in their own ways, openly collaborated with the CPA and Coalition forces, which helped them gain positions of influence. Iran did not micromanage its clients, but it worked closely with them, and continued to provide financial and other means of support. In return, both organizations, to differing extents and in different ways, served as effective extensions of Iranian influence in Iraq.

Iran began covertly moving weapons and personnel into Iraq in the weeks leading up to the invasion.[12] In keeping with its broad strategy, the IRGC aided both groups that were working with the Americans and those who opposed the occupation. Activities to harass and intimidate invading Coalition forces began soon thereafter. Early incidents were minor in scope and impact, but also messaged that Iran was not going to be a passive observer to the war. The IRGC made its presence known to U.S. forces at the outset of the invasion, and at times fired on U.S. and Coalition troops from border positions. In March 2003, as American forces advanced toward Basra, a surveillance team of eight Navy SEALs traversed up the Al-Faw Peninsula to explore the Shatt al-Arab—a waterway, also known as the Arvand River, whose thalweg marks the southern Iraq-Iran border. IRGC units monitored the Navy detachment from Iranian territory, firing rifles and mortars toward their general positions during the day and night, seeking to discourage their reconnaissance mission and test red lines. A month later, another SEALs unit was blocked from proceeding up the Shatt al-Arab by IRGC patrol boats who threatened to fire on the small American vessel if it did not reverse course. After a short standoff, the SEALs were ordered by their superiors to turn around and avoid confrontation.[13]

Small incidents such as those were lost in the noise of the invasion. Iran was an afterthought in the press, and garnered little attention in Washington. The situation in Iraq was fluid, and all parties involved explored ways to gain advantages and mitigate vulnerabilities. Iran entered the scene with a leg up on the Coalition. SCIRI's leader, Abd al-Aziz al-Hakim, was an enterprising politician, and assertively engaged with American and foreign officials. In the summer of 2003, al-Hakim met with CPA chief Paul Bremer to seek the integration of Shia forces into the Iraqi military. Bremer recalls assuring al-Hakim that Shiites would play a leading role in the new military, writing in his memoir: "'I promise you this, Sayyid,' I said, using his honorific title. 'The commander of the first battalion will be a Shiite.' The Coalition kept that promise."[14] Badr was a key beneficiary of that policy, and its fighters were absorbed into the Iraqi security services, including within the new Interior Ministry, where Badr gained a formidable presence.

Working with the Coalition increased Badr and SCIRI's political value for Iran, but it also diminished their utility in anti-Coalition militancy. To fight the occupation, and prevent the United States from gaining a lasting military presence in Iraq, Iran needed to expand its client base. That job fell to the IRGC's Quds Force, which oversaw Iran's foreign military operations. Iran's intelligence service, the lead organization in its covert operations abroad, also played an important role. Both the IRGC and Iranian intelligence pursued efforts to develop new assets in Iraq across 2003 and 2004. During that time, they focused on building networks of anti-Saddam militants within the Shia communities of Baghdad and Basra, as well as in the shrine cities of Najaf, Karbala, and Samarra. Their early clients, which included a hodgepodge of militias, criminals, and opportunists, had mixed motivations. Some sought revenge against the Baathists or shared Iran's Islamist ideology, and others were driven by monetary inducements. What most had in common was their Shia identity and willingness to pursue dangerous work in league with Iran.

Working under the cover of businessmen and diplomats, and backed by the leadership in Tehran, the IRGC and Iranian intelligence pursued overlapping but separate missions. The IRGC's main effort was to undermine the occupation by fomenting violence and instigating attacks against Coalition forces. Iranian intelligence was more invested in assassinating former Baathist officials who had had some role in the Iran-Iraq War, or been involved in the violent oppression of Shia activists in Iraq. Iranian intelligence worked closely with anti-Saddam Shia groups, such as Tharallah (Revenge of God) and the Sayyid al-Shuhada Movement, both of which were heavily involved in the ensuing assassination campaign.[15] Both groups had been active in the underground resistance to Saddam, and developed brutal reputations after his fall. Tharallah, for example, had been established in 1995 by Islamist militant Yusef Sanawi (alternatively known as both Abu Mahdi and Yousef al-Musawi), and quickly became one of the deadliest factions in southern Iraq. Through proxies and under official cover, Iranian personnel in Iraq operated in the shadows and in the daylight. The Quds Force alone reportedly had around a dozen members serving as diplomats in the Iranian embassy during this time. That included Hassan Kazemi Qomi, who became Iran's chargé d'affaires in December 2003, and later its ambassador to Iraq in 2004.[16]

Major General Qassem Soleimani, the Quds Force chief, was the architect of Iran's strategy. Although Soleimani was known to travel to Iraq regularly, he relied on field commanders, such as Abdul-Reza Shahlai (known by his nom de guerre, Hajj Yusef), Badr-associated militia leaders, such as Hamid al-Sheibani (also known as Abu Mustafa), Abu Mahdi al-Muhandis (the nom de guerre of Jamal Jaafar Ibrahimi), and skilled agents from Lebanese Hezbollah, for translating plans into effective operations on the ground.[17] Much of the effort, from planning to logistics, was overseen by Brigadier General Ahmed Foruzandeh and was coordinated out of the IRGC's Tehran-based Ramazan Corps, which he headed.[18] Day-to-day activities were run out of three forward-operating bases near the Iraqi border, each of which held responsibility for one of three regional sectors. The Nasr Command, based in Marivan, in Iran's northern Kordestan province, directed IRGC efforts in Iraqi Kurdistan and a portion of Diyala province. The Mehran-based Zafar Command, in Ilam province, held responsibility for the crucial central portion of the country, which included Baghdad, Najaf, Karbala, and smaller areas in Babil, Wasit, and Diyala. And the Fajr Command, based in Ahvaz, the capital of Khuzestan province, ran operations in the south, encompassing Basra and much of the cross-border smuggling effort used to supply militants inside Iraq.[19]

The IRGC's strategy rested on its ability to arm clients with cash and weaponry. Abu Sajjad al-Gharrawi, a trusted client since the 1980s, was the linchpin of that effort.[20] Al-Gharrawi hailed from a southern Iraqi tribe and utilized his extensive familial links to run goods through a complex of routes that weaved in and out of the vast marshes bordering Iran's Khuzestan province.[21] During the Iran-Iraq War, he had earned a reputation for being able to smuggle whatever the IRGC needed into southern Iraq. Now, as Iran began to fight a new, covert war, al-Gharrawi's network was turned to again, this time becoming the primary storehouse for outfitting the IRGC's proxies. Iranian and client commanders would submit orders directly to al-Gharrawi, whose agents would move the requested materiel into Iraq for distribution.[22] His agents used both overland crossing points, where border guards could be bribed, and intricate marsh waterways to evade Coalition forces. Once in Iraq, shipments would be brought to smaller border towns, such as Amarah, or to Basra, and then distributed to clients across the country.[23] Trusted smugglers could make $1,000 or more per delivery, which made Iran's supply line a lucrative business for some.[24]

Other clients, such as Tharallah and Badr, were also heavily involved in smuggling. Badr's point person was Hamid al-Sheibani, who led an epony-mous network that controlled some of the smaller border crossings.[25] Unlike al-Gharrawi, al-Sheibani was known to be a true believer in Iran's theocratic ide-ology and a devotee of its supreme leader. His long tenure in Iran and decades serving in Badr and the IRGC made him more an Iranian agent than an Iraqi client. He worked seamlessly within the IRGC, and was known to be finan-cially compensated better than his Iraq-based counterparts.[26] Although he was based in Iran, al-Sheibani commanded some of the underground Badr units that remained outside of the political process. His network was closely intertwined with Iranian operations from the outset, and involved in attacks on both ex-Baathists and Coalition forces.[27]

A New Proxy Army

Between Badr, its associates, and local Shia groups, Iran's reach into Iraq was al-ready extensive in the early occupation. But that network did not reach its fullest expression until the IRGC enticed factions formerly loyal to Muqtada al-Sadr to join the fold. It was from those factions that Iran developed its deadliest tools against the Coalition: the so-called Special Groups. The leaders of those militias were Shia clergy drawn from the upper ranks of the Muqtada al-Sadr's faction, and had been previously loyal to him. Along with the fighters who joined them, they had lost faith in Muqtada's leadership in the wake of the Mahdi Army's failed uprising.[28] Qais al-Khazali was the most ambitious and prominent of the new warlords. A former close aide to Muqtada, al-Khazali founded Asaib Ahl al-Haq (League of the Righteous)—a militia that became instrumental in Iran's war against the Coalition. He played a leading role in countless operations, including a deadly ambush in Karbala that killed five American troops (an episode discussed in further detail in Chapter 4), which led to his arrest by British forces in 2007. During his incarceration, al-Khazali began collaborating with U.S. forces, feeding information on Iran's activities in Iraq and the Shia insurgency in exchange for preferential treatment and other incentives. Information gained from prisoner interrogations is inherently problematic, and often unreliable. However, in al-Khazali's case, much of the information that he provided about certain aspects of Iranian operations in Iraq was corroborated by documents found when he was arrested, and confirmed by information already known at the time through numerous other sources.[29] To that extent, al-Khazali's anecdotes add flesh to the bones of an established narrative, and provide some insight into how Iran erected its lethal response to the U.S. invasion of Iraq.

According to al-Khazali, he first became acquainted with the IRGC when he and Hamid al-Sheibani accompanied Muqtada al-Sadr on a trip to Tehran in June 2003 to attend the 14th anniversary commemoration of the death of Iran's first supreme leader, Ayatollah Ruhollah Khomeini.[30] There he was introduced to Quds Force chief Qassem Soleimani, and Abdul-Reza Shahlai, the head of operations in Iraq.[31] Though contact was made, the meeting did not lead to an alliance between Muqtada and the IRGC. Instead, the upstart militant remained wary of Iran's ambitions in Iraq and wanted to keep their operatives at arm's length. However, after the Mahdi Army's humiliating defeat at Najaf, al-Sadr became open to Tehran's advances. The IRGC provided a lifeline, and Muqtada accepted the support. Soon he began sending a number of his fighters to Iran for training, and tapped al-Khazali to oversee that effort.

Al-Khazali quickly became a key node in Iran's anti-Coalition operations. Much of the new cadre of Iranian-trained militants did not return to the Mahdi Army's ranks. Instead, the IRGC forged them into a new network separate from al-Sadr's militia and leadership, which became known to Coalition forces as the Special Groups. A number of al-Sadr's deputies, such as Akram al-Kaabi, Muhammad Tabatabai, and al-Khazali himself, took on leadership roles in the Special Groups.[32] Badr associates, including Abu Mahdi al-Muhandis, Adnan al-Shahmani, and al-Sheibani, also took on leadership roles in the new formation.[33] Emerging from this were a collection of related but distinct militias, which operationally merged Sadrist factions with elements from Badr. This nexus included the Sheibani network; Asaib Ahl al-Haq, led by al-Khazali and Akram al-Kaabi; Kataib Hezbollah (Hezbollah Brigades), led by Abu Mahdi al-Muhandis; and smaller groups. Iran's patronage united these commanders and fortified the loyalty they espoused to the authority of its supreme leader, Ali Khamenei.[34]

Iran provided tens of millions of dollars in funding to its Iraqi clients every month. The funds were transferred through hawala traders, or smuggled into the country as cash.[35] Badr and SCIRI alone reportedly received $50 million from Iran every month.[36] This supplemented other forms of funding. In Badr's case, with the inclusion of its fighters in the Iraqi Security Forces, many of the monthly salaries for its personnel were likely being paid indirectly by money provided to the Iraqi government by the United States. Even as Badr-associated cliques within the Interior Ministry were linked to sectarian death squads responsible for the murders of hundreds of Sunni civilians, the group's fighters continued to be on the Iraqi government's payroll.[37] SCIRI's additional funding came through the religious institutions and pious endowments controlled by the al-Hakim family, which benefited from the legacy of Grand Ayatollah Muhsin al-Hakim, the father of the organization's leader, Ayatollah Abd al-Aziz al-Hakim, and his influential brothers.

Compared with Badr and SCIRI, the Special Groups received much less from Iran, but their operations were still generously funded. Al-Khazali claims that Iran provided the groups around $2 million per month. The money initially went to a central committee headed by Iraqi cleric Sayyid Mustafah al-Yaqubi and distributed from there. When al-Yaqubi later relocated to Iran, the funds were sent to Shaykh Jabar al-Khafaji or Shaykh Muhammad al-Sa'adi, who had headed the same logistics committee in the Mahdi Army as al-Khazali had previously.[38] The amount going to the Special Groups roughly corresponded to information found in documents seized during al-Khazali's arrest. Those documents suggested that Asaib Ahl al-Haq was receiving between $750,000 and $3 million per month from Iran.[39] It is unclear how much of those funds paid for the organization's costs, but it at least provided income for commanders and fighters, who were all paid monthly salaries.[40]

Developing a capable cadre required various forms of training. Lebanese Hezbollah was central to that effort, with its highly trained and native Arabic-speaking veterans serving as effective conduits of the IRGC. Hezbollah operatives were present in Iraq soon after the fall of the Baathist regime. They served as direct agents of the IRGC, contributing to operations in the field and providing in-country training to Iraqi counterparts. The integration of Hezbollah members into the IRGC's operations and training program evinced the importance of the organization to Iranian strategy and the intertwining of the client's interests with those of its sponsor. By July 2004, Lebanese operatives were working with the Sheibani network in Basra to help its fighters build and use explosively formed penetrators (EFPs) on the battlefield. Those weapons, which became the single deadliest piece of ordnance used against Coalition forces introduced by Iran in the war, had been smuggled into the country piecemeal by the IRGC's cross-border network and required experienced hands to be used effectively.[41] More advanced training took place at IRGC bases in Iran, including at the Imam Khomeini complex near Lowshan, in the northern Gilan province. IRGC officers oversaw courses, with instructors coming from both its ranks and from Hezbollah. Al-Khazali claims that the IRGC and Hezbollah led different aspects of the training program. Hezbollah instructors oversaw a variety of areas, including lessons in the use of EFPs, rocket-propelled grenades (RPG SA-7s), mortars (120mm, 81mm, and 60mm), and small arms. IRGC officers led more specialized courses, such as advanced explosives and tradecraft.[42] The Iraqi fighters trained in Iran were specifically schooled to combat the Coalition. Iran supported Iraqi militants that were targeting former Baathists and Sunni jihadist groups as well, but they reportedly received less involved instruction at camps inside Iraq.[43] IRGC bases thus became factories for developing soldiers for Iran's war against the occupation.

4

The Strategy of Freedom

Terrorism could not be defeated by force alone. Political violence was the outgrowth of extremism, and to defeat it, a more powerful ideology needed to take hold. For the Bush administration, spreading democracy was the cornerstone of the plan to remake the Middle East. "America is pursuing a forward strategy of freedom in the Middle East," President Bush said in a February 2004 speech. "We're challenging the enemies of reform, confronting the allies of terror, and expecting a higher standard from our friends. For too long, American policy looked away while men and women were oppressed, their rights ignored and their hopes stifled. That era is over. . . . As in Germany, and Japan, and Eastern Europe, liberty will overcome oppression in the Middle East."[1]

Iraq was the linchpin in that effort, but the war was not going according to plan. The Sunni and Shia insurgencies were bogging down Coalition troops, and jeopardizing Washington's efforts to transform the country. Violence within Iraq was mounting, and Iraqis increasingly saw the forces of occupation as part of the problem. That did not discourage Washington's quest to establish a flourishing democracy upon the ashes of the Baathist regime. President Bush routinely affirmed his determination to see the project through. As he stated six months into the war, establishing democracy in Iraq would be "a massive and difficult undertaking," but "worth our sacrifice." The United States could not afford to fail in this endeavor, the president warned, because that would "embolden terrorists around the world, increase dangers to the American people, and extinguish the hopes of millions in the region." Success, by contrast, would have a cascading and positive impact on the entire region. Bush was resolute in that vision: "Iraqi democracy will succeed—and that success will send forth the news, from Damascus to Tehran—that freedom can be the future of every nation. The establishment of a free Iraq at the heart of the Middle East will be a watershed event in the global democratic revolution."[2]

A Beacon of Hope and Fear

Central to the Bush administration's effort at overhauling Iraq's political system was returning governmental authority to Iraqi hands. The first major step toward that end came in late June 2004, when the Coalition formally transferred power to the Iraqi-led Interim Governing Council, and ended the controversial rule of the Coalition Provisional Authority. The new prime minister, Ayad Allawi, was thrust into an arduous position. He had little control over how the insurgency was being fought and little support among the occupation's detractors. His brief time in office was consumed by the end of the Mahdi Army's uprising, and the Coalition's bloody campaign against Sunni militants in Al Anbar province, which included the battles to retake Fallujah in November and December. The latter was one of the war's most massive offensives, and the second attempt to clear the city. The first effort had lasted three weeks from April to early May, and involved over 2,000 American troops. The second effort was much larger, involving almost 15,000, largely American troops, backed by Iraqi government and British forces, who encircled the city, and fought block by block, street by street, house by house, in a six-week advance aimed at clearing the city of Al-Qaeda and jihadist fighters, many of whom had fortified themselves in the city's dozens of mosques. It was the deadliest urban battle the United States fought in the war, and while it succeeded in destroying Al-Qaeda's hold of the city, it came at great cost, with an estimated 800 civilians killed, along with around 100 Coalition troops, and as many as 2,000 jihadists.[3] Hundreds more on all sides were injured. Both Fallujah campaigns became case studies for the U.S. Army's and Marine Corps' future leaders, but their destructive toll quickly reverberated negatively within Iraqi society and politics.[4]

Overseeing that part of the war earned Allawi more adversaries than allies. As its name implied, the interim government led by Allawi was merely a placeholder. In January 2005, Iraq got its first taste of post-Baathist democracy through the election of the National Assembly, which would be tasked with writing a new Iraqi constitution. The elections were boycotted by Sunni Arab political parties, who were reeling from their fall from prominence and enraged by the counter-insurgency campaign in Al Anbar province. Their boycott, and Allawi's unpopularity, gave Shia parties a distinct advantage, and allowed for the election of Ibrahim al-Jaafari, an expatriate activist from the Islamist Dawa Party. Jaafari replaced the secular-nationalist Allawi as prime minister in May, and became the head of Iraq's Transitional Government for a one-year term. President Bush hailed the achievement: "Today the people of Iraq have spoken to the world, and the world is hearing the voice of freedom from the center of the Middle East." The war was ongoing, but the Iraqi election had symbolized a victory for

Washington. "In great numbers and under great risk, Iraqis have shown their commitment to democracy. By participating in free elections, the Iraqi people have firmly rejected the anti-democratic ideology of the terrorists," Bush said in his White House address.[5]

Jaafari's government was in charge of establishing a committee to supervise the writing of a constitution. He appointed elected officials from each major constituency to the committee. Initially, this excluded Sunni Arabs due to their boycott, but Jaafari later added unelected Sunni Arab representatives to the committee to help gain their community's buy-in. Writing the constitution was a contentious process. The committee was divided by politics, sect, and mutual resentment, yet eventually managed to draft a new national pact for Iraq. The document enshrined the principles of democracy, ethnic and religious plurality, the centrality of Islam as the creed of the country's majority, and the rule of law as the basic principles of the post-Baathist state. Kurdish was adopted as Iraq's second official language after Arabic, and all ethno-linguistic minority populations were given the right to educate their students in their mother tongue in public schools.[6]

The promotion of democracy and federalism were boons to the Shia and Kurdish populations of Iraq, giving the former a demographic advantage in elections and the latter effective autonomy over Kurdish areas through the establishment of the Kurdish Regional Government (KRG). As much as those provisions meant to the Shia and Kurds in Iraq, they triggered unease in some neighboring states. The issue of Kurdish autonomy was a key concern for Turkey, whose government feared that a move toward greater independence in Iraqi Kurdistan would reinvigorate Kurdish separatism in its own country, home to 30 million Kurds. Turkish foreign minister Abdullah Gül framed Ankara's rejection of Kurdish independence as part of a larger, shared regional perspective, stating: "We will not let that go . . . neither will the Iraqi people, the neighboring countries, or the international community. While trying to solve one problem, you can't go and create another."[7]

Turkey had been at war with Kurdish insurgents for decades. The country enjoyed a relatively peaceful period since 1999, when the Kurdistan Workers' Party, or PKK, declared a ceasefire and withdrew its forces from Turkey to bases in Iraq's Qandil mountains, near the Iranian border. Unhappy with the lack of political progress in negotiations with Ankara, the PKK recommenced armed operations in June 2004, using its bases in Iraq to funnel weapons and fighters into Turkey for attacks. This led to a wave of Turkish military incursions against PKK enclaves in eastern Turkey, including operations in April and May 2005.[8] Ankara blamed the United States for the PKK's ability to operate in Iraq, and repeatedly demanded that the U.S. military target PKK positions in the country. While the United States considered the PKK a terrorist organization, the sheer scale of the insurgency in Iraq made the PKK (whose operations were focused outside of the country) a low priority.[9]

The uptick in PKK-linked terrorism in Turkey made security concerns a central factor in Turkish diplomacy with Iraqi Kurdish leaders, Baghdad, and Washington. Beyond obviating a move toward independence, Turkey wanted to prevent Iraqi Kurds from achieving the resources that could make an autonomous state possible. This meant ensuring that Iraq's northern oil-rich city of Kirkuk—considered by Kurdish leaders to be an integral part of historical Kurdistan—stayed out of Kurdish control. Kirkuk had long been an ethnically mixed city with predominant Kurdish and Turkmen communities. It also possessed the richest oil deposits in northern Iraq. To weaken Kurdish influence in the city and surrounding areas, the Baathist regime had pursued an Arabization policy, which displaced thousands of Kurdish and other non-Arab minority families and replaced them with mostly Sunni Arab émigrés.[10] Following the collapse of Baathist rule in 2003, Kurdish leaders encouraged the resettlement of Kurds in Kirkuk, particularly in the lead-up to the January 2005 elections, stoking anxieties in Ankara that Kurds would attempt to seize the city and its nearby oil fields as part of a move toward independence. Commenting on this dynamic in February 2005, Turkish prime minister Recep Tayyip Erdoğan indirectly blamed the United States for the expansion of Kurdish power in Kirkuk, saying: "Some people are looking the other way while mass migration takes place. . . . This is going to create major difficulties in the future."[11]

Erdoğan's focus on Kirkuk spoke to lingering revanchist sentiments in Turkey's political class. Kirkuk had originally been part of Turkey after the fall of the Ottoman Empire, and was later ceded to Iraq (along with Mosul) by the League of Nations. The 1926 Treaty of Ankara, which delineated the modern Turkish-Iraqi border, solidified that status. A broad segment of Turkish politicians still considered Kirkuk part of Turkey's historical geography. Combined with pan-Turkic sentiment, expressed as a commitment to protect Iraq's Turkmen population, Turkish officials set a clear red line on Kirkuk. As one Turkish diplomat put it: "Kirkuk is the number one security issue and public concern right now. . . . For us it has special status. It is like Jerusalem. It belongs to all the people. We do not want to intervene in Iraq. But we have red lines—Kirkuk and attacks on ethnic minorities."[12]

Iraq's political shift from Sunni Arab dominance to a Shia-centric democracy caused similar trepidation in neighboring Arab states. Saudi Arabia was especially vocal about what the democratic turn in Iraq could mean for the country and the region. In late September 2005, in the lead-up to the October constitutional referendum and the December parliamentary elections, Saudi Arabia's foreign minister, Saud al-Faisal, criticized U.S. steps in Iraq. He counseled that something needed to be done to bring the country's diverse peoples together, warning "elections alone won't do it . . . [a] constitution alone won't do it."[13] The marginalization of Arab Sunnis was fundamental to Iraq's insecurity, he argued, denouncing the de-Baathification policy for inherently labeling "every Sunni Baathist a criminal."[14] The Saudi official echoed concerns shared by other regional leaders, viewing the escalating violence in Iraq as a regional problem that could draw neighboring countries into the conflict.[15] More worrisome was the potential for pro-Iranian Shia groups to gain power through democratic elections. In a show of frustration, al-Faisal alluded to the long-standing Arab effort of containing Iran's regional influence, and criticized Washington's policies as benefiting Iran instead of its regional partners, stating: "We fought a war together to keep Iran out of Iraq after Iraq was driven out of Kuwait. Now we are handing the whole country over to Iran without reason."[16]

Despite regional opposition, Iraq's democratic transition progressed on schedule. The constitution was overwhelmingly approved in the October referendum, receiving more than 78 percent support from almost 10 million votes. The parliamentary election in December was similarly successful, and garnered 70 percent participation from eligible voters. The United Iraqi Alliance, a broad coalition of mostly Shia parties, including the Iran-backed SCIRI, Sadrist candidates, and the Islamic Dawa Party, dominated polls with 41.2 percent of the vote. The Kurdish coalition, under the Democratic Patriotic Alliance of Kurdistan, came in second with 21.7 percent, and the Iraqi Accord Front, a Sunni coalition, came in third with 15.1 percent. A host of disagreements, including intra-Shia factionalism, Kurdish federalist demands, and Arab Sunni discontent, stalled negotiations on forming a government for months. Eventually, Nuri al-Maliki, a veteran Dawa Party activist who had spent 24 years in exile, including 8 years in Iran and 16 in Syria, was chosen as a compromise candidate for prime minister. Maliki's government, the first under Iraq's new constitution, was approved by parliament on May 20, 2006. Even if the country was a mess, Iraqi democracy was emerging.

Iraq's political transition was a hallmark achievement for the Bush administration. Washington viewed it as part of a wider democratic wave, which had begun to challenge lingering authoritarianism in Europe and Asia. The so-called color revolutions of Georgia in 2003, Ukraine in 2004, and Kyrgyzstan in 2005, wherein pro-democracy movements made remarkable gains in former Soviet states, signaled to Washington and the world that the cause of freedom was on the march. Those developments were warmly welcomed by the Bush administration. As the president told reporters in January 2005, "I believe democracy can take hold in parts of the world that have been condemned to tyranny. And I believe when democracies take hold, it leads to peace. That's been the proven example around the world. Democracies equal peace. And that's what we're trying to advance in this administration."[17]

The Bush administration pushed for political change across the Middle East, and with some success. In Lebanon, the United States championed the popular movement against Syria's 28-year military rule, which led to a strong showing for anti-Syrian candidates in the country's May 2005 general election and precipitated an end to the occupation. In Palestine, Washington pushed for democratic elections following the death of Yasser Arafat in November 2004. A few months later, the Palestinian Authority held its first post-Arafat leadership election in January 2005, followed by a parliamentary election a year later. The result, however, was the opposite of what the Bush administration had hoped for. The election had gone to Hamas, the proscribed Islamist terrorist organization based in Gaza. While Lebanon's anti-Syria movement was hailed by the West as a triumph of popular democracy, elections in the Palestinian territories were not, and led to foreign powers and regional states boycotting the Hamas government.

Freedom on the March in Lebanon

Unlike much of the region, Lebanon had a functioning democratic system. That system was heavily restricted, however, by the combination of Syria's military occupation and the confessional structure of Lebanese politics. Based on the 1932 constitution, along with amendments following the 1989 Taif agreement, Lebanon's parliamentary system was designed to give relatively proportional representation to each of the country's main confessional communities, and equal parliamentary representation for Christians (Maronite Catholic, Greek Catholic, Greek Orthodox, Armenians, etc.) and Muslims (Sunni and Shia, but also including the Druze). The country's elected leadership was similarly derived from the 1932 founding census: the presidency was reserved for Maronite Christians, the prime minister for Sunnis, the speaker of parliament for the Shia, and, often, the foreign minister for the Druze. To that end, politicians and political parties represented, above all, their religious communities, and solicited votes largely on the basis of protecting the equities of those communities. Even so, because members of parliament were elected by all Lebanese citizens, and not just those of their confessional community, their platforms also addressed or at least spoke to shared concerns of the citizenry and issues that transcended identity.

Syria's influence hamstrung Lebanese politics. Lebanon's civil war, which lasted from 1975 to 1990, led to enduring military occupations by both Israel and Syria. Israel controlled a portion of southern Lebanon from 1982 to 2000, when it unilaterally withdrew its forces from Lebanese territory. Syria's military occupation began in 1975 when its forces entered Beirut to stabilize the city. Even after the war ended, Syria's forces remained. The Syrian government essentially controlled Lebanese politics, and acted as an outside imperial power, using established clients and loyal politicians to run the country's affairs as the Assad regime deemed fit. By the end of the 20th century, Syria's occupation seemed to be one of the constants in the Middle East, and one that was unlikely to go away. However, Israel's withdrawal in 2000 precipitated a shift in Lebanese perspectives and expectations. A political movement critical of Syria's occupation began to grow among Sunni, Druze, and some Christian politicians. Chief among them was Rafik Hariri, a billionaire who had made his fortune managing high-profile construction projects in Saudi Arabia, and a leader in Lebanon's Sunni community. Hariri was elected prime minister in 2000, and became a target of Damascus because of his stance against the occupation.

A critical juncture for Damascus was the Lebanese presidency. The post had been filled by the pro-Syrian politician Emile Lahoud since 1998, and he was barred by Lebanon's constitution from serving a consecutive six-year term. Syrian president Bashar al-Assad wanted Lahoud to remain in office and demanded that Lebanon's constitution be amended to allow it. Hariri was against this, and was summoned to Damascus in late August 2004 for a tête-à-tête with Assad. In their August 26 meeting, Assad reportedly made the proposition clear to Hariri: either Lahoud would remain president or Assad would "break Lebanon" over the heads of Hariri and Walid Jumblatt—the prominent Druze leader who had also come out against Lahoud and the Syrian occupation. A week later, under Western pressure, the UN Security Council (UNSC) passed Resolution 1559, calling on all foreign forces to withdraw from Lebanese territory, and for all militias to disband, disarm, and support free and fair elections.[18] The bill was co-sponsored by the United States and France, and aimed at pushing the Syrians out of Lebanon and disarming Hezbollah—the Shia political movement backed by both Damascus and Tehran. Hariri and Jumblatt were the key Lebanese sponsors of the resolution.

Syria's influence was almost insurmountable, and Hariri was likely to lose the parliamentary vote on Lahoud. Instead of failing in that vote, or allowing the government to collapse, Hariri unexpectedly announced his resignation in late September and left office in October. Omar Karami, a pro-Syrian Sunni politician, became prime minister the day after Hariri stepped down. Hariri switched his attention to upcoming elections in six months, and stood a good chance of returning to the prime minister's office. A few months later, on February 14, 2005, Hariri was killed along with 21 others, including several bystanders, when a bomb-laden truck detonated alongside his motorcade near Beirut's seaside corniche. The immense explosion sheered facades off nearby buildings and left a substantial crater in the road.

Hariri's supporters immediately suspected Syria and Hezbollah—suspicions that were eventually confirmed through ensuing, years-long investigations.[19]

Hariri was Saudi Arabia's main client in the country, and one of the only politicians powerful enough to attempt to challenge Syrian hegemony. A week after his death, Hariri's supporters took to the streets, calling for an end to Syria's occupation and for those responsible for the former prime minister's assassination to be held accountable. The largely Sunni and Christian demonstrators demanded that the Karami government resign, for the heads of Lebanon's six major security forces to be replaced, and for an international investigation into Hariri's assassination to be commissioned. Karami stepped down on February 28, which added fuel to the protest movement. Tens of thousands of demonstrators maintained a daily presence in Beirut's Martyr Square, and erected a tent city on the site. Their new demands focused on ending Syria's occupation, and returning Lebanon to a state of independence.

The United States and France backed the movement, and called for UNSC Resolution 1559 to be adopted by all sides, and for Syrian troops to quit Lebanon. U.S. officials likened Lebanon's popular movement with the "tulip" revolution in Ukraine and the "rose" revolution in Georgia, calling it the Cedar Revolution, an homage the country's national symbol. They also connected it to Iraq, framing it as the spread of democracy and freedom in the Middle East. As Paula J. Dobriansky, the undersecretary for global affairs at the Department of State, stated in a press conference on human rights:

> We find ourselves in an era of monumental advancement for human rights and democracy. As the President noted in Bratislava just last week, there was a rose revolution in Georgia, an orange revolution in Ukraine, and most recently, a purple revolution in Iraq. In Lebanon, we see growing momentum for a "cedar revolution" that is unifying the citizens of that nation to the cause of true democracy and freedom from foreign influence. Hopeful signs span the globe, and there should be no doubt that the years ahead will be great ones for the cause of freedom.[20]

Syria was under immense pressure to act. In early March, Syrian officials began touring the region looking for support. On March 4, Bashar al-Assad traveled to Riyadh to meet with Crown Prince Abdullah. During their meeting Abdullah reportedly asked why Syria had killed Hariri, to which Assad, feigning ignorance of the matter, suggested that had Syrians been responsible it might have been a rogue action by a section of the intelligence services. Abdullah was apparently unimpressed, and warned Assad that Syria must abandon Lebanon, including the removal of all military and security personnel, within weeks or else its relations with Saudi Arabia would be in jeopardy.[21] The next day, Assad gave a speech to Syria's parliament, and while minimizing the spiraling anti-Syrian sentiments in Lebanon, announced that Syria would abide by UNSC Resolution

1559 and withdraw its forces from the country. That departure would happen in stages: first a pullback of all forces to the Bekaa Valley, which began on March 6, and then later, forces would move across the Lebanese-Syrian border.[22]

Syria's withdrawal risked weakening the positions of its chief clients in Lebanon. Hezbollah was among those that had the most to lose, and led a last-ditch effort to rally support for its benefactor. On March 8, the party's secretary general, Hassan Nasrallah, called for a public show of solidarity with Syria, accusing the anti-Syria protestors of being tools of America and Israel. Hundreds of thousands responded to the call, with many Shia Hezbollah supporters being bussed into central Beirut from neighborhoods in the city's southside. Addressing the crowd, Nasrallah proclaimed: "Today, you decide the future of your nation and your country; today you answer the world. . . . No to American-Zionist intervention. Yes to Lebanese-Syrian brotherhood."[23] The massive demonstration was a testament to Hezbollah's influence in the country and its inseparability from its foreign patrons. It was also a panicked reaction to the sudden political shift in the country which was gaining momentum. On the same day, President Bush assured the anti-Syria movement of America's support and called on Assad to leave Lebanon or face further isolation:

> The world community, including Russia and Germany and France and Saudi Arabia and the United States, has presented the Syrian government with one of those choices: to end its nearly 30-year occupation of Lebanon or become even more isolated from the world. . . . The time has come for Syria to fully implement Security Council Resolution 1559. All Syrian military forces and intelligence personnel must withdraw before the Lebanese elections for those elections to be free and fair. . . . And that new government will have the help of the international community in building sound political, economic and military institutions so the great nation of Lebanon can move forward in security and freedom.[24]

The American president continued with a message to the Lebanese people: "All the world is witnessing your great movement of conscience. Lebanon's future belongs in your hands. And by your courage Lebanon's future will be in your hands. The American people are on your side. Millions across the Earth are on your side. The momentum of freedom is on your side. And freedom will prevail in Lebanon."[25]

In response, and to commemorate the one-month anniversary of Hariri's death, legions of anti-Syria protestors turned out on March 14 for what became the largest public gathering in Lebanon's history. An estimated one million people, largely from the Sunni, Christian, and Druze communities, made their way to Martyr's Square. It was an imposing display of Syria's unpopularity. Hezbollah could not compete on such a scale, and stopped organizing rival demonstrations. By April 26, the last of Syria's military infrastructure in Lebanon was destroyed, and its tanks and personnel carriers were sent across the border.[26] After almost three decades, the Syrian occupation of Lebanon was over. Imperial overreach had been Syria's undoing.

Isolating Gaza

The democratic moment was not all vibrant hues, flowers, and evergreens. As much as the Bush administration and Europe considered Lebanon a success for popular democracy in the Middle East, elections in the Palestinian territories dampened that enthusiasm. The death of Yasser Arafat on November 11, 2004, spurred a sea-change in Palestinian politics. The Palestinian Liberation Organization, an umbrella organization composed of the Palestinian movement's major political factions, had been headed by Arafat and dominated since 1969 by his Fatah organization. Arafat had served as the only chairman of the Palestinian Authority, the Palestinian government which held charge over Palestinian areas in the West Bank and Gaza not under direct Israeli control. Every major event in the Palestinian struggle from 1969 to 2004 had been shaped by Arafat's stewardship. Unsurprisingly, the vote to replace him as Palestinian Authority chairman in January 2005 resulted in the election of Mahmoud Abbas (commonly known as Abu Mazen), who also succeeded Arafat as the head of Fatah. Abbas had the same titles as Arafat, but lacked his predecessor's unique persona and held less sway among the competing Palestinian factions.

Arafat's absence provided Israeli politicians an opportunity to pivot on the Palestinian issue. Prime Minister Ariel Sharon pushed forward with plans to unilaterally disengage from Gaza and cede the territory to the Palestinian Authority. An early version of the proposal, which also included withdrawal from a small portion of the northern West Bank, had been approved by the Israeli government months before Arafat's death, but remained controversial. Sharon, whose rise to prominence in Israel's political establishment had followed a storied military career, including his controversial role in the 1982 invasion of Lebanon, had boldly proposed a withdrawal of the Gaza strip in 2003 as a way of avoiding a potential demographic crisis for the Jewish state.[27] With over 1.5 million residents squeezed into a territory 41 kilometers long, and only 12 kilometers across at its widest point, Gaza was among the most densely populated areas of the world. By turning Gaza over to the Palestinian Authority, Sharon and his supporters aimed to avoid a potential future scenario where the territory's mostly Muslim population could be incorporated into Israel if a two-state solution failed to be achieved. Such a situation would reduce Israel's Jewish demographic ma-jority and endanger the country's raison d'être as a Jewish state. Ehud Olmert, a member of Sharon's cabinet and eventual successor as prime minister, explained those concerns in a 2003 interview:

> More and more Palestinians are uninterested in a negotiated, two-state solution, because they want to change the essence of the conflict from an Algerian paradigm to a South African one. From a struggle against "occupation," in their parlance, to a struggle for one-man-one-vote. That is, of course, a much cleaner struggle, a much more popular struggle— and ultimately a much more powerful one. For us, it would mean the end of the Jewish state.[28]

Sharon's plan was a significant shift in Israeli policy. Gaza had been occupied by the Israeli military since 1967, and 21 Israeli settlements had been erected there over the decades. Members of Israel's far right were against the move, with the abandonment of settlements and the fear of insecurity foremost among their concerns. The proposal gained support in Washington, however, where it was seen as a step toward a two-state solution. Writing to Sharon in April 2004, President Bush described the disengagement plan as a building block for an eventual peace:

> A peace settlement negotiated between Israelis and Palestinians would be a great boon not only to those peoples but to the peoples of the entire region. Accordingly, the United States believes that all states in the region have special responsibilities: to support the building of the institutions of a Palestinian state; to fight terrorism, and cut off all forms of assistance to individuals and groups engaged in terrorism; and to begin now to move toward more normal relations with the State of Israel. These actions would be true contributions to building peace in the region.
>   Mr. Prime Minister, you have described a bold and historic initi-ative that can make an important contribution to peace. I commend your efforts and your courageous decision which I support. As a close friend and ally, the United States intends to work closely with you to help make it a success.[29]

In the face of stiff criticism from Israel's far-right settler movement and its supporters, Sharon eventually secured the necessary backing. Finance minister Benjamin Netanyahu, the Likud Party head and former prime minister, was a leading critic and argued that Gaza would become a staging ground for terrorist groups. Netanyahu seized on the issue to strengthen his position as a leading rival to Sharon within the Likud Party. He resigned in protest in August, explaining in statement: "I am not prepared to be a partner to a move which ignores reality, and proceeds blindly toward turning the Gaza Strip into a base for Islamic terrorism which will threaten the state."[30]

After its adoption by the Knesset, the disengagement plan was put into effect. Some extremist setters, who abhorred the idea of giving up any inch of land to the Palestinians, strenuously resisted abandoning the Gaza settlements. The Sharon government was unyielding, and settlers who did not vacate their homes in exchange for financial compensation and other incentives were forcefully removed by Israeli security forces. The withdrawal was completed by September 22. Gaza did not become independent as a result. Its border with Egypt was turned over to Egyptian forces, and its borders with Israel, including its coastline, remained tightly controlled. Territory within those boundaries fell under the nominal control of the Palestinian Authority, but in practice, the most direct beneficiaries were the Gaza-based militant factions Hamas and Palestinian Islamic Jihad (PIJ). Both took credit for Israel's withdrawal, claiming it to be the result of their violent resistance campaign during the Second Intifada. Public opinion polls at the time suggested that a majority of Gaza residents shared that perception.[31]

Hamas rode an upsurge in support among Gazans through Palestinian Authority elections in January 2006. Growing mistrust of Fatah, the loss of its longtime leader Arafat, and a sloppy campaign strategy led to an unanticipated result: Hamas emerged victorious by winning 74 out of 132 legislative council seats to Fatah's 45. The victory of a terrorist group through a democratic election presented a challenge to both the Knesset and Washington. The Bush administration had pushed for Palestinian democracy, but was now faced with an unanticipated outcome.[32] Instead of dealing with the new Hamas-led government, the United States, Israel, and Fatah looked for ways to undermine and circumvent it. That approach was consistent with the Bush administration's post–9/11 approach toward terrorist groups, but inconsistent with its proselytization of Middle East democracy. It was clear that democracy for the Bush administration was desired only if it led to like-minded governments. Bush himself suggested as much in a 2002 speech, urging the Palestinians to seek new leadership through democratic elections: "I call on the Palestinian people to elect new leaders, leaders not compromised by terror. I call upon them to build a practicing democracy, based on tolerance and liberty. If the Palestinian people actively pursue these goals, America and the world will actively support their efforts."[33] A democracy that led to a government opposed to core U.S. values and policies was something to be opposed, not encouraged. In Hamas's case, it was the group's refusal to abandon terrorism and accept the 1997 Oslo Agreement that made its victory dead on arrival in Washington. As Bush stated days after the election: "The Hamas party has made it clear that they do not support the right of Israel. . . . And I have made it clear that so long as that's their policy that we will not support a Palestinian government made up of Hamas."[34]

Washington was not alone in that position. The United Nations, European Union, and Russia all "conditioned continued assistance to the Palestinian Authority on Hamas's renunciation of violence, recognition of Israel, and acceptance of previous Israeli-Palestinian interim agreements."[35] Because Hamas refused to do so, outside powers and Israel began to isolate it. The United States worked with Israel to channel its previous funding of the Palestinian Authority directly to Fatah.[36] Washington and Brussels stopped financial assistance to the Palestinian Authority, and Israel withheld taxes and customs duties owed to the Palestinian Authority under the Oslo Accords. The absence of aid, and the inability for Hamas to use banks because of its terrorist designation, left the Palestinian Authority in a debilitating financial crisis. Both Israel and the United States were aiming to weaken Hamas to the point that it would be either compelled to relinquish control to Fatah or susceptible to a takeover by the same. In late 2006, the Bush administration drew up plans to provide Fatah with financial assistance, arms, and ammunition in order to help the organization gain back Gaza territory by force if necessary. Congress ultimately blocked lethal aid from reaching the Palestinians and reduced the funding from $86 million proposed by the administration to $56 million. Washington turned to Arab states to fill in the gap, with Egypt eventually providing arms and training to Fatah's security forces.[37]

Marginalizing the Hamas-led government while pumping up Fatah hastened a split in the Palestinian Authority, and led to armed clashes between the organizations in June 2007. Hamas routed its rivals in the fighting, forcing Fatah to abandon Gaza completely. The split had left Hamas with control of its home territory while Fatah reasserted authority over the West Bank. Although isolating Hamas made sense in terms of the Palestinian-Israeli peace process, because the organization was implacably against that process and unwilling to mollify its positions even after it won control of the Palestinian Authority, it also reduced Western and Arab influence in Gaza. More significantly, it opened the door for others, and Iran was happy to step in. Hamas's need for aid, combined with Iran's ambitions in the region and their mutual hostility toward Israel and the United States, created a context ripe for exploitation. Tehran already had close relations with Hamas, and had provided the group millions of dollars in funding since the mid-1990s. Flush by rising oil prices—with a barrel of crude increasing from $37.66 in 2004 to $91.48 in 2008—Tehran accelerated its support to Hamas following the exit of aid from other foreign powers.[38] While Iran had reportedly provided the group tens of millions of dollars in the past, Hamas's exiled leader

Ismail Haniyeh claimed that Iran had pledged $250 million in aid to the organiza-
tion in 2006 alone.[39] Additionally, Iran stepped up military assistance to Hamas,
which included smuggling anti-tank Katyusha rockets into Gaza. Eventually Iran
also transferred weapons-production knowhow, which enabled Hamas and PIJ
to begin a domestic rocket industry within Gaza's borders.[40] Emerging as the
main outside patron to Palestinian factions in Gaza was a significant step in Iran's
expanding regional influence, and marked a shift in the Palestinian struggle. Iran
was emerging as the center of gravity in resistance to Israel, and the influence of
Arab states was increasingly pushed to the margins.

The Path to Jerusalem

During the Iran-Iraq War of the 1980s, the IRGC developed a religious prism through which they viewed the struggle. Early in the war, the IRGC began framing the battlefield experience as a spiritual exercise, one that would not only lead its martyrs to heavenly paradise, but also lead to the fulfillment of the revolution's destiny and to Islam's victory over the forces of Satan. Those ideas were reinforced in sermons by Iran's supreme leader, Ayatollah Ruhollah Khomeini, and echoed by the regime's many clerical and lay officials. Together, they conjured a picture of the war wherein the defeat of Baathist Iraq was not an end, but the means toward a much greater victory: the liberation of Jerusalem and the destruction of Israel. "The path to Jerusalem runs through Karbala" was a slogan popularized by the IRGC during that time, and one that it regularly splashed across its assortment of internal and external propaganda. Karbala was an evocative metaphor for the war. Like Iraq's other shrine cities, Karbala was sacred ground for the Shia, the site of the martyrdom of the Prophet Muhammad's grandson Imam Husayn in 680 CE and of his consecrated tomb. The "Prince of Martyrs," as the Shia refer to Imam Husayn, is, along with his father and mother, among the most revered of Muhammad's descendants by the Shia community. He is a symbol of the struggle for justice against oppression, of right versus wrong, virtuous sacrifice, and the power of spiritual liberation. As Iranians were dying in the war, the regime's leaders told them they were forfeiting their lives for righteousness, truth, and God, just as Imam Husayn had done.[1]

Such ideas, as meaningful as they might have been to some, simply added a spiritual veneer to the regime's material objectives of removing Saddam Hussein from power and establishing a like-minded, Shia Islamist government in Baghdad. Those goals were foundational to the revolution and were articulated by Iran's civilian and military leaders since the early days of the war. Speaking to an Iranian journalist in late April 1982 during the buildup to Operation Bayt al-Muqaddas—itself a direct reference to Jerusalem—a frontline commander spoke of the IRGC's hopes of what would follow Saddam's defeat: "When that day comes, an Islamic Iran and an Islamic Iraq will work together, and aided by the people, directly confront the usurper Israel from Syrian soil."[2] Having allies governing Iraq, Iran's leaders believed, would help pave the way for the revolution to transform the Middle East from a sea of largely pro-American secular states to a collection of anti-American and anti-Zionist Islamic polities. Achieving that, they believed, would enable them to bring an end to the state of Israel, and precipitate the wider destruction of the American-led global order.

Iran failed to reach that objective in the war. And although its leadership continued to invest in proxies that threatened Israel's security, prior to 2003, the notion of expanding the revolution in any serious sense outside Iran's borders had mostly evaporated. Yet, with the end of Baathist rule, the IRGC could suddenly envision fulfilling its former dream of making Iraq a stepping stone in the revolution's unfolding and the region's transformation. Even as the IRGC feared popular democracy in its own country, it recognized its potential in Iraq, and with the election of Prime Minister Nuri al-Maliki, Iran's former archrival was now led by a fellow Shia Islamist. Maliki was not initially close to Tehran, but his politics were more in line with Iran's than those of secular-nationalists such as Ayad Allawi.

In that way, America's war in Iraq accomplished what Iran had been unable to do itself: it had replaced Iran's nemesis with a government dominated by potential friends and clients. Iran's regime viewed Iraq as key to its own security and to its larger ambitions, and sought ways to increase its influence in the country while seeking to diminish that of the United States. Acting through the IRGC, Iran relied above all on violence, particularly the ability of its militant clients to intimidate, harm, or kill adversaries. The IRGC's core strategy was to utilize lethal operations to contest the occupation, dislodge the United States from its position of power in Iraq, and frustrate efforts to transform the country into a pro-Western democracy. Toward those ends, the IRGC's operations in Iraq became intertwined with its activities elsewhere. With the war between Hezbollah and Israel in 2006, the IRGC and its proxies emerged as capable transnational actors. Whereas they relied on simpler technologies and insurgent tactics, the IRGC's regional network was a vexing challenge to the United States, its partners, and allies—and was steadily growing in strength and confidence.

War on the Occupation

Iranian-sponsored attacks against Coalition forces began to intensify in 2005 and held steady throughout the occupation. Between then and 2011, the use of explosively formed penetrators (EFPs) by Iraqi militias was responsible for the deaths of at least 196 American troops and the wounding of almost 1,000 more.[3] Deadlier than the homemade improvised explosive devices (IEDs) favored by jihadists and other Sunni insurgents, the EFPs introduced by Iran were military grade and, true to their name, could penetrate armored vehicles. Each EFP attack in Iraq averaged two deaths, and inflicted casualty rates six times greater than IEDs.[4] Those who survived often had debilitating, lifelong injuries, from severed limbs to severe brain trauma. The components for the EFPs were produced in Iranian factories, and smuggled as kits across the border along with other weaponry and materiel. Lebanese Hezbollah operatives were sent to Iraq to train militants to assemble and use the sophisticated explosives. Through this effort, Hezbollah's training contingent in Iraq grew to as many as 60 individuals by 2008, and prompted the establishment of its Iraq-focused Unit 3800. EFPs were distributed to every Iran-backed militia and their subsidiary groups, all of whom used them to devastating effect. Badr cells in the Iraqi Security Forces (ISF) and police also played a role in the use, transport, storage, and distribution of EFPs, at times even selling them outside Iran's network to Sunni insurgents.[5]

The IRGC's ground war accelerated with the election of the bombastic hardliner Mahmoud Ahmadinejad, who succeeded Mohammad Khatami as Iran's president in August 2005. Ahmadinejad's foreign policy, which was highly critical of the United States and antagonistic toward Israel, benefited from Iran flexing its muscles in Iraq and advancing its nuclear enrichment program at home. As a veteran of the Iran-Iraq War, Ahmadinejad was a strong supporter of the IRGC and provided the organization even more top-cover for its foreign operations. Throughout his tenure, Iran-supported groups grew bolder and more aggressive in their actions.

The uptick in Iran's activities was palpable, and coincided with an outbreak of sectarian violence that plunged Iraq into civil war. Jihadist groups continued to expand their attacks against Coalition forces and Iraqi civilians. The Shia community was especially targeted, with jihadists deploying suicide bombers and IEDs against population centers and government buildings. Abu Musab al-Zarqawi's Al-Qaeda affiliate focused attacks on Shia civilians in the hopes of instigating a broader sectarian war, which he believed would eventually drive Sunnis to side with the jihadist insurgency. The group were the prime suspects in the February 22, 2006, bombing of the Al-Askari shrine in Samarra, which houses the tombs of the tenth and eleventh Shia imams. The attack destroyed the shrine's emblematic golden dome, and triggered a cycle of sectarian reprisals, resulting in two years of intense communal conflict.[6] Shia militants, including Sadrists and Iranian clients, were responsible for some of the worst violence.[7] They targeted suspected Sunni militants, their families, and ordinary civilians. Although Iran did not outwardly support the reprisal attacks, it did little to prevent its clients from murdering Sunni civilians and purging them from mixed neighborhoods in Baghdad and other cities.

Communal warfare did not distract Iran from its mission to disrupt the American occupation. Iran transferred around 215 EFPs to Iraq in March 2006 alone, marking a steep escalation after having sent around 450 of the explosives across the whole of 2005. Halfway through the year, explosives linked to Iran had killed almost 70 soldiers, and injured dozens more.[8] The number of attacks against U.S. and Coalition forces attributed to Shia militias was far lower in comparison to those linked to Sunni insurgents, but the lethality of EFPs made the Iranian threat pronounced. American military commanders on the ground had no clear policy on how to handle Iranian operatives in Iraq, and that problem gradually made it to Washington. In July 2006, U.S. ambassador to Iraq Zalmay Khalilzad informed Bush administration officials about the degree of Iran's support for lethal operations against U.S. forces, which initiated a policy review. After receiving a briefing on Iranian operations in Iraq, Secretary of Defense Donald Rumsfeld wrote Chairman of the Joint Chiefs of Staff Peter Pace in frustration: "If we know so much about what Iran is doing in Iraq, why don't we do something about it?" Yet, Rumsfeld already knew the answer to that question. As he later explained: "a country strained by two wars and an administration battling criticism and declining public approval was not ready to be firm with Iran."[9] Iran was fighting a war against the United States in Iraq, and the Bush administration, overwhelmed by the occupation and domestic politics, was doing little to push back.

Hezbollah's Moment: The July War

Iran's approach in Iraq mirrored its long-standing regional strategy of making friends with like-minded entities. The Islamic Republic's two decades of Shia theocratic revolutionism put it at odds with most of its secular and monarchical neighbors. Those same politics also helped it forge some strong alliances. Syria was Iran's only state ally, and relations with Damascus grew even closer after President Bashar al-Assad succeeded his father in 2000. Relations with Syria were vital to Iran's larger strategy regarding Israel. Syria bordered both Lebanon and Israel, and was central to Iran's ongoing support to Hezbollah, its most faithful client. Since the end of Lebanon's civil war, Hezbollah had eclipsed its rivals to become the most powerful armed force in the country. In that time, Hezbollah transformed from a terrorist group into a formidable political and military organization that held quasi-state authority over its strongholds in southern Beirut, the Bekaa valley, and southern Lebanon. Iran's support to Hezbollah fueled the group's rise, and helped develop its militant wing into a military force. Iran armed Hezbollah with increasingly destructive weaponry, including rockets and long-range missiles capable of striking Israeli population centers. Those munitions were often produced in Syria or were smuggled into Lebanon from Iran through Syrian territory.[10] Hezbollah also received sophisticated weapons directly from Syria, such as shoulder-fired, anti-tank RPGs and laser-guided anti-tank missiles originally purchased from Russia.[11]

Hezbollah was a strategic investment. By providing it weapons, and funding its growth, Iran was building a proxy force that could pose a credible danger to Israel. Since Israel's withdrawal from Lebanon in 2000, it remained in a low-intensity conflict with Hezbollah, which had come to be considered by Israel's leaders to be the country's primary threat. When hostilities between the two sides erupted in July 2006, Iran's development of Hezbollah was put on full display. The 33-day conflict ignited when Hezbollah launched a cross-border operation against Israeli forces. The group used mortar fire to divert attention from its main attack, which involved a small unit infiltrating Israeli territory and striking two military patrol vehicles with RPGs and machine-gun fire. The attack was detailed, well-planned, and run with precision. Hezbollah killed three in the ambush, and abducted two wounded soldiers before escaping across the border into Lebanon. An artillery barrage followed, striking a nearby Israeli settlement and military outpost, and injuring several Israeli soldiers and civilians.[12] A four-man Israeli tank unit was killed in the immediate cross-border military response that followed, with another soldier killed by Hezbollah mortar fire in the subsequent recovery operation.[13]

The abduction came at a politically charged moment for Prime Minister Ehud Olmert, who had been in office for six months, and was only two months removed from having formed a government. Olmert had succeeded Ariel Sharon, who had been declared permanently incapacitated after suffering a stroke in January and falling into coma, but lacked the latter's gravitas. Hezbollah's attack came on the heels of a similar abduction orchestrated by Hamas in June. The Israeli Defense Forces (IDF) reservist Gilad Shalit had been abducted near the Gaza border and continued to be held. The failed operation to rescue Shalit became a symbol of Israel's vulnerability to terrorist attacks. Hezbollah's infiltration added to that perception, which likely amplified the severity of Israel's response.

Olmert considered Hezbollah's attack an act of war, and cautioned that Lebanon would suffer the consequences. Israel's response was an all-out campaign against the Iran-backed group. The objectives were extensive: to compel Hezbollah to return the soldiers, secure the northern border, eradicate the group's presence in the south, and destroy its rocket and missile capacity so that it could no longer threaten Israeli cities.[14] Over the next four weeks, Israeli forces conducted a broad aerial bombing campaign targeting Hezbollah sites and infrastructure such as bridges, roads, and airport runways. Civilian buildings associated with Hezbollah were also struck. Hezbollah had stored much of its stockpile of weapons in or adjacent to apartment buildings and other densely populated areas. Portions of Hezbollah's stronghold in southern Beirut were the hardest hit. Israel's attempt to destroy Hezbollah's military capabilities meant having to target civilian areas, and led to significant casualties. Around 1,200 people were killed and 4,400 injured during the war, the majority of which were civilians. Nearly a million more civilians were internally displaced. Hundreds of Hezbollah fighters were also killed.[15]

Despite the considerable destruction incurred from Israeli strikes, Hezbollah remained capable and undeterred throughout the conflict. The group had been well-prepared for an Israeli invasion, and its tactics proved difficult to counter. Hezbollah also benefited from Iran's on-the-ground, real-time support. Qassem Soleimani and Imad Mughniyeh, Hezbollah's operational chief, traveled to Lebanon from Syria as soon as the conflict began. Soleimani later recounted his trip, and provided a glimpse into his relationship with Hezbollah and role in the war:

> On the first day [of the conflict], I returned to Lebanon. I was in Syria, but all the roads were under attack, especially the only official . . . cross border road. It was constantly bombarded by planes and the jets wouldn't leave it [alone for] a second. So we contacted a friend through a safe line and Imad came to pick me up to move me [from] Syria to Lebanon through a [road] where we walked a part of it and drove through the rest. At that time, the main spectrum of the war included a focus on the administrative buildings of Hezbollah, the majority of the areas in the south, and some points, in the north and center. Toward the end of the first week, I was asked to go to Tehran to report on the war. I returned via a secondary road. At that time the Supreme Leader was in Mashhad. I went there to meet him at a meeting held between the heads and the senior officials of the three branches of power which were also members of the National Security Council and worked mostly in security and intelligence sectors.[16]

Beyond a personal conduit between Tehran and Hezbollah, Soleimani was involved in the war planning. Hezbollah leader Hassan Nasrallah claims that Soleimani was in the situation room during the conflict, and took a lead in operational design, both pushing his ideas and deferring to frontline commanders when they disagreed.[17]

At the heart of Hezbollah's strategy was its rocket attacks on population centers in northern Israel. Iran had supplied Hezbollah with the technology, proficiency, and materiel for its rocket program in the years leading up to the conflict. Nasrallah later acknowledged that Iran helped Hezbollah develop its rocket and missile capability after Israel's withdrawal in 2000. "This wasn't easy,"

Nasrallah said of the effort. "You needed expertise, to bring in the weapons, to build launch pads, and hide it from both Lebanese [authorities and] Israel. . . . Soleimani gets primary credit for helping us develop these advanced military capabilities during this phase."[18] Over the course of the war, approximately 4,000 rockets struck Israel, killing 44 civilians, wounding 1,500, and displacing some 300,000 more from their homes. Over 150 IDF soldiers were also killed fighting in Lebanon.[19]

The rocket attacks had a deteriorating effect on public morale. Israel's leaders were faced with the reality that the war was not achieving its aims. Its ground incursion and air campaign had failed to negate Hezbollah's ability to launch rockets, and had not meaningfully degraded its overall capabilities. Hezbollah suffered significant damage, as did Lebanon more broadly, but the group's sophisticated weapons (e.g., anti-tank missiles, EFPs, and rockets), tactics, and dispersal of weapons and forces were difficult to overcome.[20] Israel's campaign was also dragged down by contentious politics at home and an operational approach that no longer worked against an evolving adversary. Under increasing domestic and international pressure to end the conflict, Israel finally agreed to a ceasefire under the auspices of United Nations Security Council Resolution 1701. The resolution went into effect on August 14. The 33-day conflict was over, but the causes that led to it remained.[21]

Confronting Iran in Iraq

Israel's war with Hezbollah underscored the danger of Iran's proxy network. That network, to include Hezbollah, was also contesting the occupation in Iraq. Iran's involvement in Iraq muddied an already complicated conflict. By mid-2006, Iraq was seething with unrest. The Sunni insurgency was in full bloom, and sectarian violence was spiking. Foreign fighters had flooded into the country, bolstering the ranks of the Sunni insurgency. Many of those fighters came through Syria, which had quietly facilitated support to the Sunni insurgency as a way of weakening America's hold on the country. Bashar al-Assad's cynical policy provided a lifeline to jihadist groups, with Al-Qaeda in Iraq the main beneficiary.[22] American forces killed Abu Musab al-Zarqawi in June, but his fighters carried on under their new leader, Abu Ayyub al-Masri, who renamed the jihadist group the Islamic State of Iraq (ISI).

The Shia insurgency presented a different type of challenge from the jihadists, one much more tangled in politics. The military went after Shia militants the same as Sunni insurgents, but that was dealing with only the symptom of a larger problem. The source of the Shia groups' effectiveness was Iran's financial, military, and logistical support. The surest way to weaken Shia militias would be to target their capabilities and resources, which would require clamping down on the Iranian smuggling network and arresting or killing Iranian operatives, most of whom were in the country legally under diplomatic guise. They were, in other words, guests of the Iraqi government, and tightly connected to prominent Iraqi officials. Any direct action against Iranian operatives in Iraq could spark a conflagration with Iran, as well as undercut Nuri al-Maliki's government— potentially weakening the already shaky foundations of Iraq's fledgling democracy. Countering Iranian actions in Iraq was fraught with risk, and Washington's response was tentative as a result.

By late summer, the Bush administration began developing an approach to counter Iran. The process took months, and involved multiple scenarios due to the complex web of considerations at play. Vice President Dick Cheney advocated for lethal action against Iranian operatives, but others in the administration advised caution. A new policy was finally approved in mid-December, which gave American forces the greenlight to arrest Iranian agents directly tied to supporting the militias. Outside of defensive measures, lethal action would not be allowed and Iranians not linked to aiding militants could not be targeted.[23] The new authorization was quickly put into effect. U.S. Special Forces established a specific unit, eventually known as Task Force 17, to take the lead in operations against Iranian activity. The unit moved quickly, and on December 20 and 21 conducted two raids in Baghdad targeting known Iranian agents. Six Iranian nationals and seven Badr members were detained. They included three Iranian intelligence officers working under diplomatic cover, the Iranian embassy military attaché, a Quds Force colonel, and his boss, the suspected head of Iranian operations in Iraq, Brigadier General Mohsen Chizari.[24] The arrests were an embarrassment to the Iraqi government. Iraq's president, Jalal Talabani, had been responsible for bringing at least two of the Iranians into the country under formal invitation.[25] Prime Minister Maliki angrily demanded their release. Chizari, the highest ranking of those detained, was soon repatriated to Iran.

Weeks later, in a January speech on Iraq, President Bush acknowledged that disrupting Iranian activities had become a priority in the war. Linking Iran's support for Shia militants to Syria's aid to jihadists, Bush stated:

> Succeeding in Iraq also requires defending its territorial integrity and stabilizing the region in the face of extremist challenges. This begins with addressing Iran and Syria. These two regimes are allowing terrorists and insurgents to use their territory to move in and out of Iraq. Iran is providing material support for attacks on American troops. We will disrupt the attacks on our forces. We'll interrupt the flow of support from Iran and Syria. And we will seek out and destroy the networks providing advanced weaponry and training to our enemies in Iraq.[26]

Bush's speech preceded a major operation against the IRGC. On January 11, 2007, U.S. forces conducted a raid on a building in Erbil, in northern Iraq, which housed an Iranian consulate liaison office. In the early hours of the morning, American troops, backed by armored vehicles and supported by Blackhawk helicopters circling above, surrounded the building and used a loudspeaker to order the occupants to surrender. With occupants unyielding, the Americans stormed the building and detained five Iranian Quds Force operatives, seizing computers, files, and other incriminating materials that documented Iran's lethal aid to Shia militias. As the American convoy left the scene, they were stopped at a checkpoint manned by Kurdish Peshmerga forces, who had not been alerted to the operation. The confusion led to a brief standoff that was eventually resolved peacefully.[27]

Iranian officials condemned the arrests, claiming the detained were registered diplomats.[28] Kurdish officials were also upset, perhaps out of embarrassment, or because they had been left out of the loop, which implicitly suggested that the Americans did not fully trust them when it came to Iran. Fuad Hussein, the Kurdistan Regional Government (KRG) spokesman, issued a quick denunciation of the operation, calling the arrests an "abduction," adding: "These kinds of actions are totally unacceptable and the Kurdish leadership is very angry."[29] Months later, Massoud Barzani, the KRG president, claimed that the raid actually had intended to capture high-ranking IRGC commanders who had been in Erbil meeting with him around that time.[30] Iraqi foreign minister Hoshyar Zebari advanced a similar claim.[31] Mohammad Ali Jafari, who went on to become the head of the IRGC months later in September, and a Manuchehr Foruzandeh, listed as the IRGC intelligence chief (but possibly an alias for Ahmed Foruzandeh), had recently entered the country to meet with Iraqi president Jalal Talabani, the head of the Patriotic Union of Kurdistan (PUK), in Sulaymaniyah before traveling to Erbil to meet with Barzani.[32] The meetings were reportedly publicized on local television, which spoke to the openness of Iran's relationships with powerful Kurdish elites.[33] Barzani and Talabani were in the uncomfortable position of having good working relations with both the Americans and Iranians, and had been caught in the middle of escalating tensions.

Revenge in Karbala

Mounting pressure by U.S. forces had disrupted the impunity with which Iranian agents had operated in Iraq. With a small but increasing number of field agents detained, and others at risk, the IRGC needed to regain leverage. Quds Force field commander Abdul-Reza Shahlai turned to Qais al-Khazali and two Hezbollah operatives, Ali Musa Daqduq and Yusef Hashemi, who had been assisting al-Khazali's group, to develop such a plan.[34] They decided on a risky plot to kidnap American soldiers from the Provisional Joint Command Center (PJCC) in Karbala, possibly with the aim of later exchanging the hostages for the five Quds Force officers detained earlier in Erbil.[35] Hostage-taking was a tried and tested component of Iranian foreign policy. Iran had mastered the art during the 1980s in Lebanon, and continued to use the imprisonment of dual-citizens in Iran as a point of leverage in its relations with foreign states. The PJCC was targeted because it was used as a headquarters for coordinating local security matters between the ISF, Iraqi government officials, and the Coalition. Al-Khazali's group, Asaib Ahl al-Haq, provided the manpower, while the Quds Force provided funding and logistics. The IRGC might have even built a to-scale mock-up of the PJCC in Iran for training and dry runs.[36] Badr-linked units, who had better intelligence on the movement of American forces through their contacts in the ISF, were likely to have also been involved.

The operation evolved quickly. In the late afternoon of January 20, 2007, a convoy of around five black SUVs entered Karbala's PJCC complex, where American troops were meeting with Iraqi counterparts to discuss security plans for the upcoming Shia religious commemoration of Ashura, which marked the annual remembrance of the martyrdom of Imam Husayn, and would bring hundreds of thousands of pilgrims to Karbala from across the country to visit his shrine.[37] The vehicles were outfitted with antennae and other accoutrements designed to make them look like those used by security officials. The occupants spoke English and wore American military uniforms, which might explain how they got past entrance security.[38] Once inside the compound, the militants stormed the building, using automatic rifle fire and grenades to gain access to the main office where the meeting was taking place. One American serviceman was killed and at least three others were wounded in the ensuing exchange. Four other American soldiers were taken hostage. Upon exiting, three American Humvees were also destroyed in the attack, perhaps to impede a potential pursuit.

The militants fled the scene with their hostages. Hours later, the five SUVs were found abandoned along a highway near the town of Mahawil, about 40 miles east of Karbala. Three of the four Americans were dead. The other was severely wounded, and died in transport to a nearby hospital. Two of the victims had been found handcuffed in the back of one of the vehicles. All had been shot. It is unclear why the Americans had been killed after the extensive effort of taking them hostage. Iraqi police had begun pursuing the convoy at some point and the militants may have feared capture, leading them to kill the hostages in order to flee.[39] There was also speculation that the Americans might have been killed in an attempt to escape.

Regardless of the intent, the attack was sophisticated. As Lt. Col. Scott Bleichwehl, spokesman for Multinational Division Baghdad, described it at the time: "The precision of the attack, the equipment used and the possible use of explosives to destroy the military vehicles in the compound suggests that the attack was well rehearsed prior to execution."[40] The Coalition's investigation quickly focused on Iran and its Iraqi network. Ultimately, it led to a safehouse in Basra. In March, British commandos raided the home and arrested Qais al-Khazali, his brother Laith, and Daqduq. Two computers were also seized which contained files that linked al-Khazali and the Quds Force to the Karbala attack, and revealed Iran's extensive support to his militia.[41]

Out of the Shadows

Al-Khazali's arrest went far in exposing Iran's wide-ranging campaign, but it did little to weaken it. The IRGC's network had penetrated every level of Iraqi society and government. It was systematized, and had layers of redundancies which reduced the importance of individuals. Part of what made Iran's network difficult to counter was the diversification of its client base. That was also its weakness. Outside of warring against the occupation, there was no unity among Iran's clients, and many competed among themselves for influence and resources. They worked together when it suited their interests, and clashed when they disagreed. So long as they remained loyal and did not interfere in its business, they could rely on Iran's support.

By having links with all sides, Iran was able to exploit fissures within the Shia militant community to further its agenda. The struggle for control of Basra, Iraq's third largest city, was a prime example of this. With its ports and oil-shipping capacity, Basra was a vital part of the Iraqi economy. It was also important to Iran's ground campaign, central to its smuggling effort, and a relative refuge for its agents. Both the IRGC and Iranian intelligence based much of their initial activity in Basra after 2003, and the city remained a hub for operations. The city was a testing ground for anti-Coalition attacks, and where Iranian EFPs were first used.[42] Over time, Basra became dominated by three main Shia factions: Badr, Sadrists, and the Basra-based Fadhila Party led by the senior cleric Muhammad Yaqubi. Each faction received some level of support from Iran, yet they continued to compete for territory, lucrative schemes, and political influence.

Basra became a more permissive environment for Shia militants when British forces, who had represented the Coalition in the city since 2003, completed a pullback from urban patrols in the summer of 2007.[43] In the absence of a Coalition military presence, militias in the city gained more space to operate and could act with impunity. Differing agendas and greed led to surging armed violence between major factions. Sadrists seized control of entire neighborhoods, and began enforcing strict Islamic legal and social codes by targeting liquor stores, harassing uncovered women and others deemed insufficiently pious, and cracking down on religious minorities.[44] Fadhila controlled the ports.[45] And Badr, which was closely aligned with Prime Minister al-Maliki, acted as an extension of the government.[46]

By early 2008, upcoming provincial elections had shifted the competition into overdrive. Factional fighting grew into open urban war. Street battles, including with RPGs and mortars, occurred across the city.[47] To stem the violence and exert government control, Prime Minister al-Maliki called for a massive military operation. Al-Maliki wanted the campaign to showcase his government's ability to provide security, and to that end, relegated Coalition forces to a supporting role. On March 25, a mixed force of 30,000 troops from the ISF and police began an assault on Basra. With air cover provided by the United States and Britain, Iraqi government forces and local Badr elements began clearing the city of hostiles, street by street.[48] Major fighting lasted over five days, killing hundreds, and wounding hundreds more.

The government had the upper hand, but a decisive victory was unlikely. Iran stepped in and offered to mediate a ceasefire and resolve the conflict. Despite al-Maliki's earlier repeated statements that there would be no negotiations with the militants, Qassem Soleimani intervened, and worked with members of al-Maliki's United Iraqi Alliance party to arrange a sit-down in Qom, Iran. Conveniently for the Quds Force chief, almost all of the parties at the table of the March 30 meeting were on his payroll. The Iraqi government was represented by Hadi al-Ameri, the Persian-speaking Badr leader and close personal friend of Soleimani, and Dawa member Ali al-Adeeb. Without a trace of irony or sincerity, Baghdad's representatives demanded that Iran end supplying weapons to Shia militants. They also asked Soleimani to convince Muqtada al-Sadr, who had been living in Qom since May 2007 under the auspices of continuing his clerical education, to stand down his forces.[49]

The intervention succeeded, and all parties agreed on a way forward. Muqtada ordered his followers to cease hostilities on March 30, and while intermittent fighting continued for weeks and briefly spread to Baghdad, clashes gradually subsided. Soleimani's diversification strategy had paid off. With significant links to all parties involved, Iran had an inside track into Shia factionalism that neither the United States nor the Iraqi government could match. As Osama al-Nejafi, a Shiite parliamentarian involved in the government's effort in Basra put it: "An agreement was signed. . . . Iran was part of the problem and an effective part of the negotiations."[50] By showcasing his influence, Soleimani had upstaged both the Coalition and Iraq's prime minister, who was increasingly seen as ineffectual and susceptible to Iran's sway.

Soleimani's role in Basra was effectively a coming-out party for the Iranian "shadow commander." His persona grew steadily both inside Iraq and beyond, with many considering him the most powerful person in the country. That perception undercut the stature of Iraqi leaders, creating a dilemma for those who aspired to be seen as acting in Iraq's national interest as opposed to Iran's. Muqtada al-Sadr, whose nationalistic rhetoric initially differentiated his movement from those of Iran's clients, had appeared to grow closer to Iran since relocating to Qom. The Supreme Council for the Islamic Revolution in Iraq (SCIRI) moved in the opposite direction, from being Iran's best-known client in 2003 to de-emphasizing that relationship, culminating in its 2005 name change, which removed the "Revolution" from its name, and signaled its political reorientation away from the religious authority of Iran's supreme leader to that of Grand Ayatollah Ali Sistani in Najaf. Although the group remained an ally of Iran, the distance it was creating was more than symbolic. It led to a formal break with Badr in 2007, which doubled down on its ties to Iran. After Soleimani's success in Basra, officials from the rebranded Supreme Islamic Council of Iraq (SICI) were among those who tried to downplay the Iranian commander's significance. Ammar al-Hakim, the son of SICI leader Abd al-Aziz al-Hakim and his eventual successor, said of Soleimani:

> This man is like other men. . . . He may have significant intelligence capabilities, he may have his good points and his bad points. But it's not logical that we exaggerate these points to the extent of giving a surreal picture. We have all enjoyed watching the American films in which the "hero" is capable of doing the impossible, and anyone can die in the film except him, but no sooner does the film end than we return to the reality that only God is omnipotent.[51]

In other words, and despite what Iran's clients were selling, Soleimani was not some sort of Shia John Rambo or a saint worthy of worship. Ammar al-Hakim's attempt to tamp down the exaggerated views of the Quds Force chief spoke to his own inclinations, which were leading him and his family further away from Iran's orbit.

Soleimani wasted little time in promoting his own rise. In May, the Quds Force chief sent a letter to General David Petraeus, commander of Coalition forces in Iraq. In the letter, Soleimani introduced himself as Petraeus's Iranian counterpart, with a similar regional purview and responsibility for advancing Iranian policy in Iraq. Soleimani also offered to discuss the security situation in Iraq with the American general. Petraeus disregarded the proposal, but Soleimani had made his point. He had reminded the Americans that Iran had become inseparable from the situation in Iraq, and they would ignore him at their peril. Washington recognized Iran's growing role in Iraqi security dynamics and had pursued a quiet diplomatic engagement to find a way to deal with Iranian behavior.[52] Between 2007 and 2008, America's ambassador to Iraq, Ryan Crocker, met with his Iranian counterpart, Hassan Kazemi Qomi, a former Quds Force officer, toward that end. The talks amounted to little, but they were a testament to Iran's growing clout.[53]

Iran's Uncertain Victory

Iran's ascendency enabled it to push more forcefully for an American exit. Iran wanted to prevent the American military from gaining a long-term base in the country, and negotiations for a Status of Forces Agreement (SOFA) in 2008 provided an opportunity.[54] Iran employed all of its influence, including Soleimani's personal diplomacy, to scuttle any plan that would mean a lasting presence of American troops.[55] General Ray Odierno, commander of U.S. forces in Iraq, spoke of Iran's efforts at the time in an interview with reporters:

> Clearly, this is one they're having a full court press on to try to ensure there's never any bilateral agreement between the United States and Iraq. . . . We know that [the Iranians have] many relationships with people here for many years going back to when Saddam was in charge, and I think they're utilizing those contacts to attempt to influence the outcome of the potential vote in the council of representatives.

Odierno added that "there are many intelligence reports" suggesting that the Iranians were "coming in to pay off people to vote against it."[56] Indeed, as Secretary of Defense Robert M. Gates recalls, an IRGC officer had been arrested in Iraq for paying an unspecified number of parliamentarians "$250,000 each to vote against the SOFA," a sign of the resources Iran was willing to expend to block a continuation of the American military presence.[57]

Iran's influence met its limits. The majority of Iraqi politicians were in favor of such an agreement. Iran settled for less than its maximalist demands, but its pressure had an effect on the outcome. The Maliki government lobbied for a fixed departure date for American forces and the Bush administration obliged. Such an idea had been a sticking point for Muqtada al-Sadr, and was popular among pro-Iran parliamentarians and the wider Iraqi public.[58] Once finalized, the agreement specified, among other things, that all foreign military forces would withdraw from Iraqi cities by the end of June 2009, and would leave Iraq entirely by the end of 2011. Although neither Iraqi nor U.S. officials believed that would actually happen, the provision helped sell the agreement among Iraq's political class and placated Iran.[59]

By 2011, however, many things had changed. The security situation in Iraq had gradually improved. The U.S.-led counterinsurgency campaign against

Sunni militants in 2007 and 2008, nicknamed the "surge," had succeeded in destroying much of the jihadist network. Sectarian violence had slowed as a result of the weakened jihadists, and attacks by Sunni insurgents against Coalition forces were greatly reduced.[60] Shiite militias, however, increased their attacks on American forces, and eclipsed Sunni jihadists as the leading threat. American casualties were rising due to the assaults, with the death toll in June 2011 the highest of any month since 2009. With the deadline for a U.S. withdrawal looming, military officials viewed the uptick as a sign that Iran was increasing pressure in order to discourage the negotiation of another SOFA.[61]

President Barack Obama had been elected on an anti-war platform and had vowed to end the Iraq conflict. In spite of Obama's own proclivities, however, the broad assumption in Baghdad and in the Pentagon was that the United States would retain a significant, albeit decreased, force deployment past 2011 as part of an "advise and assist" mission set. There was broad desire among Iraqi officials and military commanders for American forces to remain, seeing their presence as vital in holding the country together. The U.S. military had helped crush the jihadist insurgency, and more importantly, was seen as the only countervailing force to Iran. Iran saw the American presence differently, and, in the words of American ambassador to Iraq Jim Jeffrey, "were doing all they could to ensure no residual U.S. presence" remained in Iraq, including escalating proxy attacks against U.S. forces and bribing Iraqi politicians.[62] Iran had cultivated powerful allies in Iraq, but those not on its meal ticket were wary of its influence. General Jim Mattis, the commander of U.S. Central Command (CENTCOM), recalls hearing a consistent message from Iraqis while a tentative 2011 SOFA was still being explored by Washington and Baghdad:

> [Iraqi] officials repeatedly told me they needed us there to help them "avoid the suffocating embrace of Iran." At the level below Maliki, I heard this same quote often enough to recognize an agreed-on "talking point": senior Iraqi officials wanted us to stay, even if their fractious parliament could not say so publicly, for domestic political reasons.[63]

There was serious doubt among both U.S. and Iraqi officials that the Maliki government could maintain stability without U.S. military assistance. Mattis had a particularly dour view of Iraq's prime minister, seeing him as compromised by Iranian influence, corrupt, and sectarian in mindset. That perception was routinely affirmed by Maliki's actions: "messages from my Iraqi and regional contacts and our own intelligence reports were ominous," Mattis recalls. "Maliki was stepping up the purge of Sunnis from all government posts, degrading the military in the process. Each time Maliki grossly overreached, anxious Iraqi officials complained to our advisers as if they were a court of appeals."[64]

The immunity for American servicemembers from Iraqi prosecution was a sticking point between Washington and Baghdad in negotiating a new SOFA. The Obama administration demanded it as a prerequisite for any American forces to remain, but the issue was unpopular in Iraqi society. By October 2011, it became clear to Washington and Baghdad that a deal would not get done, and by mid-December, all American forces had withdrawn from Iraq. The war, which had killed tens of thousands of Iraqis and almost 5,000 American and Coalition members, was over.[65] Despite efforts to pursue another SOFA with Iraq, the withdrawal of troops might have been the desired result for the Obama administration. Ending the Iraq War fulfilled a campaign promise, and was a common rhetorical line in his 2012 re-election campaign.[66] The departure of American forces also provided Nuri al-Maliki with an outward victory, in that he had ended the American occupation, and would be a democratic Iraq's first independent leader. Yet, he inherited a country that remained on the verge of violent disintegration. For Maliki and Iran, the gamble was worth the risk.

Iran was getting what it wanted, and what Soleimani and the Shia militias under his wing had pursued through years of lethal attacks, coercion, and subterfuge. In the minds of Soleimani, his Iraqi clients, and Iran's leadership, they had defeated the Americans. The might of the vaunted U.S. military, combined with that of its Coalition partners, could not withstand the unified efforts of Iran and its co-religionist proxies. Their determination, ingenuity, and strategy had paid off. Saddam and the Americans were gone, and Iran's Islamic revolution was on the march.

PART II

6

Upheaval

The Iraq War thrust the Middle East onto a new path—one simmering with instability and appetites for change. As the conflict raged, and later as it wound down, episodic unrest and social foment bloomed across the region. Lebanon's Cedar Revolution, the election of Hamas and its isolation in Gaza, and the 2006 Israel-Hezbollah war were examples of this. In the summer of 2009, Iran took center stage, as hundreds of thousands of Iranians took to the streets to protest the controversial re-election of the hardliner president, Mahmoud Ahmadinejad. Ahmadinejad's challenger, Mir Husayn Musavi, the country's former prime minister, had galvanized an unlikely and passionate support base among Iranians hungry for reform. The politically moderate Musavi had positioned himself as a change-agent, and took Ahmadinejad to task for his mismanagement of the country, rabble-rousing foreign policy, and egomaniacal style of leadership. On the day of Iran's elections, Musavi was widely believed to be the frontrunner and seemed all but assured of victory.

The June 12 election went another way. In a surprising result, Ahmadinejad won nearly two-thirds of the vote in every province, something unprecedented in Iranian elections. A number of inconsistencies and election-day incidents, along with the disputed final tally, gave the strong impression that the election had been rigged. The IRGC was widely blamed for interfering, and supporters of Musavi and other candidates took to the streets in protest. Demonstrations soon spread across the country, but were most visible and dramatic in Tehran, where the IRGC and its volunteer paramilitary militia, the Basij, became the blunt end of the regime's security crackdown. Militiamen used truncheons, chains, and firearms indiscriminately to disrupt and terrorize the massive crowds. At night, security forces would travel from hospital to hospital arresting the injured. Torture and sexual violence were pervasive in Iranian prisons, used to terrorize, dehumanize, and humiliate detainees, and discourage dissent. As protests intensified, so did the tenor of the protestors' message, with chants of "death to the dictator" taking aim at the supreme leader, and becoming the unofficial slogan of what became known as the "Green Movement"—named after the official color of Musavi's campaign and the one most associated with the Prophet Muhammad. Although the regime risked backlash, its vicious tactics worked. The combination of blunt violence, arrests, disappearances, and torture had the regime's desired effect: people became dejected and began staying home. Sporadic protests continued for months, but by mid-2010 the Green Movement was all but defeated. The regime crushed the snowballing popular movement before it could grow out of control.[1]

Iranian authorities also benefited from a half-hearted Western response. The United States did its best to straddle the line between appearing in moral solidarity with the protestors while avoiding escalating tensions with the regime. President Obama had spent the previous year trying to improve relations in the Middle East, and started with Iran. Early after taking office, Obama sent a letter to Iran's supreme leader, Ali Khamenei, through secret diplomatic channels. The letter had expressed a willingness to enter into bilateral negotiations on a spectrum of issues, and was meant as much to test the waters as to secure any sort of meaningful engagement. The reply from Khamenei was terse. He rejected diplomacy or compromise, and alternatively, in the words of the American president, pointed out "ways the United States could stop being an imperialist bully."[2] Earlier, in his inaugural address on January 20, 2009, Obama had announced his intentions to transform relations with the Muslim world and its leaders: "To those who cling to power through corruption and deceit and the silencing of dissent, know that you are on the wrong side of history, but that we will extend a hand if you are willing to unclench your fist."[3] Rahm Emanuel, Obama's chief of staff, referenced that line when reading an English translation of Khamenei's letter, saying to the president: "Guess he's not unclenching his fist anytime soon." To which Obama quipped: "Only enough to give me the middle finger."[4]

The president was undeterred, and pressed forward with the aim of improving relations with Iran. Taking his secret message public, Obama enunciated those intentions in a March 2009 message in honor of Naw Ruz (literally "New Day"), which marks the vernal equinox and the Iranian new year:

> So in this season of new beginnings I would like to speak clearly to Iran's leaders. We have serious differences that have grown over time. My administration is now committed to diplomacy that addresses the full range of issues before us, and to pursuing constructive ties among the United States, Iran and the international community. This process will not be advanced by threats. We seek instead engagement that is honest and grounded in mutual respect.[5]

Obama continued with a similar message to the wider region in a June 4, 2009, speech in Cairo, where he stated: "I've come here to Cairo to seek a new beginning between the United States and Muslims around the world, one based on mutual interest and mutual respect, and one based upon the truth that America and Islam are not exclusive and need not be in competition."[6] The unrest that followed Ahmadinejad's re-election a week later presented the first challenge to Obama's optimistic Middle East policy, and quickly overtook any attempt to reset relations. Obama recalls wanting to speak out forcefully against Iran's crackdown, only to be counseled against it from his inner circle of advisors. Drawing from intelligence assessments and subject matter experts, they cautioned that such an approach would "backfire" and promoted a more liminal position instead.[7] The problem that they were soon to discover is that the protests would be blamed on the United States regardless of the administration's actions. Iran's leaders reflexively blamed nearly every instance of social unrest on foreign provocateurs, and the protests, which called for democracy and condemned the rule of the supreme leader, fit squarely with that narrative. Even though Washington largely stayed out of it, the regime viewed the demonstrations as an American plot to topple Iran's theocracy. And while the Obama administration gave superficial support to the protestors, and condemned the regime's violence, it hesitated to exert much pressure. Obama's larger ambitions of improving ties with Muslim states and finding a diplomatic solution to the Iranian nuclear issue limited the extent to which Washington was willing to intercede. Iran's ability to target U.S. forces in Iraq by proxy also loomed large.[8]

The unrest in Iran was a foreshock. The following year, a seismic wave of upheaval began to sweep across the Middle East and North Africa. As it had with Iran, Washington tried to balance its responses, both encouraging reform while hesitating to intervene. The chaotic period, which became known as the Arab Spring, did not just hit America's adversaries, it also struck some of its closest regional partners and allies. That made the Obama administration's task considerably more difficult and led to uneven policy choices and plummeting relations with regional partners. Yet, the same contradictions that plagued Washington's actions also permeated the reactions of local states, who favored some protest movements while vigorously opposing others. Hypocrisy and inconsistent behavior imbued the moment with further acrimony, intensifying a divisive climate wherein regional powers viewed cascading social discontent in zero-sum terms, recognizing only existential threats or opportunities to advance parochial interests. The main cleavage was between Iran and Gulf Arab states, who perceived the region's unrest in diametrically different ways. Added to this was the intensifying pressure on Iran's nuclear program by way of sanctions, sabotage, and an assassination campaign conducted by Israel, which provoked a lethal tit-for-tat game that played out in the shadows. Clashing aims, mixed with the heat of the moment, transmuted the region's collective reaction to what had been a genuine call for justice and change by its people into a contest for its future, and fanned the flames of a conflagration that threatened to engulf their nations in conflict and war.

The Arab Spring

Mohamed Bouazizi, a 26-year-old Tunisian fruitmonger, self-immolated on a public street on December 17, 2010, in protest of his municipal government's pervasive corruption and injustice. Protests in his rural hometown of Sidi Bouzid in Tunisia's economically depressed interior began the next day, and swiftly spread throughout the country. A month later, Tunisia's leader, Zine al-Abidine Ben Ali, fled to Saudi Arabia in exile, ending 24 years of autocratic rule and opening the door to democracy. Bouazizi's desperate act triggered a tsunami of furious discontent across North Africa and the Middle East. The Arab Spring had begun. Tunisia's protests quickly inspired similar protests in neighboring Algeria, and by January, demonstrations hit Jordan, Oman, Egypt, and Sudan. In February, social upheaval expanded to Iraq, Bahrain, Libya, Kuwait, and Morocco, and by March had reached Saudi Arabia and Syria. In each country, people took to the streets out of a combination of grievance, lack of opportunity, and frustration with abusive officials. The more the protests spread, the more rousing they became. To those involved, and to those observing from the outside, the moment was filled with hope and a fevered anticipation of what might lie ahead. The youth of the Middle East were screaming for change.

It was in Egypt where the Arab Spring made its most unexpected and significant mark. Outwardly, Egypt was in a secure position when protests began in late January. President Hosni Mubarak had led the country for almost 30 years. Egypt was a vital ally of the United States, one of only two Arab states (along with Jordan) who recognized the State of Israel, and after the latter, the second largest beneficiary of American foreign and military aid. Mubarak was an example of authoritarian stability, and was widely considered immune to domestic and international pressure. Until he was not. Once images of Egyptian security forces using fierce violence against protestors amassed in Cairo's Tahrir Square reached the public, the backlash was swift. As it had been with Iran 18 months earlier, the Obama administration was initially cautious in its messaging on Egypt's unrest, with officials split between those worried about the broader consequences of interfering too strongly and those wanting to be "on the right side of history" advocating firmer backing of the protestors. The historical weight of the moment convinced Obama to push for Mubarak to step aside.[9]

On February 1, 2011, Obama addressed his decision in a televised speech from the White House:

> It is not the role of any country to determine Egypt's leaders. Only the Egyptian people can do that. . . . [But] what is clear—and what I indicated tonight to President Mubarak—is my belief that an orderly transition must be meaningful, it must be peaceful, and it must begin *now*.

"To the people of Egypt, particularly the young people of Egypt," he added: "we hear your voices."[10] The next day, Secretary of Defense Robert Gates called the head of Egypt's military, Field Marshal Mohamed Hussein Tantawi, and reiterated that a political transition should occur immediately.[11] Mubarak was unswayed by the pressure, and rejected the "foreign dictations" that called for his resignation.[12] Through daily phone calls between Obama administration officials and their Egyptian counterparts, the message got through.[13] On February 11, Egypt's military stepped in and removed Mubarak from the office he had held since 1981. The once untouchable Egyptian strongman was forced out by a combination of popular fervor and foreign pressure, achieving a template for other Arab Spring revolutions and their aspirants.

The regional implications of Mubarak's removal were vast. The UAE cautioned against removing the Egyptian leader, fearing that the absence of a secular authoritarian would empower the Islamist Muslim Brotherhood—the country's most organized opposition. As Crown Prince Mohamed Bin Zayed told Secretary Gates before Mubarak was removed, "if the regime crashes, there is only one outcome, which is Egypt to become a Sunni version of Iran."[14] Regional partners saw Washington's intervention as a betrayal. Mubarak had been thrown to the wolves. Saudi Arabia, which had been the strongest advocate for Mubarak, and the leading voice against the Arab Spring protests, was livid, and never forgave the Obama administration for what they considered to be the abandonment of a key ally. When the Muslim Brotherhood's Mohamed Morsi was elected to succeed Mubarak in June, Saudi Arabia's anger increased. As with the Emiratis, whose admonitions had been confirmed, the Saudis had deep anxieties about the Muslim Brotherhood, and deemed the group the most insidious and dangerous domestic threat to the kingdom's rule. They also did not understand the Obama administration's game plan. Washington had pushed out a long-term, secular ally, only for an Islamist party to take control of the most populated Arab state. Why did the Americans prefer such an outcome? And what assurance did any authoritarian partner have that Washington would not do the same to them some day? Most other Arab partners held similar grievances. Any observer of the Middle East who lived or spent time in the region during this period heard versions of those questions posed by Arab officials and connected insiders. With Washington's role in the Egyptian revolution, regional leaders had added motivation to prevent protests from getting out of hand in their counties, lest Western powers feel compelled to side with the popular tide.

Not all states bemoaned Mubarak's fate. At the other end of the spectrum were Iran, Turkey, and Qatar, who, each for their own reasons, saw opportunity in Egypt's revolution. As an American ally, Egypt had had an adversarial relationship with Iran. Egypt had long limited Iran's attempts to expand its influence in Gaza, and the two states held opposing regional agendas. For Iran, Mubarak's ouster was a welcomed outcome, and one it hoped to build on. Iranian officials dubbed the Arab Spring the "Islamic awakening," claiming it was the progeny of Iran's own 1979 revolution. IRGC deputy commander Hossein Salami boasted that the days of American influence in the region were all but doomed, saying: "Today a political hurricane has started in the region. . . . Today revolutionary people have pervaded on Islamic lands and have risen against the colonial and American policies and the United States' lights [i.e., allies] are being turned off one by one."[15]

Turkey was also poised to benefit from Egypt's democratic turn. Prime Minister Erdoğan had distinguished himself among his peers for encouraging Mubarak to step down, addressing his Egyptian counterpart in a February 1 speech: "Mr. Hosni Mubarak: I want to make a very sincere recommendation, a very candid warning. . . . All of us will die and will be questioned over what we left behind. . . . Listen to the shouting of the people, the extremely humane demands. Without hesitation, satisfy the people's desire for change."[16] As Erdoğan sought to position his country more squarely as a Middle Eastern power, the removal of Mubarak and the potential weakening of Egypt's regional role were likely to benefit Turkey's aspirations. Furthermore, Turkey's ruling party, the AKP, had its roots in Islamist politics, and Prime Minister Erdoğan had developed close ties with the Muslim Brotherhood. Morsi's election gave Erdoğan an ideological fellow traveler and potential regional ally.

Qatar's motivations were more opportunist. While both Iran and Turkey openly backed the popular revolution in Egypt, Qatar's support was articulated by proxy through *Aljazeera*'s wide coverage of the protests. Qatar's enterprising ruler, Emir Hamad bin Khalifa Al Thani, had also been pressing for a larger regional role, using his country's combination of wealth and media power to become a player in regional and global politics. The revolution in Egypt was, at the very least, another opportunity for Qatar to advance its regional agenda.[17] Qatar also had close ties with exiled Muslim Brotherhood leaders, and similar to Turkey, was well positioned to benefit from any political transition that favored Egyptian Islamists.[18] While the Saudis sought to isolate Morsi's Egypt, Qatar would bankroll it.

Conflicting Agendas

The impact of the Egyptian revolution was soon felt in Libya, Bahrain, and Yemen. Protests hit both countries in the days following Mubarak's ouster. Protestors were inspired by the success of Egypt's popular movement and its broad backing by the United States and the European Union. This time the international and regional responses were different. Muammar Qaddafi's 42-year rule of Libya had been defined by his eccentricities and bombast. Libya had grown alienated from most of the Arab world, but also managed to pursue working relations with a number of states. Turkey in particular had improved its relations with Libya under Erdoğan, increasing trade and cooperation between the two countries. Qaddafi had also struck compromise when it suited him, famously abandoning Libya's nuclear program and restoring full diplomatic relations with the United States in 2006.[19]

But when Qaddafi began to violently crush Libya's protest movement, support for him quickly dried up. Qatar was the first to recognize the National Transitional Council, a self-declared opposition government based in the eastern city of Benghazi, as Libya's new legitimate government. France and Britain drove the UN Security Council to adopt Resolution 1973, which, with Russia and China abstaining, approved a no-fly zone over the country and authorized "all necessary measures" to protect protestors.[20] The Obama administration was initially hesitant on Libya, aiming to avoid getting sucked into another conflict in the greater Middle East. The Pentagon had little faith in the British and French plan for a no-fly zone and believed it would have no meaningful impact on the conflict. Qaddafi's forces were doing their killing on the ground, and defending the skies would be tantamount to an empty gesture. They also feared that were the United States to relent to pressure from their European allies and get involved, it would be stuck with the lion's share of the effort and have another war on its hands. The White House was split. Secretary Gates and Admiral Mike Mullen, the chairman of the Joint Chiefs of Staff, along with Vice President Joe Biden, Deputy National Security Advisor Denis McDonough, and Homeland Security Advisor John Brennen cautioned against military action, emphasizing that another conflict would have unpredictable consequences and further strain the military's efforts in Iraq and Afghanistan. Others, including UN Ambassador Susan Rice, and National Security staffers Ben Rhodes, Antony Blinken, and Samantha Power, countered with the consequences of inaction, viewing the problem in humanitarian terms, and contrasting the specter of Qaddafi mercilessly crushing the uprising in Libya against the backdrop of America's failure to intervene in the Rwandan Genocide.[21] Through her meetings with European officials and a Libyan opposition leader in Paris, Secretary of State Hillary

Clinton had become assured of NATO and regional support, and also backed military intervention.[22]

Obama ultimately decided that in order for the war to be short and effective, America's military would need to take the lead, and European allies would need to be in charge of guiding and funding Libya's post-Qaddafi political transition.[23] Regional support was also crucial, and the willingness of Qatar, the UAE, and Jordan to take part in a NATO campaign helped ease concerns of regional fallout. For the Gulf Arab states, the campaign also presented an opportunity to gain experience in war.[24] Both states contributed military aircraft and "dropped their first bombs in combat" in Libya.[25] Saudi Arabia backed Resolution 1973, but declined material support. Turkey, which had important trade deals with Libya, eventually supported the resolution as well, while simultaneously criticizing the West's motivations for aiding the protestors. Iran similarly threw its moral support behind the protests, even as it also decried Western intervention.[26]

With the United States taking the lead, military operations in support of the Libyan opposition began on March 19, 2011. Seven months later, Qaddafi's forces had been defeated. Qaddafi was finally hunted down and killed by militia men from Misrata on October 20. The once feared despot was found injured and hiding in a drainage pipe. The militants pulled him out from his hiding spot and abused him further, sodomizing him with a rifle barrel as they detained him. Those disturbing images, a prelude to the dictator's death which soon followed, were captured on video and viewed across the globe on broadcast news and social media.[27] More than Mubarak's fall from power, Qaddafi's ignominious fate would reverberate in the minds of the region's autocrats.

Bahrain's experience with the Arab Spring was much different. Peaceful protests began in the capital Manama one day before they took place in Libya, and similarly grew in size and scope. Iran quickly emerged as the protestors' loudest champion, whereas most other regional states either denounced the unrest or stayed quiet. The Obama administration was once again torn between its desire to promote human rights and its disinclination to strain relations with regional partners. A number of factors made Bahrain a special case. Bahrain was not only a U.S. ally, it was home to the U.S. Navy's Fifth Fleet, and thereby important to the ongoing missions in Iraq and Afghanistan. Saudi Arabia and the UAE, both still reeling from Mubarak's ouster in Egypt, were also committed to ensuring that the protests got nowhere. To avoid further straining relations in the Gulf, the Obama administration voiced only lukewarm support for the protestors' desire for more representative and just governance in public statements, even as it also privately encouraged Bahrain's ruling monarch, Hamad bin Isa Al Khalifa, to make progress on those grounds. Bahrain's demographics was another inconvenient part of America's reluctance to get involved, as was Iran's interests in the country.[28] Bahrain's population is around 60 to 70 percent Shia; however, the ruling family and the country's elite hail from the Sunni minority.²⁹ The Sunni ruling class's marginalization of the island's Shia majority has been an inescapable part of the country's modern political dynamics. During the 1980s and 1990s, Iran worked to develop a loyal clientage among the Shia of the Persian Gulf, and funded the activist network associated with the Shirazi and Mudarrasi clerical families, broadly known as the Shiraziyyun, to that end. Groups such as the Movement of the Vanguard's Missionaries (*harakat al-risaliyyin al-tala'*) and the Islamic Front for the Liberation of Bahrain (*al-jabha al-islamiyya li tahrir al-bahrayn*) were active throughout the Gulf, and were involved in protest and activism in both Saudi Arabia and Bahrain, respectively. By the late 1980s, Iran had moved away from the Shiraziyyun leadership, and shifted support to some of its more militant cadre, including the Saudi-based, and IRGC-trained, Hezbollah al-Hijaz. That group was linked to several attacks, and is widely believed to have been behind the 1996 Khobar Towers bombing, which killed 19 U.S. Air Force personnel and injured hundreds more.³⁰

Iranian meddling had been a constant concern in Bahrain since 1979. Saudi Arabia and its Gulf allies had similarly feared Iran's desire to turn the Gulf's Shia against their governments. Seeing their domestic Shia populations at times as potential fifth columnists, Saudi Arabia and Bahrain adopted policies that generally worsened the sectarian divides in both countries. Shia comprise an estimated 10 to 15 percent of Saudi Arabia's total population, mostly concentrated in eastern cities and oases, such as in Qatif, Hofuf, and Awamiya, where most of the country's hydrocarbon deposits are found. The country's Shia were not allowed to celebrate their religious holidays, were prevented from gaining leadership positions in the government and security forces, and their children were educated by Wahhabi teachers who considered them infidels. In Bahrain, the Shia majority had greater religious freedoms but were similarly disenfranchised, unable to achieve high rank in the military or government work force, with their neighborhoods and villages often kept separate from the Sunni minority.

That social-economic disparity drove Bahrainis to the streets in March, and ultimately to erect a peaceful protest camp in Manama's Pearl Roundabout. Bahrain's rulers blamed the protests on Iranian machinations—something disproven in their government's own after-action investigation.³¹ The unrest nonetheless presented an opportunity for Iran, and its leaders stalwartly backed the protest movement. Neither Bahrain's government nor those of neighboring GCC states were willing to chance Iran gaining ground in the country as it had in Iraq.³² Those concerns grew when protests spread to the Shia communities of Saudi Arabia's Eastern Province on March 11. Three days later, Saudi Arabia and the UAE launched an operation to end the protests in Bahrain at the invitation of its ruling emir. The combined force, conducted under the auspices of the GCC's collective security pact, known as Peninsula Shield, included around 2,000 soldiers and hundreds of armored military vehicles.[33] GCC forces crossed the causeway from Saudi Arabia into Bahrain on March 14 and within a few days had violently removed protestors from the Pearl Roundabout and crushed the protest movement.[34] The international response to the GCC's military intervention was muted. Given their responses on violence done to protestors in Egypt and Libya, the United States and Western Europe were mostly quiet, though they voiced tempered criticism of the crackdown's harsh tactics. In contrast, Iran was unremitting in its opprobrium, and blamed the Saudis directly for the bloody campaign. IRGC chief Mohammad Ali Jafari called the intervention a "strategic mistake" for Saudi Arabia, and suggested that Iran might respond in time.[35]

The Saudi government took a similarly hard line against protests in the Eastern Province, using a massive security clampdown, arrests, and other coercive tactics to deal with the protests. Authorities arrested hundreds of demonstrators, many of them youth, over the following months.[36] That included the arrest of Shaykh Nimr Baqir al-Nimr, an outspoken Shia cleric, who, in a March 13 sermon, had criticized the Saudi royal family and called for provincial autonomy as a means to end discrimination against the Shia and restore justice in the Eastern Province. Nimr's arrest triggered further unrest in his hometown of Awamiya.[37] As with the situation in Bahrain, Saudi authorities saw the hidden hand of Iran in the disorder.[38] Although the Saudi security forces were able to prevent protests from gaining steam, sporadic instability continued through 2012, and remained a source of rising tensions with Iran.[39]

As protests in Bahrain and Saudi Arabia were being crushed, they were building steam in Yemen. What had begun in January as Arab Spring–inspired demonstrations against proposed constitutional changes snowballed into a movement calling for the end of President Ali Abdallah Saleh's decades in power.[40] Saleh had been the president of Yemen since its unification in 1990, and prior to that had ruled North Yemen since 1978. A deft manager of alliances and tribal politics, Saleh had retained the top position in the country by keeping his enemies divided and making friends with whomever he needed whenever it suited his interests. Saleh managed foreign relations similarly, staying on positive terms with the Saudis, while situating himself as an indispensable partner to Washington during the war on terror.

However, as with Mubarak and Qaddafi, Saleh could not escape the historic moment. As protests spread beyond the capital Sanaa to the southern cities of Aden and Taiz, the government's crackdown intensified. Hundreds of protestors were killed in the clashes. The GCC stepped in to seek a political compromise to end the unrest. In April, Saleh initially agreed to a deal that would see him leave office, only to refuse to step down in May.[41] The strongman's obstinance emboldened the opposition, which included factions from within his own tribe, the powerful Hashid federation, and erstwhile allies within the military.[42] Weeks later, a bomb exploded outside a Sanaa mosque where Saleh had been praying, seriously injuring him. Saleh was evacuated to Saudi Arabia for treatment. He returned to Yemen in September, but facing spiraling unrest and mounting pressure from the opposition and outside powers, Saleh was forced to resign. In exchange for the promise of immunity in a GCC-brokered deal, Yemen's longtime leader turned over power to his deputy, Vice President Abd Rabbuh Mansour Hadi.[43] Hadi ran unopposed in a subsequent election in February 2012, and became president under a two-year transitionary term.[44]

Horror Business

As the Arab Spring hit, Iran remained in a standoff with the international community regarding its nuclear enrichment program. Iran's program was concerning because Iran had pursued the program in secret, outside of its agreements under the Non-Proliferation Treaty (NPT), and because Iran was believed to have covertly pursued a nuclear weapons capability until 2003, if not beyond. Iran's intransigence, exacerbated by its regional entanglements and the antagonistic leadership of President Ahmadinejad, led to a series of sanctions imposed by the United States, the European Union, and the UN Security Council through 2012. Those sanctions targeted Iran's military programs and imposed stiff economic penalties on Iran, severely impeding its foreign financial activity and hydrocarbon exports. Combined with the poor fiscal policies of the Ahmadinejad government and endemic corruption, sanctions contributed to a significant economic downturn in Iran between 2010 and 2012.[45]

Sanctions pressure was matched by a hard-edged campaign against Iran's nuclear program. In 2010, Iran was targeted in a joint U.S.-Israeli operation against its nuclear enrichment cascades at Natanz. The effort centered on a highly sophisticated cyber-weapon that exploited "zero-day" vulnerabilities in the Siemens industrial control systems and computers that operated the facility's centrifuges. Known as Stuxnet, the worm was designed to manipulate the centrifuges, intermittently alternating their speed while hiding those changes from monitors. Through that process, the centrifuges rapidly increased speeds to the point of failure. The attack was effective, and by June, a third of the centrifuges at Natanz were destroyed or made inoperable, setting back Iran's program up to 18 months.[46]

Direct, lethal means were also used to disrupt Iran's program. In November 2011, a massive explosion at Bidganeh military base destroyed several buildings and killed 17 IRGC soldiers, including Brigadier General Hassan Tehrani Moghaddam, the architect of Iran's missile program. Iran claimed the explosion had been accidental and caused by the mishandling of ammunition in a weapons depot on the base, located 50 kilometers (30 miles) west of Tehran. Israeli officials neither confirmed nor denied involvement, but anonymous sources linked to Israeli intelligence suggested to Western reporters that it had been a Mossad operation. Either way, Israeli officials welcomed the result, with Foreign Minister Ehud Barak saying of Moghaddam's death, "May there be more like it."[47] The incident at Bidganeh occurred in the midst of a series of assassinations on nuclear scientists. In five separate attacks between 2010 and 2012, four Iranians were killed. Fereydoon Abbasi, the IRGC's top nuclear official, was the lone survivor. In November 2011, motorcycle-borne assailants attached a magnetic "sticky" bomb to Abbasi's car as he commuted to his office in Tehran, injuring him in the explosion. He was hailed as a hero by the regime, and promptly promoted to the head of Iran's Atomic Energy Organization three months later. The last assassination occurred in January 2012, and targeted 32-year-old Mostafa Ahmadi-Roshan, an academic and supervisor at Natanz. Similar to Abbasi, motorcycle-borne assailants attached a magnetic bomb to Ahmadi-Roshan's car during his work commute, with the detonation killing him and his driver.

Following the arrests of alleged conspirators linked to the killing of another nuclear scientist—35-year-old Darioush Rezaienejad, who was gunned down in July 2011 by men on motorcycles in front of his wife as they were leaving to pick up their daughter at a nearby kindergarten—Iran's intelligence minister, Heydar Moslehi, claimed that Mossad and other foreign intelligence services were behind the murders. He added that the assailants had also received training "at bases within the territories of Iran's western neighbors," insinuating possible Saudi involvement.[48] Iran's tensions with Saudi Arabia had heightened during the Arab Spring. They were on opposite sides of the rebellion in nearly every country, and the Saudi-led military intervention into Bahrain in March 2011 enraged Iranian officials. IRGC chief Mohammad Ali Jafari condemned Saudi Arabia for the violence done to Bahrain's largely Shia protestors, calling it an act of imperialism, and alluded to a response:

> One must have revolutionary patience. That is to say, for Iran to act like Saudi Arabia would not be difficult, because Iran's military capability is not at all comparable to that of a country such as Saudi Arabia; but, Iran does not need to do so. Rather, one must wait for the hand of divine revenge. God willing, to avenge in the near future the crimes they have committed.[49]

The IRGC commander's words were more than rhetoric; a plan to take revenge against the Saudis was already in process. In October 2011, U.S. officials revealed an audacious IRGC plot to kill the Saudi ambassador to Washington,

Adel al-Jubeir. Details of the scheme read like a Hollywood thriller, or perhaps dark comedy. The case centered on Mansour Arbabsiar, an Iranian-American used car salesman from Texas in his mid-fifties. Divorced, and down on his luck, Arbabsiar had recently traveled to Iran to visit family, where he reunited with his cousin, Abdul-Reza Shahlai, the high-ranking IRGC field operative. Shahlai's profile was on the rise due to his work in Iraq, where he operated under the nom de guerre Hajj Yusef. The reunited cousins concocted a plan to work together, which eventually transformed into a convoluted plan in which Arbabsiar would leverage his contacts in Mexico, where he often sold cars, to enlist the Los Zetas cartel to carry out a hit on al-Jubeir. The plan was intercepted early on when Arbabsiar's link with Los Zetas also happened to be an informant for the U.S. Drug Enforcement Administration (DEA). Much of the planning between Arbabsiar and his handler in Iran, the up-and-coming Quds Force officer Ali Gholam Shakuri, was monitored by the FBI. They planned to detonate a bomb inside the Saudi envoy's favorite restaurant in Washington, D.C., as he dined. When told by his Mexican contact that the bombing would kill a number of bystanders, Arbabsiar answered: "They want that guy done [killed], if the hundred go with him f**k 'em."[50] Arbabsiar was arrested once the IRGC forwarded payments to a bank account set up by the FBI. Despite the severity and seriousness of the conspiracy, the Obama administration chose not to respond to Iran, worried that any escalation in tensions would imperil its diplomatic effort to address the nuclear issue.[51]

Unfazed by the embarrassment, Iran pushed forward with other operations targeting Israel, including failed plots in Kenya and Azerbaijan.[52] Iran was also linked to a Hezbollah terrorist bombing in Burgas, Bulgaria, which killed five Israeli tourists, their driver, and a Lebanese-French Hezbollah operative. Dozens more were injured.[53] Iran's campaign was exposed after a set of attacks against Israeli diplomatic personnel in New Delhi and Tbilisi, as well as a bombing in Bangkok, all in a two-day stretch in mid-February 2012. The attacks in New Delhi and Tbilisi occurred on the same day and involved magnetic explosives similar to those used in the assassinations of Iran's nuclear scientists in Tehran. The explosive in Tbilisi was attached to the undercarriage of an Israeli embassy vehicle. The driver, a local Georgian, discovered the bomb when he heard a strange sound under the car after dropping off his child at a local school. The driver alerted law enforcement, who disarmed the device. No one was injured. The attack in New Delhi happened hours later, and appeared to mimic the tactics used in the operations in Tehran. A motorcyclist attached a magnetic bomb to the rear side of a vehicle leaving the Israeli embassy. The subsequent explosion seriously injured the wife of the Israeli defense attaché and her driver. The attack could have been worse, as the car was headed to pick up the Israeli official's children from school.

The next day a bomb exploded at a house in Bangkok's Sukhumvit neighborhood. At least three Iranian nationals quickly left the home, each in different directions. One boarded a plane and flew to Malaysia. Another was arrested at the airport attempting to do the same. The third, Saeed Moradi, walked away from the building barefoot and visibly injured from the explosion, carrying a large, black backpack and holding two explosive devices, one in each hand. When a taxi driver reportedly refused to drive Moradi given his injured appearance, he threw one of the bombs at the car. The explosion drew police to scene. Moradi threw the second device in an attempt to flee, but the bomb somehow failed to go very far and detonated near Moradi's feet, severing both his legs at the knees. All three Iranians were eventually arrested, and details from the subsequent investigations gradually became public. The Iranian nationals had been a cell of intelligence operatives, tasked with targeting Israeli officials in response to the assassinations of Iran's nuclear scientists. They had been preparing for an attack against Israeli officials in Bangkok when a bomb accidently exploded, exposing their team and Iran's connection to the bombings in Georgia and India.[54] Investigators concluded that Iran's clandestine field unit involved at least 12 operatives who had spent 10 months planning the attacks.[55] Iran's attempts at retaliation failed, but its willingness to respond was clear.

Rebels and Tyrants

The Arab Spring made its way to Syria by early February 2011, but protests did not spread in earnest until March. Although demonstrations began small and were limited to certain areas, they grew steadily in reaction to the brutal crackdowns by state forces. The movement galvanized in the southern city of Deraa after the arrest and torture of local teenagers who had been suspected of anti-regime graffiti. On March 15, as locals gathered to call for the teenagers' release, security forces fired into the crowd. Four civilians were killed. The next day, following the funerals of those who had died, enraged community members vandalized the local Baath Party office and other symbols of the regime. Another violent clampdown by security forces ensued, leading to more deaths and triggering further, more furious protests. That cycle of violence continued to play out, and triggered a surge of determined protests across the country, gradually leading to a broad-based rebellion against the regime.

The protests revealed widespread dissatisfaction with Syria's authoritarian ruler, President Bashar al-Assad, and the culture of corruption that he and his father had cultivated through their combined over 40 years in power. Bashar had ruled the country for more than a decade. Initially, he appeared to have reformist intentions, and focused much of his attention on privatization, transitioning the country from a socialist to a "social market" economy. He also improved relations with Turkey and Gulf Arab states, which led to increased foreign investment. Syria became a popular tourist destination for the region, and wealthy Gulf Arabs began to invest in real estate in the country, particularly for luxury summer retreats. Economic reform and the attraction of foreign capital doubled Syria's economy, boosting its GDP from nearly $30 billion in 2005 to over $60 billion in 2010.[1]

The growing economy did not translate to improved lives for most Syrians. Assad used economic privatization as an opportunity to enrich his inner circle. Relatives, confidants, and loyalists gained the lion's share of wealth generated by the reforms. Ordinary Syrians lost out, and were plagued by spiraling government corruption. At the same time, state benefits were reduced, worsening the divide between those who benefited from the system and those who did not. Factories in Aleppo were hard hit by a free trade agreement with Turkey, which advantaged the latter's southern industrial cities. Farmers and peasants were further hurt by a combination of other factors. An end of fertilizer subsidies, the tripling of diesel fuel prices after May 2008, and an enduring drought precipitated a steep decline in the agricultural sector and a steady stream of emigration of rural poor to Syrian cities. The new émigrés often lived in makeshift housing in the outskirts of major and provincial urban areas, and were among the 30 percent of Syrians living below the poverty line.[2]

The combination of poverty, emigration, and systemic corruption provoked widespread discontent across the country. The pent-up frustration felt by many Syrians was like dry tinder waiting for a spark. The Arab Spring was that spark, and it ignited pockets of unrest which were then fanned by the government's brutality. By mid-summer, security forces were confronting the protests as an insurgency, regularly firing on demonstrators and arresting large numbers, many of whom would be tortured or killed in detention. Pro-Assad militias, known as the *shabiha* (ghosts), wantonly terrorized civilians, and local Mukhabarat security forces hunted down suspected activists and protest organizers. The military used helicopter gunships in raids on towns in the northern Idlib province, leading to the first significant displacement of civilians and the first wave of refugees fleeing across the border to Turkey. By early August, over 2,000 civilians had been killed, including more than 130 during a single day of clampdowns in Deir az-Zor, Al Bukamal, and Hama.[3]

Sectarian Politics in Syria

The Assad regime sought to create a divide within the early protest movement. Syria was an ethnically and religiously diverse country, home to Alawites, Christians, Druze, Kurds, Turkmen, and Palestinians. The majority of its citizens, however, were Sunni Arabs. Comprising around 70 to 80 percent of the country's population, Sunni Arabs had dominated Syria for much of its modern history. Under the Ottoman Empire, they were preferred by their Turkish rulers, and the agricultural sector was mostly controlled by wealthy Sunni landowners and powerful Sunni tribes. The Assad family came from an Alawite background, a distinct branch of Shia Islam. Alawites had had a much different experience in Syria. Their community had been marginalized for most of their history, and relegated to living in mountain enclaves in the country's western Latakia province, along the Mediterranean. The rise of the Arab-nationalist Baath Party in the early 1960s, with its emphasis on language over sectarian identity, provided a means for Alawites and other Arab religious minorities to improve their lot. After Hafez al-Assad took power in 1971, those personally connected to the al-Assad clan—including but not exclusively Alawites—benefited the most. Bashar pushed aside most of his father's appointees, and surrounded himself with loyalists, which included a number of family members and more distant relations. By the time of the Arab Spring, Alawites were viewed by many Sunnis to be part-and-parcel of the ruling establishment, and Bashar wanted to reinforce that perception. In one common tactic, the regime would send *shabiha* groups to terrorize Sunni neighborhoods, while government agents would spread false rumors in nearby Alawite areas of an imminent Sunni reprisal. Suspicions grew between the communities, inflaming communalist attitudes.

Alawites connected to Bashar held the most sensitive leadership roles in the security services. The vast majority of Alawites, however, gained nothing from the Assads and suffered from the same corruption and lack of opportunity as other Syrians. Nonetheless, the tactic of splitting the Sunnis from minority communities worked. Anti-Alawite slogans became popular within the opposition, and anger at the regime began to take on a sectarian tone. As most of Syria's cities were mixed, but also divided into sectarian and ethnic neighborhoods, the protests grew more intense in Sunni areas, while they gradually subsided in minority ones. Assad advanced a stark narrative about the protests, positioning himself as the only bulwark protecting Alawites, Christians, Druze, and other minorities from a bloodthirsty Sunni mob. Such crude methods succeeded because they played to historically rooted anxieties within those communities. The campaign gradually split the country into oppositionists and loyalists, with Sunni Arabs making up the bulk of the former, and minority communities and Assad's allies comprising the latter.

By late summer, the protest movement had begun to transform into an armed rebellion. The state military, known as the Syrian Arab Army (SAA), was hit by mounting defections from Sunni conscripts and officers. Many of those trained soldiers joined or established the upstart militias that began popping up across the country. At the end of July, the Free Syrian Army (FSA) announced its formation, giving name to the disparate collection of armed groups who were fighting the regime. Led by former SAA officers, the FSA framed itself as the official, secular armed opposition to the Baathist state. In truth, it became more of a branding and funding mechanism for at times loosely affiliated rebel militias. The FSA manifested the transformation of Syria's protest movement into a national armed struggle. In late August, another rebel organization known as the Syrian National Council (SNC) was established by expatriates in Istanbul.[4] Intended as a deliberative body composed of representatives from militant and exiled opposition groups, the SNC provided a semblance of political structure to the nascent rebel movement.

Numerous armed groups emerged during this period. Some aligned themselves with the FSA, while others claimed independence or espoused Islamist ideologies. The rise of Islamist militias in late 2011 through 2012 quickly changed the landscape of the rebellion. Extremist Salafis and jihadists took early advantage of the unrest to build networks within the rebel community. The radicalization of the rebellion was encouraged by the Assad regime itself, both by its sectarian approach, and through calculated steps such as the mass release of Islamists from the Sednaya prison in Damascus. In late March 2011 alone, the regime released at least 260 prisoners, the vast majority of whom were known to have been jailed for connections to extremist Islamist organizations.[5] Many of those released joined the rebellion, including some who would soon lead prominent rebel groups such as Jaysh al-Islam, Liwa al-Islam, Suqur al-Sham, and Ahrar al-Sham.[6] The latter formed in December 2011, and spent the early months of the rebellion creating units across the country, giving it a more national focus than other groups.[7]

With government authority disappearing from parts of the country, a number of battle-hardened, Syrian-born militants rushed home to join the rebellion. Among them was Abu Muhammad al-Jolani (the nom de guerre for Ahmad Husayn al-Shara'a), a member of the Islamic State of Iraq (ISI) and veteran of the Iraqi insurgency, who had spent time in U.S. custody in Camp Bucca. Jolani became a key figure in ISI under the group's leader, Abu Bakr al-Baghdadi, rising to oversee operations and revenue streams in Iraq's Ninewa province. Once the rebellion began, Baghdadi dispatched Jolani to Syria to establish an ISI branch. Jolani and his lieutenants, such as the Iraqi national Abu Mariya al-Qahtani (the nom de guerre of Musa Abdullah al-Juburi), who became the group's eventual religious authority, entered Syria in August 2011 and set up shop in the northeastern Hasakah governorate. There, Jolani resurrected the same jihadist network that had funneled resources and foreign fighters into Iraq during the American occupation. That network, which stretched from Idlib and Aleppo to the border with Iraq, was now being transitioned to focus resources against the Assad regime. In January 2021, Jolani formed the Nusra Front (*jabhat al-nusra*), literally the "Support Front," to defend Syria's Sunnis from the Alawite-dominated government. The organization rapidly expanded operations across the country and became a dominant player in the conflict.[8]

Turning against Assad

The precipitous growth of state violence against innocent civilians drove most regional and Western states to turn on Assad. The Obama administration was reluctant to get involved. Assad was still viewed as a reformer by some, and

Washington had hopes that Syria could be engaged.[9] And although the United States had intervened under similar circumstances in Libya, that intervention had had mixed results. Qaddafi had been overthrown, but law and order had collapsed, and fighting between rival militias had thrust the country into civil war. The Libyan state, its military, and air defenses had also been weaker than those of Syria, which had made it a relatively more permissive target for outside intervention. Another factor that threaded through Washington's decision-making centered on Russia, which had a historically close relationship with the Assad regime. As Secretary of State Hillary Clinton observed, the "crucial difference" between the Libyan and Syrian cases was that Russia would block any action against Assad in the UN Security Council, "in large measure to prevent a replay of Libya." There was nothing straightforward or simple about Syria. Clinton described it as a "wicked problem," meaning that there were no easy answers. As she explains the administration's predicament: "Do nothing, and a humanitarian disaster envelops the region. Intervene militarily, and risk opening Pandora's box and wading into another quagmire, like Iraq. Send aid to rebels, and watch it end up in the hands of extremists. Continue with diplomacy, and run head-first into a Russian veto."[10]

With Libya, the legacy of Iraq, and the ongoing war in Afghanistan as backdrops, Obama opted for a more measured approach. His administration initially struck a similar tone on Syria as they had toward Iran in 2009, focusing calls on ending the violence and encouraging Assad to seek a political solution. Yet, as the death toll grew, so did pressure on Washington to choose a side. The administration was divided on how much to commit to the rebels, but there was broad agreement that Assad was no longer deserving of keeping his post. Even if there was no intention to pursue the matter through military force as had been done in Libya, Washington's rhetoric intensified, and openly called for Assad to step down. Some officials, such as Secretary Clinton, wanted regional states to take the lead. As she stated in a mid-August visit to the National Defense University: "It's not going to be any news if the United States says Assad needs to go. . . . Okay. Fine. What's next? If Turkey says it, if King Abdullah says it, if other people say it, there is no way the Assad regime can ignore it."[11] Obama was moved to be more direct, and a week later called for Assad to resign: "The future of Syria must be determined by its people, but President Bashar al-Assad is standing in their way. . . . For the sake of the Syrian people, the time has come for President Assad to step aside."[12] The statement was released alongside an executive order "immediately freezing all assets of the Syrian government subject to U.S. jurisdiction and prohibiting Americans from engaging in any transaction involving the government." Washington's steps coincided with a joint statement by French president Nicholas Sarkozy, German chancellor Angela Merkel, and British prime minister David Cameron, who all called for Assad to resign.[13]

America's partners in the region were more divided. Saudi Arabia was dis-inclined to see another Arab leader toppled by popular forces, and most of its attention was focused on subduing unrest in the Eastern Province, the interven-tion in Bahrain, and navigating the political transition in Egypt. Riyadh had been working to repair relations with Damascus since 2009 after they had plummeted in the wake of Rafik Hariri's assassination. By pursuing improved ties, the Saudis hoped that Assad could be encouraged to distance himself from Iran. With Iran's Shia allies rising to power in Iraq, Riyadh feared that Iran's influence would con-tinue to expand if not checked. Peeling Syria away from Iran would undermine Iran's regional ambitions by weakening the so-called axis of resistance, which became Iran's way of describing its partnership with Hezbollah, Syria, and other regional clients. Assad had showed openness to Riyadh's inducements, and reciprocated in limited, diplomatic ways.[14] The Saudis were reluctant to abandon the Syrian ruler, and were still offering him aid through March 2011, including through an offer of $140 million in loans. Turkey and Qatar, along with Saudi Arabia, had moved closer to Assad in recent years, and were similarly hesitant to leave that relationship. In the years preceding, both had developed strong economic ties with Syria. Whereas Qatar's economic relations were aimed at gaining greater political influence, Turkey's dealings with Damascus, including its free-trade agreement, were significant for the Turkish economy and a boon to its southern cities such as Gaziantep.[15]

Neither Turkey, Qatar, nor Saudi Arabia wanted to see Assad swept from power by the Arab Spring. But as the political winds began to shift in the in-ternational community, and the sectarian divide in Syria intensified, both Turkey and Qatar changed their positions. The Saudis soon abandoned hopes of rehabilitating Assad as well. Qatar closed its embassy and pulled its ambassador from Damascus in July 2011.[16] Turkey's prime minister engaged Assad person-ally, and counseled the latter to find a political off-ramp for the unrest, such as by forming a broader coalition with the Muslim Brotherhood. Erdoğan's patience eventually ran out, and in November he called for the Syrian president to resign:

> Without spilling any more blood, without causing any more injustice,
> for the sake of peace for the people, the country and the region, finally
> step down. . . . Fighting your own people until the death is not heroism,
> it's cowardice. If you want to see someone who fights his people to the
> death, look at Nazi Germany, look at Hitler, look at Mussolini.

Erdoğan further encouraged Assad to reflect on the fate of Muammar Qaddafi, saying: "look at the killed Libyan leader who turned his guns on his own people and only 32 days ago used the same expressions as you."[17] Saudi

Arabia eventually followed Qatar and Turkey's lead, but did not close its embassy in Damascus until March 2012.[18]

In late January, the Arab League's 22 member states issued a joint declaration calling for Assad to step down. While they did not endorse military intervention, they called upon the Syrian government to enter into a dialogue with the opposition, and for a unity government to oversee Syria's political transition. The Arab League's plan was taken up by the UNSC two weeks later on February 4. The United States, France, and the United Kingdom, along with 10 other non-permanent member states, all supported the measure. Russia and China were opposed and vetoed it.[19] Although both powers backed Assad, their reasons differed. Russia had enjoyed close ties with Syria since the Cold War, and the country remained a strategic interest. Syria housed Russia's only naval base outside of Russia at the Mediterranean port of Tartus. The facility was used mostly for routine repairs for Russian ships transiting to and from the Black Sea, and was important to Moscow's ambitions in the greater Mediterranean region. Russia was also the largest supplier of weaponry to Syria, accounting for some 50 percent of the latter's total arms purchases. China and North Korea supplied another 30 percent, and Iranian arms sales accounted for the remaining 20 percent. Russia increased its arms sales to Syria in 2011, despite international criticism, which amounted to a reported $960 million worth of weapons purchases through the first year of the rebellion alone.[20] Beyond that, around 8,000 Russian nationals lived and worked in Syria, a fraction of the approximately 1 million Russians living in neighboring Israel, but not an insignificant number.[21]

China had far less investment in Syria, but was consistently against supporting populist movements against sitting governments. The result of the Libyan intervention also hardened China's position on Syria.[22] Neither Beijing nor Moscow was pleased with how the NATO-led operation had been handled, especially given Qaddafi's humiliating death. Both powers were angered by the course of the Libyan intervention, and claimed that they had been misled by the West regarding the aims of the UNSC-supported mission. Neither wanted to see a repeat in Syria.[23]

Two factors helped convince regional states to turn against Assad and aid the rebellion. The first was Washington's firm stance that Assad should resign. Backed by Western Europe and Canada, the Obama administration's unequivocal position implied broad support for regime change in Syria. There was a sense at the time that it was not a question of *if* but rather *when* Assad's rule would end. What the intervention in Libya suggested, above all, was that the Arab Spring was being taken seriously by Western governments. Assad's brutality seemed to be paving the way for his eventual downfall.[24] The second factor was Iran. Iran's involvement in Syria followed soon after widespread protests broke out, and its support for Assad never wavered. Other regional states found it difficult to take an agnostic view of the rebellion once Iran had committed to backing the regime. Their logic was simple: were the rebellion to succeed, Iran would lose an important foothold in the region, and its regional influence would likely decrease. But were the rebellion to fail, Iran's position in the region would be strengthened. Iran had gained in post-Saddam Iraq, and perhaps this was a chance for Iran's competitors to gain in a post-Assad Syria. That line of thinking helped spur Saudi, Jordanian, and Turkish involvement. As Syria's neighbors, Jordan and Turkey had additional domestic concerns, as instability and refugee flows affected their security directly, but neither wanted to see Iran play a more prominent role in the country. Other Arab states, especially the UAE, Egypt, Kuwait, and Bahrain, were similarly concerned about Iran's growing influence in Syria, which helped prompt them to back the rebellion. Qatar's own ambitions led it to invest heavily in the revolt, but relative to other regional states, Iran was less of a concern.

Crisis and Opportunity for Iran

Iran had strong reasons for backing Assad. Iran's decision-makers were driven by personal sentiment, regional aims, and the regime's enduring grand strategy in the Middle East, which held Syria as its fulcrum. Syria was also Iran's only state ally. Prior to the 1979 revolution, Syria had been a safe haven for anti-Shah, Islamist activists, and a conduit for Iranian revolutionaries linking up with militant Shia and Palestinian counterparts in Lebanon. With the 1979 revolution, key members of Iran's new ruling clique had already developed extensive ties with the Assad regime. During the 1980s, Syria was the only regional state to back Iran in the war with Iraq, and the two allies grew closer with the succession of Bashar al-Assad to the Syrian presidency. Common interests in Lebanon, particularly in support of Hezbollah, combined with shared antagonisms toward Israel and, to a lesser extent, the United States, kept relations strong.

Iranian officials considered Syria to be the heart of their campaign against the United States and Israel, and thereby the foundation of the new regional order they aimed to create. Beyond seeking the eventual end of Israel as a Jewish state, Iran's ability to threaten Israel by proxy through Hezbollah had become a pillar of its deterrence against both Israel and the United States. As Hezbollah's showing in the 2006 war illustrated, its ability to strike Israeli population centers with barrages of rockets and missiles was something American and Israeli leaders had to consider when dealing with Iran. Israel's security was a bipartisan concern in Washington, and Iran had spent decades refining efforts at exploiting that vulnerability. Syria was essential to Iran's military support to Hezbollah. Most of the rockets and missiles destined for Hezbollah were produced in Syrian factories, and Russian-made weapons were procured for the Lebanese organization directly by the Syrian government.[25] IRGC commanders regularly traveled to Damascus for meetings with the Assad regime and Hezbollah counterparts, making Syria something between a logistics hub and command center for Iranian operations in Lebanon.

Syria's popular upheaval threatened the very fabric of Iran's strategic goals and prompted decisive action. By March 2011, a clandestine military effort aimed at assisting the Assad regime in putting down the growing unrest was in full swing. The IRGC led the mission, which early on focused on providing material assistance and training loyalist forces. By May, the secret campaign began to be exposed. The United States, acting on its own intelligence and information supplied by allies, issued Treasury Department designations targeting the IRGC and Iranian security officials. Qassem Soleimani was listed for being a "conduit of material support" to Syria's intelligence agencies, and Mohsen Chizari was designated for overseeing the IRGC's operations and training in Syria. In June, the Treasury Department designated the top two officers of Iran's Law Enforcement Forces, Esmail Ahmadi-Moghadam and Ahmad Reza Radan, for aiding the Assad regime's "crackdown on the Syrian people." Iranian airlines were also targeted for shuttling IRGC and security personnel to and from Damascus, and transporting weaponry and other types of material aid. The Obama administration placed sanctions on Iranian airlines four times between October 2011 and September 2012 for their links to IRGC operations in Syria.[26]

Iranian assistance grew considerably through 2012 and 2013.[27] In addition to providing funding and weapons to help bolster Assad, including giving $3.6 billion in petroleum subsidies in July 2013, Iran's effort focused on three areas: (1) deploying IRGC officers to serve as advisors, instructors, and commanders for loyalist forces; (2) organizing, training, and leading a new paramilitary force manned by pro-Assad volunteers; and (3) facilitating the involvement of non-Iranian proxies to fight alongside regime partisans. Iranian units began serving regular tours in Syria by early 2012. The precise number of IRGC troops that deployed was never clear, but estimates suggested that the Iranian presence probably grew from hundreds to thousands across 2011 and 2013. They included officers and specialists in counterinsurgency, artillery, sniper fire, and ISR (intelligence, surveillance, and reconnaissance). Although Iranian officials consistently denied reports that their military forces were active in the conflict, the IRGC acknowledged that it had a small advisory presence in the country. In May 2012, Quds Force deputy commander Esmail Qaani even advanced that the IRGC's presence in the country had actually prevented "massacres" of Syrian civilians, presumably by instructing loyalist forces in more effective crowd-control tactics.[28]

Much of the IRGC's early attention was spent on developing a paramilitary force that would augment the Syrian military, yet fall under Iran's direct command. IRGC commanders referred to this force through different terms, sometimes calling it the "popular forces" and sometimes the Syrian *Basij* ("mobilization"), directly comparing it to the IRGC's own Basij paramilitary in Iran. Eventually it became known as the National Defense Force (NDF), and was composed of Syrian loyalists from mostly Alawite, Twelver Shiite, and Christian backgrounds. In September 2012, IRGC chief Mohammad Ali Jafari claimed that the militia had a national presence across Syria and 50,000 troops.[29] NDF units were often manned by locals who hailed from the unit's primary area of operation. The opportunity to defend their neighborhoods gave the fighters added incentive to join. Iran oversaw the training of volunteers in camps in Syria and Iran, with Arabic-speaking Lebanese Hezbollah operatives often serving as instructors. As one recruit described the experience: "It was an urban warfare course that lasted 15 days. The trainers said it's the same course Hezbollah operatives normally do. . . . The course teaches you the important elements of guerrilla warfare, like several different ways to carry a rifle and shoot, and the best methods to prepare against surprise attacks."[30]

Iran also facilitated the involvement of Hezbollah and Iraqi militias. Hezbollah had a vital stake in the Assad regime and viewed the rebellion as an existential threat. Lebanese militants were likely involved in Iranian-led support efforts from the very beginning. But by early 2012, Hezbollah had begun to take a larger and direct military role in countering rebel advances. By May, the organization had begun securing border crossings and had moved into Syria to defend Shia villages along the Lebanese-Syrian border from rebel attacks. Its presence gradually expanded and became national in scope.[31] Similarly, Iraqi militias were brought in by the IRGC and became active in the war by early 2012. The same militias that had helped Iran drive the United States out of Iraq were now being mobilized to defend Assad. The sectarian tenor of the conflict helped draw thousands of Iraqi Shiites to join the fight. Initially, Iraqis were sent to help protect the Shia-majority Sayyida Zeinab suburb of Damascus, which is centered around a golden-domed shrine devoted to a great-granddaughter of the Prophet Muhammad. The suburb had long been home to foreign-born Shia, including expatriates from Iraq, Afghanistan, Iran, and Lebanon. Iraqi militias such as Kataib Hezbollah, Asaib Ahl al-Haq, and Badr all sent fighters to Syria under the guise of "defending the shrine of Sayyida Zeinab." That same slogan was adopted by the IRGC as a euphemism to describe its own involvement in Syria.[32] New militias with a specific Syrian focus, such as Liwa Abu Fadl al-Abbas, Harakat Hezbollah al-Nujaba, and Kataib Sayyid al-Shuhada, were also established at the time and became active in the conflict. By late 2013, the IRGC began to introduce Afghan Shia into its burgeoning foreign legion in Syria, and formed them into a militia called Fatemiyoun. Like Lebanese Hezbollah and Iraqi militias, the Fatemiyoun militants—who were mostly recruited from the Afghan refugee population in Iran—became a constituent part of Iranian-led operations across the country.

The use of proxies allowed Iran to keep its troop levels in Syria to a minimum. They also masked, to some extent, the IRGC's involvement in the fighting. The IRGC maintained an ambiguous line regarding its participation, often waffling between outright denial and partial admissions that spoke of a purely advisory role. But evidence indicating that Iran's troops were involved in the fighting gradually emerged. IRGC forces began to sustain casualties in Syria, as did Hezbollah and Iraqi militias. Most Iranian casualties occurred on the frontlines of the war in clashes with rebel groups. But deaths of some high-ranking commanders, such as Hassan Shateri, who oversaw the IRGC's day-to-day operations with Hezbollah, might have been the result of Israeli covert operations aimed at discouraging Iran's buildup in Syria.[33] More details of Iran's role in the war came in mid-2013 after Syrian rebels ambushed an IRGC unit near Aleppo and killed some of its officers. After the battle, the rebels seized footage from an IRGC videographer and shared it with the British Broadcasting Corporation (BBC) to call attention to Iran's military involvement. The footage, which was authenticated through an investigation by BBC Persian, focused on an IRGC unit in charge of operations near the southern Aleppo front. In the video's final scenes, an IRGC commander, Esmail Ali Taqi Heydari, leads Iranian and Syrian NDF troops in a mission aimed at intercepting a small rebel advance. Unknown to the commanders and the cameraman, IRGC officer Hadi Baghbani, their unit was walking into a trap. The concluding images recorded by Baghbani are of the IRGC unit exchanging fire with rebel forces before retreating. Baghbani and Heydari were both killed in the exchange and buried in their hometown of Amol in northern Iran days later.[34]

Fueling the Fire of Rebellion

As the rebellion spread through 2012, the nature of the conflict transitioned from a domestic affair to a regional one. The rebellion continued to gain ground with each month, breaking up the country into Sunni-majority, opposition-controlled enclaves, and areas that remained under regime control. By the end of the year, and into 2013, Syria's conflict had become a civil war, pitting mostly Sunni Arab rebel groups against loyalists of the Assad regime. Kurds, who dominated Syria's northeast, as well as smaller pockets of the northern periphery, had long been alienated by the Baath Party's Arab-nationalist ideology. They remained mostly outside of either camp, focusing instead on moving toward greater autonomy in Kurdish domains. The Druze, the majority community in the southern Suweida province, remained nominally loyal to the regime but concentrated on defending their own communities by establishing local militias and pulling back from participation in the Syrian Arab Army.[35] This reduced the loyalist camp to a constituency of minorities and beneficiaries of the system: a coalition of mostly Alawites, Christians, Sunni Arab elites, and other smaller groups, such as Shiites and Palestinians, who all feared losing out or being targeted for retribution in any political transition.

The rebels were firmly intertwined with Sunni Arab communities and, more broadly, with regional Sunni patrons. Their fight against a non-Sunni government, supported vigorously by Shiite Iran, was an inescapable dynamic of the fighting and the prism through which many in the country and the wider Middle East viewed the conflict. Sympathy for the rebels led to increased foreign aid. Rebel groups were sustained by direct and indirect assistance provided by foreign states and private donors. Saudi Arabia and Qatar became the two primary funders of the opposition, while Turkey used its long border with Syria to shape the development of the rebellion in the northern part of the country. Jordan became active in the south, engaging rebels, and focusing on its own border security. Wealthy donors from the Gulf states, including Syrian expats and prominent Salafi clergy from Saudi Arabia, Qatar, Bahrain, and Kuwait, supplied crucial financial aid to rebel groups, who used that money to purchase weapons on the black market and to attract and pay the salaries of fighters.

The flood of cash provided the necessary resources for the protest movement to develop into a national armed resistance. It also helped factionalize the rebellion by encouraging competition for outside resources. The dynamic playing out on the ground was fairly simple: the more money a group had, the more weapons it could purchase, the more fighters it could recruit, and the more it could pay them. The more weapons and fighters a group controlled, the more powerful it became, and the more territory it could carve out for itself. The more secure a militia's area of control was, the more effective its operational planning could be. And the more effective its operations, the more credible it became to both recruits and, crucially, to foreign sponsors, who wanted to see a return on their investment by way of rebel victories on the battlefield.[36]

Throughout 2012, outside backers focused on strengthening the fledgling FSA. Rebel groups started receiving weapons supplies by at least January 2012. Saudi Arabia and Qatar were the leading purveyors, with Turkey's National Intelligence Agency (Millî İstihbarat Teşkilatı in Turkish, or MİT) serving as the chief conduit funneling foreign-bought arms to rebel groups across the border in Syria.[37] Jordan played a similar role in transferring arms across the southern border. Much of the weaponry, particularly that supplied by Qatar, was purchased through middlemen from Libya's stockpiles. Other weapons came from former Eastern Bloc countries. An early challenge for outside state supporters was ensuring that the weapons were going to the right groups. The FSA was the main target of support, but as an umbrella organization, it lacked both the centralization and coordination to facilitate an effective supply of arms to its many members. The Syrian National Council (SNC) positioned itself as the political representative and coordinating institution for the FSA. However, the SNC's role was contested early on by a number of FSA groups who accused it of being dominated by the Muslim Brotherhood and of favoring Brotherhood-linked groups in the distribution of aid. Some groups further accused the SNC of using funds provided by foreign states to build up the Brotherhood's network and operations in Syria, which had been severely weakened by decades of Baathist suppression.[38] The inefficiencies of the SNC continued to annoy foreign sponsors, who pressed rebel groups to further unify. By the fall, another front organization, the National Coalition for Revolutionary Forces and the Syrian Opposition, which was designed to be more inclusive and to reduce the dominance of the Muslim Brotherhood, was established to address that concern.[39]

Despite efforts to coordinate support to the rebellion, the project suffered from a lack of unity on both sides of the project. The proliferation of front groups, along with their militia counterparts, and the distance between those on the ground and those engaging foreign officials undermined cohesion. The failure to come together was fueled as much by parochial interests as fundamental questions about the war. There was little agreement on a number of issues. Were Assad to fall, what system would replace him, who would get what, and who would be in charge? Conflicting ideologies and aspirations of the groups and their sponsors also played a role. What did they want for Syria? How would they change the country's direction should they be victorious? Aside from the goal of toppling Assad, the rebels were not unified on any of those questions. Foreign backers were similarly divided.

The United States was hesitant to flow too much aid to the rebellion too quickly. Washington did not understand the landscape of Syria's opposition well, and the scene was rapidly evolving. The fear of inadvertently funneling arms to Islamists, especially those with connections to Al-Qaeda and other jihadist networks, was a warranted concern. Islamist groups, such as Ahrar al-Sham and Suqur al-Sham, emerged early in the conflict, and FSA militias associated with the Muslim Brotherhood were also active. Washington was apprehensive about providing sophisticated weaponry to the rebellion, especially shoulder-fire anti-air rockets, commonly known as MANPADS, for fear of such arms falling into the hands of terrorists or anti-Israel militants.

Despite those misgivings, the Obama administration was still committed to providing some non-lethal support to the rebellion, while helping facilitate or at least tacitly approve of arms transfers to the opposition through regional partners.[40] A CIA effort, codenamed *Timber Sycamore*, was greenlit by Washington in mid-2012 to train and provide non-lethal aid to the rebels. This kept the CIA on the sidelines of the arming effort, and created a vacuum for Saudi Arabia, Qatar, and Turkey to fill. In August, there were reports that a rebel group had received shoulder-fire anti-aircraft munitions from Turkey, possibly through Qatar. The notion that such weapons were getting to rebels despite Washington's objections evinced how little leverage or oversight the United States actually had in the effort. In response to the relative free-for-all of arms transfer to rebel groups, the Obama administration sent CIA director General David Petraeus to reprimand his Arab counterparts for "sending arms into Syria without coordinating with one another or with C.I.A. officers in Jordan and Turkey."[41] By November, Washington continued its push for greater coordination, establishing a train-and-equip program for vetted rebels across the border in Jordan, as well as a reportedly smaller but similar effort in Turkey. The program for rebels in Jordan was overseen by American, Jordanian, and French military instructors, who trained the rebels in small arms, anti-tank TOW systems, and tactics.[42]

The disjointed campaign fueled entrepreneurship and competition among rebel commanders. Fighters' loyalties and ideologies could shift with little more than a paycheck, and commanders shopped their groups to a host of potential sponsors in the hopes of obtaining cash and weapons. As a Syrian financier explained in August 2012:

> The local brigade commanders on the ground swear allegiance to whoever supports them and the expat community sending them money is divided. These are [Syrian] expats in the States and the Gulf using their own trusted channels for getting money through, so the money is pouring in from many different pockets. The number of fighters each commander can summon wax and wane with his ability to arm and pay them and their families, so there is no particular leader with enough clout to bring the brigades together. . . . All the other money comes from multiple sources and multiple channels. You can only unify these units with a unified source of money.[43]

The influx of private money flowing to the rebels competed with that provided by the United States, Saudi Arabia, and Qatar, and further undermined efforts to consolidate the opposition.

To gain better control over the flow of support, the Obama administration expanded *Timber Sycamore* to allow lethal aid in 2013. The effort, heavily backed by Saudi funding, and to a lesser extent Qatar, focused on providing aid and training to rebel fighters individually vetted by U.S. Special Forces.[44] Training took place in bases in Jordan and Turkey, and reportedly consisted of a two-week course for 20 to 45 fighters that concentrated on anti-tank and anti-aircraft weapons. Finding acceptable rebels who were willing to work closely with the United States and could pass vetting protocols was difficult. The program in Jordan, for example, trained around 100 fighters from Daraa in southwestern Syria, near the Jordanian border, between November 2012 and June 2013. The rebels were apparently promised ample weaponry, including anti-tank rockets, but by June, Daraa's FSA military council had received only a small portion of what they expected, which consisted of "four or five Russian-made heavy Concourse antitank missiles, 18 14.5-millimeter guns mounted on the backs of pickup trucks and 30 82-millimeter recoil-less rifles." As one rebel commander complained to American reporters, "I'm telling you, this amount of weapons, once they are spread across the province [of Daraa], is considered nothing. . . . We need more than this to tip the balance or for there to even be a balance of power."[45]

Cash, Guns, and Beards

The U.S.-led training effort was meant to accomplish two things: to strengthen the chances of FSA forces in the conflict, and to keep the weapons provided by U.S. regional partners out of the hands of Islamists. It was not, however, designed to help the rebels win the war. That would have required far more robust and much less constrained support. Even more aspiring plans discussed within the administration did not envision helping the rebels win on the battlefield. Secretary Clinton was among those in favor of expanding military aid to the rebels, but as she explains, the options considered were not intended "to build up a force strong enough to defeat the regime. Rather, the idea was to give us a partner on the ground that we could work with that could do enough to convince Assad and his backers that a military victory was impossible."[46] In the end, privileging vetted rebels over all others limited the types of groups that would receive support, and similarly hindered, to differing degrees, how regional partners distributed their largesse. Although Qatar, Turkey, and Saudi Arabia continued to aid Islamist groups, the channeling of the bulk of foreign state funds to a set of FSA-associated rebel organizations left space for entrepreneurs to make their mark. Private donors seized the opportunity and directed much of their aid to Islamists. The jihadist Ahrar al-Sham, for example, was provided funds by Syrian expatriates in the Gulf as well as from wealthy Gulf clerics and Islamic charities. Smaller groups promptly recognized that sporting an Islamist agenda and branding could help bring in more money. Some nominally secular groups shifted their focus and appearance, growing beards and renaming their groups with Islamic names to attract pious sponsors.[47] Through videos posted to YouTube or regularly updated feeds on Twitter, social media allowed for these groups to advertise their new Islamic bona fides to would-be patrons.

The millions of dollars flowing to Islamist groups from expatriates and Salafi networks in the Gulf increased rivalry among the opposition. It also facilitated the rise of jihadist rebel groups over their secular and non-jihadist counterparts, and encouraged foreigners to travel to Syria to participate in the "jihad" against the Assad regime. Aspiring holy warriors traveled from across the region and the globe to take part in the fight. Jihadist groups were the main beneficiaries of the influx of foreign fighters and, given their transnational outlook and ideology, were the best equipped to merge foreigners into their ranks. Fighters entered Syria mostly through Turkey, whose government turned a blind eye to, if not facilitated, the flow of volunteer manpower to rebel militias. Once in Syria, foreigners would link up with jihadist groups and be transported to camps across the country.

Nusra Front profited from both the support of private funding and foreign fighters. The group rapidly rose to become one of the largest, best resourced, and most effective rebel organizations. It was also known for its brutality and suicide operations against civilians, which set it apart from most of the Syrian opposition at the time. The experience its leaders had gained through years of fighting the coalition in Iraq gave Nusra an advantage on the battlefield, and by proving its effectiveness in war, it became a prime recipient of private donations. Although Nusra was nominally independent, it coordinated operations with other Islamist groups, such as Ahrar al-Sham and the Tawhid Brigade, both of which received state funding from Qatar.[48] Rebel groups participated in a collective arms bazaar, buying and selling weapons from each other, including those donated by foreign states or liberated from Syrian stockpiles. Unsurprisingly, weapons provided by Qatar and Saudi Arabia soon made their way to jihadist groups.

Nusra's rise was challenged by a rupture in its ranks. Although Nusra was partially funded by Abu Bakr al-Baghdadi's Islamic State of Iraq (ISI), it had effectively become an independent operation, and perhaps the single most powerful militia in the Syrian conflict. Baghdadi tried to reassert control over his erstwhile associate, sending a deputy known as Haji Bakr to convince Jolani to re-enter the fold and publicly announce Nusra's affiliation with ISI. As Jolani hesitated, Haji Bakr quietly secured the loyalties of a number of Nusra commanders and prominent foreign fighters. With much of the organization's loyalty secured, Baghdadi announced in April 2013 that Nusra and ISI were merging into a single organization that would be renamed the Islamic State of Iraq and al-Sham (ISIS), using the Arabic term for greater Syria (al-Sham). Jolani rejected the merger, and claimed allegiance to Al-Qaeda and its leader Ayman al-Zawahiri instead. This was news to Zawahiri, who had not been informed of Jolani's intention to affiliate Nusra with Al-Qaeda.[49] Spurned by his former underling's disloyalty, Baghdadi protested to Zawahiri directly, demanding the Al-Qaeda emir compel Jolani to agree to the merger, and alluding to his intention to fight Jolani's forces if he did not fall back in line:

> It has just now reached me that [Jolani] has released an audio message announcing his direct oath of allegiance to you. . . . This poor servant [Baghdadi] and those brothers with him here in al-Sham believe it is up to our shaykhs in Khorasan [i.e., Zawahiri and Al-Qaeda leadership in Afghanistan and Pakistan] to announce a clear, unambiguous position in order to bury this conspiracy before it causes blood to flow and we [*sic*] become the reason for a new calamity for the *umma*.
>
> We believe that any support for what this traitor has done, even tac-itly, will lead to a great fitna, which will thwart the program for which the blood of Muslims has been shed. Delaying the announcement of the correct position will lead to . . . splitting the ranks of the Muslims and diminishing the prestige of the group such that there will be no healthy cure afterward except by shedding more blood.[50]

Zawahiri attempted to stem the feud by chastising both Jolani and Baghdadi, ruling that Nusra would remain Al-Qaeda's affiliate in Syria, and Baghdadi's Islamic State was to remain in Iraq only. Baghdadi balked at the ruling, and released a public statement that read: "I have chosen the command of my Lord over the command in [Zawahiri's] message. . . ."[51] Baghdadi's decision divided Nusra in two, with the Islamic State leader getting the better of his rebellious lieutenant. Jolani's inner circle and the bulk of his Syrian fighters remained in the Nusra camp, but the majority of Nusra's ranks, including top commanders and foreign fighters, followed Baghdadi and took on the mantle of ISIS. The split severely weakened Nusra for months and led to lasting hostilities between the two organizations.[52]

ISIS's arrival on the scene was swift and bloody. The break with Nusra fueled tensions between Baghdadi and Zawahiri, leading to a complete break between their organizations. The jihadist community, which had long held Al-Qaeda to be the leader of the movement, now had to choose between competing factions, with Al-Qaeda and ISIS becoming the "Coke and Pepsi" of jihad in the violent competition that emerged. By absorbing much of the insurgent network Nusra had built in Syria, ISIS was able to hit the ground running. Perhaps more impor-tantly, the split between Nusra and ISIS was also meaningful for revealing how dominant the Islamist rebels had become in the war. Between Nusra, the Islamic Front headed by Ahrar al-Sham, and ISIS, Islamists had become the main power brokers in rebel territory. Their independence from foreign state donors, and ability to draw funds from both private networks and internal sources, gave them virtual autonomy. Their strength further undermined the rebel organizations more beholden to the West and regional states. The military councils, groups connected to the FSA, and other front organizations were increasingly sidelined, further weakening the influence of the United States and its allies in the war.[53]

Testing Obama's Red Line

Rebel forces made substantial gains from late 2012 through 2013. With efforts focused in the northern and eastern parts of the country, opposition groups developed an effective strategy of seizing critical infrastructure, military bases, and towns located along key transportation routes, imposing a slow bleed of the regime and reducing its ability to project power. In November 2012, rebels took the Syrian army's 46th regiment military base near Aleppo, known as Base 46—the largest base in the Aleppo governate. Rebels gained a massive supply of weapons, armored vehicles, and tanks from the base's stores.[54] The regime's hold on Aleppo deteriorated, and much of the northern suburbs were lost to the rebellion. A week later, rebels pushed government forces out of a major artillery base near Deir az-Zor, expanding their control east of the city all the way to the Iraq border.[55] That same week, militants seized the Tirshin dam, which sits on the Euphrates north of Aleppo, a vital source of electricity for much of the country.[56] In February 2013, rebels took the town al-Thawra and the nearby Taqba dam, which gave them control of Lake Assad, Syria's largest fresh water reservoir, and another source of hydroelectricity. Those holdings strengthened the links between rebel operations in the north with those in the east. Islamist rebels exploited the moment to advance against Syrian military forces in Raqqa, 40 kilometers to the south of Taqba. By March, Islamist rebels had driven regime forces out of Raqqa, and gained complete control of the city. Raqqa became the first provincial capital to fall to the rebellion.[57] The city and its environs expanded the rebellion's reach across eastern Syria, strengthening its positions near Deir az-Zor to the Iraqi border.

Such territorial gains might have been greater had rebel disunity not impeded the advance. The bloody rivalry between ISIS and Nusra slowed the momentum of the Islamists, with ISIS seizing territory and resources from Nusra and its allies such as Ahrar al-Sham. ISIS and Nusra also clashed with FSA groups, leading to inter-rebel turf battles in Raqqa and Aleppo.[58] By the spring, Iran and the Assad regime shifted focus to western Syria, prioritizing Damascus, the border with Lebanon, the Latakia coastal region, and the supply route connecting Aleppo with the capital. Backed by Iran, Iraqi militias, and Hezbollah, the loyalist camp conducted a series of effective operations through the spring and fall of 2013. Hezbollah intervened in large numbers across the Lebanese-Syrian border, retaking a number of villages and small towns in April, and capturing the city of Qusayr in June, which rebels had held for nearly a year.[59] Qusayr was a major loss for the rebellion, signaling vulnerability during a period when it had been otherwise ascendant. It further enhanced the perception that Iran and its Shia proxies were the backbone of the regime, which further heightened the war's sectarianism.[60] Loyalist forces made additional gains around Damascus, Aleppo, and Latakia through the summer and fall, which reinforced the regime's control over supply routes between Damascus and its western strongholds.

With the rebellion gaining momentum, the Syrian military resorted to using chemical weapons as part of its urban warfare strategy. The August 21 attack on rebels and civilians in the Damascus suburbs of western and eastern Ghouta was gruesome. Although there had been reports of chemical agents being used by the Assad regime since at least December 2012, the carnage in Ghouta became impossible to conceal.[61] It was far larger in scale than previous attacks and its effects were rapidly made public through numerous videos and pictures posted to social media and provided to nongovernmental organizations (NGOs).[62] The U.S. intelligence community conducted a thorough review of the evidence, and in just over a week, released a public report that concluded, with "high confidence," that "the Syrian government carried out the chemical weapons attack against opposition elements." The report further determined "that 1,429 people were killed in the chemical weapons attack, including at least 426 children."[63]

This development defied a statement President Obama made a year earlier regarding the question of U.S. military intervention in Syria, when he stated: "We have been very clear to the Assad regime, but also to other players on the ground, that a red line for us is we start seeing a whole bunch of chemical weapons moving around or being utilized. That would change my calculus. That would change my equation."[64] From that moment on, the perception in the U.S. foreign policy establishment, internationally, and on the ground in Syria, was that any clear use of chemical weapons by Assad would trigger strikes on Syria, if not a broader military intervention. That perception, whether it accurately reflected Obama's meaning of the term "red line" or not, obliged the Obama administration to act.[65] Such thinking was widely shared by key members of the administration, including the new secretary of state, John Kerry, who had succeeded Hillary Clinton months earlier. As Kerry recalls, after the intelligence community's assessment that the Syrian military was responsible for the Ghouta attack, he believed Obama "would decide to strike." For Kerry, the rationale was clear: "A targeted, surgical military response was proportional to Assad's atrocity," and had the "bigger potential value" to trigger diplomatic engagement. To that end, Kerry believed that "military strikes could achieve a number of goals," because:

> They would send an unequivocal message that the Unites States stood by the red line and would enforce it with or without our allies. They would signal that international norms regarding the use of weapons of mass destruction were ironclad and that we would defend them, an important message for a number of regimes, including Iran, to hear loud and clear. And I believed they might finally give us leverage to change Assad's calculation, beginning by making it plain to him just how badly he'd misjudged the world's tolerance for his barbarity. I also thought that these strikes could create a diplomatic opening and bring countries together around an endgame that could lead to a post-Assad Syria with the institutions of the state preserved. Assad's protectors in Iran and Russia would learn there were limits to Assad's freedom of action and ability to gain advantage on the ground. I knew Assad had acted out of weakness, not strength. There was no military solution to the war, but the opposition was doing well enough to worry him. I believed that if Russia's calculation changed, they might encourage either a negotiated exit for Assad and the creation of a transition government . . . or an election in which the people of Syria could select their future leader. Most of all, Assad might see that he couldn't gas his way out of a civil war.[66]

There was broad agreement among Obama's national security team that a military response was necessary. Whereas Kerry and others pushed for quick, decisive action, reasoning that time would only aid Syria and Russia in their attempts to cover up the attack and obfuscate the truth through disinformation, Obama's chief of staff, Denis McDonough, cautioned against it, and worried that any direct military involvement would see the United States slide into yet another Middle Eastern conflict.[67] Obama shared those misgivings, and was disinclined to rush into anything. Instead, he sought to involve Congress, hoping to secure a broader mandate from the representatives of the American people, and asked for more options. More than anything, Obama felt deep unease about entering into another military engagement, and felt that past American administrations had taken the wrong path in the name of retaining credibility. He was also not convinced that military strikes would achieve much more than making good on a threat. In that way, Obama's own red line had created what he viewed as a trap, one that he wanted to avoid but also one that he felt he was being dragged into by some of his cabinet members, the military, European allies, and regional partners, such as Jordan and Saudi Arabia, who had been advocating for Washington to follow through with defending the boundary it had publicly enunciated.[68]

A decisive moment came when British prime minister David Cameron, who had, along with France, agreed to take part in the strikes, failed to win support from Parliament. With the United Kingdom out of a potential military campaign, the United States would be acting more alone. Losing a coalition partner further entrenched Obama's belief that congressional support was vital. Yet, there was still belief within the administration that the president would green-light military action. The next day, Kerry made the case to the American people in a August 30 televised speech, stating: "As previous storms in history have gathered, when unspeakable crimes were within our power to stop them, we have been warned against the temptations of looking the other way. History is full of leaders who have warned against inaction, indifference and especially against silence when it mattered most." Kerry summed up the dilemma: "The primary question is no longer what do we know. The question is what is the free world going to do about it?" That visceral framing could not overcome the zero-sum politics of Washington. The path for seeking authorization through Congress was fraught with both the enmity of Republicans and the regrets still haunting Democrats from the Iraq War. Although the Senate Foreign Relations Committee voted in favor of a resolution authorizing military action in Syria by a 10–7 margin, there was no hope that the White House would win a wider vote.[69]

Following the committee's decision, Kerry held a regular phone call with Russia's foreign minister, Sergei Lavrov. During the conversation, Kerry floated an offhand idea that aside from military strikes, the only conceivable option to deal with the chemical weapons issue would be for Assad to ship his remaining stockpile out of the country. Kerry had not been offering an actual policy position, but rather thinking out loud of ways short of war that could address the crisis. Lavrov dismissed the idea, but later that night, during a meeting of G20 leaders in Moscow, Obama pitched the idea to Putin directly. For Obama, it was an opportunity to use the threat of military intervention to get Russia to compromise on the diplomatic front. Russia was on board. Sensing an opportunity to increase its influence in the conflict and stem potential American military involvement, President Putin took Obama's suggestion and offered to broker a deal with Assad to remove the country's chemical weapons stockpile.[70] Obama continued to make the case for a military response to the American people, while also opening the door for the Russian initiative. In a public address on September 10, Obama said:

> If we fail to act, the Assad regime will see no reason to stop using chemical weapons. . . . And that is why, after careful deliberation, I determined that it is in the national security interests of the United States to respond to the Assad regime's use of chemical weapons through a targeted military strike. The purpose of this strike would be to deter

Assad from using chemical weapons, to degrade his regime's ability to use them, and to make clear to the world that we will not tolerate their use.

With the legitimacy and necessity of a military response as the backdrop, Obama then addressed the Russian initiative as a way to avoid further bloodshed. As he reasoned, "this initiative has the potential to remove the threat of chemical weapons without the use of force, particularly because Russia is one of Assad's strongest allies. I have, therefore, asked the leaders of Congress to postpone a vote to authorize the use of force while we pursue this diplomatic path."[71]

Obama's decision to pursue a diplomatic solution over a military one was controversial. On the one hand, the president had found a way to navigate past the slippery slope of military intervention, and in the process, had outwardly addressed the Syrian chemical weapons threat. On the other hand, Assad had effectively called America's bluff and gotten away with it. Russia further advanced its standing in Syria and prevented the United States from changing the game. Even though much of Syria's stockpile was removed during the following year, Assad never stopped using chemical weapons. By late 2014, attacks against civilians and rebels using agents such as chlorine gas and sarin were again being attributed to Syria's military.[72] Even so, Obama later called the decision to not strike Syria one of his proudest moments as president.[73] As he told Jeffrey Goldberg of *The Atlantic*:

> The overwhelming weight of conventional wisdom and the machinery of our national-security apparatus had gone fairly far. The perception was that my credibility was at stake, that America's credibility was at stake. And so for me to press the pause button at that moment, I knew, would cost me politically. And the fact that I was able to pull back from the immediate pressures and think through in my own mind what was in America's interest, not only with respect to Syria but also with respect to our democracy, was as tough a decision as I've made—and I believe ultimately it was the right decision to make.[74]

Critics of the decision saw it differently.[75] The failure to enforce a stated red line, particularly on an issue as dire as a dictator's flagrant use of chemical weapons against civilians, was seen by many as an abdication of American leadership. Arab states, already exasperated with the Obama administration for its role in Hosni Mubarak's resignation, were incredulous that the United States had hesitated at such a definitive moment. "I think I believe in American power more than Obama does," Jordan's King Abdullah II reportedly quipped. Adel al-Jubeir, Saudi Arabia's ambassador to Washington, complained that the move undermined American influence in the region, reportedly telling his bosses back home: "Iran is the new great power of the Middle East, and the U.S. is the old."[76] More broadly, it signaled to Assad that the United States would not intervene for any reason, no matter how egregious his regime's behavior. It betrayed the toothlessness of Washington's support to the rebellion, and ceded the role of foreign powerbroker to Russia, thereby strengthening the positions of Assad, Russia, and Iran in the conflict. For the rebels it became evident that, unlike in Libya, the West had no intention of toppling Assad.

As the war raged on, the United States and Russia continued to advocate for a political solution to end hostilities. Yet, without an agreement between the two powers on the future of Assad, and the rebellion divided, there was no obvious path to reach such a resolution. The United States lacked influence on the ground, and could not compel a compromise even if it could offer one.[77] Absent a credible threat of Western intervention, and with the Assad regime realizing fresh momentum, no progress was made on the political front. The rebellion's prospects were still favorable. Rebel forces controlled vital border crossings with Turkey and Iraq, and a vast stretch of territory in between, from Idlib and parts of Aleppo in the northwest to Raqqa and the environs of Deir az-Zor in the east. But by early 2014, the world's attention began to shift from the rebellion to the rapid rise of ISIS. The organization that emerged from the ashes of the once-defeated Al-Qaeda network in Iraq steadily grew to become the most powerful independent actor in Syria and a simmering regional threat. It straddled two countries, and as it gained strength in Syria, it returned to Iraq with a vengeance.

8

Firestorm

The Islamic State of Iraq and al-Sham (ISIS) exploded on the scene like a fire-storm. Between the summer of 2013 and 2014, the group expanded its war on all parties, gaining large swaths of territory in both Syria and Iraq in the process. Territorial gains paralleled a rapid increase in the group's recruitment, as fighters from other rebel forces, foreign adventurers, and civilians living under the group's dominion joined its ranks. To fund its enterprise, ISIS looted banks, seized vital dams and oil fields from rivals, sold stolen antiquities on the black market, and taxed the population under its control. With swelling coffers and thousands of new recruits, the group set out to conquer as much territory as possible and eradicate all who stood in its way. Some of the group's victims faced a choice: bow to its authority or be killed. Others did not, especially Shia Muslims and religious minorities, whom the group targeted with genocidal barbarity. What ISIS's leaders saw as a campaign to purify their domains of infidels and insufficiently pious Sunnis, the rest of the world rightly recognized as barbarism and butchery.

ISIS's rise in Syria coincided with a deteriorating political situation in Iraq. Since the departure of American forces in December 2011, Iraq's sectarian divide continued to widen. Shielded by Iran, backed by ruthless Shia militias, and emboldened by the absence of an American counterweight, Prime Minister Nuri al-Maliki's vengeful and communalist dispositions stoked Sunni discontent. Maliki made little effort to engage constituencies outside of his own Shia activist base, and enforced policies that both antagonized and marginalized the Sunni Arab community. That sectarian approach sparked a series of furious protests in the largely Sunni Anbar province. Demonstrations began in Fallujah in late December 2012 and quickly spread. ISIS took advantage of the uproar and conducted a string of attacks, hoping to galvanize the anger among its frustrated co-religionists into a broader movement. In late July 2013, ISIS struck the infamous Abu Ghraib prison, freeing hundreds of inmates, including seasoned jihadist fighters and commanders. In September, the group also began operations against Kurdish Regional Government forces in Erbil, claiming the attacks were in response to the expulsion of jihadist rebels from Ras al-Ayn in northern Syria by Kurdish groups in that country.[1]

Maliki used the terrorist attacks as a pretext to move against the protests, claiming that Al-Qaeda was using the protest camp in Ramadi as its base of operations. In late December, Iraqi security personnel stormed the encampment, igniting clashes that left 17 dead.[2] The operation further enraged the Sunni population, and spurred activists to respond. A widespread crackdown on Sunni dissent led by Iran-backed militias, who had been given free rein by Maliki, soon followed. The militias outwardly sought to uproot jihadist cells, but also targeted the remnants of the Sons of Iraq, the prominent Sunni tribal groups who had supported the United States during the 2006–2008 surge against the jihadist insurgency.[3] Although the Shia militias operated with de facto state authority, they often did so from the shadows, engaging in abductions, torture, and extrajudicial murder. Jihadists, suspected collaborators, and innocent civilians were all swept up in the dragnet. Scores of Sunnis were disappeared or killed across Baghdad, Hilla, and Diyala provinces. In the Baghdad area alone, there were 48 documented killings of Sunni men between March and April 2014.[4]

The violence fueled social unrest. ISIS capitalized on the chaos, unifying a broad collection of Islamist and tribal militants against the Iraqi government. The militants seized Fallujah and parts of Ramadi in a quick and direct retort to the government's crackdown. That served as prelude to ISIS's improbable seizure of Mosul, Iraq's second largest city, months later. The group's rapid assault on June 6 overpowered the city's local security forces and triggered panic in the military's ranks. Within three days, top army commanders had abandoned their posts, leaving soldiers to fend for themselves or flee. When the dust settled, it became obvious that Iraq's political and military officials had relinquished the country's second city to a comparatively small force of impassioned insurgents without much of a fight.[5] ISIS followed with an advance on Tikrit days later, seizing Camp Speicher airbase and capturing thousands of its retreating troops and cadets, who had been deserted by their commanders once again. Jihadist militants separated their captives by religious affiliation, setting Sunnis free while killing Shiites and non-Muslims without hesitation. ISIS is believed to have executed around 1,700 captives that day, burying the dead in shallow, mass graves.[6]

By the end of the month, Abu Bakr al-Baghdadi had declared himself caliph—the successor to the Prophet Muhammad and the leader of all Muslims. The Islamic world had not had a caliph since the end of the Ottoman caliphate in 1924. What had been, after Islam's first generation, a mostly ceremonial position adopted by emperors of the past was now being claimed by a terrorist. With the self-declaration, Baghdadi also renamed his group the Islamic State, thereby indicating its intended transformation from a geographically bound entity into a boundless, independent nation. Baghdadi likewise abandoned his nom de guerre for the aspirational title Caliph Ibrahim, enunciating, in a rare public sermon on July 4 at Mosul's Great al-Nuri Mosque, that the Islamic State and its dominion would be firmly under his authority.[7] Over the following weeks and months, the Islamic State continued its march, capturing towns and villages across northern Iraq. By the end of the year, the group had nominal control of over 88,000 square kilometers (or around 34,000 square miles) of contiguous territory that stretched from Syria across northern Iraq—an area the size of neighboring Jordan.[8]

Baghdad Calling

The rise of ISIS dramatically changed how the war in Syria was seen from the outside. The rebellion had spawned a monster which donned itself in religious garb and acted the part of an End Times prophecy made flesh. Washington's fears that the rebellion would incubate extremism had been confirmed. The war had spread to Iraq, overwhelming the country's fragile socio-religious fabric and flooding its landscape with sectarian strife. Iraq was fighting for its survival, as well as its identity as a multiconfessional, multiethnic society. Both Iran and the United States had a stake in safeguarding the country, and held intersecting views on ISIS, but their opposing aims in Syria complicated their responses.

Iran did not hesitate to aid the Maliki government. By early June, as the tempo of jihadist attacks was increasing, the IRGC was moving assets, advisors, and equipment into Iraq. Qassem Soleimani oversaw the intervention and worked closely with client militias and partners. KRG president Masoud Barzani credited Iran for being the first outside power to answer their calls for help. In the early days of fighting, the IRGC reportedly delivered two cargo planes full of weaponry to supply Peshmerga forces fighting ISIS across Kirkuk, Sinjar, Baiji, and other fronts.[9] The bulk of Iran's support went to Shia militias. Soleimani and other IRGC commanders worked directly with militia leaders, organizing, training, and operationalizing their campaign. The militias were further aided by an influx of new recruits. Following the fall of Mosul, Grand Ayatollah Sistani issued a religious edict that called on Iraqis to mobilize and defend their country. It was a powerful message from the country's leading Shia authority, and given Sistani's reluctance to enter the political fray, epitomized the existential crisis ISIS posed to Iraq.[10]

ISIS's rapid ascent across the country provoked a fevered response from Iraq's Shia community. Young men volunteered in droves to defend their homeland and their religious brethren. Recruits were funneled into the ranks of various militias, including those close to Sistani, those loyal to Muqtada al-Sadr, and those backed by Iran. The militias also recalled thousands of their troops from Syria. Between returning forces and the surge of volunteers, the militias grew substantially in size and ability. Prime Minister al-Maliki brought the militias together to form the Popular Mobilization Forces (*hashd al-shaabi*, or PMF), an official paramilitary organization established to help coordination between its over 60 participating groups. The PMF ostensibly fell under the charge of the Interior Ministry, but that veneer did not extinguish the independent nature of the militias, whose leaders were more loyal to their patrons than the government. That was especially true for Iran's clients and for the militants loyal to Muqtada al-Sadr. The military's collapse provided the militias an opportunity to take an early lead in the campaign. By extension, Iran was given a principal role in the war. Soleimani personally attended operational planning sessions with other militia leaders, and helped guide the militias' strategy throughout the war.

Compared to Iran, the United States was more reluctant to get involved, but that hesitancy dissipated once ISIS laid waste to the Yazidi religious minority community of Sinjar and Zumar in northeastern Iraq in early August 2014.[11] The violence done to Yazidi civilians was genocidal. Hundreds of men, women, and children were tortured and killed. Reports indicated that some women and children were even buried alive. Hundreds of younger females were raped and taken as plunder, later to become the sexual captives of powerful commanders or sold in open slave markets to the highest bidder in ISIS strongholds.[12] The audacious cruelty was like something out of humanity's past—a re-enactment of Abrahamic mythology that only the most spiritually ill and deluded could attempt to justify. Those fortunate to escape were driven to the barren climbs of Mount Sinjar, bereft of steady access to food or water, and blocked from leaving by jihadists waiting downslope. The horror stories of the Yazidis, and the images of those seemingly left to die of starvation and thirst on a desolate mountainside, sparked an international outcry and spurred the Obama administration to act. American forces began striking ISIS positions near Sinjar on August 9.[13] The air campaign was followed by the limited insertion of Marines and Special Forces on Mount Sinjar and other areas, who assisted a ground rescue effort led by the Peshmerga.[14]

The Obama administration made broader support contingent on the resignation of Prime Minister al-Maliki, viewing the latter responsible for the country's slide into chaos. American officials engaged in behind-the-scenes diplomacy to help gain a consensus among Iraqi officials to promote a change in the executive. As Secretary of State Kerry explains, "We sent a clear message: the sustained support they needed was unlikely to come with Maliki in charge. Iraq needed a leader who would govern in an inclusive, nonsectarian manner."[15] Maliki was strongly backed by Iran, but the utter failure of his political appointments in the military, and the mess of his governance, undermined

Iran's position. With its project in Iraq on the brink of disintegration, Tehran acquiesced to Washington's position. The return of American troops to Iraq was an inconvenient necessity for Iran and prompted a shift in its calculus. Without Iran's support, Maliki had no options but to resign. On August 14, the embattled prime minister stepped down and handed power to Haider al-Abadi, a fellow Dawa Party veteran, who had maintained positive relations with both Washington and Tehran.[16]

As the political transition in Baghdad developed, the Obama administration turned its attention to building a broad coalition to defeat ISIS, focused heavily on gaining the involvement of regional partners. Arab states remained frustrated with Washington's handling of the Syrian conflict, but most viewed ISIS as a mutual and pressing concern. Maliki's resignation also helped ease tensions between Sunni states and the Iraqi government, and paved the way for a regional response.[17] In a September 10 speech, Obama announced the assemblage of a broad, American-led coalition of "some 60 countries," which included a number of Arab partners.[18] The president's message was straightforward: "We will degrade, and ultimately destroy, ISIL through a comprehensive and sustained counterterrorism strategy." In addition to expanding humanitarian and counterterrorism missions, the strategy had two main lines of effort: providing military support to Iraqi forces fighting ISIS on the ground, and deploying U.S. troops to aid Iraq's military through "training, intelligence, and equipment." Obama stressed the limited nature of this assistance, and intimated his disinclination to send troops back to Iraq, saying: "As I have said before, these American forces will not have a combat mission—we will not get dragged into another ground war in Iraq."[19] Regardless of how the intervention was framed, the reality of the moment was inescapable: after less than three years, the American military was returning to Iraq—this time to save it from collapse.

Iran's intervention in Iraq was more robust and open than in Syria. The universal condemnation of ISIS had provided Iran more political space and greater legitimacy to act. Iran hurriedly moved soldiers, advisors, and commanders, along with weapons, equipment, and surveillance drones, into Iraq. The IRGC relocated its small fleet of Sukhoi Su-25s to Iraqi airbases and flew combat missions against ISIS in the battles at Baiji, Ramadi, and Fallujah.[20] The Iranian military's regular air force also flew limited missions with their vintage F-4 Phantoms over Saadia and Jalawla.[21] Through involvement on the ground and in the air, Iranian and American forces were in the uncomfortable position of overlapping operationally in the war. In the battle to liberate the town of Amerli, the coalition's first major success against ISIS, the United States provided air support to Kurdish Peshmerga forces advancing from the north. Those strikes similarly benefited Iran-backed Shia militias who were advancing from the south. To avoid mishap, the American and Iranian forces eventually coordinated and deconflicted operational activity through Kurdish and Iraqi military intermediaries.

The speed and relative openness of Iran's support to Iraq mirrored the outward confidence portrayed by Soleimani and Iran's leaders. Iran had good reason to intervene. ISIS had managed to capture territory across the breadth of northern Iraq up to the villages of Jalawla and Sadiyah in Diyala province, only 40 kilometers from the Iranian border. The jihadists were implacably anti-Shia, and advocated the genocide of Muslim and non-Muslim minorities. But ISIS was also an outcome of Iran's own policies in Syria and Iraq. After U.S. forces left Iraq in 2011, Iran's influence in the country was unchecked. Politicians backed by Iran and militiamen on Iran's payroll excelled in corruption, marginalizing the opposition, and abusing civilians caught in the middle, but failed at governance. Iran's policies in Syria were equally to blame. ISIS not only flourished in the chaos of the civil war, it benefited from a joint IRGC and Assad strategy, which largely left the group alone and allowed jihadists space and time to strengthen relative to the non-Islamist rebels who received the brunt of the loyalist war effort.[22] That strategy helped energize extremism within the rebellion, which in turn reinforced the Assad regime's narrative that the opposition was a movement of terrorists who would exterminate non-Sunnis were they to take power. Jihadism was also plainly unpalatable to the West, and as it grew in prominence within the rebellion, so too did Western reluctance to get involved. Even as that Machiavellian scheme helped polarize the war and dilute Western passions for regime change, it spawned the scourge that was now threatening the very existence of a friendly, neighboring state and closing in on Iranian territory. The irony of the moment seemed to escape Soleimani and Iran's leaders. Iraq was on the brink of implosion largely due to the war waged by Soleimani in Syria and by the sectarianism and mismanagement of Iran's allies in Baghdad. By overseeing Iran's policies in both countries, Soleimani was both the arsonist and the firefighter. Soleimani presented himself as a savior when Iraq most needed one, but the conflagration consuming the country was one he had stoked.

North of Aden

As much of the world's attention was focused on ISIS and another war in Iraq, Yemen's political cohesion was deteriorating. The situation in Sanaa had remained fluid and unsettled since President Abd Rabbuh Mansour Hadi had taken over from Ali Abdallah Saleh for an initial two-year transitional period in February 2012. Hadi's main task was to oversee a national dialogue aimed at developing an inclusive reform agenda for the post-Saleh Yemeni state. The dialogue brought together the country's major tribes, political parties, and armed factions, whose leaders and representatives traveled to the capital to promote their interests. The European Union and Gulf Cooperation Council were heavily invested in the dialogue, and within the confines of Sanaa's Movenpick hotel, where most of the deliberations took place, the mood was hopeful. Yet, outside of the capital, ambitious warlords, militias, and extremist groups looked for ways to exploit the waning of state power.[23] Among Hadi's early efforts were reforming Yemen's national military, and pursuing a military campaign against Al-Qaeda in the southern governorates of Abyan and Shabwa.[24] Those efforts, combined with the political turbidity of the moment, had reduced the military's presence and effectiveness in much of the rest of the country, and contributed to a further decline in state authority. The national dialogue culminated in January 2014 with a set of 1,800 recommendations delivered to President Hadi, including a two-year extension to the latter's term.[25] By that time, the government in Sanaa had grown weak, and no longer benefited from the same relationships and deals that had previously buttressed its authority under Saleh.

That vacuum of power provided room for determined actors to expand their reach. In the northern province of Saada, the Houthis, under the leadership of Abdulmalik al-Houthi, the youngest son of the movement's founder, seized the opportunity to move against his archrivals: the Salafis at Dammaj. Dammaj was home to the Dar al-Hadith, a leading Salafi theological institute funded primarily by wealthy Saudi and Gulf patrons. The institute attracted thousands of students from across the country, region, and abroad, including people such as John Walker Lindh, who studied there in the early part of his youthful sojourn before traveling to Afghanistan and joining ranks with the Taliban.[26] Dar al-Hadith was established in the early 1980s by Muqbil bin Hadi al-Wadi'i, a Saada local who lived in Saudi Arabia for almost two decades and adopted the Salafi persuasion before returning to his home province in 1979. Guided by Muqbil's religious puritanism, Dar al-Hadith students regularly antagonized Saada's majority Zaydi Shia community through sectarian proselytizing and activism, such as the vandalism of Zaydi cemeteries and other forms of small-scale violence. Muqbil died in 2001, and his successor, Yahya al-Hajuri, forged a de facto alliance with the Saleh government, wherein he ensured the obedience of his school's students to governmental authority in exchange for Saleh's support and protection.[27] Beneath that security umbrella, the institute's antagonism toward the local Zaydi Shia community increased unimpeded. Their rivalry with the Zaydi revivalists helped spark a series of six conflicts between 2004 and 2010, known as the Saada wars, which pitted the Houthi family and their supporters against the Saleh government. The Dammaj Salafis assisted the government in those conflicts, the last of which, known as the sixth Saada war, also included a Saudi military intervention in support of the Yemeni government.

With Saleh out of office, and the government's authority contracting, the Houthis recognized a golden opportunity to settle old scores. In October 2013, Houthi forces moved against their local foes, expelling the Salafis from Dammaj and shuttering Dar al-Hadith. With no one to hold them back, the Houthis expanded their aims and set their sights on shaping the dialogue process unfolding in the country's capital. In their southward advance, the Houthis clashed with and defeated tribal adversaries who had previously supported the government against them. That included militias aligned with the Hashid tribe's al-Ahmar clan and those of the powerful Sunni Islamist Islah Party. From late 2013 through early 2015, Houthi forces steadily progressed toward Sanaa—overwhelming foes and forging new tribal alliances along the way. Upon reaching the capital, the Houthi-led forces took up defensive positions outside of the city and maintained a regular presence within it, using intimidation to influence politicians during the dialogue process. The Houthis were not alone in using such tactics, but they exploited the situation more deftly than their rivals.

Fundamental to the Houthis' success was a behind-the-scenes alliance with their former adversary, the ousted former president, Ali Abdallah Saleh. Saleh was above all an opportunist and retained a powerful constituency in parts of the military. He and the Houthis shared enemies in the al-Ahmar clan and Islah Party, and held similar distrust of President Hadi. General Ali Muhsin Saleh al-Ahmar, a relative of Saleh, but of no relation to the al-Ahmar clan, was also a shared adversary. As former commander of the First Armored Division, Ali Muhsin had led the government's campaigns against the Houthis in the Saada wars. Once Saleh's closest ally and likely successor, Ali Muhsin had been marginalized politically over the previous decade as Saleh began to groom his eldest son, Ahmed Ali Saleh, for the role instead. Ali Muhsin's political ambitions had sharpened his rivalry with his former boss, whom he turned against as the 2012 protest movement gained steam. After Saleh's fall, Ali Muhsin had become a chief challenger of both the former president and the Houthis. Saleh retained his own support base, however, which included forces controlled by his General People's Congress (GPC) party and his son, Ahmed Ali, the Republican Guard commander. Those supporters helped facilitate the Houthis' advance toward Sanaa and augmented the group's presence in the capital.[28]

The Houthi Revolution

The Houthis and Saleh were indirectly aided by the policies of Hadi's external allies. In March 2014, Saudi Arabia had designated the Muslim Brotherhood a terrorist organization, and sought to marginalize it regionally as well.[29] The UAE followed suit, and outlawed the Brotherhood in November.[30] ISIS's dramatic and murderous territorial expansion provided the Saudis and Emiratis with an international context seemingly sympathetic to a crackdown on Islamist extremism. But their policies were driven less by their concerns about the wider impact of Islamism than by their own anxieties regarding the stability of their monarchies at home. Having seen the Muslim Brotherhood propelled to power in Egypt by Arab Spring protests, and its disastrous, short-lived rule under Mohamed Morsi, Saudi Arabia and the UAE feared the Brotherhood's potential as a political force both domestically and regionally. The Saudis and Emiratis, as well as Kuwait, were the first states to provide billions of dollars in aid to Egypt following the military coup d'état, led by General Abdel Fattah al-Sisi, which toppled Morsi in July 2013. Sisi had close ties to Riyadh, having served as Egypt's defense attaché there earlier in his career, and closely aligned himself with the Saudis after he succeeded Morsi as president in May 2014.[31] In June 2014, King Abdullah even traveled to Egypt to meet with Sisi after his election, symbolizing both the new closeness in Saudi-Egyptian relations, as well as its asymmetry. The short meeting took place entirely on the aging monarch's private jet, which he never left before returning home.[32]

The turn against the Muslim Brotherhood seemed at odds with Saudi Arabia's long-standing policy of favoring Salafism and like-minded Islamic movements. Yet, even though the Saudis had strongly promoted and financed the spread of an intolerant Sunni religiosity across the region and globally for decades, the populist power of Islamists evinced in the Arab uprisings quickened a shift in Saudi thinking that neither the 9/11 attacks nor the rise of jihadism had succeeded to motivate.[33] Populism of any stripe that called for a change to the authoritarian status quo was considered the real threat, and the Muslim Brotherhood was viewed as the most potent political movement in the region and therefore the most dangerous.

The Saudi and Emirati position on Egypt, and on the Muslim Brotherhood more broadly, put them at odds with Qatar and Turkey, both of whom had been leading supporters of Morsi, and had garnered close relations with Muslim Brotherhood political parties and leaders across the region.[34] But in Yemen, the Saudi stance threatened to undermine the country's largest political party, al-Islah, and the traditional influence of the party's leadership and tribal patrons, especially the al-Ahmar clan. Islah was a major player in Yemen, and dominated the country's Islamist political landscape. The party had gained influence through its alliance with many of the military and tribal heavyweights who had held positions of power under Saleh, which included Hamid al-Ahmar, a brother to the Hashid tribal confederation's chief, Sadiq al-Ahmar, and one of the wealthiest and most influential elites in Yemen. Islah and the Ahmars were facing potential marginalization by Yemen's richest neighbors.[35]

With their rivals vulnerable, and their fortunes strengthened by the alliance with pro-Saleh forces, the Houthis used a combination of armed violence, street protests, and populist messaging to increase pressure on President Hadi. By late summer 2015, when it became clear to the Houthis that Hadi would not fall in line with their agenda, the Houthis began to move against the government.[36] In September, a series of clashes between the Houthis and pro-government forces left scores dead. On September 21, Houthi militants stormed government offices and effectively took control of the capital.[37] These events added a new crisis to the region's turmoil. Less than two weeks later, President Obama announced the formation of the international coalition to defeat ISIS in Iraq. The Middle East was facing yet another armed conflict.

The United Nations stepped in to halt the violence in Sanaa, brokering a ceasefire agreement which called for Houthi forces to leave the capital in exchange for the establishment of a unity government and other concessions.[38] In reality, while some forces left the city, the Houthis remained the de facto power in Sanaa and retained a chokehold on the Hadi government. They wasted no time in striking against their opponents, capturing the First Armored Division's military base, and ransacking the home of the division's former commander, Ali Muhsin. With their main rival defeated, the Houthis soon had enough strength to seize control of government buildings and ministries, prompting an exodus of prominent politicians from the capital.[39]

Initially, the Houthis expressed no intention to maintain control of the government, but rather sought a larger voice within it. That did little to reassure the international community. In November, the United Nations Security Council (UNSC) came down firmly on the side of President Hadi's government, and issued sanctions against two Houthi military leaders, Abdulkhaliq al-Houthi and Abdullah Yahya al-Hakim, for their role in the coup. The UNSC also sanctioned Saleh for aiding the Houthis, as well as for secretly working with Al-Qaeda in the Arabian Peninsula (Al-Qaeda's affiliate in Yemen, also known by the acronym AQAP) in an assassination campaign that targeted common rivals. In January 2015, the Houthis tightened their grip on the government, placing President Hadi and a number of cabinet officials under house arrest, and forcing their resignations. A month later, the Houthis announced a new government headed by a new executive body, the Supreme Revolutionary Committee, led by Muhammad al-Houthi, making the coup d'état complete. Speaking to the BBC about the newly formed government, Yahya al-Houthi, a former member of parliament from Saleh's GPC party and Abdulmalik al-Houthi's half-brother, stated: "This declaration will found a new era, an historic state, politically and economically, in the history of the Yemeni people." Yet, Houthi leaders still denied seeking full control of the government. As senior Houthi official Saleh

Ali al-Sammad told the *New York Times* in February: "[we] do not want anything more than partnership, not control. . . . This was not a coup."[40]

To showcase their populist credentials, the Houthis focused efforts on fighting jihadist terrorism and exposing the systemic corruption that had continued under President Hadi. The Houthis even signaled some openness to establishing relations with the United States. Any semblance of a honeymoon was short-lived. Washington withdrew its ambassador and closed its Sanaa embassy in February. Outside states similarly refused to recognize the Houthi-led government's legitimacy.[41] Within the capital, and in other parts of the country, Houthi rule soon became synonymous with government oppression. Anyone deemed a threat was liable to be arrested and jailed on dubious charges. Activists, journalists, religious minorities, and conservative Sunni preachers were all targeted. A more severe social code was also imposed, making it clear that the Houthis' intentions went well beyond improving transparency in government spending. Hadi eventually escaped house arrest and left Sanaa—reportedly in the guise of a woman—for the southern port city of Aden. Once in the south, Hadi renounced his resignation, and declared Aden the capital of a government-in-exile. The international community continued to regard Hadi and his Aden-based government as the only legitimate authority in Yemen.[42]

Revenge of the Nobles

Sanaa proved to be more way station than end point for the Houthi-Saleh nexus. As the Houthis were preparing the ground in Sanaa, their forces were expanding into western and central parts of the country. After toppling the government, their forces continued advancing southward toward Aden under the banner of fighting corruption and terrorism. The Houthis were nominally in pursuit of Al-Qaeda, which had remained a fixture of Yemen's political scene and was growing stronger in the absence of state power. Despite the U.S. military's enduring drone campaign against the group's leadership, and more recent pressure by the Yemeni military under the Hadi government, Al-Qaeda had managed to enmesh itself in local communities. The group strengthened ties with political elites opposed to the Houthi-Saleh nexus, and formed cooperative agreements with nearby tribes, primarily the al-Awaleq, al-Nu'man, and al-Kazemi. In the wake of Hadi's ouster, the jihadist group again emerged as a formidable power in Abyan and Shabwa, and effectively controlled the seaport of al-Mukalla, the capital city of the southeastern Hadhramaut governorate, after its front group, Ansar al-Sharia (Helpers of Sharia), seized it in early April 2015.[43]

Added to this was the emergence of an ISIS affiliate in Yemen in late 2014. The rise of ISIS in Iraq and Syria spurred a franchising effect, with jihadist groups across the greater Middle East and North Africa announcing their allegiance to Abu Bakr al-Baghdadi and the Islamic State. In late March 2015, the group conducted its first high-profile attack in Yemen when a suicide bomber detonated his explosive vest in a packed Zaydi mosque in Sanaa during Friday prayers, killing 137 civilians. The group claimed responsibility in a Twitter post, stating: "Let the polytheist Houthis know that the soldiers of the Islamic State will not rest and will not stay still until they extirpate them. . . . God willing, this operation is only a part of the coming flood."[44]

Two days after the attack in Sanaa, pro-Houthi militants took the city of Taiz, an Islah Party stronghold, and quickly closed in on Aden. The impending collapse of Aden, which sits adjacent to the strategic sea lanes of the Bab al-Mandab strait, along with the likely defeat of the Hadi government, compelled a reaction from Yemen's neighbors. Saudi Arabia considered its southern neighbor central to its interests. The Saudis had focused their Yemen policy on building links with the powerful elite through patronage lubricated with financial inducements. That had included President Saleh, before his leadership became untenable, and a variety of tribal and Sunni Islamist leaders. The Houthis, whose northern home territory abuts the Saudi border, share historical ties with Zaydi communities in the southern Saudi provinces of Jizan, Asir, and Najran. They were distrusted by the Saudis for their independence, willingness to rebel against the state, and Zaydi Shia affiliation. But it was the Houthis' close political relationship with Iran that caused the most concern in Riyadh. The Saudis had assisted Saleh in the Saada wars, and intervened militarily against the Houthis in 2009, engaging in land operations along the border and bombing Houthi positions from the air.

Those wars had kept the Houthis mostly confined to the north. But they also provided an opportunity for Iran, which became the only outside power to support the Houthis. Saleh had promoted a narrative of the Houthis being an Iran proxy since the first Saada war in 2004. Yet, because the claims were often exaggerated, and because the vast majority of Iran's regional activities were in the covert realm, there was virtually no public evidence proving Iranian involvement. Even so, there was something to the Houthi-Iran relationship, and it stretched back to the 1980s, when Badr al-Din, the Houthi patriarch, along with his family and sons, Husayn and Abd al-Malik, resided in Iran for some time. There are substantial religious and cultural differences between the Zaydi Shiism in Yemen and Twelver Shiism in Iran, but Badr al-Din, a prominent Zaydi scholar, had been inspired by the political power of Iran's revolutionary ideology. After his family returned to Yemen, Husayn al-Houthi, who had become a religious scholar like his father, established a Zaydi revivalist organization in the 1990s called Believing Youth (Shabab al-Momenin). The group ultimately split in 2001 due to disagreements among its leadership, and the faction loyal to Husayn evolved into the Houthi movement. The Houthis adopted aspects of Iranian political ideology, particularly by linking their Zaydi revivalism to anti-American and anti-Semitic politics, which they epitomized in their official slogan adopted in 2001: "Death to America! Death to Israel! Curse upon the Jews! Victory for Islam!" Israel's harsh policies toward the Palestinians and the American invasions of Iraq and Afghanistan fueled the attractiveness of those core sentiments within Yemen, as well as regionally. The Houthis later rebranded their movement in 2011 to Ansar Allah (Helpers of God), but continued to be known generally by their familial epithet.[45]

Despite the appropriation of aspects of Iranian ideology, Husayn al-Houthi's ambitions were distinct from those of Iran, and were inextricably tied to the unique conditions of Yemen's Zaydi community. For a millennium, Zaydi Shiites in Yemen had been led by a separate social caste, the Sayyids, who communally trace their descent back to the Prophet Muhammad. During that time, the Sayyids had been a privileged nobility, set apart from their Zaydi tribal counterparts, who both provided them protection and deferred to them in religious and political matters. A central belief in Zaydism is that any Sayyid who is both a scholar and a warrior fighting in the path of justice can claim the mantle of imam—or supreme religious authority—over the entirety of the Muslim community. But it is only the most learned and just Sayyid who would be deserving of the position. Following that basic framework, the institution of the Imam, known as the Imamate, ruled much of Yemen from the 10th century through 1962. By the time of its dissolution, the Imamate in Yemen had ceased to bear much relationship to Zaydi concepts of religious authority or even Shia religiosity.[46] Rather, it had become a hereditary monarchy closely associated with corruption, backwardness, and greed. The last Zaydi Imam, Muhammad al-Badr, was also the final ruling monarch of the Mutawakkilite Kingdom of Yemen. He was overthrown in a palace coup that established the Yemen Arab Republic, and after a failed rebellion by Zaydi supporters in Saada, the Imamate was dissolved. After that point, political power in Yemen shifted to the tribes, and the fortunes and influence of the Sayyids, who had been the upper crust of Yemeni society for a millennium, declined.

For the Houthis, resurrecting the traditional status of the Sayyids in Yemen was a main goal. They aimed to achieve that through establishing a resurgent religious identity within the wider Zaydi (both Sayyid and tribal) community. In a previous era, the Houthi leaders could have asserted a claim to the Imamate. However, by the 1980s the Imamate continued to suffer from a poor reputation among the tribes, and the idea of re-establishing the institution remained unpopular as well as politically untenable. Instead, the Houthis looked to populist ideology as a way of resurrecting communal Zaydi identity and thwarting the growing challenge of Sunni Islamism, which had expanded within traditionally Zaydi areas over previous decades through Saudi funding and patronage. Their anti-American and anti-Israeli rallying cry became a summation of their simplistic, but effective Iran-inspired platform.

During the Saada wars, the Houthis' affiliation with Iran gradually led to rumors of Iranian involvement in Yemen. Saleh used the Iran connection to entice greater military aid from Washington in each of those conflicts, framing the Houthis as a terrorist group linked to Iran and Hezbollah, which made fighting them part of Yemen's writ in the larger war on terror. Yemen received regular military aid from the United States over this time due to prevailing Bush and Obama administration policies, but countering Iran had little to do with it. The main focus for U.S. policy was countering the presence of Al-Qaeda-linked groups in Yemen. Iran's involvement in the country was also minor; however, the Saudi intervention into Saada in 2009, combined with the Arab Spring, changed Iran's calculus. By 2011, more credible reports of Iranian arms shipments and other forms of aid started to appear.[47] As Arab uprisings convulsed across the region, Yemen became another zone of competition. Although Iran's efforts in support of the Houthis were modest compared to its push into Syria, its involvement increased alongside the rise of its allies. As the Houthis fought to gain power through 2015, Iran's level of support grew to encompass an IRGC advisory mission and steady shipments of weaponry—an effort headed by the veteran Quds Force field commander Abdul-Reza Shahlai, and partly staffed by Lebanese Hezbollah operatives.[48]

Iran's expanding role in Yemen was the fulfillment of long-held regional fears. Neighboring states viewed the Houthis as direct proxies of Iran, and worried that they could develop into a peninsular version of Hezbollah. For many outside observers, this perception seemed misplaced. The Houthis' objectives were rooted in social, political, and religious dynamics unique to Yemen, and their regional interests and ideological connection to Iran seemed to begin and end with their official slogan. However, for Iran, the Houthis' aims and beliefs mattered less than who their adversaries were. To the extent that the Houthis' aims ran counter to those of the Saudis in Yemen was reason enough for Iran to see value in cultivating stronger ties to them through increased military aid and financial support. Iran was the only state aiding the Houthis, and therefore was in a strong position to use its largesse as leverage with the group and as a means of gaining a foothold on the Arabian Peninsula. There was another angle to Iran's adventurism: Syria. Iran's main challenge in that conflict came from Gulf Arab support to the rebellion. By stoking a fire in Saudi Arabia's backyard, Iran was giving its neighbors a more pressing concern, one that could potentially distract them away from Syria, and shift their attention, military support, and coin to Yemen.

Nuclear Clouds

In the midst of regional turmoil, another, more hopeful process was playing out. With the election of President Hassan Rouhani in 2013, the United States and Iran began talks on Iran's nuclear enrichment program. A low-level, bilateral diplomatic effort led by veteran diplomat Bill Burns, and brokered by Oman, had begun two years earlier and continued through the end of Mahmoud Ahmadinejad's presidency. Those meetings helped establish a modicum of engagement between Washington and Tehran, but produced little more. The divide between the Americans and Iranians was vast. Burns's assessment following the final round of talks with the Ahmadinejad government suggested bleak prospects: "The Iranians were wildly unrealistic in their expectations; they weren't in the same ballpark, or even playing the same sport . . . ."[1] Yet, those secret meetings, which concluded in early March 2013, succeeded in changing the conversation. The Obama administration signaled to Tehran for the first time that its position on the latter's enrichment program was open to compromise. Previously, Washington had been adamant that Iran should not be allowed to enrich uranium within its facilities, and instead should use fuel imported from Russia in its reactors—a limitation Iran rejected out of hand. The gulf between the American and Iranian positions on the question of enrichment had been one of the main hurdles in multilateral efforts to engage Iran on the nuclear issue. Without informing its allies in Europe, the Obama administration had communicated to Iran that its position could evolve were Iran willing to accept certain, verifiable constraints.[2]

Given the change in government in Iran, Washington hoped the more pragmatic Rouhani administration, and its foreign minister, Mohammad Javad Zarif, would be an easier side to deal with. Anticipating a tonal shift from Tehran, the Obama administration reached out to the Rouhani government once it took office in August 2013. A one-on-one meeting between Secretary of State John Kerry and Zarif on the sidelines of the UN General Assembly in September, followed by a brief phone conversation between Obama and Rouhani the next day, the first direct communication between respective leaders of the two countries since the 1979 revolution, jump-started the process.[3] As Kerry explains of his meeting with Zarif:

> We talked pleasantries at first—his years in New York, the UN, life in Iran and his family, our politics, my job, the Senate. Then we got down to business. I made it clear that the administration was prepared to be serious but didn't feel either rushed or compelled to reach an agreement on Iran's nuclear program. No deal was better than a bad deal, and it would be vital that Iran be prepared to prove it would live by the International Atomic Energy Agency (IAEA) standards and more, or we would be wasting our time. He said Iran was not desperate for a deal. He mentioned [Khamenei's] fatwa, made public in 2003, declaring that Iran would not pursue a nuclear weapon. I said we obviously needed one of the most verifiable international agreements ever made. It was understood: we each had clear bottom lines that would never be crossed, but we were also both serious about trying to find a way forward.[4]

Those modest but promising interactions reinvigorated diplomacy. The two countries, along with Britain, France, China, Russia, and Germany—the so-called P5 + 1—began negotiations to address the nuclear dilemma. By January 2014, an interim deal, which imposed minor restrictions on Iran's enrichment program and increased inspections of its facilities by the International Atomic Energy Agency (IAEA), in exchange for partial sanctions relief, took effect. With growing trust between both sides, talks on a more substantial agreement continued. Over 18 months of contentious diplomacy, punctuated with numerous setbacks and some moments of optimism, the multilateral talks achieved an outcome acceptable to both Washington and Tehran. In July 2015, all members of the P5 + 1 signed the Joint Comprehensive Plan of Action (JCPOA)—a document that delineated the parameters that would be imposed on Iran's nuclear program and authorized the IAEA's monitoring effort that would verify that Tehran's commitments were held. The agreement took effect six months later, in mid-January 2016. Under the deal, Iran agreed to roll back and freeze various aspects of its nuclear program for periods ranging between 10 to 15 years. It also agreed to cap its enrichment levels to 3.67 percent and allow for extensive monitoring of its nuclear facilities by the IAEA. In exchange, nuclear-related economic sanctions against Iran were lifted. Iran also received other promises to incentivize its continued cooperation with the agreement, including the scheduled removal of an arms embargo by 2020, which would allow Tehran to buy and sell weaponry on the open market without UN Security Council (UNSC) approval, and an end to corresponding restrictions on its ballistic missile program by late 2023.[5]

The JCPOA was the landmark foreign policy achievement of the Obama administration, and the fruit of the administration's careful approach toward Iran. Once negotiations began in late summer 2013, the goal of reaching a deal, and later, the preservation of that agreement after its implementation, became primary factors influencing the White House's Middle East policy. Across the major crises churning in the region, the administration's actions were shaped by a combination of a general wariness for intervention and a desire to safeguard the fragile engagement with Iran. Another consideration was that war against ISIS in Iraq had once again brought U.S. forces in close proximity to Iranian proxies. Although both sides were generally working to defeat ISIS, their ultimate objectives were discordant. Seeking to avoid potential flare-ups with Iran-backed militias further constrained American behavior.

By contrast, caution did not define Iran's behavior. Instead, Iran pursued its regional interests with renewed confidence. Even as the nuclear deal limited one of Iran's key programs, it insulated other strategic behavior from American action, thereby providing Iran a measure of deterrence against outside aggression. As Washington worked to balance its leading concerns and limit its involvement in the Middle East, in part to avoid escalation with Iran, regional and foreign powers acted with increasing assertiveness. With the Saudi-led intervention in Yemen, and Russia's move to back Bashar al-Assad with direct military power in Syria, competition in the Middle East entered a new, more complicated phase—one which both heightened America's challenge and presented Iran with new opportunities.

The Crown Prince's War

As the components of the nuclear deal were being hashed out in European hotels, Saudi Arabia was on the cusp of a historic transition. The ruling monarch, King Abdullah, whose cautious hand had guided the country through the turbulence of 9/11 and the Arab Spring, died in January 2015. His death was a turning point for both Saudi Arabia and the region. Under Abdullah, Saudi foreign policy had been largely conservative and risk-averse. But the tempo of regional dynamics and a mounting rivalry with Iran had prompted a gradual shift, leading Riyadh to come around to supporting the rebels in Syria and bankrolling the return of military authoritarianism in Egypt under President Sisi. With the ascension of Abdullah's half-brother, Salman bin Abdul-Aziz al-Saud, to the throne, Riyadh doubled down on its activist turn in regional affairs. Salman delegated much of the kingdom's decision-making in foreign and strategic affairs to his favorite son, Mohammed bin Salman (more commonly known as MBS), who replaced his father as Minister of Defense and assumed a central decision-making position. A year and a half later, in June 2017, MBS was promoted to crown prince, and took control of all major policy, foreign and domestic.

With the rise of the Houthis, Yemen was now the top concern. For decades the Saudis had managed relations with their poorer, southern neighbor through monetary and religious patronage. The Saudis relied on having elites on the payroll, using their purse strings to nudge policy this way or that. The Houthis fell outside of Riyadh's sway, and worse, were close to Iran. The prospect of the Houthis transforming Yemen into an Iran-friendly country, along the lines of Syria or Iraq, was not something the Saudis would acquiesce. Saudi Arabia had fought the Houthis in 2009, and the two sides continued to view each other as enemies. By gaining control of Yemen's government, and expanding its circle of domestic allies, the Zaidi Shia group posed a problem for Saudi Arabia with no obvious fix.

MBS was unencumbered by the risk aversion of his father's generation. The 29-year-old wanted to be decisive and bold, and no longer cede the first step in regional competition to Iran. Rather, he would do what Iran had done in Syria and Iraq. He would commit to one side and make a move. Saudi Arabia had one of the most expensive and technologically advanced militaries in the region, and sought to use it. In late March 2015, Riyadh did just that, and began a direct military intervention into Yemen in support of the ousted Hadi government. The crown prince put together a coalition of Arab allies, including the UAE, Bahrain, Qatar, Egypt, Jordan, Sudan, and Morocco, to back the effort. The specter of the pro-Iran Houthis gaining ground on the Arabian Peninsula deeply concerned surrounding states who were already reeling from Tehran's expanding influence elsewhere. A common refrain within Gulf Arab states at the time was that with the Houthis' rise to power, Iran now controlled four Arab capitals: Baghdad, Damascus, Beirut, and Sanaa.[6] That sentiment expressed a widely held perspective in the region that the Arab world was standing by as more and more territory fell to Iran and its Shia proxies. Yet, the Houthis were not only seizing territorial control, they were gaining tribal allies, and taking possession of airports, military bases, vast stores of arms, and some of Yemen's most sophisticated weaponry. The group was quickly expanding its power and capabilities, and openly courting Iran, such as by announcing the establishment of daily flights between Tehran and Sanaa. The group's advance on Aden was a red line, and the broad coalition assembled by MBS was a testament to the trepidation the Houthis had triggered within the region.

Those fears were not shared by all of Riyadh's allies. The Saudis also approached Pakistan in the assumption that Islamabad would provide the forces and military know-how needed to defeat the Houthis. The Saudis had close ties with Pakistan's military, and had served as benefactor to Pakistan's political elite for decades. Unlike the Saudi armed forces, which had never deployed beyond the country's borders nor fought a significant conflict, Pakistan's military was powerful and experienced in both conventional and counterinsurgency warfare. Pakistan had defense agreements with Saudi Arabia, which the Saudis believed would extend to the situation in Yemen. However, with the complexity of the situation on the ground, and the involvement of Iran, the Yemen conflict was not a straightforward affair.

Iran and Pakistan had tense and complex relations. Iran's advocacy for the Shia minority in Pakistan, nearly a fifth of country's population, and Pakistani military intelligence's links to Sunni extremist organizations, such as the anti-Shia Sipah-e-Sahaba, were continual sources of acrimony. Yet, they were also neighbors, and had intersecting security concerns along their shared border and in Afghanistan. In late March, Pakistani prime minister Nawaz Sharif met with King Salman and President Hadi in Riyadh, where he was formally asked to join the Saudi-led coalition.[7] Sharif punted the issue to Pakistan's parliament, which voted against joining the coalition two weeks later, in early April.[8] Two days prior to the vote, Iran's foreign minister, Mohammad Javad Zarif, traveled to Islamabad to urge the Pakistanis to reject the Saudi request.[9] In lieu of sending troops to Yemen, Sharif expressed solidarity with Saudi Arabia, and traveled to Riyadh with military leaders to reassure the Saudis that Pakistan remained committed to protecting the country's territorial integrity. Pakistani forces would not, however, be drawn into a regional war between fellow Muslim states.[10]

In the build-up to intervention, the Saudis informed Washington of their plans to conduct an air campaign against the Houthis. The war-wary Obama administration was in a delicate spot, and defaulted to a familiar middle position, neither publicly joining the Saudi-led intervention nor seriously trying to prevent it. Instead, the administration opted to offer certain forms of non-lethal assistance to the effort, in the hopes that some amount of coordination would sharpen the precision of Saudi military action while also potentially constraining it. The United States was already involved in ongoing counterterrorism operations in Yemen, focused on killing Al-Qaeda operatives and disrupting jihadist networks through drone strikes and limited special operations.[11] Even with low-level involvement, the war against the Houthis promised to deepen American engagement in the country.

The Saudi air force began striking Houthi positions in Sanaa on March 26, 2015, commencing Operation Decisive Storm, the code name for the first stage of the intervention. In a press conference in Washington, the Saudi ambassador to the United States, Adel al-Jubeir, provided an official statement on the campaign:

> Saudi Arabia has launched military operations in Yemen, as part of a
> coalition of over ten countries in response to a direct request from the

legitimate government of Yemen. The operation will be limited in nature, and designed to protect the people of Yemen and its legitimate
government from a takeover by the Houthis. A violent extremist militia. The Gulf Cooperation Council (GCC) countries tried to facilitate
a peaceful transition of government in Yemen, but the Houthis have
continuously undercut the process by occupying territory and seizing
weapons belonging to the government. . . . Based on the appeal from
President Hadi, and based on the Kingdom's responsibility to Yemen
and its people, the Kingdom of Saudi Arabia, along with its allies within
the GCC and outside the GCC, launched military operations in support of the people of Yemen and their legitimate government.[12]

Vociferous responses from Houthis and Iran soon followed. Houthi leader
Abdulmalik al-Houthi accused the "oppressive forces led by Saudi Arabia" of
"trying to carry out the will of the United States and Israel by attacking Yemen."
He called on the Yemeni people to "stand up against this oppressive attack,"
declaring, "the Yemeni people will not suffer being slaves of the Saudi regime."[13]
IRGC deputy commander Hossein Salami pushed a similar line, and linked
the Saudi intervention to the conflicts in Iraq, Syria, and Gaza, thereby reifying
Yemen as a zone of competition between Iran and its adversaries. He hailed the
Houthis for possessing "the same logic and ideology as [Iran's] Islamic revolu-
tion," calling Yemen the "Achilles' heel of American politics in the region."[14]

With Operation Decisive Storm, the wealthiest country in the Arab world
was now at war with the poorest. Over the next few weeks, the Saudis focused
their assault on Houthi-controlled military sites, destroying runways, aircraft,
radar, and missile sites, with the aim of degrading the Houthis' capabilities and
impeding its advances. In mid-April, the UNSC adopted Resolution 2216, which
called for the Houthis to disarm, withdraw forces from cities under their control,
and for all parties to pursue a political process to end the conflict. The resolution
received 14 affirmative votes and one abstention from Russia, and also placed
sanctions on Abdulmalik al-Houthi and on Ahmed Ali Saleh for their role in
the conflict.[15] The Houthis rejected the resolution. A week later, the Saudi-led
air campaign broadened and began to hit the country's critical infrastructure.
Civilian airports, roads, bridges, and ports were all targeted and destroyed. Such
strikes wrought destruction but initially did little to shift momentum in the conflict. For Yemen's civilian population, however, the situation went from bad to
worse. As the veteran Yemen reporter Ginny Hill explains:

After nine months of civil war and Coalition airstrikes, the poorest
country in the region was significantly poorer still. Oil production had
halted and exports fell to zero. The economy was in ruins, following a de

facto port blockade that restricted food and fuel imports, and decimated commercial shipping. The scarcity of fuel, combined with widespread damage to transport infrastructure made it extremely difficult to move people and goods to the market. Hunger, always widespread, became increasingly prevalent. Thousands of schools were closed, while hospital workers were struggling to treat an influx of war casualties with fewer and fewer resources.[16]

The Saudi-led coalition also spearheaded a ground invasion to dislodge the Houthis from Aden and drive their forces back north. The Saudi portion of the campaign focused on Houthi positions in the northern parts of Yemen. The UAE took control of southern operations and the coasts. Under the leadership of Crown Prince Mohamed bin Zayed, known commonly by the acronym MBZ, the UAE was equally concerned with Iranian influence in Yemen but less committed to President Hadi. That lack of commitment shaped the UAE's approach to the war. The UAE had a modern, well-trained military, but it was also small, and had limited expeditionary capabilities. To play to its strengths, the UAE committed its special forces to Yemen, and augmented their involvement with foreign mercenaries and local armed groups, including pro-secessionist Southern Movement (hiraki) militias and Salafi militants, many of whom were displaced students from the Dar al-Hadtih seminary in Dammaj. Hadi had courted the Salafis as well, appointing Hani bin Breik, a Dar al-Hadtih graduate and prominent cleric from the south, as the minister of state for security.[17]

The UAE's southern campaign was effective, and by late July, had succeeded in driving out pro-Houthi forces from Aden. Houthi forces fell back to Taiz, which settled into a frontline. The UAE's advance made steady progress against the Houthis in Taiz through the summer, but failed to dislodge them from key positions in and around the city. Despite success in Aden, the overall effort gradually stalled and Houthi defenses became entrenched. The Emiratis focused on expanding a buffer around Aden and on improving security within it. Emirati special forces concentrated on establishing local militias composed of southern Yemenis who were adversarial both to the Houthis and to the Muslim Brotherhood–associated Islah Party. Among the UAE's new clients were fighters associated with the Al-Qaeda-affiliated groups Ansar al-Sharia and the Sons of Hadhramaut. The Emiratis convinced militia leaders to split from Al-Qaeda and rebrand their groups as independent southern militias, nominally loyal to the Hadi government. That approach helped pro-Emirati forces weaken Al-Qaeda's presence around Aden, Abyan, and in al-Mukalla. Through its military presence, and control of numerous proxy militias, the Emiratis had become the de facto power in Aden. The Yemeni government, with its president residing mostly in Riyadh, exercised authority in the temporary capital in name only.

Through the end of 2015, the Saudi-led coalition pressured pro-Houthi forces across the north and south. Brief ceasefires in the summer and in December, as well as efforts to establish UN-sponsored peace talks, did little to end the conflict.[18] The intermittent bombardment of pro-Houthi positions failed to dislodge their forces, and had no discernible impact on their hold of the north. Over time it became evident that the Saudi-led intervention stood little chance of achieving its aims and would struggle to win many substantial battles on the ground. Poor planning, targeting, and execution, combined with the complexities of Yemen's social and political fabric, which at times blurred the conflict's dividing lines, all contributed to the morass. The Houthis benefited from their adversaries' inability to direct an effective combined campaign, and their relative coherence as an indigenous sociopolitical movement gave them the upper hand over the Hadi government's tenuous coalition. Those political divisions mattered little to the civilians suffering from the conflict, which was taking a serious and deadly toll on Yemeni society. For the people caught in the middle, the fighting brought only destruction, misery, and famine. By December, less than nine months into the war, a United Nations report estimated that over 6,000 civilians had been injured in the war, and over 2,700 others had been killed. A further two million people were internally displaced, fleeing bombs, armed clashes, and the general insecurity unleashed by the fighting.[19]

Obama's Delicate Dance in Syria

More than in Yemen, navigating engagement with Iran loomed large in the United States' approach to Syria. Prior to the outbreak of ISIS, the Obama administration had settled on a middle-ground approach: supporting the rebellion without a commitment to rebel victory. This helped the rebellion take shape and gain strength but denied the rebels the backing needed to overthrow Assad. That policy kept U.S. troops out of the conflict, and skirted a potential clash with Iran. Iranian leaders had repeatedly warned the United States against intervening in Syria, and threatened retaliation if it did. When it appeared that the Obama administration might strike Syria in response to the Assad regime's use of chemical weapons in August 2013, which contravened both international law and the president's red line, the newly appointed deputy foreign minister, Abbas Araghchi, cautioned that an attack could lead to a wider imbroglio, saying: "We want to strongly warn against any military attack in Syria. There will definitely be perilous consequences for the region. . . . These complications and consequences will not be restricted to Syria. It will engulf the whole region."[20] IRGC chief Mohammad Ali Jafari was less diplomatic: "Despite the bitter experiences of Afghanistan and Iraq, should the Americans conduct military

action in Syria . . . they will encounter the most humiliating defeat in history. . . .
Syria would become a second Vietnam for the United States." He then expanded
the threat to Israel, saying: "The Zionists should know an American military
strike on Syria will not save their invented regime from the talons of the resistance. Rather, an attack on Syria will lead to the imminent annihilation of Israel."[21]

The Obama administration had tip-toed around Iran in Syria since the rebellion began, and such threats reinforced that approach. The rise of ISIS, however,
changed Washington's calculations. ISIS was a transnational problem. Its leaders
did not recognize boundaries or norms, nor did they distinguish between innocent civilians and combatants. As Obama stated in September 2014 in the
lead-up to the U.S.-led intervention in Iraq, "[ISIS] poses a threat to the people
of Iraq and Syria, and the broader Middle East—including American citizens,
personnel and facilities. If left unchecked, these terrorists could pose a growing
threat beyond that region, including to the United States."[22]

The war against ISIS shifted the United States' thinking on Syria. Intervention
was necessary but had to be calibrated to target ISIS in isolation. The prospect
of Assad's fall was now even more fraught, and aiding the rebellion in a more significant manner was still unpopular in the White House and across Washington.
Yet, something had to be done. So, to complement the campaign in Iraq, the
United States began a clandestine effort to train and equip Kurdish and Arab
militias in northwestern Syria to counter ISIS. The Kurdish People's Protection
Units, more commonly known by the acronym YPG, were at the heart of
the campaign. U.S. Special Forces forged partnerships with the YPG, which
functioned as the armed wing of the Democratic Union Party, or PYD, the most
powerful Kurdish political organization in Syria and the de facto authority over
the country's northeastern Kurdish region, known in Kurdish as Rojava. The
partnership proved effective. Kurdish militias, backed by American advisors and
air power, turned the tide against the Islamic State. The first major victory was
the defeat and withdrawal of jihadist forces from the town of Kobane in January
2015 after a four-month campaign.[23] ISIS remained powerful in the area, but
American backing provided the Kurds with the tools necessary to stem jihadist
advances and gradually extricate Islamic State fighters from their strongholds.

The American-led effort also included Arab armed groups from the area.
Kurdish and Arab contingents became the two halves of the 65,000-member Syrian
Democratic Forces (SDF), the establishment of which was announced in October
2015.[24] The SDF became America's main partner in combating the Islamic State in
Syria. Combining Kurdish and Arab fighters into a single front organization was in
part designed to reflect the local demographics of northern Syria. It was also an at-
tempt to placate Turkey, which considered the YPG an offshoot of the PKK.[25] The
YPG and PYD claimed to be independent from the PKK and to have no role in
Kurdish activism in Turkey.[26] The Obama administration accepted this view, and

hoped that by merging Kurdish and Arab militias, they could make the case that the counter-ISIS coalition in Syria was just that, and not a group that would turn its attention toward Turkey after the war with ISIS was over.[27]

That line of reasoning did nothing to assuage the concerns of Prime Minister Erdoğan, who viewed American support of the SDF as a betrayal. Two weeks after the announced formation of the SDF, Turkish aircraft bombed YPG positions near the Turkish border in Syria. Erdoğan justified the operations by accusing the YPG of ethnically cleansing Turkmen from areas under their control, and of advancing west of the Euphrates—Ankara's red line. In defiance of a NATO ally, Erdoğan warned, "Turkey doesn't need permission from anyone—we will do what is necessary. . . . We are determined to [combat] anything that threatens us along the Syrian border, inside or out." He further accused the United States of hypocrisy, complaining, "They don't even accept the PYD as a terrorist organization. What kind of nonsense is this? . . . The West still has the mentality of 'My terrorist is good, yours is bad.' "[28]

Russia Intervenes

Despite the Islamic State's setbacks, the rebellion gained momentum against the Assad regime in other parts of Syria through the first half of 2015. In late March, Islamist rebels led by the Nusra Front captured the provincial capital of Idlib and much of the territory north of the city stretching to the Turkish border. In April, Islamist rebels took the city of Jisr al-Shughur, 50 kilometers to the west of Idlib. Idlib and its environs were the most important victories of the rebellion to date, and hardened rebel positions in western Syria. This provided them more geographical control between Aleppo and Damascus, and afforded them with uncontested smuggling and supply routes to Turkey.[29] Positions in Idlib also strengthened rebel operations in neighboring Latakia province, the Alawite-majority ancestral home of the Assads. The regime suffered another blow when the Islamic State seized the ancient city of Palmyra in central Syria in May. Islamic State militants turned the sacking of Palmyra into a public relations spectacle, decapitating the city's former lead conservator, the 81-year old Khaled al-Asaad, and destroying ancient Roman statues and edifices that had defined the city for over 1,500 years and made it, prior to the war, a global tourist destination.[30] Beyond the iconoclasm and opportunistic looting of antiquities, which became a lucrative resource stream, Palmyra offered the Islamic State a strategic foothold at the intersection of two major highways, which could be used to strike the heart of the regime in Damascus, 250 kilometers to the southwest.

The combined advances of the Islamist rebels and Islamic State had reversed the regime's momentum in the conflict. The rebellion was on the march and loyalist forces were weakening. Assad's backers in Tehran and Moscow could see where the trend lines were headed. Syrian military forces were exhausted and depleted due to mass desertions and battlefield losses. Iranian-led forces helped stem the tide, but were insufficient to hold the rebellion back. America's intervention against ISIS in northeastern Syria was another concern. Iran could ill-afford further setbacks and scrambled for a way to save the Assad regime from defeat. Qassem Soleimani traveled to Moscow in July with a simple message: if Russia did not step in, Assad would fall.[31] Within weeks, Russia began deploying forces and equipment to the Hmeimim airbase in Latakia, and by late September, Russian forces began conducting airstrikes against rebel positions in Syria. President Putin was now at war in the Middle East.

The Russian intervention in Syria marked its first military action outside of the former Soviet Union since the Cold War, and reinvigorated loyalist forces.[32] Prior to Russia's involvement, the Syrian military had been unable to combine air and ground offensives into effective campaigns. Syria's air fleet was limited, and its infantry had struggled to stop rebel advances or extricate rebel forces from hardened positions. Russia's advanced platforms, superior Intelligence, Surveillance and Reconnaissance (ISR) capabilities, and greater resources brought air power and combined operations to the center of the war. Buoyed by that support, loyalist forces began to turn the tide against the rebels and make progress on the ground.

Russia's involvement was a direct challenge to the American and Turkish efforts in Syria. Moscow claimed that its air campaign was focused on terrorist groups, and ISIS in particular, yet its military's actions in theater suggested otherwise. Russian air sorties routinely targeted non-jihadist rebel groups, including pro-Turkish and pro-U.S. rebel factions, while largely sparing ISIS.[33] Such airstrikes were condemned by the U.S.-led coalition and Turkey, which both understood the danger Russia posed to the rebellion.[34] Further aggravating Ankara were its claims that Russian military aircraft had been violating Turkish airspace. Those tensions culminated in November, when a Turkish F-16 shot down a Russian Su-24 that had briefly strayed into Turkish territory near the Syrian border, killing its crew. Though Putin condemned the incident, he eventually opted for de-escalatory measures and began to seek ways to mollify his Turkish counterpart. Turkey had enforced its red line with Russia, but neither country could afford to escalate the matter. Turkey had extensive economic relations with Russia, and Russia recognized the advantage that relations with Turkey could provide, both in Syria and as a potential weak link in NATO.[35]

Russia's intervention similarly complicated American activity in the country. Washington criticized Russian involvement and the targeting of non-jihadist rebel groups, but also sought to avoid unintentional interactions between their forces, especially in the air. Russia shared a desire to de-conflict military operations, and following negotiations begun by presidents Obama and Putin at the United Nations General Assembly in September, both countries signed a memorandum of understanding on air safety in October. The memorandum established "specific safety protocols for air crews to follow" but fell short of an agreement to avoid contact or to cooperate.[36]

The United States and its allies continued to push for a political solution to the conflict. The UNSC also pursued avenues that could reduce fighting and lead to an end to the conflict. The differing agendas of Russia and the United States, France, and the United Kingdom proved impossible to align. Even so, in December, the UNSC adopted Resolution 2254, which called on parties of the conflict to cease hostilities and to allow humanitarian aid to reach Syria's besieged civilian populations. Major rebel groups, along with the Syrian government and Russia, were parties to the resolution. However, groups already designated as terrorists, including ISIS, Nusra, "and all other individuals, groups, undertakings, and entities associated" with those groups, remained outside of the political process and therefore continued to be legitimate targets of U.S. and Russian counterterrorism operations.[37] In practice, this meant that Russia could continue to strike most rebel positions—including in Aleppo and Idlib—because Nusra or its allies operated in those areas. The United States could also continue its war with ISIS in eastern Syria unconstrained.

Over the next several months, the infusion of Russian military power enabled the Assad regime to make steady progress against the rebellion. The first major victory for the loyalist camp was the retaking of Palmyra from ISIS in March 2016. Russian air power paved the way for Iranian-led forces (including Syrian, Iraqi, Lebanese, and Afghan militias), who did much of the heavy fighting on the ground.[38] With Palmyra behind them, loyalist forces focused their attention on retaking rebel-held eastern Aleppo. The rebels controlled much of the city, but parts of its southern and western neighborhoods had remained in regime hands. As Syria's second-largest urban area, and once financial hub, the regime devoted enormous resources and manpower to retain a foothold in the city. Russian military support gave Assad a chance to break the stalemate. The combined effort to retake the city, which again centered on Iranian-led ground forces and Russian air power, established a style of combined operations that the loyalist camp would use to expel rebels in future campaigns. This operational approach was incremental in its design, and effective in its execution. Loyalist forces began by severing rebel supply lines into Aleppo and preventing "humanitarian assistance provided for under UNSCR 2254 from reaching it."[39] An aerial bombing campaign followed, which, as Robert Hamilton, Chris Miller, and Aaron Stein explain:

> [did] not discriminate between terrorist groups and legitimate opposition groups that were parties to the cessation of hostilities. Russian

and Syrian bombing also did not discriminate between legitimate military targets and civilian targets, such as schools, hospitals, and residential areas. Having choked off humanitarian assistance to the city and subjecting it to relentless and indiscriminate bombing, the Russian military then offered to open "humanitarian corridors," allowing rebel fighters to leave along with civilians. In most cases, these people were moved to Idlib Province, which was filled with opposition groups— from moderate, Western-backed groups, to Turkish-backed groups and UN-designated terrorist groups.[40]

After months of intense fighting, and aerial and artillery bombardments, the city's remaining rebel forces, which were starved of food and supplies, began to gradually retreat. By early December, a ceasefire deal brokered by Russia and Turkey was reached.[41] Remaining rebel forces and their families were evacuated on buses, with most heading to rebel-controlled Idlib. The Assad regime declared victory on December 13. Pro-Assad forces retook parts of the city that had been under rebel control since 2012. Regime soldiers and Iranian-led militiamen marched through the crumbling, depopulated neighborhoods as conquerors, but it had been Russian air power, and the sheer destruction of civilian areas, that had determined the outcome. Rebel defeat in Aleppo turned the war in Assad's favor.

Perhaps sensing that the rebellion would not be able to overcome the imbalance of power that Russia's involvement had produced, outside involvement in the conflict also began to shift. Turkey's position evolved considerably after the Russian intervention. President Erdoğan did not abandon pro-Turkish rebels, but his aims pivoted from the goal of overthrowing Assad to securing influence and territorial control over much of the northern border region. Turkey redoubled its efforts to expand its political dominance in northern Syria through the support of client rebel groups. Even as Turkish-backed groups continued to fight ISIS, they concentrated operations on checking the advance of Kurdish militias west of the Euphrates and denying any routinization of Kurdish control near the Syrian border.[42]

Ankara's aims ran counter to those of Washington, and strained bilateral relations. With tensions rising, Erdoğan began to accede to the Russian position in Syria. After the rebel defeat in Aleppo, Turkey's priorities in Syria became more centered on securing interests in the north than on regime change. Erdoğan was in a better spot to strike bargains with Putin; even though Russia's aims in the country ran counter to Turkey's, Russia's support to Assad was deemed less of a threat than America's support to the Kurds.[43] To that end, Erdoğan joined a Russian-led diplomatic initiative ostensibly founded to seek an end to the conflict. Dubbed the Astana Process, due to the group's first meeting in the Kazakh capital in January 2017, the initiative included Russia, Iran, and Turkey, and left out the United States and Gulf Arab partners.[44] Although ineffectual, the Astana Process signaled Turkey's distancing from the United States, its NATO ally, and its emerging, yet fragile cooperation with Russia. Above all, Erdoğan wanted to be on the winning side and would not brook the rising power of Syria's Kurds facilitated by Washington.

PART III

America First

In America's 2016 presidential election, Donald Trump campaigned as a populist catering to the grievances of a dwindling middle class. He packaged issues such as immigration and rampant opioid addiction with promises to reinvigorate America's crumbling industries. Playing to the economic and cultural anxieties of his mostly White supporters, Trump promised to resurrect steel plants in the Rust Belt and return the coal mines of Appalachia to their former glory, while using reactionary and racist tropes that fanned the flames of America's divisions. Those positions were combined into a potent nationalism, reduced and commodified by his campaign's two slogans: "Make America Great Again" and "America First."

Trump's domestic agenda was matched by an ambitious foreign policy that sought to reduce U.S. commitments abroad while also increasing pressure on adversaries. Trump articulated that vision in his campaign's first foreign policy speech—an event hosted by the Center for the National Interest, a small think tank in Washington, D.C., whose anti-interventionist and Moscow-friendly positions were echoed uncoincidentally in Trump's comments. Russian ambassador Sergey Kislyak was in attendance, adding an early layer of intrigue to the future president's controversial relationship with Russia.[1] In his talk, Trump decried the interventionist policies of the Bush and Obama administrations and vowed "to put the interests of the American people and American security above all else." "It has to be," he continued: "That will be the foundation of every decision that I will make. . . . America First will be the major and overriding theme of my administration."[2]

Trump presented his approach as the contradistinction of Obama's. Where Obama had turned left, Trump would turn right. The Middle East was of special importance because it had been the focus of post–9/11 U.S. foreign policy, and where its greatest failures—the wars in Iraq and Afghanistan—lay. As Trump argued:

> It all began with the dangerous idea that we could make Western
> democracies out of countries that had no experience or interest in

becoming a Western democracy. We tore up what institutions they had and then were surprised at what we unleashed. Civil war, religious fanaticism; thousands of American lives, and many trillions of dollars, were lost as a result. The vacuum was created that ISIS would fill. Iran, too, would rush in and fill the void, much to their unjust enrichment. Our foreign policy is a complete and total disaster. No vision, no purpose, no direction, no strategy.[3]

Using Obama as the foil, Trump identified what he called the "five main weaknesses" of American foreign policy. First, he argued, America's commitments around the globe had left it overextended and incurring massive debt. Second, allies had grown accustomed to the United States leading and footing much of the bill for their security. They needed to pay "their fair share" and increase their defense spending so that the burden of costs would be shared more equitably. "[A]nd if not," he warned, "the U.S. must be prepared to let these countries defend themselves. We have no choice." Third, America must back its other friends. Obama's approach to the Middle East, such as during the Arab Spring and in signing the nuclear deal with Iran, had caused America's regional partners—especially Israel and Arab states—to lose trust in Washington. Fourth, American power was no longer respected by rivals and competitors, and that needed to change.

Finally, Trump called for a "clear understanding of [America's] foreign policy goals." Concerning the Middle East, that meant, above all, avoiding costly military interventions and adopting an orientation that prioritized securing the region's authoritarian status quo over promoting democracy or human rights. As Trump saw it: "One day, we're bombing Libya and getting rid of a dictator to foster democracy for civilians. The next day, we're watching the same civilians suffer while that country falls and absolutely falls apart." Added to this, Trump's Middle East policy sought to identify "radical Islam" as the real enemy, support Christian communities, and back Israel unconditionally.

Upon taking office in January 2017, such sentiments guided Trump's presidency. Although he aimed to establish a coherent approach to foreign policy, one which put America's interests, so far as they were understood by him, at the heart of every decision, his policies were fraught with contradicting desires and impulsive decisions. Nowhere was this more apparent than in the Middle East, where Trump's vitriol for his predecessors was strongest. Trump wanted to end American military involvement in the region while also amplifying pressure on Iran, getting tougher on jihadists, and throwing even more support behind Israel—efforts undergirded by the U.S. regional military presence.

In pursuing that agenda, his administration became mired in the same tangled problem set as its predecessors, and U.S. influence continued to slacken. Trump's desire to de-militarize U.S. policy in the region, along with his disinclination to criticize or challenge the policies of regional partners, further encouraged a climate of foreign policy entrepreneurship. Middle East states had already been moving in that direction. Iran's behavior had shown its neighbors that a forward-leaning posture could bring strategic benefits, and that no foreign power, to include the United States, any longer had the will to prevent regional states from pursuing extraterritorial influence through military means. With the United States stepping back from the region, its partners rightly understood that they could no longer sit by and expect Washington to solve—or create—their problems for them. They would need to do that themselves. And with Trump moving away from the hallmarks of previous administrations, particularly in the promotion of human rights and democracy, regional states had more latitude to behave in ways that contravened those ideals. Turkey, Saudi Arabia, and the UAE grew more ambitious and assertive as they faced less pushback from Washington, further stoking competition in the region's simmering conflicts.

Turkey and the War on ISIS

Trump's election followed the beginning of major U.S.-led offensives against the Islamic State in Raqqa and Mosul. Launched in October and November 2016 by the Obama administration as part of Operation Inherent Resolve (OIR), the campaigns targeted ISIS's main geographic footholds. By squeezing the terrorist organization from the east and west, the effort aimed at destroying the territorial integrity of the self-proclaimed caliphate, while reducing ISIS's access to resources and safe havens. The war was a transnational effort, with foreign powers backing both state security forces and non-state militias against a terrorist insurgency pretending to be a state. The U.S. military provided most of the air support, funding, and intelligence for the ground campaign, with Coalition partners playing important yet more discrete roles. U.S. and Coalition troops were also on the ground in smaller numbers, working closely with local partners. In Syria, the Coalition backed the Kurdish-dominated SDF in the retaking of Raqqa. In Iraq, the Coalition worked with Iraqi federal forces, including the military and police, as well as with Kurdish Peshmerga forces under the authority of the Kurdish Regional Government (KRG), in the liberation of Mosul. Those campaigns were complicated by other patron–client efforts involved in the conflict. Iran-backed Shia militias, which had become part of the larger Popular Mobilization Forces (PMF), represented another nexus contending to be involved in the Mosul campaign.

The move to liberate Raqqa coincided with Turkey's ongoing onslaught against Kurdish positions in northern Syria under Operation Euphrates Shield. Clashes between Turkish-backed Syrian rebels and SDF factions occurred across parts of the northern border, and around Manbij. Turkey aimed to seize the entirety of Manbij from Kurdish elements, but failed to fully expel them. When Operation Euphrates Shield formally ended in late March, Turkey nonetheless claimed victory. The end of the code-named operation was not the end of Turkish ambitions in Syria. As Prime Minister Binali Yildirim told Turkish state television, "Operation Euphrates Shield has been successful and is finished. Any operation following this one will have a different name."[4]

The effort to liberate Mosul was also complicated by the geopolitical context. The PMF's close links to Iran, and the prominence of Shia militias with a history of anti-Sunni sectarian violence within it, made the paramilitary umbrella organization controversial, especially among Iraqi Sunnis and Sunni regional states. The campaign to oust ISIS from Mosul and surrounding environs brought that criticism to the fore. Turkey in particular warned against the potential involvement of the Shia militias in Mosul, and that stance threatened to be more than bluster. President Erdoğan had deployed around 2,000 Turkish troops to northern Iraq in 2015 as part of counterterrorism operations against the PKK. From its firebase near the town of Bashiqa, around 12 kilometers north of Mosul, Turkish forces trained Sunni Arab militiamen and Kurdish Peshmerga fighters.[5] Turkey's military presence had come at the invitation of the KRG, but without the consent of the federal government in Baghdad, it added another obstacle to the already complex landscape of the war.[6]

Turkey's operations in Iraq were part of an evolving strategy. By 2010, Ankara began moving away from the idea of supporting a united, federal Iraq, in favor of increasing links with regional partners in Kurdistan and the northern Nineveh Governorate, along with its capital Mosul. KRG president Masoud Barzani and his KDP organization had developed extensive ties to Ankara over the preceding decade, as had Sunni Arab politicians, including the powerful al-Nujaifi brothers, Atheel and Osama. Atheel, who was governor of Ninewa when Mosul fell to ISIS, had moved to Erbil and organized a loose-knit militia known as Hashd al-Watani (National Mobilization Forces) composed of Sunni Arabs from the area. After 2015, the militia's few thousand fighters began receiving training from the Turkish military.[7]

The Bashiqa base gave the Turks a card to play; Baghdad, however, rejected any prospect of a Turkish role in the war.[8] The Iraqi government was officially in charge of the campaign, and had been angered by the unapproved Turkish deployment. In October 2016, Prime Minister Abadi condemned the Turkish military presence as an "occupying force." Erdoğan responded by warning his Iraqi counterpart to "know his place." Adding, "You are not at my level . . . the army of the Turkish republic has not lost such standing as to receive instructions from you. . . . You should know that we will do what we want to do."[9]

Erdoğan's primary interest was having a say in the future of northwestern Iraq, especially regarding Mosul and Tal Afar—a mostly ethnically Turkmen enclave near the Syrian border. Under the Ottoman Empire, Mosul had been the capital of its own administrative district (*vilayet*), and a segment of Turkish nationalists considered it to be an integral part of the Turkish homeland. Erdoğan played to those revanchist sentiments in a speech railing against the detractors of Turkey's military involvement in Iraq, stating: "Some ignorant people come and say, 'What relation could you have with Iraq?' Those geographies that we talk about now are part of our soul. . . . Even if it weighs on our hearts [to no longer possess them], we respect every nation's geographical borders." Beyond possible imperialist designs in northern Iraq, Turkey's gambit afforded it a degree of leverage in how the conflict might play out.

Turkish advocacy against the PMF's potential involvement in the Mosul campaign paralleled a similar diplomatic effort by the U.S.-led Coalition, which succeeded in convincing Baghdad to limit the role of the militias. Baghdad prevented the PMF from having a direct role in the operations to liberate Mosul, but they were allowed to participate in the wider effort to clear the surrounding countryside of ISIS cells.[10] They played a larger role in Tal Afar, dislodging ISIS from the environs around the city, retaking the local airport, and establishing positions outside of town to counteract ISIS's ability to resupply.[11]

The encroachment around Tal Afar alarmed Ankara. Erdoğan warned against any invasion by the militias:

> Tal Afar is a very sensitive issue for us. We definitely do not regard [the militia's involvement] positively in Tal Afar and Sinjar. [It is] a totally Turkmen city, with half Shia and half Sunni Muslims. We do not judge people by their religious affiliation, we regard them all as Muslims. . . . But if Hashd al-Shaabi terrorizes the region, our response would be different.[12]

Badr chief Haider al-Amiri cautioned Turkey against intervening: "Tal Afar will be the cemetery of Turkish soldiers should Turkey attempt to take part in the battle."[13] Months later, Erdoğan revealed his dour view of the pro-Iran militias, implying in an interview with *Aljazeera* that they were nothing more than terrorists. That earned a formal protest from Baghdad, with the Iraqi Foreign Ministry summoning Turkey's ambassador in response.[14]

End of a Caliphate

The Mosul campaign began in October 2016. U.S.-led Coalition forces, both on the ground and in the air, backed a combined local force of over 100,000 troops. Iraq's elite Counter Terrorism Service (CTS), military, and police, along with KRG Peshmerga, spearheaded the ground advance. ISIS was estimated to have around 5,000 to 12,000 fighters tightly embedded across the city.[15] The Coalition's strategy focused on surrounding Mosul while gradually pushing forward, using airstrikes to soften enemy targets and prepare the way for a ground assault. It took six weeks for Coalition forces to establish a security perimeter around the city, and even with vastly superior numbers, the Coalition could not fully cut off ISIS's logistical pipeline. Through the first four months of the campaign, the jihadists maintained links with Tal Afar, around 65 kilometers to the west, and strongholds in Syria, affording them open lines of communication with leadership and resupply. ISIS used the urban topography to its advantage, fashioning underground tunnels to funnel resources into the city, and using civilian buildings, such as schools, hospitals, warehouses, and mosques, to store arms and shield fighters.[16]

Air power was heavily used in the effort. Precision strikes by Coalition aircraft and drones weakened the Islamic State's positions, and aided the forward progress of troops. Yet, because ISIS's positions were intentionally co-located within civilian neighborhoods, the utility of airstrikes came at a heavy cost. The Iraqi government estimated that as many as 1,260 civilians were killed by airstrikes during the campaign.[17] The effect of air power was also limited, which necessitated a grinding infantry assault. The battles to retake the city occurred in dense urban spaces, making it easy for jihadists to hide and move, and use the city's population as de facto human shields. The Islamic State's dogged and elaborate defenses, which relied on vehicle-borne improvised explosive devices (VBIEDs), booby traps, subterranean tunnels, and a complex of hidden passageways interwoven throughout the city's densely packed apartment buildings, made the fight a slog. As one U.S. Army report notes: "As the coalition fought deeper into Mosul, the rate of gains decelerated from kilometers per day at the outset to single-digit meters per day by the end of the operation."[18] Iraqi and Kurdish forces took heavy casualties—the elite CTS alone suffered a 40 to 60 percent attrition during the campaign.[19]

Gradually, over weeks and months, the Islamic State's defenses began to soften, and militants retreated west across the Tigris River to the western part of the city. By January, the Coalition had liberated east Mosul, and in July, after nine months of intense fighting, Coalition forces had liberated most of the city's western part. Fighting continued through August until the remaining ISIS cells in Mosul were destroyed. Coalition forces incurred 8,200 casualties during the campaign, the vast majority of which were Iraqi troops. Three-quarters of that number were killed in the effort to capture the western part of the city.[20]

With ISIS defeated in Mosul, the fight shifted to Tal Afar and lasted only a week. Jihadists initially offered stiff resistance, but after days of intense fighting could not hold out. The fall of Tal Afar in late August signaled the end of the

Islamic State's ability to hold significant territory in Iraq. ISIS fighters retreated into the desert and embraced a "strategy of evasion," making identifying and eliminating them more challenging.[21] By early November, after an 11-month effort, Raqqa was also liberated by the U.S.-led Coalition and SDF forces. The final blow to the Islamic State's aspiration as a territorial power came in Deir az-Zour and at the hands of the loyalists. ISIS had laid siege to the city for three years, but never fully controlled it. With Russian air power, and the support of Iranian-backed militias on the ground, the pro-Assad front succeeded in retaking all parts of the city by mid-November. The Islamic State was a state no more.

Turkey's Gambit in Syria

The Islamic State's territorial demise in Syria did not sit well with Turkey. President Erdoğan bitterly objected to U.S. backing of the Kurdish YPG, and in mid-December 2018, threatened to launch military operations to expel Kurdish militias from northeast Syria, regardless of the U.S. military's presence there.[22] White House staff organized a phone call between Trump and Erdoğan to impress upon the latter the need to avoid such unilateral action. The call did not go as planned. Erdoğan reiterated Turkey's view of the YPG, and pressed the American president to explain his rationale for continuing to support Kurdish forces. Instead of making such a case, Trump was swayed by the Turkish leader's arguments, and rather than pushing back or raising concerns about ISIS's ability to regenerate were Kurdish militias removed from the area, he reversed course and pledged to withdraw U.S. forces from Syria. "You know what? It's yours. I'm leaving," Trump reportedly told his Turkish counterpart.[23]

National Security Advisor John Bolton, who was at the president's side and listening in during the call, recollects a conversation less scandalous in its details if not similar in its conclusion. According to Bolton, Trump expressed a desire to remove troops from Syria in the lead-up to the call, telling his advisor during the preparatory brief, "We should get the hell out of there," and did not need any convincing from his Turkish counterpart to that end. As Bolton recalls, the conversation played out more like a bargain:

> Trump said [to Erdoğan] he was ready to leave Syria if Turkey wanted to handle the rest of ISIS; Turkey could do the rest and we would just get out. Erdogan promised his word on that point, but said his forces need logistical support. Then came the painful part. Trump said he would ask me (I was listening to the call, as was customary) to immediately work on a plan for US withdrawal, with Turkey taking over the fight against ISIS.[24]

Trump's deal with Erdoğan sent a shock wave across Washington. This was in part due to how the information was announced, with the president posting his decision on Twitter before many of his advisors or Congress had been informed. In a follow-up video message, Trump declared total victory against the Islamic State: "We have won against ISIS. . . . We've beaten them badly, and now it's time for our troops to come back home."[25] Leading members of Congress denounced the move. A bipartisan letter signed by five senators implored the president to rethink his decision: "Any sign of weakness perceived by Iran or Russia will only result in their increased presence in the region and a decrease in the trust of our partners and allies." Lindsey Graham, one of the signatories of the letter, was among the most outspoken, tweeting: "If Obama had done this we'd be going nuts right now: how weak, how dangerous."[26] The fallout spread to the Pentagon and contributed to the resignation, days later, of Secretary of Defense Jim Mattis, who had long counseled the president away from abandoning America's partners, including the Kurds in Syria.

Tweets aside, White House advisors and defense officials succeeded in stalling any significant action for almost a year. Bolton was particularly invested in the issue, and considered the U.S. presence in Syria to be important not only for operations against ISIS, but also for competition with Iran. The archipelago of U.S. bases in eastern and southern Syria, especially the exclusion zone in Al-Tanf near Syria's border with Jordan and Iraq, complicated Iran's ability to operate and move resources into the country. As Bolton describes his thinking, which he argued to the president and key administration officials, including Secretary of State Mike Pompeo and Mattis:

> With most of the ISIS territorial caliphate gone (although the ISIS threat itself was far from eliminated), the big picture was stopping Iran. Now, however, if the U.S. abandoned the Kurds, they would either have to ally with Assad against Turkey, which the Kurds rightly considered the greater threat (thereby enhancing Assad, Iran's proxy), or fight alone, facing almost certain defeat, caught in the vise between Assad and Erdogan.[27]

Even though Trump was not swayed by Bolton's logic, such thinking, combined with the inertia of U.S. operations in Syria, stymied the effort to fully withdraw forces from the country.

Further complicating the matter were lingering problems in the Turkish-U.S. relationship. Several factors had exacerbated tensions, and the failed 2016 coup d'état against Erdoğan by factions of the Turkish military continued to loom large. Erdoğan blamed the coup on supporters of the reclusive Sufi leader Muhammed Fethullah Gülen, who had left Turkey in 1999, and lived in self-imposed exile in a sprawling compound in the Pocono Mountains, near Saylorsburg, Pennsylvania. Gülen led a large spiritual movement in Turkey, known as Hizmet, whose members had permeated the military, education, and civil services. Erdoğan mistrusted the Gülenists, and used the coup attempt as pretext to purge thousands of suspected members from the Turkish civil sector and the military. Erdoğan demanded that Gülen be extradited to face charges of supporting a terrorist movement. As Bolton recalls, in one phone call between the American and Turkish leaders that touched on the issue, Erdoğan asked "yet again that he be extradited to Turkey. Trump hypothesized that Gulen would last for only one day if he were returned to Turkey. The Turks laughed but said Gulen needn't worry, since Turkey had no death penalty."[28] Without firm evidence linking Gülen to the events of the coup attempt or any other crime, however, the United States could not legally expel him from the country.

Erdoğan's frustrations drew him closer to Russia, leading to the procurement of the sophisticated S-400 surface-to-air system, despite fierce objections from Washington. The S-400 was considered a red line by the United States because of Turkey's NATO membership and role in the production program of the F-35 multirole combat aircraft. Defense planners worried that were Turkey to possess both the F-35 and S-400, Russia could use Turkey's experience with its air defense system to learn how to better target the fifth-generation American aircraft. Washington threatened Erdoğan with sanctions and expulsion from the F-35 program to discourage the move. When Turkey did not back down, and received the S-400 shipment from Russia in July 2019, the Trump administration ended its role in the F-35 program and prohibited the Turkish military from receiving any of the aircraft in the future.[29]

As bilateral tensions climbed, Turkey hardened its position on Syria. Facing the prospect of an imminent Turkish military offensive, Trump followed through with his original commitment to remove troops from the country. The decision counteracted months of planning by the White House and the Pentagon, which had developed a plan to withdraw a few hundred troops from northeastern Syria and sought assurances from Ankara that Turkish troops would not cross the border.[30] Yet, Trump forced the issue, and in early October 2019, the administration announced the withdrawal of around 1,000 American troops from northern Syria, signaling an apparent end to the U.S. military's support of the Kurdish-led SDF. Reaction from lawmakers was swift, with Senate Majority Leader Mitch McConnell saying the move "would only benefit Russia, Iran, and the Assad regime." Lindsey Graham called the decision "a disaster in the making," and "a stain on America's honor for abandoning the Kurds." He further tweeted that Ankara's impending military invasion "destroys Turkey's relationship with U.S. congress."[31] Trump's response was initially guarded. He issued a statement calling Turkey's invasion "a bad idea," but added: "From the first day I entered the political arena, I made it clear that I did not want to fight these endless, senseless wars—especially those that don't benefit the United States."[32] In an effort to quell his detractors, Trump took to Twitter, warning: "if Turkey does anything that I, in my great and unmatched wisdom, consider to be off limits, I will totally destroy and obliterate the Economy of Turkey (I've done before!) [*sic*]."[33]

Turkey's offensive began days later. The Turkish air force pounded SDF positions along the border as mechanized infantry advanced on the ground. The Turkish-allied Syrian National Army (SNA), an umbrella organization comprising mostly former Free Syrian Army militias and Islamist groups of northern Syria, such as Ahrar al-Sharqiya, made up a bulk of the ground element. Hundreds of Kurdish fighters and civilians were killed in the incursion, and nearly 300,000 mostly ethnic Kurdish residents were expelled from the area.[34] The result was a Turkish military occupation of a long stretch of northern Syria, which extended 30 kilometers deep into Syrian territory. Turkey and Russia brokered an agreement to divide areas of control in parts of the north, thereby demarcating boundaries of the Turkish-controlled zone. The Turkish military and its proxies became the administrators of the occupied border region, which also included disconnected parts in Idlib and Afrin established through previous operations. All of those areas became politically and economically interconnected with Turkey, and dependent on its largesse and support.[35]

Western governments condemned Turkey's campaign against the YPG. Reports of war crimes by the Turkish military and their rebel proxies, such as the use of white phosphorus munitions, and the execution of civilians and captives, added cause to the opprobrium.[36] The European Union threatened a number of sanctions against Turkey, including a total arms embargo, but settled on limiting arms sales to Turkey instead.[37] European leaders were further angered by Erdoğan's threat to "open the gates" and send over 3.5 million Syrian refugees to Europe if they did not support Turkey's position.[38] Fear of Erdoğan's threat, which hung like the Sword of Damocles over the heads of European officials, who had been struggling with waves of refugees fleeing war and insecurity in the Middle East and Africa, likely mitigated their response. Washington's reaction was more severe. Even though Trump helped prepare the ground for Turkey's invasion, his administration admonished Erdoğan by imposing tariffs on steel imports, ending negotiations on a trade deal, and issuing financial sanctions on the Turkish defense and energy ministries as well as their leaders.[39] Senator Graham sponsored the "Countering Turkish Aggression Act," which imposed wide-ranging economic and military sanctions on Turkey and Turkish officials. The bill was adopted with strong bipartisan support in both houses of Congress.[40] Erdoğan was winning in Syria, but losing Washington.

Peninsular Woes

The passions of the Arab Spring supercharged tensions between competing regional powers. Nowhere was this more apparent than in Iran's feuds with its Gulf Arab neighbors. Tensions between Riyadh and Tehran spiked in early January 2016 after the former carried out its death sentence on Shaykh Nimr Baqir al-Nimr, the dissident senior Shia cleric who had been arrested following protests against the monarchy in 2012. The execution was roundly criticized by Iran and its clients, with the supreme leader, Ali Khamenei, proclaiming that "divine revenge" awaited the Saudi throne.[1] Hardliners in Iran's regime quickly organized a fervent demonstration of thousands outside the Saudi consulate in Mashhad. Whether a calculated act by officials, or in an impromptu act of rage, a group of protestors broke through the gates and ransacked the building, ultimately setting it on fire. Iran's government formally condemned the assault, and blamed it on rogue elements, but that contrition could not stem the fallout. Such a breach of norms provoked a cascade of rebukes by Arab states. With the exception of Oman, all members of the Gulf Cooperation Council (GCC), as well as Morocco, Jordan, and Sudan, downgraded relations with Iran or, as with Saudi Arabia and Bahrain, severed them entirely.[2]

Mohammad Javad Zarif, Iran's foreign minister, issued a response to the Saudi-led effort to isolate his country through an op-ed published in the *New York Times*. In his letter, Zarif strives to shift the spotlight away from Iran by focusing on Saudi Arabia's harsh human rights record and "active sponsorship of violent extremists." "The barbarism is clear," he writes. "At home, state executioners sever heads with swords. . . . Abroad, masked men sever heads with knives."[3] Those bold accusations, which likened the Saudi state to ISIS, prompted a retort from Adel al-Jubeir, now the Saudi foreign minister, and whom the IRGC had plotted to assassinate years earlier. As al-Jubeir writes:

> While Iran claims its top foreign policy priority is friendship, its behavior shows the opposite is true. Iran is the single-most-belligerent-actor

in the region, and its actions display both a commitment to regional hegemony and a deeply held view that conciliatory gestures signal weakness either on Iran's part or on the part of its adversaries.

The Saudi envoy enumerates Iran's known connections to terrorism throughout the article, and in making reference to the plot against his life, further argues:

> We are not the nation under international sanctions for supporting terrorism; Iran is. We are not the nation whose officials are on terrorism lists; Iran is. We don't have an agent sentenced to jail for 25 years by a New York federal court for plotting to assassinate an ambassador in Washington in 2011; Iran does.[4]

As their diplomats squabbled in the open, and aimed to draw attention to their cause in Washington, it was clear that neither side was keen to back down, and that the competition spurred by the Arab Spring was provoking rash decisions by the region's most powerful actors.

The Qatar Blockade

With relations severed, the Saudi-Iranian rivalry entered a new, more dangerous phase. Yet, even as Riyadh sought to isolate Iran, long-standing grievances and differing policies toward the Arab Spring drove a similar effort against Qatar. On June 5, 2017, as the war against the Islamic State was reaching its zenith, Saudi Arabia, the UAE, Bahrain, and Egypt announced they were severing diplomatic relations with Qatar, and would impose upon it an air, land, and trade blockade. The drastic action had been the culmination of years of frustration and deteriorating relations between Qatar and its Arab neighbors. Saudi Arabia and the UAE led the effort, each with their own grievances with Doha and how it ran its affairs.[5] President Trump's mercurial leadership, which encouraged breaking norms, along with his hawkish rhetoric on Iran and radical Islam, might have given leaders in Riyadh and Abu Dhabi the impression that Washington would back any action were it framed the right way. Trump suggested as much after the blockade was announced, tweeting: "During my recent trip to the Middle East I stated that there can no longer be funding of Radical Ideology. Leaders pointed to Qatar—look!"[6] Behind the scenes, however, Secretary of State Rex Tillerson and Secretary of Defense Jim Mattis sought to calm the situation, and reportedly nixed a Saudi plan to militarily invade Qatar.[7]

Using Kuwait as an intermediary, the Saudi-led bloc submitted 13 demands before relations could be restored and the blockade lifted. Severing relations with Iran and ceasing any cooperation with the IRGC was top of the list, followed by a call to cut all ties with terrorist groups, including the Muslim Brotherhood, ISIS, Al-Qaeda, and Hezbollah. Shuttering *Aljazeera* and all other Qatari-funded news sites, such as *Middle East Eye*, was also prioritized.[8] *Aljazeera* regularly ran unflattering coverage on neighboring states, and its Arabic service provided a platform for Islamist commentary, which rankled the Saudi and Emirati leadership. Qatar's relationship with Muslim Brotherhood leaders and regional affiliates was particularly vexing. Both the UAE and Saudi Arabia considered the banned group the most potent threat to their monarchical systems. In sum, the blockade's leaders argued that by maintaining ties to a plethora of nefarious actors, Qatar had become a leading source of regional instability. As the UAE's ambassador to the United States, Yousef Al-Otaiba, described the purpose of the campaign: "It's not to isolate or marginalize Qatar—it's to protect ourselves from Qatar." He continued:

> Outside of Iran, Qatar hosts the second-largest number of designated terrorists in the world, including 59 people that we've just designated, of which 12 are on the U.S. list and 14 are on the UN list. They're not in jail, they're not under house arrest, they're moving around freely and openly and raising money for al-Nusra and al-Qaeda, Libyan militias, and many many others.[9]

One episode highlighted by the blockading states, meant to showcase Qatar's support to terrorists and connections to Iran, concerned the freeing of Qatari royals from captivity in Iraq. The royals and their attendants were kidnapped in December 2015 when their hunting camp was ambushed by heavily armed militants in Iraq's remote southwestern desert. Details were opaque: why the Qatari royals were on a falconry trip in southern Iraq while much of the country was in the midst of war with ISIS; the scale and precision of the militia's ambush; and Iran's potential connection to all of it. How Qatar eventually secured the release of the royal party after lengthy negotiations and the price it had to pay were equally obscured by rumor and innuendo.

What soon became clear to Doha was that the ambush had been premeditated. Qatar's support to jihadist rebels in Syria had put it in the crosshairs of Iran and its proxies. The royals had been kidnapped by Kataib Hezbollah, and were to be used as leverage. Iran's demands were gradually communicated to Qatar through Lebanese Hezbollah. Tehran wanted to force through a proposal it had previously offered to rebel factions a couple of months earlier, which called for a population transfer of the residents of two Shiite towns in northern Syria (Fua and Kefraya) for the residents of two Sunni towns near the Lebanese border (Madaya and Zabadani). All four towns were besieged by enemy forces, and the trade would have ended the sieges peacefully. The rebels rejected the offer out of hand in part because it would have been an act of sectarian cleansing engineered and orchestrated by foreign powers.[10]

The royals gave Iran a card to play with the benefactor of those jihadist rebel factions: Qatar. Through months of negotiations and possibly payments of up to $50 million to the rebels, Qatar brokered a compromise between Iran, Hezbollah, and Hayat al-Tahrir al-Sham (HTS), the Al-Qaeda-linked umbrella organization whose forces had been besieging Fua and Kefraya. In mid-April 2017, instead of a population swap, thousands of residents from the four towns were escorted onto buses and moved to safe zones in Idlib and Aleppo, respectively controlled by HTS and pro-Assad forces.[11] The evacuations coincided with another ransom payment: $360 million in cash delivered to Iraq by an official Qatari delegation. The Iraqi government was unaware of the deal and customs officials impounded the cash, which was packed into 23 identical duffel bags, upon inspection at Baghdad International Airport. The Qatari delegation spent several days working through intermediaries to get the money released by the government, but to no avail. Baghdad held on to the cash, persuading Qatar to reportedly dispatch another payment of a similar amount directly to Hezbollah in Beirut, where government oversight was easily avoided. The money reached its intended destination, and after a 16-month imprisonment, the royals and their non-royal attendants were released. The final exchange is believed to have been authorized by none other than Qassem Soleimani.[12]

Those events testified to the tangled web of politics and rivalry the Syrian and Iraqi wars had engendered. Regional states and non-state proxies had become intertwined and, to some extent, could no longer be easily differentiated. The business of Hezbollah and Iraqi militias was Iran's business. And the behavior of Syrian rebel groups could be swayed by pressure and payments from Qatar. The conflicts were multifaceted and multilayered, and transcended national borders. By being a player in the Syrian conflict, Qatar had also set itself up to be a target.

The blockade was intended to coerce Qatar's emir, Tamim bin Hamad Al Thani, to yield to the will of his neighbors, and reverse course on a number of fronts. Qatar's growing alignment with Turkey was among their pressing concerns. The two states held similar interests regarding the Muslim Brotherhood and other Islamist groups, and were aligned in Egypt, Libya, and Syria. Both had backed Mohamed Morsi's short-lived presidency, and had lost out when Saudi Arabia and the UAE financed the Egyptian military's counter-revolution. That experience underpinned the signing of a defense cooperation agreement between Doha and Ankara in 2014. A year later, Qatar announced it would host a Turkish military detachment of 3,000 troops, "as well as air and naval units, military trainers and special operations forces."[13] Closing the Turkish military base was one of the blockading states' 13 demands. Saudi Arabia's ambassador to Turkey, Walid al-Khuraiji, criticized the base, stating: "We hoped that Ankara would stay impartial for the sake of keeping good relations with all the Gulf countries. . . . When Ankara sided with Doha, it lost its neutrality as an unbiased party."[14]

Over the first year of the blockade, the rhetoric against Qatar grew menacing. For a period, Saudi officials floated ideas such as digging a canal along the Saudi-Qatar border to turn Qatar into an island. Saud al-Qahtani, a senior advisor to Mohammed bin Salman (MBS), euphemistically called the plan "the East Salwa island project," and hinted it could include new ports, private beach resorts, or perhaps even a nuclear waste site.[15] The problem with threats is that they only work if the recipient gives in, and Qatar did not. The country's policies, and *Aljazeera*'s critical coverage, remained unchanged. Instead of reducing its ties to Turkey and Iran, Qatar strengthened them, with both countries becoming key to reducing the blockade's impact. Imports from Turkey and Iran quickly increased. Food and produce that had once entered the country over land from Saudi Arabia were now brought by sea from Turkey and Iran. Qatar also expanded its security ties with Turkey. The Turkish parliament approved the rapid deployment of additional troops to Qatar just a few weeks after the Saudi-led blockade began. Those troops arrived six months later, and joined the growing Turkish detachment at Tariq bin Ziyad military base south of Doha.[16]

Qatar proved that it could not be easily isolated by its neighbors. It was too rich, too well-integrated globally, and had extensive security ties with the United States. Qatar hosted the largest U.S. military base in the region at Al Udeid, home to U.S. Central Command's forward headquarters and 10,000 troops. The Turkish military base hardly registered at that scale, but hosting it signaled a similar intent and strategy. Qatar needed the protection, and Turkey sought the prestige and influence that its military footprint might bring. It also needed the money. Qatari investment had helped offset the negative impact of the Syrian war on Turkey's economy.[17] The failed 2016 coup d'état hardened President Erdoğan's resolve to grow Turkey into a regional power, and amplified his mistrust of domestic opponents and regional competitors. Engaging in contentious politics with neighbors and the West, as well as showing strength in the international arena, represented a means of burnishing popularity with Erdoğan's nationalist and religiously conservative electorate.[18] Increasing defense ties with Qatar was an opportunity to expand Turkey's footprint, gain leverage with Gulf states, and increase the perception of its strategic power. With the Saudi-led blockade attempting to marginalize Qatar's political reach, Erdoğan recognized an opportunity to both expand Turkish influence and strengthen its partnership with the region's leading benefactor.[19] Turkey had the muscle and Qatar had the wealth. They stood a better chance at competing in their neighborhood together than they would apart.

A Murder in Istanbul

The killing of Jamal Khashoggi was another drag on Turkey-Saudi relations. Khashoggi was a veteran journalist and erstwhile Islamist fellow-traveler best known for his personal relationship with Osama Bin Laden, whom he had interviewed several times across the 1980s and 1990s. The Saudi national became a familiar commentator after 9/11, seen as someone who could both explain the peculiar jihadi movement from an insider perspective as well as identify its failures. His personal and political evolution led him to become an outspoken advocate for progressive reform in Saudi Arabia, particularly the need for greater freedom of speech. Pressure from the Saudi royal family to cease such commentary inspired Khashoggi to leave his homeland in 2017 and live in exile in Washington, D.C., where he became an occasional global affairs columnist for the *Washington Post*. In his columns, Khashoggi wrote about issues concerning Saudi Arabia, from free speech to the merits of engaging the Muslim Brotherhood. In one of his final pieces, Khashoggi condemned the war in Yemen, citing its humanitarian toll, and called on MBS to end Saudi Arabia's involvement in the conflict, arguing:

> The longer this cruel war lasts in Yemen, the more permanent the damage will be. The people of Yemen will be busy fighting poverty, cholera and water scarcity and rebuilding their country. The crown prince must bring an end to the violence and restore the dignity of the birthplace of Islam.[20]

Fears that MBS sought to forcibly return him to the country to face retribution did not prevent Khashoggi from visiting the Saudi consulate in Istanbul in order to secure documents needed to marry his Turkish fiancé, Hatice Cengiz. The dissident journalist entered the consulate in the afternoon of October 2, 2018, and was never seen again.[21] Rumors of Khashoggi's disappearance quickly spread on social media. Despite persistent denials from the Saudi authorities that anything untoward had occurred, grisly details of Khashoggi's fate gradually began to be leaked to the press. Within weeks, it became clear that Khashoggi had been murdered by a Saudi hit squad shortly after he had entered the consulate. He was forcibly restrained and injected with drugs before being suffocated with a plastic bag. The 15-person assassination team included two of MBS's "closest aides and five probable members of his security detail."[22] The team also included a forensic pathologist who promptly dismembered Khashoggi's body with a bone saw.[23] Another Saudi team member served as a body double, donning Khashoggi's clothes, a fake beard, and glasses, before leaving the consulate through the back exit in an attempt to establish a false narrative.[24] Khashoggi's body was either dissolved in acid on the grounds or packed into suitcases and returned to Saudi Arabia later that night by his assassins.

Khashoggi's murder infuriated President Erdoğan, who considered it an epic betrayal by Saudi Arabia and its upstart crown prince. As Erdoğan stated in a speech in late October: "This murder might have been committed at a consulate building which may be considered Saudi Arabian land, but it rests within the borders of Turkey." With Saudi officials pursuing a line of deflection and dissimulation, the Turkish government forced the issue, feeding information to the Turkish press that implicated the Saudi state—and by extension, MBS—in the killing.[25] Turkish media released details of the assassination drip by drip, creating a steady stream of controversy and melodrama. Much of Turkey's information came from audio recordings from inside the compound, some of which were shared with Washington. Turkish officials later made some of the recordings public, and provided a play-by-play of how the murder went down, including Khashoggi's last words, "I can't breathe," which he uttered as he was being suffocated to death. The recording suggested that Turkish intelligence had had the consulate bugged, and probably knew more about what had happened to Khashoggi—and many other matters—than had been revealed.

With evidence about the operation mounting, Riyadh finally admitted that Khashoggi had been killed in a "rogue operation" by a security team, but denied that it had been ordered by the throne.[26] The partial admission did little to stem the backlash. By November, reports claimed a leaked CIA investigation had concluded that MBS had most likely authorized the operation. President Trump attempted to brush away the story, writing in a statement: "It could very well be that the crown prince had knowledge of this tragic event—maybe he did and maybe he didn't! . . . In any case, our relationship is with the Kingdom of Saudi Arabia." The president's awkward deflection triggered a vociferous counter from members of Congress, including from close ally Lindsey Graham, who stated: "The behavior of the crown prince—in multiple ways—has shown disrespect for the relationship and made him, in my view, beyond toxic."[27] In an example of how deep the grievance against the Saudi government lay in the American capital, the district's council voted in 2021 to rename the street in front of the Saudi embassy "Jamal Khashoggi Way."[28]

Popular and congressional ire fixated on MBS and the foreign policies most associated with him, particularly the issue of weapons sales and the war in Yemen. In March, the Senate voted to end U.S. support for the Saudi-led coalition. Democratic senator Chris Murphy typified the message Congress was

sending to President Trump: "We should not be associated with a bombing campaign that the U.N. tells us is likely a gross violation of human rights."[29] Trump
vetoed the bill once it reached his desk in April, stating that the resolution was
"an unnecessary, dangerous attempt to weaken my constitutional authorities."[30]
Undeterred, Congress next targeted weapons sales, and in June, voted to block
arms sales to Saudi Arabia and the UAE. The resolutions were co-sponsored by
Democratic senator Bob Menendez and Republican senator Lindsey Graham.
Graham said the bills were intended to communicate to Saudi Arabia that "if
you act the way you're acting there is no space for a strategic relations [sic]." He
added, "There is no amount of oil you can produce that will get me and others
to give you a pass on chopping somebody up in a consulate."[31] Trump vetoed the
bills in July. It was only his third veto in office, but his second sheltering MBS
from the wrath of Washington lawmakers in as many months.

Damage Control: The UAE Pivots in Yemen

Khashoggi's murder put a spotlight on Saudi Arabia's egregious effort to silence dissenters, especially journalists and activists, who opposed the kingdom's
policies. It also invigorated opposition to the war in Yemen in Washington and
Western capitals. To whatever extent this might have worried MBS was unclear,
but there was little adjustment to Saudi policy in response to U.S. congressional
pressure and the broader international fallout from Khashoggi's assassination.
The UAE, however, was beginning to rethink its strategy in the war.

The UAE stood as a loyal ally of Saudi Arabia, and backed the kingdom in the
wake of the Khashoggi debacle. Yet, in Yemen, the UAE's actions deviated from
the Saudi line. As Saudi Arabia focused on backing the government of President
Hadi against the Houthis and their Iranian patrons, the UAE sought to solidify
its control over the country's south, exercising its influence through militias
aligned with the southern secessionist movement and non-jihadist Salafis.
That effort brought the UAE into conflict with the Houthis and jihadi terrorist
groups, which overlapped the Saudi effort, but it also deliberately undermined
the Yemeni government's already anemic authority. The Emiratis had no confidence in President Hadi, and did not see him capable of holding the country together. Hadi's reliance on Islah Party militias was also a point of contention, with
the UAE inflexibly against allowing the Muslim Brotherhood affiliate to return
to a position of prominence in a future Yemeni state.[32]

With little desire to support Hadi, the UAE pursued a strategy it thought had
a chance of succeeding: empowering the south to stand on its own in order to
secure the coastline. Yemen was also a springboard for the UAE's ambitions. The
UAE sought to become the premier power in the wider Horn of Africa, Gulf

of Aden, and Arabian Sea region. This meant, above all, controlling the Yemeni coast, particularly Aden and the Bab al-Mandab, and the surest way to do that was to back the locals. In April 2018, the UAE also established control over Socotra, a Yemeni island and UNESCO heritage site best known for its unique flora located at the mouth of the Gulf of Aden.[33] Following backlash from the Hadi government, and amid reports amplified by Qatari media that the UAE had occupied Socotra in a way that smacked of colonial conquest, the island was officially handed to Saudi forces a month later.[34] The UAE, however, retained its military position on the island, as well as de facto control.[35]

Expanding its military power and maritime presence across the region was part of the UAE's broader strategy. The UAE established naval bases and military installations in Eritrea, and in Somaliland and Puntland (both unrecognized breakaway states of Somalia); and, through its state subsidiary DP World, operated ports in Jeddah, Djibouti, Pakistan, and India. Beyond gaining a military foothold in unstable regional states, and creating a transregional maritime network, the approach was designed to safeguard the UAE's economy, which revolved around the country's ability to serve as a logistics hub for the region, and ensure the country's position as a top player in global commerce.[36] Securing shipping lanes and littoral spaces was central to that effort, and Yemen's geographic position made it of key interest.

Pursuing that strategy saw the UAE test the depth of its aspirations in Yemen and revealed its realist inclinations. By summer 2018, the Saudi-led coalition's attention had turned to depriving the Houthis of resources. With the coalition having fortified most of the Yemeni coastline, the western port city of Hodeidah was the Houthis' only major maritime outlet and its main source of resupply. Hodeidah was also critically important to the rest of the country, with 90 percent of Yemen's food and supplies transiting through its port. The Houthis' control over the port made it a strategic target in the war, and in June, Saudi- and Emirati-backed forces began an offensive to seize Hodeidah and sever Houthi access to the sea. The advance began despite calls from the international community against it. The United Nations and aid agencies cautioned that warring against the city of 600,000 people was likely to intensify Yemen's severe humanitarian crisis. Contesting the city would cut off aid shipments from reaching Yemen's most vulnerable communities, and further displace tens of thousands of more civilians.[37]

The outside pressure did not dissuade the Saudis and Emiratis from advancing toward Hodeidah. Initial gains were gradual, with much of the fighting focused on Hodeidah's airport, southwest of the city. A UN-brokered peace effort allowed for a brief pause in major hostilities, but by late August, the offensive was back in full swing. Emirati-led forces reached the southern outskirts of the city, and by mid-September, established an arc of control along its western perimeter. That

effectively cut the Houthis' main access route to the city. The coalition's strategy
was to encircle Hodeidah to compel Houthi forces inside the city to negotiate
a retreat. Weeks of heavy fighting and continual bombardment from coalition
aircraft failed to achieve that goal. The effort to take Hodeidah slowed and the
Houthis showed no sign of wavering.[38] With civilian casualties mounting and
international condemnation increasing, the UAE's resolve began to falter. By
December, the Emiratis encouraged the Saudis to commit to the UN-brokered
peace process, which led to a ceasefire agreement in January 2019.[39] The agreement included a number of provisions designed as compromises between the
two sides, but essentially ceded Hodeidah to the Houthis.

That failure became a turning point for the UAE. Faced with mounting dis-
approval of the war in Washington and Europe, the UAE shifted its attention
toward solidifying the position of its allies in the south and reducing its military footprint. The UAE had made significant advances in the conflict. It had
pushed the Houthis out of the south, retained firm control over Aden, and developed strong client forces who provided the UAE with the coastal zone of influence it had sought. By July 2019, the UAE began withdrawing most of its 3,500
troops from the country.[40] A residual force of a few hundred remained, serving
in mostly command and advisory capacities. The pivot allowed the UAE to take
a step back from the conflict, yield most of the negative attention from the war
to Saudi Arabia, and manage its interests from the outside. With its withdrawal,
the UAE was moving to a new stage in the conflict, one that turned focus away
from fighting the Houthis directly, and concentrated on routinizing its stake in
the south.[41] The UAE's clients, comprising around 90,000 fighters, remained
dependent on it for arms, training, and financial resources; and as long as that
support continued, the UAE's foothold in Yemen was likely to endure.[42] The
UAE's departure also helped it to concentrate its attention elsewhere, particularly Libya, where factional fighting was once again heating up.

The Quest for Tripoli

Some of the same feuds animating the Qatar blockade interspersed other regional and international affairs. Nowhere was this clash fiercer than in Libya, which continued to pulsate with armed violence and was descending deeper into another civil war. As with the Middle East's other conflagrations, Libya's situation attracted the involvement of outside powers, all of whom partnered with local clients in an attempt to steer the outcomes of the fighting to suit their divergent agendas. In pursuit of their own interests, Turkey, Qatar, the UAE, Egypt, and Russia, as well as Western powers France, Italy, the United Kingdom, and the United States, all opted to back the opposing sides, with some supporting the UN-recognized government in Tripoli and others their Tobruk-based rivals. The involvement of Turkey and Gulf Arab states not only extended their competition to North Africa, it also further entangled Libya's internal problems with those of the contending foreign interveners.

For Libya, the demise of Muammar Qaddafi solved one challenge and introduced sundry more. The country's 2011 civil war had succeeded in part by bringing a measure of democratic change to the country. In July 2012, hopeful Libyans cast their vote for a new parliamentary government called the General National Congress (GNC). The GNC was tasked with drafting a national constitution, which would later be ratified through a popular referendum. The international community backed the GNC, hoping it would bring peace and opportunity to the Libyan people. Unfortunately, the GNC's authority was challenged by the numerous armed groups who had fought against Qaddafi's regime and had been empowered by its collapse. Tribal militias, gangs, and Islamist groups continued to compete for territory and resources, and used violence and coercion to push their will on the GNC. The country was fragmented by politics, ideology, and geography. Armed groups in places such as Misrata, Benghazi, Derna, and Tripoli controlled important resources and territory, and acted with autonomy and impunity. The government held little sway outside of the capital, and did not even control the country's oil industry. Jihadists were also active across the country, expanding their networks through a number of eastern cities. The seriousness of the jihadist threat was put in sharp relief on September 11, 2012, when militants attacked an American diplomatic compound in Benghazi, killing the U.S. ambassador to Libya, Christopher Stevens, and two CIA contractors. The attack was blamed on Ansar al-Sharia, a group linked to Al-Qaeda, and underpinned the growing terrorism threat in Libya.

Political unrest across parts of the country undermined Libya's political development, and set the stage for a second civil war. An inflection point came in June 2014 as Libyans went to the polls to elect a new parliamentary body called the House of Representatives (HoR), which was to replace the GNC. Violence marred the election, which resulted in low voter turnout and contributed to a strong showing for secular liberals and federalists. That result was deemed unacceptable to the Islamist-dominated GNC, which refused to recognize the election's outcome. With the newly elected HoR and GNC factions unwilling to strike compromise, violence was soon to follow. In August, pro-GNC Islamist militias from Misrata occupied the capital, prompting members of the HoR to flee to the eastern city of Tobruk.[1] In November, Libya's supreme court sided with the GNC and invalidated the election result, ruling it unconstitutional. The HoR rejected the court's decision, and instead claimed to be Libya's legitimate federal government. Rivalry between the HoR and GNC split Libya's nascent political system into two contending bodies, one based in the western part of the country and the other in the east.[2] Each faction considered itself to be the rightful government, but drew their support from different constituencies. The GNC held together a coalition of tribal and Islamist allies, and retained control of the capital and a swath of western Libya, including Misrata, whose militias made up a vital part of its fighting force. The HoR controlled Tobruk and parts of the east. Its chief ally was the former head of the Libyan Army, Khalifa Haftar, who left the GNC and re-constituted a parallel military coalition called the Libyan National Army (LNA), composed of breakaway army units and local tribal militias based in Benghazi.

At stake was more than legitimacy. Key to each side's strategy was aiming to seize control over Libya's scattered oil fields to secure hydrocarbon revenues. A fight over Libya's oil industry had plagued the country since the ancien régime's ouster. As Frederic Wehrey explains, this "was a legacy of Qaddafi's misrule." Qaddafi's state had been "founded on the distribution of oil rents. There were no political structures, institutions, or civil society." After Qaddafi's demise, "the prize of the oil revenues came up for grabs" and became "a major theme" in the political infighting that followed.[3]

The quest for power and petro-dollars fueled a return to conflict, and the United Nations once again pushed for compromise. In 2015, the United Nations spearheaded the Libyan Political Agreement as an effort to unify the country's armed factions. By December, the process resulted in the establishment of the Government of National Accord (GNA), which the UN Security Council recognized as Libya's new official government.[4] Within it were two novel institutions: the Presidential Committee, which included the prime minister and eight other executives, and the High State Council, designed as an advisory body with the power to endorse or check certain decisions and appointments made by the HoR. The GNC was formally dissolved under the new framework, with much of the body moving into positions in the High State Council. Tensions remained, however, between the former GNC coalition and the HoR. The two sides resumed their fight in early 2016, and within months, the HoR, which had initially pledged its support to the GNA, broke away from the UN-backed government and renewed its claim to be the rightful head of the Libyan state.

Adding to the turmoil was the growing influence of jihadists in the country's east. The Shura Council of Benghazi Revolutionaries, an umbrella group that included Ansar al-Sharia, was the most powerful of the jihadist organizations. Sidelined by the political process, the Shura Council asserted its own claims to authority and aggressively expanded its control over parts of eastern Libya. By summer 2014, the council had seized most of Benghazi and expelled pro-Haftar military forces from the city. With the victory, the Shura Council announced the formation of their own quasi-government and declared Benghazi—the country's second largest city—to be an Islamic emirate.[5] ISIS also sought a stake in Libya's fortunes, and funneled hundreds of foreign fighters into the country to capitalize on the chaos. Just as it had done in Syria and Iraq, ISIS quickly focused on fighting fellow Islamists, especially Al-Qaeda-aligned rivals.[6] By summer 2015, ISIS had seized control over much of the city of Sirte, and dominated pockets of Derna and Benghazi.[7]

Libya's Belligerents: Foreign and Domestic

As Libya's evolving conflict attracted outside involvement, the composition of the belligerents, and their respective political and ideological associations, shaped international and regional responses. Another factor influencing outside involvement was the arms embargo placed on Libya in 2011 by the UN Security Council, which banned the flow of arms to and from Libya, with only certain exceptions made for non-lethal aid. The embargo made nearly all foreign military assistance to Libya's warring parties, to include its internationally recognized government, officially prohibited.[8] Yet, without an adequate enforcement mechanism, the ban proved ineffective.

Libya's UN-recognized government retained the support of most former GNC factions and the western militias. Although its largest political bloc included moderates and liberals, the Muslim Brotherhood, through the Justice and Construction Party, was an integral component of the new government. Turkey and Qatar quickly emerged as the GNA's most assertive backers, and became leading conduits of military and economic support to the Tripoli-based government. Following the UN's mandate, the United States, the United Kingdom, and Italy also backed the GNA. With a continued focus on counterterrorism operations, U.S. involvement in Libya transcended the political dispute. Those operations were concentrated in eastern Libya, and as such benefited both sides, even indirectly paving the way for Haftar's Libyan National Army to make gains against jihadist groups in Sirte and other parts of the east.[9]

Haftar was an x-factor in the conflict. He possessed an unusual background: a former Libyan military officer who had helped bring Qaddafi to power in the 1969 revolution, only to turn against the autocrat later in his career. Haftar emigrated to the United States in 1990, and spent the next two decades living in northern Virginia, gaining U.S. citizenship, and serving as an occasional CIA asset. Once he returned to Libya in 2011, Haftar quickly became a formidable leader among the hodgepodge of revolutionaries, and eventually took command of the Libyan military. It was in that capacity that he sided with the HoR and began to oppose the GNC in 2014, in part due to the latter's Islamist orientation. His strident anti-Islamist rhetoric and vocal hostility to the Muslim Brotherhood endeared him to outside backers such as the UAE and Egypt. Even so, Haftar also partnered with some Islamist militias, such as the Madkhali Salafis, who followed the religious guidance of Sheikh Rabi' al-Madkhal, the former head of Sunna studies at the Islamic University of Medina, the center of Saudi-aligned Salafi scholarship. The Madkhalis differed from pro-GNA Islamists in two important ways: they rejected participation in democracy, and they were implacably antagonistic to the Muslim Brotherhood.[10] The latter position likely made them more palatable to Haftar's primary foreign backers. And although Haftar was allied with the HoR, the self-styled field marshal of the Libyan National Army displayed the persona of an aspiring strongman. Those qualities might have endeared him to his supporters, but they were viewed as equally problematic by his detractors, including those in Washington.[11]

With Haftar's backing, the LNA secured strong outside patronage. The UAE, Egypt, Russia, and to a lesser (and murkier) extent France, were the primary providers of arms and military assistance to Haftar's forces. For the UAE and Egypt, the GNA's alignment with the Muslim Brotherhood made it an untenable option. Under President Abdel Fattah al-Sisi, Egypt's government had outlawed the Muslim Brotherhood and deemed it the leading threat to domestic and regional order. With its western border approximately 150 kilometers from the Tobruk-based HoR, Egypt became a vital node in the supply chain for Haftar's forces. The UAE viewed the Muslim Brotherhood similarly, but its support to

Haftar was also motivated by a desire to deny Turkey and Qatar from securing a foothold in Libya. Haftar received further aid from neighboring Chad, which contributed a few thousand troops to the LNA; and from the American war profiteer Erik Prince, whom the United Nations' Expert Panel on Libya identified as having overseen a botched effort to funnel helicopters, aircraft, weapons, and mercenaries into the country—a scheme likely funded by the UAE.[12]

French and Russian motivations were less straightforward. France officially recognized the GNA, but also provided training and weaponry to Haftar's forces in support of the LNA's counterterrorism efforts in areas such as Benghazi.[13] The prospect of enduring instability in an important Mediterranean state, and of growing jihadist activity in the country, drove France's double-game in support of the would-be strongman, whom Paris saw as a better option than the GNA.[14] Russia had a similarly qualified position; as part of the UN Security Council, it recognized the GNA, while supporting the LNA through the Wagner Group.[15] Russia's penchant for exploiting insecure environments with the aim of expanding its influence when and where it could, especially without expending much coin or political capital, both motivated and mitigated the extent of its involvement. By funneling support through Wagner, the mercenary army owned by close Putin confidant Yevgeny Prigozhin, Russia also distanced itself from any official role in the conflict.[16]

The Second Civil War

The LNA's advance toward Tripoli in the spring of 2019 intensified the war. Haftar's strategy was in part designed to discourage support for the GNA among its less committed supporters, with the hope that once the LNA's victory was all but certain, associated militias would begin to peel away from the government and join his side. The gamble produced the opposite effect, and forced western militias into closer cooperation.[17] Another problem for Haftar was that the offensive could be perceived as an act of war against Libya's internationally recognized government. The longer the fighting lasted, the weaker his position was likely to grow with the government's foreign backers. Yet, the field marshal and his patrons believed that were the capital to be taken, and the GNA deposed, the international community, and especially Washington, would have little choice but to accept the outcome as a fait accompli and acquiesce to a Haftar-led government, whatever shape that might take.

As Antonio Gutierrez, the UN Secretary General, was visiting Tripoli on April 4, 2019, Haftar's offensive to take the city began. The UAE and Russia heavily supported the effort, pumping cargo planes full of materiel and mercenaries to aid the LNA. Between April 2019 and January 2020, Russia alone conducted over 350 military supply flights to Libya. On January 19, as the UAE's Mohamed bin Zayed and other world leaders attended a UN-sponsored Libyan peace conference in Berlin, four Emirati cargo planes full of weapons landed in Libya. The conference ended with all attendees, including Turkey, Russia, Egypt, and France, signing a pledge to respect the 2011 arms embargo, and "commit to refraining from interference in the armed conflict or in the internal affairs of Libya and urge all international actors to do the same."[18] The pronouncement proved disingenuous. The UAE continued to bankroll Haftar's fight, which, according to an internal Pentagon report, even encompassed funding the Wagner Group's involvement.[19] The UAE also experimented with cultivating its own cadre of foreign mercenaries to augment LNA forces. An Emirati security firm, Black Shield, was the conduit for at least a portion of that foreign fighting contingent, including the disconcerting case of hundreds of Sudanese who were reportedly hired under false pretenses and sent to military training camps before arriving in Libya as unwitting combatants.[20]

Foreign support gave the LNA a military advantage, especially in the skies. The UAE had supplied Haftar's forces with Chinese Wing Loong II combat drones and the personnel to operate them. The UAE and Egypt were also suspected of flying air sorties over the capital in Mirage 2000-9 combat aircraft in support of the LNA's advance. Additionally, the LNA possessed aging Soviet-era MiG-21 and MiG-23 fighter jets, which were operated by Libyan pilots.[21] According to the UN Support Mission in Libya (UNSMIL), the UAE and pro-Haftar forces "conducted some 850 precision airstrikes by drones and another 170 by fighter-bomber, among them some 60 precision airstrikes by foreign fighter aircraft." By comparison, during the same period, pro-Tripoli forces "conducted some 250 air strikes."[22] The technological divide helped the LNA make steady gains through 2019—advancing across the western and southern parts of the country, seizing territory, oil fields, and strategic airbases, until it closed in on the southern suburbs of Tripoli by early spring.[23]

Turkey's Military Intervention

Support flowed to the GNA as well, but was initially hindered by the diverging interests of Western states. The United States, the United Kingdom, and Italy were the GNA's leading supporters, but lacking the political appetite for intervention, none increased military support to stop Haftar's advance. Washington's response was also muddled by President Trump's continued praise of Haftar as a champion in the fight against terrorism, even as the latter's war against the government in Tripoli progressed.[24] France also retained links to Haftar while still upholding its recognition of the GNA's legitimacy. With Western states sitting idle, or in disagreement, regional states jockeyed to steer the conflict toward their preferred ends.

Turkey acted with the least reservation, and by January 2020, had directly intervened in the war. The introduction of Turkish troops to Libyan soil expanded the support Ankara was already providing to GNA forces, which had included 24 combat drones and some anti-air platforms, most of which had been destroyed by that point in the war. Turkey further deployed 2,000 soldiers, as well as aircraft, naval vessels, tanks, self-propelled howitzers, and other weapons systems.[25] Turkey augmented its forces with "at least 5,000" Syrian mercenaries drawn from its client, the Syrian National Army (SNA). SNA fighters were reportedly hired by the Turkish private military firm Sadat, and offered incentives such as $2,000 monthly salaries and financial death benefits for their families.[26] Unlike their Turkish counterparts, the Syrians were quickly sent to the frontlines, and by June 2020 had sustained heavy losses, with over 500 killed and 2,000 injured, mostly in action around Tripoli.[27] Turkey's mercenaries were not the only Syrians fighting in the conflict. The Wagner Group also hired an estimated 2,000 pro-Assad militiamen to serve as combatants in support of the LNA.[28] The introduction of Syrians into both sides of Libya's civil war was a sad testament to the new marketplace for mercenaries in the region's pulsating belligerencies, and an illustration of how much warfighting had become a privatized industry, with area powers possessing an increasing share.

Turkey's assertiveness stemmed from overlapping strategic and economic concerns. Libya presented President Erdoğan with an opportunity to attempt to restructure his country's role in the Eastern Mediterranean, and to secure greater access to subsea gas deposits. Turkey had ongoing maritime boundary disputes with neighboring Greece and Cyprus, in part driven by differing interpretations of the roles that islands play in helping define exclusive economic zones (EEZs). In October 2018, Ankara began forcing the issue by sending the *Barbaros*, a seismic research vessel, with a naval accompaniment, to explore waters in the Mediterranean and the Aegean seas internationally recognized as Greek and Cypriot territory, but contested by Turkey.[29] Tense naval interactions with its neighbors, threats, and international rebuke from the United States and the European Union did not stop Turkey's provocations.[30] The discovery of undersea gas deposits over the previous decade by Israel, Cyprus, and Egypt had invigorated the regional energy market, and Turkey feared losing out. That anxiety was compounded by Turkey's energy-centered trade deficit. As Galip Dalay explains:

> Energy trade is the main source of the country's budget deficit. Turkey imported 72.4 percent of its energy needs as of 2018, while energy constituted 16.8 percent of its overall imports as of June 2020. In the last

five years, Turkey's total budget deficit amounted to $220 billion [and in] the same period, Turkey's overall energy bill stood at $213 billion. Through hydrocarbon exploration, Turkey hopes to address its chronic economic problems; to this end, the country has doubled down on its energy exploration activities both in the eastern Mediterranean and the Black Sea.[31]

In drawing closer to Libya's government, diplomatically and militarily, Turkey aimed to address some of those concerns. In November 2019, Erdoğan and his Libyan counterpart, GNA president Fayez al-Serraj, signed accords that established a security cooperation agreement between the two states that recognized Turkey's claim to an exclusive economic zone stretching from the Turkish to Libyan coasts—a zone that included Greek territorial waters.[32] The deal was condemned by the United States, Russia, Egypt, Israel, and the European Union, who all backed Greece's position and considered Turkey's claim to be a contravention of international law.[33] Turkey's move was yet another signal to its neighbors that it would aggressively pursue a greater portion of the eastern Mediterranean's hydrocarbon market, and was willing to employ strategic means if necessary. In this case, and in addition to its maritime activity, that meant leading a military intervention into the Libyan war.[34]

Erdoğan's gambit changed the trajectory of the conflict. By the end of 2019, the LNA was in the ascendency. Haftar's forces dominated Libya's skies with drones and aircraft, and controlled over 90 percent of the country's oil installations.[35] The LNA had laid siege to the southern suburbs of the capital since April, and was poised for eventual victory.[36] Turkey's intervention tipped the balance of military power in Tripoli's favor, and burnished the already strong coordination among pro-GNA militias. A crucial step was the installation of HAWK XXI surface-to-air missile (SAM) batteries in Misrata and Tripoli in mid-January, which served as the backbone of a multipronged air defense system that also included Korkut 35mm anti-aircraft guns, American Stinger MANPADS, and off-shore Gabya-class missile frigates. Those Turkish-controlled weapons and platforms ended the LNA's air dominance over pro-GNA territory, and removed their key advantage. Turkish artillery and jamming systems further neutralized and destroyed much of the Wagner-operated Russian anti-air batteries, which opened the skies for offensive strikes against LNA positions.[37] Over the following months, the LNA's gains were steadily reversed. As Jason Pack and Wolfgang Pusztai characterize the turning tide against Haftar's forces: "With air superiority achieved and the LNA defenders open to continual artillery or aerial barrages, they simply fled, continuing a pattern that has characterized Libyan warfare since 2011."[38]

Haftar was forced to quit the fight. By August 2020, both sides announced an end to hostilities, and in October signed a UN-sponsored ceasefire agreement.[39]

The agreement called for a return of the belligerents to their camps, the departure of foreign fighters from the country, and the establishment of a number of joint-operated, national institutions to oversee the country's security, resources, and transportation lines. It also called for future presidential elections in 2021, which in theory would give the country a single, national leader.[40] What the agreement did not do, however, was give either side a clear victory. It was a compromise that required neither side to relinquish much power over their areas of control. The pro-GNA forces still controlled areas west of Sirte to the Tunisian border, including Misrata and Tripoli, and the LNA dominated the eastern half of the country, including Sirte, Benghazi, and Tobruk, as well as much of the country's southern interior. Foreign forces mostly stayed put. The ceasefire thus returned Libya to its previous political divide. The modicum of hope that the agreement brought was tempered by the toothlessness of earlier agreements, and the reluctance of foreign and local players to abide by them. Successful elections were unlikely to occur, and the peace would remain fragile.

Libya's second civil war once again showed the effectiveness and limits of foreign intervention. Unlike in Syria and Iraq, where Russian and American air power shifted the momentum of those conflicts, the military power of regional states, Turkey and the UAE, determined the course of Libya's second civil war. In a competitive environment, foreign involvement is only as strong as the commitment and resources of the intervening party. In this case, despite robust Emirati, Russian, and Egyptian participation, Turkey's intervention demonstrated that, compared to its regional rivals, it was willing to take greater risks, was more willing to contest the conflict openly and directly, and was more invested in securing a favorable outcome in the war. Turkey's military might, NATO-derived expertise, and ability to intervene at a scale that the UAE could not, and Russia and Egypt would not, proved to be the difference. Turkey also retained a stronger grip on its ally in the conflict, effectively trading a security guarantee for economic and strategic compacts that could strengthen Ankara's influence in the eastern Mediterranean and pay dividends in the future should the UN-backed government survive. By comparison, the UAE and Russia held less sway over Haftar and had less desire, and less need, to manifest their objectives.[41] In short, Turkey simply wanted it more, and had the wherewithal to advance its interests. Haftar's failure to take Tripoli, however, was not an outright defeat for the Russian and Emirati projects in the country. It simply constrained their areas of influence, at least for a time.

PART IV

13

The Razor's Edge

On January 2, 2020, a U.S. MQ-9 Reaper drone fired four Hellfire missiles at two vehicles leaving Baghdad International Airport. Killed in the pre-dawn explosion was the Middle East's most influential strategist, Qassem Soleimani, and his confidant, Abu Mahdi al-Muhandis. Soleimani's death ended his over 20-year tenure as Iran's man in the shadows. The Quds Force commander made his name by exploiting the chaos that followed the U.S. invasion of Iraq and the Arab Spring. Through personal charisma, risk-taking, and a deft understanding of his enemies, Soleimani led Iran's rise as a regional power. His sudden and violent death punctuated a career spent overseeing the violent deaths of others. To Iran's regime he was a hero and a martyr, who, almost single-handedly, had pulled Iran from a position of weakness to one of strength. To his detractors, especially wide publics in Syria and Iraq, he was a sectarian warlord, who sided with barbaric authoritarians and oversaw a mafia-style enterprise that subjugated everyday citizens in the furtherance of Iran's neo-imperialistic aspirations. In many ways, he was all those things. And now he was dead.

The assassination was the culmination of the Trump administration's pressure campaign against Iran, which relied on economic sanctions designed to persuade a change in behavior. Iran was faced with a choice: submit to the will of a greater power and reap the rewards of integration with the West, or press forward and risk the prospect of bankruptcy and military escalation. Iran's leaders had long flirted with war with the United States. Such a showdown had been rhetorically, if disingenuously, courted since the 1979 revolution; but as the Islamic Republic's project gained momentum in the 21st century, its hubris grew and its fear of the United States diminished. Through its foreign clients and domestic military industries, Iran possessed the ability to both strike its enemies by proxy and deter military aggression against the homeland. The Trump administration hoped Iran would blink. Iran's leaders bet that the United States had no stomach for a conflict, and would seek to avoid one.

Such a dynamic transformed U.S.-Iranian relations into a test of wills. Washington needed to convince Iran's leaders that their economy would be ruined if they did not alter course. Tehran needed to persuade the Trump administration that sanctions would not work, and moreover, would cost the United States and its allies more pain than it would Iran. Israel was also part of the equation, and pursued its own strategy against the Islamic Republic, striking IRGC positions in Syria and working in the darkness to expose Iran's porous internal security. Iran's behavior and that of its clients grew more aggressive as a result, leading to audacious attacks by proxy and at sea, targeting neighboring adversaries and U.S. forces in the region. With neither side capitulating, tensions skyrocketed, and the prospect of open war grew perilously close.

Maximum Pressure

In late April 2018, Israeli prime minister Benjamin Netanyahu made a stunning announcement: Mossad spies had stolen highly classified documents on Iran's nuclear program from a secret storage facility in Tehran. Netanyahu claimed the documents, which amounted to 55,000 paper files and 183 compact discs, proved Iran had pursued a nuclear weapons program—something Iran's leaders had consistently denied. "These files conclusively prove that Iran is brazenly lying when it said it never had a nuclear weapons program," he charged.[1] Highlighting some documents during the elaborate press conference, Netanyahu sought to shift public opinion on the Iran issue. Tehran could not be trusted, he argued, and the nuclear deal that constrained Iran's nuclear enrichment program was insufficient. Above all, this pitch was aimed at President Trump, who was already skeptical of the agreement, and close to deciding whether to remain party to it or not.

Trump pulled the United States out of the nuclear deal a week later. Leaving the deal was part of the administration's evolving approach toward Iran, which ostensibly sought to compel the regime into a more comprehensive agreement. The strategy's champions were Trump's new national security advisor, John Bolton, who replaced Lieutenant General H. R. McMaster earlier that month, and new secretary of state, Mike Pompeo, who had been promoted from his post as CIA director in March after Rex Tillerson was fired due to policy disagreements and heightening tensions with the president. Since arriving at the White House, Bolton had pushed for a rethink of Iran policy which hinged on withdrawing from the JCPOA and reintroducing sanctions.[2] Playing to Trump's own distaste for the deal, Bolton succeeded in bringing the administration around to his position within a month. Defense Secretary Jim Mattis had been the Trump team's main holdout, fearing that escalating tensions could lead to

blowback against U.S. forces in Syria and Iraq by Iran's proxies, but quietly accepted the decision.[3]

The administration's new strategy was enunciated by Secretary Pompeo
two weeks later in a May 21 speech at the Heritage Foundation, a conservative
Washington think tank. "President Trump withdrew from the deal for a simple
reason: it failed to guarantee the safety of the American people from the risk
created by the leaders of the Islamic Republic of Iran," he said. The deal would
not prevent Iran from gaining a nuclear weapon, but "merely delayed" it; and
failed to address Iran's other dangerous behavior—its support to proxies, involvement in regional wars, and ballistic missile program. Moreover, by ending
economic sanctions on Iran, the Obama administration had enabled Iran to finance those activities:

> The JCPOA permitted the Iranian regime to use the money from the
> JCPOA to boost the economic fortunes of a struggling people, but the
> regime's leaders refused to do so. Instead, the government spent its
> newfound treasure fueling proxy wars across the Middle East and lining
> the pockets of the Islamic Revolutionary Guard Corps, Hizballah,
> Hamas, and the Houthis. Remember: Iran advanced its march across
> the Middle East during the JCPOA. Qasem Soleimani has been playing
> with house money that has become blood money. Wealth created by
> the West has fueled his campaigns.
>
> Strategically, the Obama administration made a bet that the deal
> would spur Iran to stop its rogue state actions and conform to interna-
> tional norms. That bet was a loser with massive repercussions for all of
> the people living in the Middle East. . . . [It] was a bad one for America,
> for Europe, for the Middle East, and indeed for the entire world. It is
> clear that the JCPOA has not ended Iran's nuclear ambitions, nor did it
> deter its quest for a regional hegemony. Iran's leaders saw the deal as the
> starting gun for the march across the Middle East.[4]

To counteract Iran, Pompeo promised that the Trump administration would
exert "painful" and "unprecedented financial pressure" on the regime. The
United States would unilaterally reimpose the sanctions that had been removed
by the previous administration as part of the nuclear deal, and would work to
re-establish multilateral sanctions on Iran. "These will indeed end up being the
strongest sanctions in history when we are complete," he said. Without UN
Security Council backing, which was unlikely to happen, American sanctions
would only bite if other countries who did business with Iran willingly enforced
them by cutting trade ties. That would require the United States to pressure its
friends in Europe and Asia, as well as adversaries such as China, to halt financial

transactions with Iran and end all energy-related imports. Pompeo acknowledged that the effort would negatively impact the economies of partner states, but cautioned "we will hold those doing prohibited business in Iran to account." Hard power would also be used:

> I will work closely with the Department of Defense and our regional allies to deter Iranian aggression. . . We will ensure freedom of navigation on the waters in the region. We will work to prevent and counteract any Iranian malign cyber activity. We will track down Iranian operatives and their Hizballah proxies operating around the world and we will crush them. Iran will never again have carte blanche to dominate the Middle East.[5]

Pompeo issued a list of 12 demands, which called for the release of all Americans held hostage by the regime and the cessation of Iran's main strategic efforts, including its support to proxies in the region, role in regional conflicts, nuclear enrichment program, and ballistic missile development. Those maximalist demands, if met, would be matched with a maximalist reward: full normalization of ties. Were Iran to capitulate in each area, Pompeo assured that the United States would end all sanctions and be "happy at that point to re-establish full diplomatic and commercial relationships with Iran. And we're prepared to admit Iran to have advanced technology. If Iran makes this fundamental strategic shift, we, too, are prepared to support the modernization and reintegration of the Iranian economy into the international economic system."[6]

The Trump administration's strategy became known as the "maximum pressure campaign." It reinstituted and expanded an architecture of economic sanctions on Iran, aiming to either compel the regime into submission or have it risk economic collapse. Iranian officials rejected the proposition. Not to be outdone by his counterpart, Iran's foreign minister, Mohammad Javad Zarif, released his own, even longer list of demands. He suggested that the Trump administration's new strategy contravened international law and was an attempt to "divert international public opinion," writing: "Mr. Pompeo's 12 preconditions for Iran to follow are especially preposterous as the U.S. administration itself is increasingly isolated internationally due to its effort to undermine diplomacy and multilateralism."[7]

Protests in Iraq and Retaliation in Syria

The maximum pressure campaign further complicated regional dynamics. Iraq was the most vulnerable to the new sanctions given its extensive trade with its neighbor, and the reliance on water and electricity from Iran. The United States routinely gave Iraq temporary waivers, which allowed it to maintain its financial ties to Iran, but the unintended economic disruption that U.S. sanctions caused increased Iraq's sense of vulnerability and the anxiety of its citizens.[8] Tensions with Iraqi Shia militias mounted, leading to threats and sporadic rocket attacks near U.S. installations in the country. With Mosul liberated, and the war against ISIS winding down, the future of U.S. troops in Iraq remained uncertain. The Iraqi government wanted to retain a limited presence of U.S. and Coalition forces to help maintain security and military training.[9] Iranian clients, however, were adamantly opposed to such an arrangement, regardless of sanctions. As Jafar al-Hussaini, Kataib Hezbollah's spokesman, warned in a February interview: "Our combatants have limited weapons but a confrontation with the American forces may begin at any moment. Unlike in the past, the Americans this time will not benefit from any mediation."[10]

Iraq was set for a social and political reckoning. The country had been sliding toward unrest, and the war had only compounded discontentment in the country. Regular Iraqis had witnessed how corruption had brought their country to the brink of collapse, and empowered greedy militias. Fresh off their victory, the militias felt entitled to influence, stature, and power. They began to operate more like mafias, extracting money and resources from both the state and citizenry. Everyday citizens were squeezed out of employment opportunities in the public sector, which remained the largest employer in the country. Militiamen and their families controlled most of the jobs, and thereby hoarded much of the money available to younger people eager to enter the workforce and make a life for themselves. Aided by low turnout, the parliamentary elections in May 2018 were dominated by Shia militias and their political allies. Muqtada al-Sadr's list gained the most votes (54 seats), followed closely by the list headed by Hadi al-Ameri (48 seats), which encompassed most of the Iran-allied militias and associated politicians. That made the two most powerful militia networks the two most influential political blocs in the new parliament. The list headed by Prime Minister Haider al-Abadi came in third (42 seats).[11] His position grew tenuous, and after months of deadlock, he was succeeded in October by a compromise candidate, the former vice president and oil minister Adil Abdul-Mahdi, who was also a veteran member of the Supreme Islamic Council of Iraq.

Life in Iraqi cities was increasingly grim. Continual power outages, water insecurity, and surging unemployment had created a restive environment. Resentment against the militias, the government that emboldened them, and Iran, which appeared to be the one pulling the strings, and was the source of the country's unreliable electricity and unsafe drinking water, was spiraling. The oppressive summer heat inflamed tensions, which by July, boiled over into furious protests across Shia-majority cities in the south. In one episode, protestors in

Basra set fire to the Iranian consulate, chanting "Iran, out, out!" as they stormed the building.[12] The protests coincided with, or perhaps motivated, renewed militia operations against U.S. forces. In September, rockets struck near the U.S. consulate in Basra and the U.S. embassy in Baghdad.[13] The unguided strikes missed buildings, and resulted in no injuries to American personnel, but sent a message: Iran and its allies were prepared to raise the stakes.

The maximum pressure campaign also affected the American role in Syria. U.S. forces remained in smaller numbers in the country, where operations aimed at uprooting ISIS from its remaining strongholds in the Euphrates Valley continued. Although the U.S. mission was to aid the SDF in defeating ISIS, the idea that the American force presence in Syria could somehow be used against Iran—a line promoted by John Bolton until his resignation in September 2019—gained some adherents in the White House, even if Mattis and the president were less convinced.[14] A common argument was that by maintaining a U.S. force presence in eastern Syria, especially near the border with Iraq, the IRGC could be blocked from establishing a contiguous supply line from Iran to Syria. The American mission was limited, however, and engaging loyalist and pro-Iranian forces was beyond its scope. The battlespace in Syria was congested with competing forces, and minor encounters between U.S. troops and Iran-backed forces nonetheless occurred. The most significant exchange happened in February 2018, when a firefight broke out between regime forces, Iranian-backed militias, and Russian Wagner Group mercenaries, and a small U.S. Special Forces detachment operating out of an SDF base in the village of Khasham near Deir az-Zour. Loyalist forces advanced toward the American position shortly after dawn, transgressing a deconfliction line agreed upon by the U.S. and Russian militaries. American troops defended their position with machine-gun fire and artillery barrages, and called in airstrikes. The battle lasted hours. When the dust settled, over 100 pro-regime soldiers had been killed, including several Russian nationals from the Wagner Group. U.S. forces sustained no casualties.[15]

As the rebellion continued to lose ground, it was becoming evident that the IRGC would have an enduring role in Syria. That posed a problem for Israel's security. The IRGC continued its efforts to build up military capabilities in Syria, and to use Syria as a means of delivering weapons to Hezbollah in Lebanon, including advanced rockets and missiles. To discourage that behavior, the Israeli Defense Forces (IDF) began striking IRGC weapons shipments early in the conflict. That campaign expanded by 2017, with IDF aircraft regularly hitting weapons transfers, depots, and other Hezbollah and IRGC-linked targets across Syria. Through the first six years of the war, IDF officials acknowledged having conducted around 100 attacks inside Syria.[16] Between 2017 and September 2018, Israel claimed to have conducted over 200 more strikes.[17] The IRGC and its proxies had little answer for these attacks, and IDF officials believed their strategy had disrupted some Iranian positions and forced them to relocate to more distant parts of Syria.

The IRGC and its allies attempted a few counteroperations, with most ending in failure. A notable exception occurred in February 2018, following the interception in Israeli airspace of an Iranian drone launched from the T-4 airbase near Homs. Israeli F-16s responded to the breach by striking the trailer that had launched the drone. Syria targeted the Israeli aircraft with a heavy barrage of surface-to-air missiles from four different batteries. One F-16 was hit, forcing its pilot and co-pilot to eject over Israeli airspace. Iranian officials denied a drone had been flown into Israel but hailed the downing as a victory. A statement from Iran-led Joint Operations Command in Syria called the attack "a clear warning to Israel. The era of Israeli strikes on Syria is over."[18] Israel responded soon after by striking 12 targets inside Syria, including several IRGC positions and the four anti-air platforms that had been used, thereby seriously degrading Syria's air defenses.[19] Israel's strikes in Syria were not over.

Cracks in the Revolution

The Trump administration had reason to believe that economic pressure could stimulate change in Iran. Iran's economy, due to decades of mismanagement, corruption, and poor relations with major powers, was a mess. Years of economic sanctions exacerbated those problems, and slumping oil prices contributed to a declining GDP. Despite a brief boost in foreign investment between 2016 and 2017 following the signing of the JCPOA, Iran's foreign entanglements continued to drag down its economy. Complicating matters was the U.S. Treasury Department's terrorist designation of the IRGC in October 2017.[20] With the IRGC intertwined with Iran's state industries and commercial enterprises, it was difficult for Iranian entities to regain access to foreign banks after the UN sanctions were lifted, because financial institutions did not want to risk U.S. penalties by inadvertently doing business with Iran's sanctioned military sector.

Iran did not get the economic lift the JCPOA was anticipated to bring, and the regime's hardliners sought to play that to their advantage by pinning the blame on the Rouhani government, which had won re-election in June. An ill-fated effort to scapegoat Rouhani began with an anti-government protest in the city of Mashhad, the home of Ebrahim Raisi, a hardline cleric and regime insider who had unsuccessfully opposed Rouhani in the election.[21] With the irony it deserved, the protest merited little locally; however, it unintentionally inspired a wave of popular discontent. Protests erupted across the country in late December. To the hardliners' dismay, the demonstrators did not single out the Rouhani government for their ire, as had been done in Mashhad; rather, they blamed the entire system, from the supreme leader on down.[22] Iran's security forces moved against the protests swiftly and violently, killing around two dozen civilians in the process. The protests were over by mid-January, but hinted at the potential magnitude of the anger seething within Iranian society.[23]

When mass protests broke out again in November 2019, the Trump administration might have believed their strategy was working. The return of economic sanctions was having a severe negative impact on Iran's economy and society.[24] Instead of trying to shield its population from sanctions, the regime passed the buck, betting on the idea that a humanitarian crisis would either sway the Trump administration to relent, or build up antipathy among Iranians for the United States while burnishing support for the supreme leader's anti-American project. Everyday citizens were caught in the crossfire and suffered most. Pharmaceuticals were especially in short supply, which added to the distress of those dealing with illnesses such as cancer or diabetes.[25] Unemployment and inflation were also on the rise, with the poor and working classes most affected. Official numbers pegged unemployment at 12.5 percent, but it was likely double that for younger Iranians.[26]

Unlike the year before, the 2019 protests began organically after the government announced a 200 percent increase in gasoline prices. Within hours, demonstrations broke out across Iranian cities, from Mashhad in the north to Ahvaz in the south. The protests were angrier, more violent, and more destructive than anything Iran had experienced since the revolution. They were also distinctly anti-regime, with slogans that called for the supreme leader's death and an end to the Islamic Republic. Protests were strongest in the blue-collar towns of poorer provinces, which were often neglected by Tehran, and had been hardest hit by the country's economic slide. Young people with few prospects and little opportunity to advance in life blamed Iran's leaders and their agenda for their lot. Chants against Iran's support for Hezbollah and Hamas could be heard alongside other anti-regime slogans, including some that even called for a return of the Pahlavi monarchy. Although the protestors were not sympathetic to the Trump administration, they nonetheless rejected the regime's sacred totems.

More worrisome for the regime was where the demonstrations were taking place. In the past, mass protests, such as the 2009 post-election unrest, had been concentrated in major cities, and most prominent in Tehran. For that reason, the regime wrote them off as the crocodile tears of a privileged elite, and not representative of their pious base. But the demonstrations in 2018 and 2019 occurred in some of Iran's most traditionally conservative and religious towns, scattered across 29 of the country's 31 provinces.[27] The pious poor, who had backed the revolution in 1979 and remained the core constituency of the Islamic system, were turning against the theocracy. The regime was losing its young. Generation

Z did not care about the shah, Israel, or America. They did not experience the war with Saddam or the glimmers of hope of the reformist 1990s. Rather, they had grown up in the post–9/11 world, and had only known a life shaped by war, alienation, and above all, the regime's bellicosity.

Concerned about the disorder, Iran's supreme leader convened a meeting with senior officials, during which he reportedly said: "The Islamic Republic is in danger. Do whatever it takes to end it. You have my order." Whether those were his actual words or not, the regime's response aligned with those sentiments and was brutal. The southern city of Mahshahr was particularly hard hit, with IRGC armor units and tanks moving into the city, and troops using machine-gun fire to kill protestors in the streets, alleys, and in the marshes where some sought refuge.[28] Similar operations crushed other protests across Iran. The death toll from the countrywide crackdown was staggering, with reports suggesting upwards of 1,500 civilians, including 17 teenagers and 400 women, killed by Iranian security forces.[29]

Challenging Trump's Resolve

It was within that charged climate that Iran's leaders sought to thwart foreign pressure. Iran had a restive population at home, its allies in Iraq were the target of a growing youth-driven protest movement, Israel was increasing its barrage on Iranian military positions and weapons smuggling in Syria, and the Trump administration seemed hell-bent on twisting the screws even further. Iran's response included three main efforts: first, it sought to reduce its commitments under the JCPOA and gradually advance its nuclear enrichment program to raise the stakes of Trump's strategy. Second, the IRGC pursued aggressive operations against its adversaries, using both direct means and working through proxies, to spread the pain and dampen regional support for Washington's pressure campaign. Finally, Iran sought to sell its oil and gas on the black market to whomever was willing to buck U.S. sanctions. That included China, who became the leading importer of Iranian oil, as well as Iraq and Syria.

In early May 2019, Iran announced it would begin walking back its nuclear commitments and threatened more steps in 60 days so long as sanctions were upheld.[30] It followed through with those threats in July, messaging that it would no longer abide by the limits imposed by the JCPOA, and would begin increasing its enrichment levels beyond the 3.67 percent cap. It promised additional steps in two months if sanctions were not lifted.[31] In November, with the Trump administration unmoved, Iran announced the installment of advanced centrifuges and the start of enrichment at its Fordow facility, which had been banned from processing uranium under the nuclear deal.[32]

As Iran's government took these steps, the IRGC was pursuing another approach. Key to Washington's influence in the Middle East were its close relations with Arab states. Saudi Arabia and the UAE had pushed the Trump administration to be tougher on Iran, and were held partly accountable by Tehran. The IRGC aimed to discourage the complicity of these states by exposing the vulnerabilities in their own economies, namely commercial shipping and hydrocarbons. The IRGC began to target shipping vessels with sabotage attacks in May, when four tankers off the coast of the UAE's Fujairah port were struck by explosions in the middle of the night. The UAE blamed the attacks on a "state actor," which ruled out the Houthis and terrorist groups, but did not elaborate further.[33] Although Iran was suspected, no evidence was provided to link it to the incidents. A month later, two more tankers were struck in similar limpet mine attacks in the Gulf of Oman. In responding to one of the vessel's distress calls, the U.S. Navy spotted an IRGC patrol boat returning to the scene to retrieve a limpet mine that had failed to explode from the ship's hull. The entire episode was filmed and released publicly.[34] Iran maintained its denials, but the IRGC was clearly the culprit.

On June 20, the IRGC announced that it had downed an American surveillance drone over its national airspace near the Strait of Hormuz. "Our borders are our red line," stated newly promoted IRGC chief Hossein Salami regarding the operation. "Iran is not seeking war with any country, but we are fully prepared to defend Iran." The U.S. Navy soon confirmed that a RQ-4A Global Hawk had been shot down, but disputed Iran's claim of territorial transgression, calling the incident an "unprovoked attack on a U.S. surveillance asset in international airspace." President Trump tweeted a terse warning—"Iran made a very big mistake!"—and seemed determined to act. The U.S. military announced that it was deploying an additional 1,000 troops to the region in response to Iran's "hostile behavior."[35] Military planners provided the president with an array of options, including striking anti-air launch sites inside Iran, which would likely inflict casualties, or striking an IRGC smuggling vessel laden with missiles, which after a warning given to the crew to abandon ship, would incur no causalities.[36] A meeting of the National Security Council debated the issue later that morning. A broad consensus was reached among the principals, who settled on a plan to strike three military sites along Iran's Gulf coast (which included potentially Russian-manned anti-air batteries) and "other measures." Trump agreed to the proposal and the military began preparations.[37] As Bolton explains, the plan was remarkable on three levels:

> (1) we were hitting functioning military targets . . . not merely symbolic ones; (2) we were hitting inside Iran, crossing an Iranian red line, and were certainly going to test their repeated assertions that such an attack

would be met by a full-scale response; and (3) we were hitting targets likely entailing casualties, which question we had confronted, Trump having heard that the attacks he had ordered meant dead Iranians (and, possibly, dead Russians).[38]

By the afternoon, Trump told Republican lawmakers that he had decided to respond, without specifying the details of the plan. Early the next morning, U.S. Navy ships and aircraft were in position to carry out the president's order. Ten minutes before the operation was to commence, Trump changed his mind and called it off.[39]

Explaining his decision the next day, Trump reasoned: "I thought about it for a second and I said, you know what, they shot down an unmanned drone, plane, whatever you want to call it, and here we are sitting with 150 dead people, that would have taken place probably within a half an hour after I said go ahead." "And I didn't like it. I didn't think—I didn't think it was proportionate," he said.[40] The number of potential casualties had been devised by lawyers in the Pentagon who used rough estimates that assumed a maximum of 50 soldiers per anti-air battery. They communicated that number to Trump's deputy counsel, John Eisenberg, who in turn informed the president and argued that such an attack would be illegal and disproportionate. When Trump called to confer with General Joseph Dunford, the chairman of the Joint Chiefs of Staff, the chairman explained to him that the estimated figure was a maximal projection and that the actual number killed would likely be considerably less than 150. The president's misgivings were not assuaged, and he remained uneasy with the idea of inflicting death in response to the downing of an unmanned aircraft, telling Bolton and Pompeo that their plan would mean "too many body bags." Perhaps sensing Bolton's disappointment, Trump said: "Don't worry, we can always attack later, and if we do it'll be much tougher."[41]

Escalating with Missiles and Drones

A more dangerous and potentially escalatory attack occurred in mid-September, when 18 kamikaze drones and 7 cruise missiles struck Saudi Arabia's Aramco facilities at Abqaiq and Khurais, respectively. The attack, which came in two waves and lasted 17 minutes, severely damaged processing tanks and infrastructure in both plants, halting Saudi oil production and reducing output by 50 percent for weeks. The attack was sophisticated and precise, with the vast majority of weapons hitting their targets. The Saudis were caught off guard, and either failed to adequately detect the attack or respond with nearby anti-air systems.[42] Some reports suggested that the air defense systems were concentrated on intercepting attacks from Yemen in the south, and may have not anticipated an attack from the north. Other reports suggested that Saudi air defense systems were not designed to counter low-flying targets such as cruise missiles and drones.[43] Whatever the reason, the attack exposed Saudi Arabia's susceptibility to such strikes. The drones and missiles hit the lifeblood of the Saudi economy and within minutes reduced global oil production by 5 percent. Had the swarm been larger, or had the weapons carried larger payloads, the damage could have been devastating. Saudi Arabia had to contend with that knowledge in planning for any potential retaliation.

There was also some question about the culprit of the attack.[44] The Houthis quickly claimed responsibility, and threatened more attacks, but that claim was roundly dismissed. Although the Houthis had repeatedly, albeit mostly unsuccessfully, attacked Saudi territory throughout 2018 and 2019 with ballistic missiles and drones, the September attack was too complex for the Houthis to have credibly been behind it.[45] Further, neither the types of drones nor cruise missiles used were a known part of the Houthis' arsenal.[46] The United States asserted that Iran had been behind the attack, and suggested that intelligence showed that the strike had originated from Ahvaz in southern Iran, with the drones and missiles flying over Iraqi and Kuwaiti airspace before reaching Saudi Arabia.[47] Saudi officials were less declarative, with the military's spokesperson calling the attack "unquestionably sponsored by Iran," and affirming that the munitions had come from the north, but falling short of holding Iran directly responsible. The main evidence linking Iran to the attack, provided to the public by the Saudis, was Iranian-made parts and electronics found in the wreckage of the drones and missiles.[48] Citing unnamed high-ranking sources in Iran, Reuters provided a detailed confirmation of Iran's involvement, claiming that the attack had been planned by the IRGC and greenlit by the supreme leader, with the missiles and drones taking circuitous routes over Iraq and Kuwait to obscure their point of origin in southwestern Iran.[49] Iranian officials rejected all allegations, and backed the Houthis' claim.

Although it could not be definitively proven that Iran had been responsible for the attack, at least not based on the information that Saudi Arabia made available, no state believed that the perpetrator was anyone but Iran. Saudi authorities, however, were reluctant to lay blame publicly. Part of that hesitation might have been due to the ramifications of such an accusation. Were Iran to be behind the attack, it would have been an act of war, and something that required a response. When President Trump was pressed on whether or not the United States would react, the president reiterated his disinclination for war, saying, "How did going into Iraq work out?" He added: "There's plenty of time to do some dastardly things. It's very easy to start. And we'll see what happens." Washington pledged sanctions and more diplomatic pressure, but if Saudi Arabia wanted to retaliate militarily, it would need to take the lead and confirm Iran's responsibility.[50] Trump also reiterated that there was no promise or treaty obliging the United States to defend Saudi Arabia. Telling reporters that if anything is to be done, his administration would "have to sit down with the Saudis and work something out." "They'll be very much involved, and that includes payment. And they understand that fully."[51] With Washington uncommitted, the ball was in the kingdom's court. Riyadh would need to be the initiator if it desired a military response. It did not, and the attack remained clouded by a hint of uncertainty.

If Iran was the culprit, as is believed, its attack on Saudi Arabia was effective. It was a successful display of Iran's increasingly sophisticated over-the-horizon strike capability. Low-flying cruise missiles and inexpensive "delta wing" drones were used, and in the Abqaiq strike, all but one of the munitions hit their target. Iran's practice of exporting weapons technology to its regional clients also gave some merit to the idea that the attack had been conducted by proxy. Even if no one really believed that to be the case, Iran had established a semblance of deniability which complicated responses to its aggressive actions. For Saudi Arabia, the attack exposed the vulnerability of its oil industry, and by extension, its economy. It was also evident that Saudi Arabia was not willing to engage Iran militarily, and that hesitation redefined the Saudi-Iran conflict into a one-sided contest. Saudi Arabia had no military answer to Iran, which inherently emboldened the posture adopted by Iran and its clients, especially the Houthis. Finally, and perhaps more importantly, the attack helped clarify the limits of the United States' security relationship with Saudi Arabia. The United States would not go to war with Iran on Saudi Arabia's behalf. It might have supported retaliatory actions against Iran by the Saudis, but it would not take the lead. From that point on, Iran's leaders could safely bet that an attack on Saudi Arabia or on any other regional adversary—with Israel being a possible exception—would not escalate into a war with the United States. U.S. military presence in the Persian Gulf might deter some Iranian aggression, but it did not guarantee the security of its Arab partners.

Lethal Exchanges in Iraq

While the Aramco attack succeeded in those ways, it failed to motivate a change in U.S. policy. If anything, it reinforced the Trump administration's argument that Iran's regime was dangerous. Iran's predicament remained the same, so the IRGC shifted focus to proxies in Iraq. Since the end of major operations against ISIS, Iraqi militias had been regularly targeting the American presence by launching rockets into military bases and the Green Zone compound. Unlike missiles, the Iran-supplied Katyusha rockets used by Iraqi militias were unguided munitions, with a wider radius of potential impact. Often Iraqi militias would launch rockets into relatively empty areas where there was a low probability of inflicting causalities. These attacks were perceived as symbolic warnings. American forces did not respond to them in kind, because they remained nonlethal, and conducting operations against the militias, who were also part of the official Popular Mobilization Forces, would undermine the government in Baghdad and upset the country's delicate political balance. U.S. forces also understood that Iraqi militias could change tactics and target populated areas if they wanted to. And in a late December 2019 attack on K-1 base near Kirkuk, they did just that. A barrage of 30 rockets hit an area housing Coalition forces, injuring several American and Iraqi servicemembers, and killing Nawres Hamid, an American civilian linguist and father of two.[52]

Hamid's death changed the game for the Trump administration. Until now, the attacks ascribed to Iran following the reimposition of sanctions were nonlethal or targeted foreign interests. The lethal strike shifted Washington's calculus, and Trump allowed for a kinetic response. Two days later, American F-15s launched strikes against Kataib Hezbollah, hitting sites in western Iraq and across the border in Syria described as a regional headquarters, weapons depot, and command-and-control post. Early reports suggested that 25 militiamen were killed, including four local commanders, with dozens more wounded. Secretary Pompeo said of the strikes: "We will not stand for the Islamic Republic of Iran to take actions that put American men and women in jeopardy."[53]

Iran-backed militias quickly responded. On December 31, a funeral procession for the those killed in the U.S. airstrikes in Baghdad turned into a march of thousands of militiamen toward the U.S. embassy compound—the most fortified American embassy in the world. Pro-Iranian militants forced their way into the Green Zone and gathered outside of the embassy, with some penetrating the outer perimeter gate, hurling Molotov cocktails into the compound, and torching the reception center. As American diplomats and staff took shelter in a safe room, Blackhawk helicopters brought in 100 additional Marines as reinforcements. There was no attempt to use force against the protestors, and the latter seemed content to not push further. The crowd was led by Iran's top clients in Iraq: Abu Mahdi al-Muhandis, the leader of Kataib Hezbollah; Qais al-Khazali, the leader of Asaib Ahl al-Haq; Hadi al-Ameri, the Badr chief and PMF deputy commander; and Faleh al-Fayyadh, the head of the PMF. All were in attendance, and gave impassioned speeches calling for an end to the American military presence. By evening, the militants had erected a camp outside the embassy's entrance, suggesting that they intended to stay.[54] Trump blamed the siege on Iran, tweeting: "Iran will be held fully responsible for lives lost, or damage incurred, at any of our facilities. They will pay a very BIG PRICE! This is not a Warning, it is a Threat. Happy New Year!"[55] Iran's supreme leader replied with a tweet of his

own: "You are wrong! If Iran wants to fight another state, it will do so unequivo-
cally. We adhere to the interests and honor of our nation, and whoever threatens
it will be confronted and struck without the least hesitation."[56]

The protest ended the next day, almost as quickly as it began. The militants
had used their siege as leverage with Iraq's prime minister, Adil Abdul-Mahdi,
who was put in a nearly impossible position of trying to quell the passions of
the militias while also retaining positive working relations with Washington.
Finally, in exchange for ending the protest, Abdul-Mahdi gave militia leaders
assurances that he would put forward legislation that would end the American
military presence. A standoff was avoided. While protestors settled for a political solution, they left their mark on the embassy: with scorched buildings, damaged fences, and graffiti that denounced the United States and praised Qassem
Soleimani. One line seemed to imagine the Iranian military leader's presence
among the fray, reading: "He passed through here."[57]

The Brink of War

Soleimani and Abu Mahdi al-Muhandis were killed the next day. Around the
same time, a U.S. drone strike in Yemen targeted—but failed to hit—another
IRGC commander: Abdul-Reza Shahlai, best known for his link to the foiled
murder plot on Saudi ambassador Adel al-Jubeir.[58] Those attacks set the tone for
what was to become a very dangerous year for Iran. The chronology of escalatory
events suggested that Soleimani had been assassinated in retaliation for the embassy protest. American officials, including the president, painted a different
version of events, claiming the action was taken to prevent an imminent attack
on U.S. forces being plotted by Soleimani at the time. Eventually it was revealed
that the decision had actually been made by Trump seven months prior, and
that an extensive intelligence operation, which also involved Israel's Mossad, had
been monitoring the Iranian general's movements.[59] When Soleimani boarded
Cham Wings Airlines Flight 6Q501 in Damascus, an informant alerted intelligence operatives, who passed the report up the chain. Soleimani's flight landed
in Baghdad at 00:36 local time, and taxied to a quiet section of the airfield closed
off for his arrival. He was received by Abu Mahdi and a small entourage, who
entered two cars. Unbeknownst to the Iranian commander, his movements had
been tracked minute-by-minute by Israeli and American military intelligence.
A Delta Force sniper team lay in wait hundreds of yards away, with scopes
trained on their targets, and three U.S. drones circled overheard. The vehicles
and occupants were identified by informants on the ground, who relayed the information to the Americans. Minutes later, the vehicles were struck leaving the
tarmac along a service road, killing 10, including Soleimani and Abu Mahdi.[60]

Soleimani's death sent a shock wave through Iran and the region. He had played an outsized role in Iran's strategic posture, and was uniquely responsible for its proxy network. Iran's supreme leader praised Soleimani for having "no fear of anyone or anything," saying that he achieved martyrdom for "performing his duty and fighting for the cause of God."[61] He also warned: "With his departure and with God's power, his work and path will not cease, and severe revenge awaits those criminals who have tainted their filthy hands with his blood and the blood of the other martyrs of last night's incident."[62] The regime organized countrywide commemorations in honor of the fallen commander, including massive processions in Tehran and Kerman, Soleimani's former stomping ground and home province.

Iran soon retaliated in an operation codenamed "Martyr Soleimani." In the early hours of January 8, IRGC forces fired at least 16 Fateh-313 and Qiam-1 ballistic missiles at American troops in Iraq. All but one of the missiles, which came in three successive waves, were aimed at Ayn al-Asad airbase in Anbar province, around 230 kilometers west of Baghdad and home to 2,000 American troops and personnel. A lone missile targeted a facility at the Erbil airport in northern Iraq. American intelligence satellites had observed the IRGC readying missiles in western Iran and moving them into position, suggesting a westward attack was imminent, which gave U.S. forces a couple of hours to prepare. Base commanders at Ayn al-Asad removed around half of their troops as well as 50 aircraft from the base. Most of the remaining troops packed into overcrowded bunkers, which, despite being insufficient protection for ballistic missiles, were still the safest locations on base. A smaller number of troops took up sentry posts to watch for a potential coordinated land attack. Missiles began to hit the base at 01:35, with the whole attack lasting over an hour. The assault did extensive damage to the base, destroying a barracks, airplane hangars, and other buildings.[63] Over a hundred servicemembers were injured, most with traumatic brain injuries, but there were no immediate deaths. At least 68 troops were awarded Purple Hearts for the severe and lasting injuries they sustained.[64]

The strikes on Ayn al-Assad were the largest ballistic missile attack on U.S. forces in history. It was audacious, potentially highly lethal, and put Iran's missile capabilities on full display. Eleven missiles hit their targets with destructive precision. The accuracy surprised even the closest outside observers of Iran's missile program, something IRGC media was happy to highlight in its own coverage of the attack, which they called the greatest attack on America since Pearl Harbor.[65] When the attack concluded, Iran messaged Washington through the Swiss Embassy that that would be the extent of their retaliation. IRGC air defense systems were at the ready and expecting an American response. U.S. forces in the region were primed to retaliate, and military planners had already briefed the president on a list of targets in Iran for such a scenario.

Iran's skies remained open to civilian flights—a bewildering decision given the careful planning of the attack, which was greenlit by Iran's supreme leader and done with the Rouhani government's full knowledge, and the high likelihood for American counterstrikes. That choice, either done to better obscure Iran's intention to attack, or sheer ineptitude, proved catastrophic. Shortly after 06:00 local time, only a few hours after the end of Operation Martyr Soleimani, an IRGC Russian-made Tor-M1 battery fired two surface-to-air missiles at a civilian airline that had departed Tehran's Imam Khomeini International Airport minutes earlier. The 176 mostly Iranian passengers and crew on board Ukraine Air Flight 752, including 15 children, were killed as the plane broke apart and crashed.[66]

The downing of the Ukraine Air flight was an inexcusable tragedy—it might have also helped avert war. U.S. forces in the region were ready to respond to the attack on Ayn al-Asad. President Trump, however, downplayed the severity of the ballistic missile strikes, and framed the missile barrage as something akin to a cathartic gesture, something that the Iranians needed to get out of their system. With no Americans killed, Trump considered the matter closed. "Iran appears to be standing down which is a good thing for all parties concerned," Trump said in an address to the nation hours after the attack, adding: "I'm pleased to inform you the American people should be extremely grateful and happy. . . . No Americans were harmed in last night's attack by the Iranian regime." Iran had had their fun, and that would be that. Washington would respond with additional sanctions, a pallid gesture given the totality of economic sanctions already imposed on Iran, but would not retaliate militarily.[67]

It is impossible to disentangle how the downing of Ukraine Air Flight 752 factored into Trump's decision-making. Within hours the IRGC had gone from its most impressive military operation to its ugliest mistake. There were no victory parades, no swelling of national pride. Iranians were instead reminded of the regime's incompetence and malice. The brief moment of sympathy that the killing of Soleimani had engendered vanished instantly. It was replaced with another round of limited, yet stridently anti-regime protests calling for justice for the flight's victims and their families.[68] A heated political scandal and cover-up followed, which further tarnished the reputation of Iran's government, and especially that of its foreign minister, Mohammad Javad Zarif, who was the public face of Iran's duplicitousness, despite knowing the IRGC was responsible.[69] Although the most plausible scenario was that the IRGC hastily mistook the Ukraine Air flight for a U.S. military jet or missile, and that a severe breakdown in command-and-control failed to prevent the strike, Iran's reluctance to come clean about the matter, including in the official report it provided the international community, led to the persistence of speculation that the strike had been intentional and a Machiavellian attempt to preempt U.S. military retaliation and avoid war.[70]

The episode displayed both the IRGC's power and incompetence. The man behind it all was Brigadier General Amir Ali Hajizadeh, the chief of the IRGC's Aerospace Force. Even though he led Iran's most important military efforts, including its drone and missile programs, Hajizadeh remained overshadowed by Soleimani. He had neither the following, the charisma, nor the sanctification of his renowned colleague, but he was responsible for Iran's growing military might. Soleimani's death and subsequent eponymous operation thrust Hajizadeh into the limelight. In one interview, Hajizadeh spoke of the strategic ramifications of the Ayn al-Assad attack. From his perspective, the attack exposed the United States as a paper tiger. U.S. forces were susceptible to aggression, and Washington lacked the will to respond. Hajizadeh contrasted the American restraint to the Trump administration's threats of military action in the past, calling such rhetoric a "bluff." "The whole world saw that America could not do anything," he said.[71]

An Undeclared War

As Iran avoided war with the United States, its conflict with Israel was intensifying. Israel considered Iran its leading security challenge, and adopted a proactive strategy aimed at steadily raising the costs of Iran's behavior. In Syria, Israel expanded its air operations against the IRGC and Hezbollah, hitting weapons shipments, storehouses, and logistics bases. Those operations were part of Israel's routine maintenance of the Syrian conflict, but did little to alter Iran's approach. Israel amplified the pressure through covert operations in Iran. As one senior Israeli diplomat later described the approach, "Our goal is to harass them at home, so they will be busy with that," adding that the effort is "primarily economic, through a number of activities, financial, diplomatic, preemptory actions, covert and open, in cyberspace and other areas."[1] Iran dealt with a string of incidents and sabotage attacks across 2020 and 2021 that betrayed its porous national security. Israel was believed to be behind the most damaging of those incidents. Added to this was the COVID-19 pandemic, which hit Iran in February, making it the first country outside of China to struggle with what rapidly became a global public health emergency. Even as the pandemic aggravated political crises across the globe, it did little to slow the undeclared war between Iran and Israel.

For Iran, the pandemic coincided with a series of mysterious explosions across the country, some severely damaging sensitive sites located within secure military bases. As the summer heat took hold in late June and July 2020, explosions and blackouts began to hit governmental facilities. Many of the incidents seemed to involve compressed gas and oxygen cylinders, and were described by officials as accidents. Most occurred at government buildings, and harmed no one; however, an explosion in late June blamed on a leaking gas tank at the Sina Athar clinic in Tehran killed at least 19 people and injured many more.[2] A week earlier, a blast torched a staging area and adjacent hillside used in engine testing at the IRGC's Khojir missile complex. The explosion could be seen lighting up the night sky by residents in Tehran, 20 kilometers to the west, and was likely centered on a compressed missile fuel storage tank. At around the same time, a blackout hit the city of Shiraz, over 900 kilometers to the south, which was linked to an unexplained fire at the city's main electrical plant.[3] Those incidents might have been coincidences, accidents, or both; yet, the tempo of what followed suggested that at least some were part of an organized campaign by a foreign state adversary.

A week following the accident at Khojir, a massive explosion ripped apart a building at the Natanz nuclear complex near Esfahan. The blast destroyed much of the Iran Centre for Advanced Centrifuges (ICAC) warehouse, a key part of Iran's nuclear enrichment infrastructure. Iranian officials acknowledged that the incident had been caused by an explosive charge, but downplayed the severity of the damage. Israel was again suspected. When asked during a radio interview if Israel had been involved, defense minister Benny Gantz coyly replied: "Everyone can suspect us in everything and all the time, but I don't think that's correct," adding: "Not every event that happens in Iran is necessarily related to us."[4] Later, Israeli intelligence sources told the *Jewish Chronicle* that the incident was the result of a covert multiyear effort to infiltrate Iran's strategic programs through front companies, informants, and well-placed operatives on the ground, including workers and scientists within Iran's nuclear facilities. Mossad operatives acting as a third-party construction wholesale company sold Iran building materials that secretly contained explosives. The materials were used in the construction of the warehouse's interior and remained in place for over a year until they were remotely detonated.[5] Fereydoon Abbasi, the former head of Iran's Atomic Energy Organization, and the survivor of a 2010 assassination attempt blamed on Israel, claimed the explosive had been sealed inside a steel table that had been brought into the facility.[6] Either way, it was clear that explosives had been inserted deep into one of Iran's most secure buildings—a disconcerting lapse of security that underscored Israel's ability to carry out covert operations on Iranian soil.

Holiday Road

Israel's disruption campaign extended beyond industrial sabotage. On November 27, 2020, a remote-operated 7.62mm machine gun sat concealed in the back of a Nissan pickup along the side of a rural road near Absard, a small town 90 kilometers east of Tehran. Its target was Mohsen Fakhrizadeh, a high-ranking IRGC officer believed to be the head of Iran's murky nuclear weapons effort. Fakhrizadeh had been mentioned by name during Prime Minster Netanyahu's 2018 news conference where he announced Mossad's successful operation seizing nuclear files from a storage facility in Tehran. "Remember that name," Netanyahu said, "Fakhrizadeh." While traveling back to Tehran after a regular holiday spent at his vacation home near the Caspian Sea in the lush province of Mazandaran, a burst of gunfire hit the driver's side windshield, striking Fakhrizadeh at least once. Fakhrizadeh exited the driver's side door and was struck again several times, killing him on the road. His wife, who had been sitting just inches away in the passenger's seat, was unharmed. The security detail which had escorted Fakhrizadeh, staffed by the IRGC's elite Ansar al-Mahdi protection unit, was unable to identify where the shots had come from. Soon after, the Nissan pickup exploded, partially destroying the weapon that had been used to assassinate Iran's leading nuclear scientist.[7]

Details released by Iranian officials about the incident sounded like science fiction. Ali Fadavi, the IRGC's deputy commander, blamed the attack on a high-tech, satellite-operated machine gun, which had used facial recognition technology and artificial intelligence (AI) to identify its victim and avoid collateral damage.[8] At first blush, such details seemed geared toward relieving the IRGC of any failure in preventing the plot. The IRGC seemed to be saying the only way one of their country's most important military officials could be assassinated in broad daylight during a routine weekend holiday was by a never-before-seen futuristic robot weapon. As strange as the tale sounded, it was broadly corroborated by Western journalists citing unnamed Israeli intelligence sources in two reports: one by the *Jewish Chronicle* and the other by the *New York Times*. According to those sources, the operation took over eight months to plan, and involved logistics teams in Israel and operatives in Iran. An intelligence unit monitored Fakhrizadeh's daily routines and weekly movements during that time. The weapon, which weighed around a ton due to the explosive package contained within it, was smuggled into Iran piecemeal and gradually assembled by Mossad agents in the country. The two reports differ on how the weapon was triggered, with one claiming it had not been satellite-operated, but rather controlled remotely by a nearby ground team who had used the bomb explosion as a distraction to escape undetected.[9] The other report confirmed the IRGC's findings that the weapon had been satellite-operated and AI-controlled, and claimed that the operation had been overseen by a team in Israel using feeds from cameras mounted on the weapon, rather than by a nearby ground team.[10] The operation had been designed to avoid causalities beyond its target, and seems to have largely succeeded on that front, as no one else was reported to have been killed (the IRGC claimed that one security officer was struck by four bullets, which the Israeli sources refuted).[11]

The narrative promoted by the IRGC and anonymous Israeli intelligence sources both described a highly complex operation—one that revealed as much about Israel's prioritization of Iran's nuclear program as it did Israel's ability to permeate Iran's security sector. Israel was determined to thwart, discourage, counter, and impede Iran's nuclear progress by any means short of large-scale, direct military action. The assassination of Fakhrizadeh was one point along the continuum of that effort. Israeli officials believed that his removal would delay Iran's timeline toward developing a nuclear weapon by up to two years. More than a delaying tactic, it was another signal that Israel was willing to play Iran's dangerous game, and that the IRGC's top brass could be targeted.

Nuclear Advancements and Tit-for-Tat Attacks

Despite Israel's escalatory actions, Iran remained unmoved and defiant. Yet, with limited ability to conduct complex covert operations, Iran was unable to respond in kind. Instead, Iran continued its strategy of distributed pushback through difficult-to-attribute attacks. Such behavior messaged Iran's resolve, and discouraged aggression from Arab neighbors, but it did little to sway Israel and the United States. The election of Joe Biden in November 2021 had the potential to change that. Even though Biden retained a tough line on Iran, his national security team was believed to be predisposed to restoring the nuclear deal. Whereas the Trump administration had emphasized the spectrum of its strategic behavior in dealing with Iran—encompassing nuclear enrichment, missiles, regional presence, and support to proxies—Biden was expected to return the nuclear issue to the forefront. The Biden administration's formal position was that it wanted to forge a new deal with Iran that would incorporate the nuclear issue as well as missiles and other matters. Iran rebuffed the proposition, arguing instead for a return to the JCPOA and an end to all sanctions imposed by Trump, which would include numerous non-nuclear sanctions.

To get Washington to act, Iran pushed its nuclear program forward and stirred the narrative that it was speedily moving toward the point of no return—that is, possessing sufficient highly enriched fissile material to build a nuclear weapon. The specter of Iran crossing the threshold of a nuclear-armed state was the only thing that had the potential of unsettling Western capitals enough to relent on sanctions. To that end, on April 10, 2021, Iranian president Hassan Rouhani announced the installment of 164 IR-6 and 30 IR-5 advanced centrifuges at Natanz, which would rapidly increase Iran's ability to produce highly enriched uranium. Iran also began testing its IR-9 centrifuges, which had the capacity to enrich 50 times the amount of uranium as its first-generation centrifuges, the IR-1.[12] The move was in clear violation of the JCPOA, but that was the point. American and Iranian diplomats had just concluded a week of talks the day before in Vienna, where Iran once again demanded full sanctions relief before the return to any sort of nuclear agreement.[13] If the United States did not fall back in line, Iran's nuclear program would press ahead.

Hours after Rouhani's announcement, Natanz was rocked by a massive explosion. Iranian officials quickly acknowledged that it had been no accident, with Ali Akbar Salehi, the head of Iran's Atomic Energy Organization, calling the incident an act of "nuclear terrorism." The explosion occurred 50 meters below ground and appeared to target the internal electrical distribution nodes and back-up systems powering the cascades of centrifuges in the plant's heavily secured facilities. Most Iranian officials downplayed the damage, which caused a blackout and destroyed an unspecified number of centrifuges. Western officials believed it would set back Iran's enrichment program up to nine months. Iran promised to replace the damaged centrifuges with advanced versions, and increase its enrichment levels from 20 to 60 percent.[14] Fereydoon Abbasi grudgingly admired the operation, calling it "very beautiful." He explained: "I'm looking at it from a scientific point of view. They thought about this and used their experts and planned the explosion so both the central power and the emergency power cable would be damaged." Foreign Minister Zarif blamed the Israelis for aiming to scuttle nuclear talks, warning, "We will take our revenge on the Zionists."[15]

Months later, details of the operation were leaked to reporters. According to that narrative, Mossad had amassed a team of over a thousand scientists, engineers, and field operatives in the planning and execution of the attack. Key to the operation were Iranian scientists at Natanz who had been recruited to knowingly sabotage the facility. They believed they were working with Iranian expatriates, not Israel, but were knowledgeable about the basic plan. Explosives were smuggled into the facility using elaborate means, and installed gradually by Iranian scientists who possessed the clearances to access some of the most secure parts of the plant.[16] Iran acknowledged that at least one scientist at Natanz was suspected to have been a part of the plot. As it had done a year earlier, Israel detonated the explosives at a politically expedient time. In this case, it served as a direct retort to Iran's installation of advanced centrifuges. The message was unmistakable: Israel had found ways to infiltrate Iran's most secure and sensitive buildings. It had done it before, and could do it again.

Beyond attacks at home, Iran was also struggling with sabotage attacks against its tankers at sea. Selling oil to a small cadre of willing buyers was mitigating the economic impact of sanctions. Much of Iran's oil went to Chinese buyers, but Iran was also selling oil to Iraq and shipping it to Syria as part its support to Bashar al-Assad. Since 2019, suspected Israeli attacks had damaged Iranian tankers and cargo ships headed to Syria. By March 2021, Israel was believed to have been behind 12 such incidents, including against the Shahr-e Kord cargo vessel, which had been possibly struck by missiles in the port of Latakia that same month.[17] Weeks later, Israel was suspected of a mine attack on the IRGC's *Saviz*, a converted shipping vessel that served as an intelligence platform and staging base in the Red Sea.[18] Combined with intermittent aerial assaults on IRGC weapons

depots and arms transfers in Syria, and the covert attacks on Natanz and potentially other sites inside Iran, Israel's strategy of steadily bleeding Iran was playing
out from the eastern Mediterranean to some of the most secure sites inside Iran.

Iran had limited means with which to respond without triggering escalation.
The IRGC is believed to have been behind a string of tit-for-tat assaults against
Israeli shipping, including a suspected limpet mine attack in February 2021 on
the MV *Helios Ray*, a cargo vessel operated by the eponymous Tel Aviv–based
company;[19] and possible missile attacks in the Gulf of Oman in March and July
on the container vessels *Lori*, operated by Haifa-based XT Management Ltd.,
and *Tyndall*, which had been previously operated by Israeli billionaire Eyal Ofer's
Zodiac Maritime before being sold months earlier.[20] Also in July, a suicide drone
struck the *Mercer Street* tanker off the coast of Oman, killing the ship's Romanian
captain and British security officer. Iran was identified as the culprit, and a semi-
official Iranian news site claimed the attack was in response to an Israeli bombing
in Syria days earlier which had killed two commanders, one from Hezbollah and
another from the IRGC.[21]

Gazan Spear: The 11-Day War

Those limited attacks messaged Iran's tenacity, but also betrayed its limitations
in countering Israeli aggression. While Israel hit targets deep in Iranian territory,
and assassinated prominent officials, Iran responded with attacks on merchant
vessels owned or formerly owned by Israeli nationals. Iran could not run operations inside Israel, and as its 2012 spree of operations from Georgia to Thailand
showed, Iran could not easily hit Israeli officials in third-party countries either.
As much as Iran aspired to have such capability and reach, it did not need it to
threaten Israel. Iran's clients in Lebanon and Gaza served that purpose. Iran's
strategic approach toward Israel was similarly long term, but instead of bleeding
Israel slowly, Iran focused on building its clients into formidable militaries that
Israel could not easily defeat. The IRGC was steadily improving the weapons
and weapons-production capacity of its clients, and even designed rocket and
missile variants specifically for their use. Those variants were simpler, cheaper,
and easier to produce for groups that lacked the resources and industrial infrastructure of a state. Following that approach, Iran updated and expanded the
arsenals of Hezbollah in Lebanon, and Hamas and Palestinian Islamic Jihad
(PIJ) in Gaza.

The 11-day war between Gaza factions and Israel in mid-May showcased
the fruits of that labor. Following several restive weeks between Arabs and Jews
marked by protests and communal violence, Hamas began a series of massive
rocket barrages into Israel. Throughout the short engagement, Hamas and PIJ

launched over 4,300 rockets from Gaza, most aimed at southern Israeli cities, such as Ashkelon, Ashdod, and Beersheba, but others striking as far as Tel Aviv and Jerusalem. The sheer scale of the volleys was unprecedented. In one five-minute stretch alone, Hamas and PIJ fired over 130 rockets at Tel Aviv.[22] Hamas unveiled a new suicide drone variant during the fight, nicknamed the "Shahab" ("meteor"), which became the first precision-guided munition to be used by the Gaza factions. At least six were flown into Israel during the short conflict and all were intercepted by air defenses.[23] Another armed drone was shot down as it entered Israeli airspace over Beit She'an near the border with Jordan. Israeli officials blamed Iran, claiming the drone had been launched from either Syria or Iraq.[24] (The next week a major explosion occurred at a petrochemical plant near Esfahan linked to Iran's drone program, injuring nine workers. The cause of the explosion was unclear, but it was suspected to be Israeli retaliation.)[25] The immense volleys of explosive projectiles and drones were intended to strain and evade Israel's state-of-the-art Iron Dome air defense system, which until then had a nearly flawless 99 percent kill rate. Iron Dome proved largely effective, eliminating 90 percent of strikes entering Israeli territory, but the barrages also succeeded in overwhelming the system, increasing the failure rate. In all, around 130 rockets landed inside Israel and killed 11 civilians, including two children.

Israel responded to the attacks with hundreds of airstrikes against Hamas and PIJ positions in Gaza, many of which were intentionally located within multistory civilian buildings. In total, the IDF destroyed 258 buildings, severely damaging hundreds of others, and struck over 100 kilometers of underground tunnels. For Israel's military, this was likened to "mowing the grass," a routine, periodic, and necessary degrading of the enemy's military strength and capabilities.[26] The damage done to Hamas and PIJ was indeed severe, but so too was the civilian toll. Around 200 civilians in Gaza were killed, a third of whom were children.[27] Another 52,000 civilians were displaced, most of whom sought refuge in UN-run schools.[28]

Hamas declared the operation victorious, despite ordinary Gazans suffering disproportionately as a result. Outwardly, the war achieved little for Hamas and PIJ. Many of their factories, warehouses, launch sites, and tunnels were destroyed, and an estimated 200 of their fighters were killed. The Israeli military inflicted much more damage on Gaza than Hamas and PIJ managed to exact on Israel. Yet, proportional carnage was not the aim. Rather, Hamas and PIJ were able to display their enhancing capabilities and massive stockpile of domestically built munitions. Their arsenal of Badr-3 rockets and Shahab drones were the product of Iranian assistance.[29] Hamas and PIJ managed to retain much of their arsenal despite the immensity of Israel's counteroffensive. Israeli officials estimated the collective stockpile of the Gazan factions to be around 29,000 rockets prior to the conflict, with at least half of those surviving. That stockpile was likely to rapidly increase once production facilities were brought back online.[30]

The conflict made one thing clear: Gaza was steadily advancing its military industries with Iran's help. Their rockets were cheap, easy to build, concealable, and when launched en masse, could penetrate Iron Dome defenses. Tel Aviv and Jerusalem could be hit. Iran had sharpened its spear, and its proxies were holding it. Although it could not respond to Israel's covert attacks in kind, Iran had honed its clients into a vexing threat to Israel. Israel had no easy solutions to the challenges posed by Hezbollah and the Gazan factions, and their steadily improving aerial capabilities and expanding stockpiles were putting Israel's population centers in increasing danger. Even though Israel held an edge when it came to escalatory options and abilities, Iran's quest to encircle Israel was steadily progressing. Neither side had effectively deterred the other, and their war was far from over.

Shifting Sands of a New Era

Iran's forward-leaning posture had advanced its strategic aims in certain respects. Through the IRGC, Iran had become a major player in several regional states. With its network of clients and forward-deployed military advisors and assets, the IRGC had established a near-contiguous bloc of allied geography from Iran to the Mediterranean. That success produced the semblance of a burgeoning, formidable challenge to the United States and its partners, wherein Iran's self-styled "Axis of Resistance" could be seen—particularly by Tehran and its satellites—as an alternative to the U.S.-dominated status quo. The addition of the Houthis in Yemen to that matrix expanded the scope of what Iran could achieve. Beyond its northern arc of Iraq, Syria, and Lebanon, with Gaza as a nearby outpost, Yemen provided Iran access to the Red Sea and the Gulf of Aden, and enabled it to threaten the states of the Arabian Peninsula. Were Iran playing a game of Risk, its pieces would be covering a good portion of the board and replacing those of other players one by one.

Yet, the same behavior that had spread Iran's military power across the region was also pushing its adversaries closer together. With the United States messaging a desire to reduce its Middle East engagements, Arab states concerned about Iran were forced to reconsider their options. Donald Trump in many ways had been a false messiah for those seeking a muscular solution to the Iran problem. He spoke tough words, took rash actions, and was enthusiastic about imposing harsh economic sanctions and, at least initially, assassinating Soleimani.[1] When those steps did not compel Iran to concede, however, Trump was reluctant to push further. He was not willing to go to war with Iran, neither in a limited or open manner. For all of his bluster, Trump was wary of war, at least as he understood it. After the attacks on Saudi Arabia's Aramco complex and on U.S. forces at Ayn al-Assad, it became evident to regional leaders that the Trump administration would not pursue its Iran agenda any further. Were Iran to be contained, it would need to be either placated through détentes, which would likely occur only if Arab states conceded to Iran, or through a more focused regional security arrangement. Some mixture of the two might also be necessary.

Such an idea was not new. Arab states had originally organized the Gulf Cooperation Council (GCC) as a retort to Iran's 1979 revolution. The GCC had not amounted to the security bloc its architects envisioned. While Gulf states were able to utilize GCC security mechanisms to end Bahrain's protest movement during the Arab Spring, there was no unity when it came to Iran, and even less confidence in the prospect of military confrontation. Israel was the only regional state that actively pushed back against Iran through military means, and took the threat posed by Iran more seriously than any other. It possessed the most technologically advanced and capable military in the region, and was unmatched in terms of espionage and covert operations. For the Gulf Arabs to develop a regionally based approach to contain Iran's reach and deter its aggressive behavior, partnering with Israel would be essential.

The Abraham Accords

Saudi Arabia and the UAE had already been growing closer to Israel over the past decade, and had developed bilateral connections through their military and intelligence services. The domestic political hurdles that had previously hindered engagement with Israel had been slowly ebbing, especially among younger Arabs in the Gulf. Although sympathy for the Palestinians remained strong, support for the Gaza factions had dampened due to their association with Iran, particularly in the wake of the Syrian conflict. Hezbollah had lost much of its appeal among Sunnis for the same reason, and was regarded more for its role in oppressing Sunni Arabs than for its stance against Israel. The outlawing of the Muslim Brotherhood in Saudi Arabia and the UAE also made it risky to express any outward support for Hamas and its associates.

The only thing keeping certain Gulf states and Israel apart were the vestiges of 20th-century politics and a lack of will. For some states, the menace of an unchecked Iran motivated change. The Trump administration's Israel-centered regional diplomacy helped facilitate a coming together of both sides. From August through December 2020, Washington helped foster the normalization of relations between Israel and four Arab states. The effort was billed as the Abraham Accords, drawing on the shared ancestral and religious lineages that both Arabs and Jews share with the prophet Abraham.

The UAE was the first to initiate formal ties with Israel. That effort was put in jeopardy when Prime Minister Netanyahu announced in May his intention to annex parts of the West Bank, including the whole of the Jordan River valley. Seeking to stop Israel from effectively killing the prospect of a future and viable

Palestinian state, as well as enraging much of the region, the UAE's ambassador to the United States, Yousef al-Otaiba, published an op-ed in Hebrew that ran on the front page of the *Yedioth Ahronoth* newspaper in late June. Addressing the Israeli people, al-Otaiba described both the benefits that normalization would bring and its impossibility were annexation of the West Bank to go forward. "Recently, Israeli leaders have promoted excited talk about normalization of relations with the United Arab Emirates and other Arab states. But Israeli plans for annexation and talk of normalization are a contradiction," he wrote. The ambassador cautioned:

> A unilateral and deliberate act, annexation is the illegal seizure of Palestinian land. It defies the Arab—and indeed the international—consensus on the Palestinian right to self-determination. It will ignite violence and rouse extremists. It will send shockwaves around the region, especially in Jordan, whose stability—often taken for granted—benefits the entire region, particularly Israel.

The Emirati envoy further described how Emirati-Israeli relations could bring strategic and economic benefits to both sides, writing:

> With the region's two most capable militaries, common concerns about terrorism and aggression, and a deep and long relationship with the United States, the UAE and Israel could form closer and more effective security cooperation. . . . As the two most advanced and diversified economies in the region, expanded business and financial ties could accelerate growth and stability across the Middle East.[2]

Al-Otaiba's gesture and message connected with Israel's leadership. Netanyahu put the annexation plan on hold and pursued formal relations with Arab states instead. The UAE and Israel announced a normalization in ties in August.[3] Bahrain followed, and established normalization with Israel a month later. The Trump administration then pressed for additional commitments from other Arab states, granting quid pro quos as inducements. Sudan established relations with Israel in October, and in return, was removed from the U.S. State Department's list of terrorism-supporting states (which also required a $335 million payment for restitution) and gained access to $1 billion in annual loans from the World Bank.[4] In December, Morocco agreed to normalize ties in exchange for the Trump administration's controversial recognition of its claim to Western Sahara.[5]

Riyadh also explored establishing formal relations with Israel. In November, Netanyahu made an unannounced trip to Saudi Arabia, where he held a secret meeting with Mohammed bin Salman (MBS) in a northern seaside town along the Red Sea—an area renamed Neom by the crown prince and envisioned as a future economic and social hub for the country. Yossi Cohen, the head of Israel's Mossad, attended the two-hour meeting, which was believed to have been facilitated by Secretary of State Mike Pompeo, who had visited Jerusalem days earlier, and was also in Saudi Arabia at the time. The Israeli and Saudi leaders reportedly discussed a number of issues, from the prospect of normalization to how to deal with Iran. Much anticipation surrounded the event once it was revealed by Israeli Army radio soon after, as it appeared to be setting the stage for normalization—but it was not.[6] There was some speculation that, given Trump's electoral defeat and the election of Joe Biden earlier that month, the Saudis were hesitant to squander what could be a point of leverage with the new American administration. Biden's team was known to be supportive of the Abraham Accords and had little choice but to pursue those efforts further, which made the prospect of normalization a valuable chip that could be played later.[7] The meeting nonetheless revealed an already functioning Saudi-Israeli relationship centered on intelligence and security and active at the highest level.

The Abraham Accords gave name to something that had been slowly manifesting in the region: a convergence of Arab and Israeli strategic interests. Normalization was about more than Iran. Other factors, including Turkey's assertive behavior across the region, as well as trade and investment opportunities, also played a role. But concerns about Iran were at the forefront. There was irony to this. Since 1979, Iran's overriding strategic ambitions were twofold: to overturn the U.S.-dominated status quo in the region, and to destroy the Israeli state as a Jewish enterprise. Iran's leadership had closely held on to its anti-Zionist position, putting it front and center in foreign policy, seeing the issue as one that could unify the Muslim world against Israel and against the American power which they believed safeguarded Israel's existence. Since the 1980s, Iran had devoted much of its energy in the region to providing weapons, training, and cash to groups who sought Israel's demise. The wars of the early 21st century allowed Iran to further expand its ability to threaten the Jewish state. From Tehran's perspective, Israel's days were numbered.

Yet, while Iran was winning the zero-sum competition in the region's ground wars, it was losing politically and diplomatically. Instead of seeing Iran's march across the Middle East as a fait accompli, Arab states were pivoting in order to better deal with Iran for the long haul. Iran had helped to push Arab states and Israel closer together and to recognize their shared interests. Both Israel and the Gulf Arabs wanted to contain Iran's assertive behavior and curb its power. Israel's ties to Gulf Arab states were not new, but with normalization they would expand and lead to Israel gaining more military access to the Persian Gulf. Through its single-minded strategy, Iran had made Israel an indispensable partner for Arab states. Instead of inspiring its neighbors into adopting a shared ideological position, or coercing them to step aside, Iran's push to isolate Israel accomplished the precise opposite. Israel was more integrated than ever, and Iran remained alienated.

Regional Recalibration

The Abraham Accords were part of a broader recalibration among regional powers coinciding with the election of Joe Biden. In January 2021, the Saudi-led blockade of Qatar ended with a multilateral agreement brokered by Kuwait and the United States, which reopened borders and airspaces in exchange for a withdrawal of Qatar's international lawsuits against Saudi Arabia and vague assurances about toning down negative media coverage. Qatar had not relented on any of its neighbors' original 13 demands.[8] Saudi Arabia also began a series of security talks with Iran hosted by Iraq's prime minister, Mustafa al-Kadhimi, in Baghdad. Through six rounds of talks in 2021, the Saudis and Iranians addressed a number of issues, but failed to reach compromise. Iran's regional behavior remained the same, and the Houthis continued to attack Saudi Arabia with increasingly destructive drone and missile strikes, which undermined any Iranian assurances.[9] The talks were nonetheless a sign of both states' willingness to engage. Relatedly, the UAE spearheaded an effort to rehabilitate Bashar al-Assad and bring him back into the Arab fold. The UAE's efforts, along with Jordan, signaled that some of the rebels' early backers had reversed their positions on the conflict, and viewed Assad's victory as all but complete.[10] Not wanting to lose out to Iran, the Arab states were once again looking for ways to increase linkages with Assad, and incentivize him, through aid and investment, away from Tehran's orbit—the same approach Saudi Arabia had spearheaded prior to the rebellion.

After two decades, the United States had also ended the war in Afghanistan, deepening its de-prioritization of the region. President Biden carried through with his campaign pledge, and guided by a deadline imposed by his predecessor, started to withdraw troops from Afghanistan in the summer of 2021. Afghan security forces began to cede territory and provincial cities across the country to the emboldened Taliban, with most giving up without a fight. The Afghan state quickly collapsed. On August 6 the Taliban entered Kabul, forcing the U.S. embassy to evacuate its staff by helicopter. Afghanistan's president, Ashraf Ghani, most of his cabinet, and other prominent officials fled the country, taking suitcases full of cash and other valuables with them as they abandoned their compatriots in a final act of dereliction. Over the next three weeks, the remaining U.S. forces made a hasty retreat, as desperate Afghans fearing reprisals from the Taliban, and foreign and dual-citizens anxious to return home, swarmed Kabul's airport hoping to make one of the final departing flights. On August 26, in the last days of evacuations, a suicide bomber from the Islamic State's regional affiliate struck the massive crowd outside the airport's entrance, killing 13 American troops and at least 170 civilians.[11] Anticipating more terrorist activity, a U.S. drone fired on a vehicle suspected of carrying a suicide bomb intended for another airport attack two days later. The strike killed at least 10, including seven children who were nearby. An investigation concluded that the car's occupants had not been terrorists, but rather ordinary civilians, whose cargo of water canisters had been mistaken for explosives.[12] It was an ugly end to a Sisyphean war. American forces were out of the country by the end of August, and the Taliban was back in power.

In the wake of its success in Libya, Turkey also sought to lower tensions in the region, leading to a series of bilateral engagements. In February 2022, Erdoğan traveled to Abu Dhabi, where he met with Mohamed bin Zayed. Beyond mutual gestures of goodwill, the two leaders explored a possible trade and investment deal between their countries. "The dialogue and cooperation of Turkey and the United Arab Emirates carries [sic] great importance for the peace and stability of our entire region," Erdoğan told reporters after the meeting.[13] A month later, Erdoğan hosted Israel's president, Isaac Herzog, in Ankara, marking the highest-level interaction between the two states in 14 years. Both leaders gave hopeful statements about improving ties, with Herzog stating: "I feel it is a great privilege for both of us to lay the foundations for the cultivation of friendly relations between our states and our peoples . . . and to build bridges that are critical for all of us."[14] In June, MBS traveled to Turkey to meet with Erdoğan, ending the feud that had been sparked by the murder of Jamal Khashoggi. In a joint statement, both leaders spoke warmly of a "new period of cooperation," and described the state of Saudi-Turkish ties as "the depth of the perfect relations."[15]

As its neighbors looked to mend fences, Iran sought a stronger partnership with China to reinforce its position in the region. To that end, Tehran and Beijing signed a 25-year strategic cooperation agreement in March 2021. The publicized portions of the deal, which had first been broached by Chinese premier Xi Jinping in a visit to Iran five years earlier, spoke more to possibilities than specifics. China pledged to invest billions in Iran through trade, infrastructure, development, security, and other programs in exchange for certain guarantees on Iranian hydrocarbons. "China is a friend for hard times," said Iran's foreign minister, Mohammad Javad Zarif, of the deal. "The history of cooperation between two ancient cultures of Iran and China dates back centuries. Signing the cooperation agreement will further strengthen the ties of the two nations."[16]

The deal was more significant for Iran than China, and was indicative of Iran's desire for Eurasian powers to serve as a bulwark to Western pressure. Even though Iran and China were in harmony when it came to the United States, China's interests in the Middle East were broad. China was the top trading partner with the GCC, including with Saudi Arabia and the UAE.[17] The oil and wealth of Gulf Arab states made them important, and China was unlikely to upset those relations by tipping the regional balance in Iran's favor. That dynamic made the agreement a curiosity with an uncertain future. An early result, however, was Iran's admission to the Shanghai Cooperation Organization (SCO) in September. Iran first applied to become a member of the China-led group—which also included Russia, India, Pakistan, and Central Asian states—in 2008, after having obtained observer status in 2004.[18] The realization of that ambition was a moment of prestige for Iran, and came at a time when it was otherwise isolated. In true balancing fashion, China paired Iran's membership with inviting Saudi Arabia, Qatar, and Egypt into the SCO as "dialogue partners."[19]

Biden's Inheritance

Upon taking office, President Biden sought to reverse the missteps of his predecessor. In foreign policy, that meant pivoting away from Trump's transactional approach, and recommitting the United States to its international allies and partners. The shift was starkest in Europe and the Middle East, where Trump's policies had weakened the NATO alliance and had heightened the standoff with Iran. The nuclear issue plagued the United States' Middle East policy. Biden's administration believed the JCPOA had addressed the problem, and Trump's withdrawal from the deal had proved fruitless. Biden was inclined to return to the agreement, and appointed Rob Malley as his Iran envoy and chief negotiator. In an interview with *MSNBC*'s Ayman Mohyeldin in early February 2022, Malley explained the administration's rationale for pursuing a deal with Iran:

> If we're not in the deal, Iran is unconstrained in its nuclear advances, and that's why we see that as of today, they are only a few weeks away from enough enriched uranium for a bomb. . . . [But] the position of Secretary Blinken and all the rest of the team, is that as of today, it is still well worth getting back into the deal. There's much still that can be salvaged, not for much longer, but as of today, our view is getting back into the deal will be profoundly [in] our national security interests, profoundly in our interests to avoid seeing Iran advance towards a bomb, and avoiding more tension and . . . another conflagration in the Middle East.[20]

The challenge for the Biden administration was that Iran was in a stronger position than when the JCPOA had been first negotiated. Iran's new president, Ebrahim Raisi—a hardline cleric and rumored possible successor to Ali

Khamenei as supreme leader—was a critic of the original agreement and un-likely to encourage compromise. Hossein Amir-Abdollahian, Iran's new foreign minister, was close to the IRGC and a strong supporter of its proxy clients. The IRGC's regional ventures were also going strong. Syria's rebellion was no longer a danger to Assad, the Gaza factions had showed their strength against Israel, the Houthis had stabilized their gains and were on the front foot in Yemen, ISIS remained territorially defeated in Iraq, and the United States had withdrawn forces from Afghanistan. Sanctions continued to dampen Iran's economy, but they were no longer a dire threat. Iran managed to steady its economy through oil sales to China and a host of complex financial schemes, including a clandes-tine banking system that enabled it "to handle tens of billions of dollars in annual trade" prohibited under American sanctions.[21] Were the Biden administration to succeed in negotiating a new agreement, the latter would likely be weaker than the original and come at the cost of sanctions, which were the most significant consequences short of military force that the United States and its regional part-ners could impose on Iran in response to its aggressive behavior.

The Biden administration also wanted to further extricate the United States from any association with the war in Yemen, which remained unpopular in Washington. The war was inexorably linked to Saudi Arabia and its crown prince, whose reputation still suffered from the murder of Jamal Khashoggi. Secretary of State Antony Blinken removed the Houthis from the State Department's list of foreign terrorist organizations shortly upon taking office. His predecessor, Mike Pompeo, had designated the Houthis only a couple of weeks earlier as a favor to Riyadh and Abu Dhabi, as well as to further ensnare Iran's foreign entanglements into the web of sanctions.[22] The Biden administration had no love for the Houthis, but was concerned, along with international aid organ-izations, that their designation would achieve little aside from complicating the distribution of aid in the country and worsening the war's toll on Yemen's people.[23] The true impact of the designation remained untested, it having lasted less than a month.

The Biden administration's pivot on Iran and Yemen chafed regional part-ners. The war in Yemen was unsettled, and the Houthis continued to attack Saudi Arabia and the UAE with destructive strikes. A Houthi missile attack on Jizan in southern Saudi Arabia killed two in December 2021, and in March 2022, a series of missiles and drones hit a desalination plant in Al Shaqeeq, a power station in Dhahran, and an Aramco distribution facility near Jeddah, among other locations.[24] The Houthis also targeted the UAE. In January, the Houthis struck Abu Dhabi's international airport and a nearby industrial area with missiles and drones, killing three; and in February 2022, Houthi missiles struck Al Dhafra Air Base. U.S.-supplied Patriot and Terminal High-Altitude Area Defense (THAAD) anti-air systems engaged the missiles in the attacks, marking THAAD's first use in combat.[25] Those attacks were outwardly part of the conflict in Yemen, but also were related to Iran, whose technology transfers and military support had enabled the Houthis' long-distance strike capability and steadily improved the effectiveness of their attacks.[26]

Although Iran's aid to non-state groups was a problem, Washington and Western Europe were more concerned about its nuclear program. The nuclear issue concerned regional partners, too, but the pressing threat remained Iran's direct aggression and support to proxies. Were a nuclear deal to be robust and expansive, to include Iran's regional behavior and its missile program, it would have been welcomed in the region. However, initial rumors about the Biden administration's intentions suggested that any agreement was likely to be more permissive than its predecessor, with shorter timelines, fewer limitations, and no meaningful rollbacks of Iran's enrichment capabilities. America's partners were not happy. Israel, Saudi Arabia, and the UAE all wanted to keep the pressure on Iran, and in lieu of any better ideas, keep sanctions in place. While Israel actively engaged in covert attacks to disrupt Iran's nuclear and strategic programs, the Arab states felt unable to challenge Iran on their own.

Those concerns increased as Iran's actions grew bolder. On March 12, 2022, Iran fired missiles into Iraq for the second time in as many years. The strike came as retribution for a sabotage attack on an IRGC drone facility in Kermanshah a month earlier, which had been blamed on Israel. In a predawn operation, the IRGC launched a barrage of 12 cruise missiles at a gated compound in Erbil. The missiles struck a large mansion owned by a prominent Kurdish businessman, whose family had been away. No one was injured despite the home being destroyed. Iran claimed the building had been used by Mossad operatives as a control center, but no evidence supported it.[27] Iraq's government condemned the strike, as did Washington. There were no other consequences. Iran's attack, regardless of the target, reaffirmed Iran's resolve to retaliate with force, and further displayed its ability to strike accurately beyond its borders. Iraq was caught in the middle and was powerless to respond.

In the midst of the provocations by Iran and its proxies, the U.S. military held quiet talks with Arab and Israeli counterparts in March to discuss ways of countering aerial threats. Held in the Egyptian tourist enclave of Sharm El Sheikh, the meeting brought together the military chiefs of Saudi Arabia, Egypt, Jordan, and Qatar, along with a military representative from the UAE, to explore avenues for regional military coordination for defending against air attacks from Iran. General Frank McKenzie, the outgoing CENTCOM commander, served as the American envoy and was charged with advancing an idea of how Arab governments and Israel could integrate, to some limited extent, their radars, early warning systems, and perhaps anti-air networks to develop a larger security umbrella for all involved. As had been the case in other American-led attempts

to encourage coordination and interoperability among regional partners, parochial interests, disagreements, and worries about antagonizing Iran, particularly
by the UAE, all reduced what could be achieved. Although the participants reportedly "reached agreement in principle on procedures for rapid notification
when aerial threats are detected," the agreement was non-binding. Yet, even if
the meeting did not move the needle toward any sort of Israeli-Arab military alliance, it did reinforce that Israel and leading Arab states shared certain concerns
and were at least open to considering how to deal with them collectively.[28]

Partnerships in Crisis and China's Deepening Role

In late March 2022, Israel hosted a public-facing event in the Negev desert that
highlighted how quickly its relations with certain Arab states had transformed.
The inaugural Arab-Israeli summit brought together the top diplomats from
Israel, the United States, Bahrain, Egypt, Morocco, and the UAE for the first time
to discuss common concerns. Ostensibly, the Negev Forum (as the Biden administration would later call it) was a continuation of the ongoing discussions about
how to build on the Abraham Accords and deal with Iran. Israel was the most
bullish about forging a coordinated network among its newfound Arab partners.
As Yair Lapid, Israel's foreign minister, told reporters: "What we are doing here
is making history—building a new regional architecture based on progress, technology, religious tolerance, security and intelligence cooperation. . . . This new
architecture, the shared capabilities we are [building] intimidates and deters
our common enemies, first and foremost Iran and its proxies." Privately, the
discussions provided an opportunity for regional envoys to press for assurances
from the United States on its commitments to the region, and for the United
States to seek support from its partners on an issue which had become both the
Biden administration's foreign policy priority and something that had further
strained its regional relations: Russia's war on Ukraine.[29]

   The Russian invasion of Ukraine a month earlier had been a naked imperialist effort driven by Vladimir Putin and his inner circle. It involved a greater
power using its might to deny autonomy to a smaller neighbor and incorporate
its territory. For the West and its allies, Ukraine's pro-democracy movement was
an inspiring and sympathetic cause. The blowback against Russia was necessarily swift, as Western states and leading Asian democracies placed extensive
economic sanctions on Russia, which replaced Iran as the most sanctioned state
in the world.[30] With one decision, Putin had forced the proponents of democracy back together. The gradual weakening of NATO and disunification of the
West that had been ongoing since 9/11 and that had intensified under President
Trump almost instantaneously reversed. At least for a time, democracies had a

common cause and a common enemy. The threat of authoritarianism and where it could lead was plain for all to see.

Reactions were more mixed in the Global South and among authoritarian regimes. In the immediate wake of the invasion, 141 member states voted to adopt a UN General Assembly motion calling for Russia's unilateral withdrawal from Ukrainian territory. Syria was one of five countries to vote against the UN resolution, and Iran and Iraq were among 35 others who abstained. The rest of the Middle East voted in favor.[31] However, that early willingness to condemn Russia's actions did not translate to an appetite for isolating Russia through sanctions and boycotts. Instead of galvanizing support for Ukraine, the war exposed the region's indifference. Iran relied on Russian support in a number of areas, and was not about to join hands with the West. Turkey condemned the war, but its broad economic ties with Russia, and overlapping interests in Syria, inhibited support for sanctions. Israel's relationship was also complicated. Russian-speaking Jews were Israel's largest minority community, and Israel relied on Russia's acquiescence in Syria to allow for strikes against the IRGC and Hezbollah. Saudi Arabia and the UAE viewed Russia as a useful counter-weight to the United States, an important defense partner, and given its status as a permanent member of the UN Security Council, a relationship too valuable to disregard. The UAE and Russia also had shared interests in Libya. And even though one would suspect that Riyadh and Abu Dhabi, given their experience with Iran, would side with Ukraine out of solidarity with smaller states standing up to bullying neighbors, they did not.

The Ukraine crisis sharpened contradictions in the region and exposed lingering tensions with the West. As a rotating member of the UN Security Council, the UAE refused to censure Russia's invasion. When oil prices spiked early in the war, neither Saudi Arabia nor the UAE was willing to discuss increasing petroleum output with the Biden administration, with their de facto rulers reportedly declining to take calls from the U.S. president.[32] Further, Saudi Arabia provocatively announced intentions to possibly begin pricing some of its oil sales to China in yuan, which would help make the latter a reserve currency and challenge the U.S. dollar.[33] Those moves were taken as signs of Saudi and Emirati discontent, particularly over Biden's policies toward Iran and Yemen, but also highlighted their penchant of blaming the United States for their security dilemmas. After all, the United States was supporting their defense more than any other foreign power. By contrast, Russia and China were the main enablers of Iran's adventurism. Both powers helped insulate Iran's regime from outside pressure, including through their seats on the UN Security Council and through sanctions busting. Both also pushed for a return to the nuclear deal, and required less compromise from Iran than Western states in the P5 + 1 construct. Iran's regional empowerment had been facilitated by the support and acquiescence of

Moscow and Beijing, both of which refused to press Tehran to change its beha-vior. If Russia and China were alternative partners to the United States for the Gulf Arabs, they promised little relief regarding Iran.

An unintended consequence of the West's sanctions campaign against Russia was spiking inflation and energy costs. High oil prices also diminished the impact of sanctions, with Russia still able to sell oil to China, India, and other willing buyers. To help limit inflationary pressures and bring down the cost of fuel, Washington needed the Saudi-led Organization of the Petroleum Exporting Countries (OPEC) to agree to a substantial increase in oil production. However, relations remained tense between Washington and Riyadh. During his campaign, Biden had pledged to reduce Saudi influence in Washington, end arms sales related to the war in Yemen, and hold MBS accountable for his role in Khashoggi's murder. In one debate in 2019, Biden was particularly im-politic to that end, stating that there was "very little social redeeming value in the present government in Saudi Arabia," calling the government a "pariah," and describing its war in Yemen as "murdering children."[34] In February 2021, shortly after taking office, the Biden administration released a declassified report on Khashoggi's death by the intelligence community, which concluded: "We assess that Saudi Arabia's Crown Prince Muhammad bin Salman approved an opera-tion in Istanbul, Turkey to capture or kill Saudi journalist Jamal Khashoggi."[35] The administration followed the report with a series of sanctions imposed on some of the security officials and operatives involved in the murder, including a travel ban on the former Saudi intelligence chief, but stopped short of taking actions against the crown prince. Relations with Saudi Arabia were deemed too important, and the White House feared any sanctions against MBS would risk a rupture in ties.[36]

Bilateral relations suffered nonetheless. President Biden's statements and the publicized intelligence report cast a pall over Saudi-American engagement, and undermined Washington's attempts to encourage the kingdom's support fol-lowing the Ukraine crisis. Yet, even as problems with Washington lingered, MBS took steps to reduce his country's tensions elsewhere, and sought ways to end the quagmire in Yemen—a chief concern in Washington. In early April, a UN-brokered ceasefire between Yemen's warring parties took effect. The truce was the first significant break in the six-year conflict, and included provisions that allowed for a resumption of fuel ships to the Houthi-controlled Hodeidah port and for the resumption of international flights to and from Sanaa.[37] Days later, Yemen's president, Abd Rabbuh Mansour Hadi, announced his intention to step down from office in favor of a new eight-person governing council composed of representatives from parts of the political and tribal spectrum. Hadi's resignation and the council's establishment had been orchestrated by Saudi Arabia as a way to expedite a shift in the conflict. The council, with half its members chosen by

Riyadh and the other half by Abu Dhabi, became the head of Yemen's internationally recognized government, and although its prospects were uncertain, it signaled Riyadh's desire to find a way out of the war.[38]

In June, MBS traveled to Ankara, where he met with President Erdoğan. The visit had come as part of Saudi-Turkish efforts to repair relations severely damaged by the Khashoggi affair. Whatever ill-will might have lingered was put aside for the visit, which presented a warm and fraternal relationship between the Saudi and Turkish leaders. In the end, the bitter rivalry was resolved through mutual pragmatism. Turkey's soaring inflation necessitated increased foreign trade and investment, and Saudi Arabia's desire to reposition itself and diversify its economy required a reset in its regional approach.[39]

Relations with Washington were less easily repaired, even if both sides grudgingly desired it. The Biden administration hailed Saudi Arabia's steps to end the war in Yemen, which helped pave the way for the president's visit to Saudi Arabia in mid-July. That visit, where he met with MBS and King Salman in an attempt to smooth ties and encourage an increase in oil production, was a significant change in posture from the American president and a testament to how critical Saudi Arabia remained to broader U.S. foreign policy. The tension in Biden's short and cordial meeting with MBS in Jeddah was symbolized in their greeting, with the two leaders preferring a pandemic-appropriate fist bump in lieu of a traditional handshake. Speaking to the press after the meeting, Biden stated that he had confronted MBS about Khashoggi's assassination, and stated that he believed the latter had been personally involved—a claim denied by Saudi officials. Despite disagreements over the details in that exchange, the meeting resulted in several small gestures between the two sides. The most significant concerned relations with Israel, and included Saudi Arabia's decision to open its airspace to civilian aircraft flying to and from Israel; and the withdrawal of a small U.S. peacekeeping detachment from the Red Sea islands of Tiran and Sanafir, which required Israeli approval due to their strategic location near the Gulf of Aqabah. Those moves were small, and short of normalization, but important steps toward a potential Israeli-Saudi rapprochement.[40]

The next day Biden held a conference with the heads of the five GCC states, plus Jordan, Egypt, and Iraq. Above all, the purpose of the meeting was to reassure the attendees of the United States' enduring commitment to them and to the region. As the president stated in his remarks:

> Let me state clearly that the United States is going to remain an active, engaged partner in the Middle East. As the world grows more competitive and the challenges we face more complex, it is only becoming clearer to me that—how closely interwoven America's interests are with the successes of the Middle East. We will not walk away and leave

a vacuum to be filled by China, Russia, or Iran. And we'll seek to build
on this moment with active, principled American leadership.[41]

Biden detailed America's security engagement and defense cooperation in the
Middle East, including in the maritime domain and in air defense. He also spoke
to America's long-standing counterterrorism effort, military capacity to meet
new and existing challenges, the common interests that the United States and
regional partners shared in the "rules-based international order," and that while
his administration was pursuing diplomatic avenues to constrain Iran's nuclear
program, it remained "committed to ensuring that Iran never gets a nuclear
weapon." The message from Washington was firm: it was invested in the region's
security and committed to its future.[42]

If the president's remarks were any indication, it was clear that he understood
that partner states in the Middle East had severe doubts about America's commitment to the region, and that this doubt was damaging relations and hastening
a political separation. Had simply delivering that message been the main goal
of Biden's visit, it might well have been achieved. However, if it had been to improve relations with Saudi Arabia and motivate it to side with the West in OPEC,
it failed. In its next meeting weeks later, OPEC agreed to raise oil production
by a negligible amount. The 100,000-barrels-per-day increase announced in
early August was far less than the almost 650,000 barrels per day the cartel had
agreed to in its previous meetings, and would have no meaningful impact on
global oil prices or inflation. The move was roundly considered a snub to Biden
by the Saudi-led organization.[43] It was evident that Biden's charm offensive had
not swayed the kingdom, or other Gulf states, to take a greater role in isolating
Russia, and that relations were far from repaired.

When OPEC decided to cut oil production two months later, Saudi Arabia
reaffirmed its disinterest in catering to Washington's requests. The announcement to reduce production by 2 million barrels per day came after OPEC's
meeting in early October 2022, and further tested the elasticity of the U.S.-
Saudi relationship. It was the cartel's largest reduction in two years, and testi-
mony to MBS's lingering resentment toward Washington. The cut would not
only increase inflation and fuel costs, it would directly aid Russia and prolong its war on Ukraine. Adding to the outrage was a statement put out by
the Saudis that claimed the Biden administration had asked it to delay the cut
by a month. With U.S. midterm elections coming in November, the implication of the Saudi statement was that the Biden administration was trying to
get some help for Democrats in domestic politics; however, by making that
innuendo, the Saudis were seen as trying to aid the Republicans and therefore interfering in the election. Riyadh maintained that the decision had been
a purely economic one, and was driven by the decrease in crude oil prices.

Washington saw it differently.[44] As John Kirby, the National Security Council (NSC)'s spokesman, explained:

> In recent weeks, the Saudis conveyed to us—privately and publicly— their intention to reduce oil production, which they knew would increase Russian revenues and blunt the effectiveness of sanctions. That is the wrong direction. . . . We presented Saudi Arabia with analysis to show that there was no market basis to cut production targets, and that they could easily wait for the next OPEC meeting to see how things developed.[45]

Democratic lawmakers were furious. Senator Bob Menendez of New Jersey, the chairman of the Senate Foreign Relations Committee, wrote in a statement: "The United States must immediately freeze all aspects of our cooperation with Saudi Arabia, including any arms sales and security cooperation beyond what is absolutely necessary to defend U.S. personnel and interests."[46] He framed Riyadh's decision in binary terms regarding Russia's war on Ukraine, stating:

> There simply is no room to play both sides of this conflict—either you support the rest of the free world in trying to stop a war criminal from violently wiping off an entire country off of the map, or you support him. The Kingdom of Saudi Arabia chose the latter in a terrible decision driven by economic self-interest.

Senate Majority Leader Chuck Schumer took to social media to echo those sentiments, writing: "What Saudi Arabia did to help Putin continue to wage his despicable, vicious war against Ukraine will long be remembered by Americans."[47] Senator Dick Durbin of Illinois, the second-highest-ranking Democrat in the Senate, accused Saudi Arabia of never being "a trustworthy ally," and said: "It's time for our foreign policy to imagine a world without this alliance with these royal backstabbers."[48]

President Biden was similarly reflective, if not more circumspect in his comments. In an interview with *CNN*'s Jake Tapper, the president agreed that a "rethink" was in order regarding the relationship with Saudi Arabia, and warned "there's going to be some consequences for what they've done with Russia." Biden maintained that his visit to the kingdom in July was about reassuring America's partners, not trying to make a deal on oil.[49] But the divide between Washington and its Gulf Arab partners had become apparent. Those relationships were no longer partnerships or alliances based on mutual loyalties. Regional states wanted more independence and wanted to compromise less. As Bernard Haykel wrote about Saudi decision-making concerning OPEC in the wake of Russia's invasion: "When the Saudis increase output, it will be because doing so is in their own interest. They will not risk alienating Russia by taking America's side. But they will not risk their own economic future, either."[50] With their cut in October, the Saudis enunciated that placating the United States was no longer in their interest. In doing so, the kingdom accelerated the decline in its relations with America, and positioned itself as a transactional actor whose policy choices would no longer be determined by a desire for partnership with the West.

As Riyadh was distancing from Washington, it was drawing closer to Beijing. With his visit to Saudi Arabia in December as part of a broader Middle East summit, Chinese premier Xi Jinping signaled China's ambition to deepen relations within the region. Xi's tête-à-tête with MBS was markedly different from the latter's brief meeting with President Biden in July. Pictures of the two leaders showed friendly exchanges, smiles, and mutual affection. Their meeting resulted in a lengthy joint statement, which reflected extensive alignment on numerous political, economic, and strategic issues. Perhaps most importantly to Xi, Saudi Arabia declared its commitment to China's "one China" policy, which meant opposing the West's positions on Taiwan and Hong Kong. The two sides also agreed to deepen commitment to China's Belt and Road initiative, which entailed both increased investment from Saudi companies and "enhancing the Kingdom's location as a regional center for Chinese companies in producing and exporting the products of energy sector [sic]." On defense and security, both countries "affirmed their determination to develop cooperation and coordination," and agreed to develop initiatives related to nuclear energy, space, and artificial intelligence, among many more. For its part, China pledged support for the kingdom's security and opposition to "any actions that would interfere in the internal affairs of the Kingdom of Saudi Arabia," and rejected "any attacks targeting civilians, civilian facilities, territories, and Saudi interests"—an unsubtle yet impotent rebuke of Iran.[51]

The next day, Xi held a broader Chinese-Arab summit in Riyadh, which brought together officials from 21 Arab states and the Palestinian Authority for a series of multilateral conferences and bilateral meetings. By the end of the summit, China had "signed at least thirty-four agreements with regional firms during the tour, valued at about $50 billion."[52] The final communiqué, released jointly by China and the participating Arab governments, again showed broad alignment on numerous areas where there was disagreement with the West. On the issue of human rights, the joint statement called for "rejecting the politicization of human rights issues and using them as a tool to put pressure on states and interfere in their internal affairs." Similarly, on the issues of democracy and governance, the statement called for respecting independence, and "refusing to interfere in the internal affairs of states under the pretext of preserving democracy."

Finally, as it had with Saudi Arabia, China got the attendees to pledge their commitment to the "one China" policy, and affirm China's positions on Taiwan and Hong Kong.[53] Xi summed up the tenor of his visit in an article published by the Saudi newspaper *Al Riyadh*, wherein he wrote that the trip "will usher in a new era in China's relations with the Arab world, with Arab states of the Gulf and with Saudi Arabia." He also took aim at Washington, writing "the Arab people value independence, oppose external interference, stand up to power politics and high-handedness, and always seek to make progress."[54]

Iran under Pressure

Xi Jinping's Arab tour showcased China's attempt to balance its interests between Iran and Gulf Arab states. That allowed Xi to engage with Arab states on a number of fronts, but it also limited what China could deliver in terms of security. Iran was under no real pressure from China to abandon its strategic policies or alter its behavior. On the contrary, Iran's belligerence toward the West suited Beijing. It also suited Russia, to whom Iran became a valuable ally in the war on Ukraine. Unlike its neighbors, Iran did not hide its support for Russia behind a smokescreen of neutrality. Iran engaged in the same semantic gymnastics in its statements on the war as many other states, in that it called for peace without holding Russia accountable for its aggression, but through other actions, its military support in particular, its partisanship was betrayed. Aiding Russia's war, even as it was still mired in hostilities elsewhere, made Iran's gambit dangerous and the outcome uncertain. Involvement in Ukraine had expanded the scope of Iran's strategic behavior, and presaged a possible future for the Islamic Republic as an extra-regional player and a stalwart partisan in the competition between the United States and Eurasian powers. Given Iran's other ventures, especially its conflict with Israel and nuclear showdown with the West, engaging in further adventurism underscored the risks the regime was willing to take in pursuit of its objectives.

In that way, the Ukraine conflict came at a perilous time for Iran, and coincided with its intensifying shadow war with Israel. Iran's thirst for revenge for the assassination of Mohsen Fakhrizadeh and other attacks attributed to Israel was ongoing and unsated. In February 2022, two weeks before Russia's invasion of Ukraine, Israeli media drew attention to Iran's persistent pursuit of retaliation by reporting that Mossad had foiled 12 assassination plots over the previous two years in Turkey alone with the help of Turkish intelligence.[55] A peculiar incident in April drew further attention to that issue. Israeli television aired a video confession of an alleged Quds Force operative named Mansour Rasouli, who had been detained and interrogated by Mossad agents, most remarkably, inside

Iran. In the video, Rasouli admits to having been involved in plans to kill several individuals—an Israeli diplomat in Turkey, an American general stationed in Germany, and a French intellectual—before apologizing for his actions and disavowing any further involvement.[56] Rasouli was released after his confession, but later recanted those statements in a video posted to social media during which he claimed to have been coerced to give false statements under torture and threats.[57]

Weeks later, Israeli intelligence reportedly assassinated Colonel Hassan Sayyad Khodaei, a senior Quds Force officer and veteran of the Syrian war, who was shot to death in May outside his Tehran home by motorcycle-borne assailants. Iranian media called Khodaei's death a martyrdom, and suggested a foreign hand.[58] Reports in Western media cited unnamed Israeli officials who acknowledged Mossad's role, and alleged that Khodaei had played a pivotal part in Unit 840, a section of the Quds Force charged with assassination and terrorism operations, and had been involved in the same failed plots described by Rasouli.[59] Days later, another high-ranking Quds Force officer, Colonel Ali Ismailzadeh, died under mysterious circumstances at his home in Karaj. The Saudi-funded, London-based news organization *Iran International* cited unnamed sources in claiming that Ismailzadeh had been killed by IRGC counterintelligence for his connection to Khodaei's case.[60] Iranian media rejected those allegations as "fake news," but gave conflicting accounts of his death, with most suggesting that Ismailzadeh had fallen from the balcony of his home accidentally, while others called it a suicide.[61]

The ongoing attacks inside Iran were part of an evolving campaign by Israel against the IRGC. Israeli prime minister Naftali Bennett dubbed the effort the "Octopus Doctrine," using the metaphor of an octopod as Iran's regime with regional proxies as its limbs. As Bennett said in a briefing to a Knesset committee in June:

> In the past year, the state of Israel has taken action against the head of the terrorist octopus and not just against the arms as was done in previous decades. . . . The days of immunity, in which Iran attacks Israel and spreads terrorism via its regional proxies but remains unscathed, are over.[62]

The steady drip of destructive and lethal attacks inside Iran linked to Israel were the products of that approach. That included assassinations and attacks against military-linked programs, such as a quadcopter attack on a drone research facility at the Parchin military complex in late May, which killed an engineer and injured another person; and a cyber-attack on steel plants that supplied the IRGC in June.[63]

Iran was finding it difficult to respond to such incursions, but continued to seek retribution outside its borders. A vivid illustration of that effort was the botched scheme by an Iranian cell to kill Israeli tourists in Turkey. The plot was exposed by the Israeli government in early June when Foreign Minister Yair Lapid called on vacationing Israelis to avoid Istanbul and return from Turkey if possible, warning that Iranian operatives had set their sights on Israeli tourists. "They are selecting, in a random but deliberate manner, Israeli citizens with a view to kidnapping or murdering them," he said.[64] Turkish and Israeli intelligence worked together to uproot the cell, culminating in the arrest of five Iranian nationals in late June, along with the confiscation of two pistols with silencers, maps, and other targeting information. The successful counterintelligence operation was another sign of warming Turkish-Israeli relations, as well as a setback for Iran.[65] Such a visible failure was an embarrassment to the regime, and led to the sacking of the head of the IRGC's intelligence branch, Hossein Taeb, the next day. One of the supreme leader's most trusted clerical lieutenants, and a former head of the Basij paramilitary, Taeb had overseen IRGC intelligence operations for 13 years, and was the highest-ranking political casualty of Iran's inability to defend against Israeli aggression or respond to it in kind.[66] He was reassigned to the ceremonial post of advisor to IRGC chief Hossein Salami, and replaced by a senior officer, Brigadier General Mohammad Kazemi.[67]

With Iran's attempts to respond directly to Israel obstructed, it turned again to proxy forces. In mid-August, Iran-sponsored militants conducted an attack involving two Iranian-made KAS04 suicide drones on U.S. forces stationed at the al-Tanf garrison in southern Syria. The unsuccessful attack, which had been intended to inflict casualties, highlighted the small but continuing U.S. presence in Syria, where it supported partner forces in ongoing operations against the remnants of ISIS. The base at al-Tanf included U.S. troops and hundreds of fighters from the Maghaweir al-Thowra (Commandos of the Revolution) Syrian rebel group, who were responsible for a 55-kilometer zone surrounding the border crossings.[68] That strategic location kept the base in the crosshairs of the IRGC-backed militias operating on both sides of the Iraq-Syria divide. The drones used were known to be a variant associated with Kataib Hezbollah, and with the launch site of the attack occurring in Iraq's Babil province, an area where the group controls a highly secure base, the probability of the militia's involvement was high.[69] It was unclear to American officials if the strikes had been in response to an Israeli attack on positions associated with the IRGC in Syria days earlier, or if it had been more general retaliation to the ongoing pressure campaign against Iran. Either way, the Biden administration moved to establish a clear red line against such aggression, and nine days after the attack, sent two pairs of F-15E and F-16E aircraft to strike nine bunkers associated with the militia in northeast Syria. The strikes destroyed ammunition dumps and logistical facilities, and were calibrated to deter further aggression while also avoiding causalities.[70] Seeking to draw a red line of their own, IRGC-led militias replied the next day with rocket attacks against two U.S. bases near Deir Ezzor—Mission Support Sites Conoco and Green Village—which injured three U.S. servicemembers. In the resulting exchange, U.S. forces used artillery, AC-130 gunships, and Ah-64 Apache helicopters against enemy positions, destroying vehicles, equipment, rocket launchers, and killing at least four militants.[71]

The Pentagon believed the IRGC had directed the Syria assaults, which further complicated U.S.-Iranian relations at a time when the Biden administration was seeking to restore the nuclear deal. Both sides had been holding indirect talks concerning aspects of a new agreement, and while progress had been made, gaps remained.[72] Seeing itself as the aggrieved party due to the Trump administration's unilateral withdrawal from the JCPOA, Iran's position had hardened, and prospects for an agreement as strong as the original were slim. Concerns had spread among the deal's critics that Washington's diplomats, and its chief Iran envoy, Rob Malley, in particular, had softened demands in order to secure Iran's participation. The attacks in Syria, as well as the Biden administration's forceful response to them, were the backdrop for renewed calls by Israel to bolster the terms of any future deal and reinforce it with a credible military threat. As Prime Minister Yair Lapid—who had succeeded Naftali Bennet in July as part of their power-sharing accord—stated in late August, a good deal for Israel "would not have an end date," and "the oversight would be tighter and it would also deal with Iran's ballistic missile program and its involvement in terror around the Middle East."[73] Lapid's comments came after Israeli defense minister Benny Gantz had met with U.S. national security advisor Jake Sullivan in Washington, wherein he pressed Israel's case to expand the parameters of negotiations and retain kinetic pressure on Iran to increase a deal's deterrent effect. Gantz left the meeting with the sense that Israel had gotten through to the Americans, but still worried that the deal Washington was willing to make would not serve Israel's security interests.[74] As Prime Minister Lapid warned: "We will act to prevent Iran from becoming a nuclear state. . . . We are not prepared to live with a nuclear threat above our heads from an extremist, violent Islamist regime."[75] Israel's actions against Iran's strategic programs were therefore unlikely to change inside a multilateral nuclear framework to which it was not a party.

A more serious hurdle to restoring the deal was Iran's decision to aid Russia. The Biden administration began warning of Iran's plan to transfer weapons to Russia in July 2022, and in August announced that Russian troops were undergoing training on drone systems in Iran.[76] Russia's war on Ukraine had not gone according to plan, and its stockpile of missiles and other munitions was dwindling. Iran was an unlikely source of resupply, but it possessed the technology, know-how, and most importantly, was willing to risk the West's wrath by becoming a party to the war. Shipments of drones reportedly began in August, and were introduced to the battlefield by Russian forces in early September. Iran vigorously denied supplying Russia with weapons initially, only to partially confess in November to having sent "a limited number" of drones to Russia before the war started. In making that confession, Iran's foreign minister, Hossein Amir-Abdollahian, feigned concern that Russia might actually be using the weapons, saying: "If [Ukraine] has any documents in their possession that Russia used Iranian drones in Ukraine, they should provide them to us. . . . If it is proven to us that Russia used Iranian drones in the war against Ukraine, we will not be indifferent to this issue."[77]

Such statements proved disingenuous. Iranian drones quickly became a cornerstone of Russia's strategy to destroy and degrade Ukraine's civilian infrastructure and power grid. The weapons were cheap, could be deployed in swarms and receive targeting coordinates while in flight. Even though they were slow, low-flying, and loud, Iran's drones overwhelmed Ukrainian anti-air defenses by sheer numbers, and their payloads, which were specifically designed for infrastructure, could be devastating upon impact.[78] Further undermining Iran's attempt at contrition, American officials announced in October that IRGC advisors had deployed to occupied Crimea to assist Russian forces in drone operations. NSC spokesman John Kirby explained in a briefing that Russian forces had encountered a number of problems in trying to use the weapons systems in battle, which prompted Iran to supply its own technical experts to improve the lethality of drone operations in the war. "The fact is this," he said. "Tehran is now directly engaged on the ground and through the provision of weapons that are impacting civilians and civilian infrastructure in Ukraine—in fact, that are killing civilians and destroying civilian infrastructure in Ukraine."[79] Later that month, a Ukrainian official told Israel's *KAN* news that 10 Iranian military advisors had been killed in strikes on Russian positions in Crimea, without providing evidence. That report was confirmed, still without evidence, by Ukraine's top security official, Oleksiy Danilov, in an interview with the *Guardian* in late November.[80]

Iran's support to Russia was part of a larger strategic convergence between the two allies. The gradual coming together of Iranian and Russian interests, from the Syrian conflict to Ukraine, was rooted in a shared aim of overturning the American-centered global order, which had produced a number of intersecting interests both in the Middle East and more broadly. The two countries had signed a general cooperation agreement in 2001, and a more detailed military cooperation pact in 2015; however, Iran's support in Ukraine signaled a turn toward a deeper and more meaningful strategic relationship.[81] In December 2022, U.S. officials reported that Iran's drone shipments were enticed by Russian pledges to provide Iran with access to sophisticated weapons systems, platforms, and technology, which could include helicopters and advanced fourth-generation fighter aircraft, for which Iranian pilots had already begun training in Russia. That corresponded with an announcement in September by Brigadier General Hamid Vahidi, Iran's air force chief, that Iran would purchase two dozen Sukhoi Su-35 multirole aircraft from Russia, which would be a marked improvement over Iran's Cold War–era fleet, deepening its air defenses and advancing its ability to use air power beyond its borders. And in January 2023, an Iranian parliamentary official stated that they expected to receive those aircraft later that year.[82] In February, Iranian military officials announced the new "Eagle 44" underground airbase in Hormozgan province, strategically located 100 miles from the Strait of Hormuz. Satellite imagery of the base, which showed an at-scale mockup of an Su-35, suggested that the base had been designed for or was being retrofitted to house a new fleet of Su-35s or similar aircraft.[83] Beyond military transfers, U.S. officials reported that Iran and Russia had plans to begin co-production of an advanced drone variant and had begun building a factory in Yelabuga, Russia, to that end.[84] Through such ventures, it became evident that Iran's participation in the war on Ukraine transcended political alignment: it was an investment in Iran's future strategic and military development. By making itself indispensable to Russia, Russia had become indebted to Iran, which had given Iran more leverage in their relationship. Iran was thus willing to risk prolonged estrangement from the West by partnering with Russia, because in so doing, Iran was expediting the benefits it would receive from their expanding partnership. Iran's actions aggravated its feud with the West, but its military and the strategic umbrella provided by Russia were both likely to grow stronger as a result.

The Iran Dilemma

As Iran was playing with fire in Ukraine, the flames of internal unrest returned to its streets at home. In mid-September 2022, furious protests erupted in response to reports of the murder of 22-year-old Mahsa Amini—a young woman who had been beaten to death by morality police for the crime of wearing insufficiently pious trousers. The cruel circumstances of Amini's death were all too familiar to the Iranian people, and especially Iranian women, who had long suffered the oppression of state security forces charged with enforcing the regime's interpretation of Islamic social mores. Within days, Amini's death reignited a new wave of anti-regime protests across the country. Demonstrations began in Tehran and spread throughout the country. Much like the protests of 2018 and 2019, young people fueled the unrest, and directed their ire against the Islamic system. They took to the streets, rebelled at their schools, and destroyed regime symbols, targeting the ubiquitous icons of the supreme leader and torching large billboards of Qassem Soleimani—an emphatic reminder of the regime's failure to cultivate a national hero.

With protests came more state violence. Civilians were beaten on the streets by security forces, as well as arrested, tortured, and disappeared. The regime's response was strongest in the provinces of Iran's periphery, where the country's ethnic minorities are most concentrated. The IRGC led militarized crackdowns, involving armored vehicles and live fire, in the Kurdish west, which included Amini's hometown of Saqqez, and in the heavily Baloch southeast.[85] Along with familiar anti-regime chants, which took aim against the supreme leader and Iranian foreign policy, the paramount rallying cry of the protests became "Zan, Zendegi, Azadi," or "Women, Life, Freedom." That simple but powerful combination of words transformed into an international symbol of the depths of discontent that had been swelling inside Iran. The regime understood that it sat on a powder keg, and calibrated its response accordingly. While regime forces used brute force and lethal tactics to quell demonstrations in minority areas where media attention did not generally focus, it relied on arrests, torture, and meting out death sentences to convicted protestors to suppress unrest more broadly. By February 2023, after months of disorder, the regime's tactics had proven partly effective. Sporadic protests continued, particularly in Zahedan, but also declined in frequency and scope.[86] Nevertheless, the protests were a stark reminder that the regime no longer had the support of the people and had failed to make inroads with post-Boomer generations. Those who had grown up under the Islamic Republic, and had no connection to life before the revolution, had come to broadly reject its sacred cows of Shiite theocracy and resistance to the West, and therefore stood against the very premise of the regime's legitimacy. What the protests and those that preceded them in earlier years had made plain was that even though another wave of heated discontent had passed, barring serious and systematic reform by the regime to its external policies and internal governance, more were bound to follow and their vehemence was likely to increase.

Combined with the regime's persistent aggression, support to Russia's war, unrelenting repression of its women, and violent crackdown on another widespread protest movement, the West's appetite to pursue diplomatic engagement with Iran dampened and the desire for punitive action intensified. The European Union adopted a series of sanctions on Iranian security officials for their role in human rights violations, and the United Kingdom debated listing the IRGC as a proscribed terrorist group.[87] Efforts to renegotiate a nuclear deal also suffered. Much of the onus of failing to reach another agreement fell on Tehran, whose diplomats remained intransigent to the types of compromise required by the United States. As Rob Malley explained in late October 2022, due to Iran's support of Russia and suppression of protests in Iran, nuclear talks were no longer a focus, stating: "It is not on our agenda. We are not going to focus on something which is inert when other things are happening . . . and we are not going to waste our time on [it] if Iran has taken the position it has taken."[88] The next month, President Biden called nuclear negotiations "dead" in an informal exchange during an election rally in California.[89] Whether an acknowledgment of the obvious or an overstatement, Biden's comment suggested dire prospects for reaching another nuclear accord.

As important as the nuclear issue was, the mounting divide between the West and Iran had made bridging that gap fraught with contradicting aims. Washington sought both to deter Iranian aggression and impose strict limitations on the regime's enrichment. It wanted to do those things to help ensure the security of its allies and partners, as well as to allow it to expend less energy in the Middle East and more in dealing with Russia and China. America's regional allies and partners, however, viewed Iran as a clear and present danger, and were much less concerned about Russian aggression in Europe or China's aspirations in the Indo-Pacific. Their advocacy to strengthen the deal prioritized their interests—interests they viewed as inadequately represented in the West's engagement with Iran.

Israel was the most vocal and influential in that regard, and had good reason to fear a deal that constrained but did not end Iran's nuclear program. A new deal would provide sanctions relief and likely insulate Iran from the threat of pressure from the West, at least for a time. And unless the agreement required significant compromises beyond the nuclear domain, Iran's behavior in other areas would not only remain unchanged, it would be further safeguarded and infused with more resources. Hostilities between Israel and Iran would endure, and Iran would have greater finances to fund its side of the conflict. Iran's wars would not end, and its ability to coerce its neighbors would not diminish. Rather, it would be in a stronger position, and more likely to press for further gains than settle for what had been achieved. A nuclear-armed Iran would be worse for the region; but a nuclear-constrained Iran would still preserve an untenable status quo.

There was no easy solution to the challenge Iran presented. A stark reminder of that came in a report by the IAEA in late February 2023, in which the agency announced that it had detected traces of uranium enriched to nearly 84 percent in Iran's Fordow facility. That number was just shy of the 90 percent threshold for weapons-grade uranium—a difference that could be made up quickly with Iran's advanced centrifuges, and a steep increase from the 60 percent enrichment level Iran claimed to be producing. Iran acknowledged the findings but denied it had been intentional. Although fluctuations in the enrichment process can occur, a variance of that degree was uncommon and worrisome. The IAEA report also found that Iran's possession of highly enriched uranium had increased by 87.1 kilograms since its last report in November, for a total stockpile of 3,760 kilograms. Of that, 87.5 kilograms were enriched to the 60 percent level, more than enough for a nuclear weapon. Altogether, the report highlighted Iran's steady escalation of its nuclear program since U.S. withdrawal from the JCPOA. As Colin Kahl, the undersecretary of defense for policy, said in a briefing to a congressional armed services committee after the IAEA's findings were released: "Iran's nuclear progress since we left the [deal] has been remarkable.... Back in 2018, when the previous administration decided to leave the [deal], it would have taken Iran about 12 months to produce one bomb's worth of fissile material. Now it would take about 12 days."[90]

Publicly the Biden administration believed that Iran still had not decided to go down the path of weaponization. But it now possessed the fissile material for several weapons and possibly, given its past and potentially secret weapons research, the knowledge for building a nuclear warhead. That progress ensured that the clock toward confrontation would continue to tick. The nuclear question, unsolved and simmering, was one part of a much larger problem. Absent fundamental change in its behavior, policies, and strategic trajectory, conflict involving Iran would endure. The nuclear question was the issue most likely to trigger military escalation, particularly with Israel, but not the only one. The tit-for-tat shadow conflict, intensifying proxy attacks, and Iran's direct aggression beyond its borders were all kindling that could spark a larger conflagration— one that could easily draw in the United States and envelop the wider region. The prospects for peace were few, the pathways to war were many.

Yet, even as Iran's approach continued at pace, many of its neighbors were looking for ways to reduce their involvement in regional hostilities. The Abraham Accords, rapprochements between Turkey, Israel, and Saudi Arabia, the end of the Qatar blockade, Saudi Arabia's desire to seek a truce in Yemen, the UAE's willingness to rehabilitate Bashar al-Assad's image and re-engage with Syria, along with its declining appetite for confronting Iran, all signaled a broad desire to move away from conflict and toward a renewed pragmatism. Parallel to those movements was China's increasing engagement in the region, which stressed economic investment and respect for sovereignty, and was unhindered by any pretense for concerns regarding human rights, democracy, or wars in Europe. Whereas the Arab-Israeli convergence and thawing inter-regional relations benefited the interests of the United States, China's engagement portended a slackening of the status quo that Washington had sought to maintain. The growing non-alignment of regional states benefited Iran most of all. As its neighbors pursued balance in their relations with foreign powers, the Islamic Republic could relish the prospect that the de-Americanization of the Middle East that it had pursued for decades was inching closer to realization.

Epilogue

On March 10, 2023, representatives of Saudi Arabia and Iran announced a surprising agreement to restore bilateral relations. The deal had been brokered by China and was the product of four days of secret meetings in Beijing. Riyadh had been exploring ways to extricate itself from its conflict with Iran since mid-2021, including through bilateral talks hosted by Iraq, but with Iran unwilling to compromise, and Houthi attacks continuing, those talks were seemingly unproductive. China's offer of mediation broke the stalemate, and brought the two sides together under a trusted, more powerful third party.[1] With China in the room, Iran's pledges were given more credibility and Saudi Arabia's promises more weight. Although the specifics of the agreement were not released, unnamed officials from both countries, as well as from the United States, suggested that it included at least assurances that Tehran would no longer facilitate attacks on Saudi Arabia by the Houthis, and that Riyadh would ensure that critical coverage on Iran's regime would be curtailed in the Saudi-funded, Persian-language *Iran International*.[2] Diplomats involved in the deal initially described it in generic terms, but soon both Saudi and Iranian officials excitedly enumerated the many ways in which bilateral cooperation could grow, including through economic, environmental, and security collaboration.[3]

Iran's détente with Saudi Arabia followed its quieter rapprochement with the UAE in August 2022, which received less fanfare from both sides.[4] Along with restored relations with Kuwait, and improving ties with Bahrain, Iran's diplomatic isolation by its Persian Gulf neighbors, which had been ongoing since 2016, was nearly over.[5] Outwardly, such overtures were signs that regional players were aiming to move past the era of competition that had heated up with the Arab Spring. Opposing Iran had not worked out well for its neighbors, and Iran's belligerence had weakened their resolve. To that end, these rapprochements were less a settling of differences than a settling of the status quo. Saudi Arabia and the UAE were no longer looking for Iran to change its ways; they simply wanted Iran to stop targeting them. Should re-establishing ties achieve that, then they were willing to live with Iran's activities elsewhere. Ending its diplomatic isolation was a victory for Iran. Not only were its adversaries seeking peace, they had capitulated in their struggle to compete and were now inclined to step aside and allow Iran's campaign to proceed in the region unmolested. Iran was the dominant power in the Persian Gulf, and its neighbors were finally coming around to that reality. They might not have seen it that way, but the leadership in Tehran undoubtedly did.

Furthermore, and especially due to the détente with Saudi Arabia, Iran was beginning to glimpse the regionwide change it had so vigorously sought. Through numerous areas where bilateral and multilateral exchanges were anticipated to occur, Iran's leaders envisioned the Arab-Iranian convergence to be setting the stage for a much broader restructuring. As Ali-Reza Enayati, Iran's newly appointed ambassador to Saudi Arabia, told Iranian reporters, "we will enter a new stage based on the formation of, or the development of arrangements for, the new regional order. This cooperation is unquestionably necessary to create a new orientation for the Persian Gulf region." Central to that was the question of regional security and how it would be policed. As Enayati describes it, "the new concept of establishing security" in the Persian Gulf should be based on cooperation instead of competition, and rely on "endogenous" militaries instead of "the presence of foreign forces." Impediments remained, however, including Israel's growing relations with Gulf Arab states. To Enayati, the "foothold" that Israel had gained in the Persian Gulf, through its defense ties with the UAE and Bahrain, was a problem in transregional cooperation and "both a threat and an obstacle to the formation of a new order."[6]

There was also the problem of the U.S. military, which remained a fixed presence in the region.

Maritime security, the central writ of the Bahrain-based U.S. Navy's Fifth Fleet, was a key area of concern that both Iran and its neighbors wanted to address, although for different reasons and in completely different ways. Iranian officials had long maintained that the Persian Gulf did not need an outside power, and the United States in particular, to protect its waters. Rather, that mission should fall to the governments of the area. Because Iran's behavior was seen by its neighbors to be the main threat to Gulf security, and the military power of the United States as the best way to address that threat, Iran's calls for a local solution to regional security rang hollow. Even as Iran was resolving its diplomatic isolation with its neighbors, its aggression at sea continued unabated. Since it stepped up its retaliation against ongoing U.S. sanctions on its oil exports in 2021, Iran's navies had "harassed, attacked or seized nearly 20 internationally flagged merchant vessels" near the Strait of Hormuz and in the Gulf of Oman.[7] Iranian authorities justified those actions by accusing the ships' operators of various infringements, from unpaid fines to smuggling oil. U.S. Navy vessels in the area often responded to distress calls by the ships targeted by Iran, and succeeded in interrupting Iranian assaults when they were able to arrive at the scene in time. But Iran's persistence also paid off, and when it did, such as in the seizure of a tanker in May that had recently left Dubai, it was a reminder that the United States could only do so much.

The UAE was particularly angry about such incidents and protested to Washington about the latter's inability to deter Iranian aggression.[8] That frustration, mixed with a strong desire to pull back from its confrontation with Iran, prompted the UAE to announce its departure from the Combined Maritime Force (CMF) in late May 2023. Even though it remained a member, that the UAE pulled its military contribution from that U.S.-led multinational maritime coalition, which was designed in part to counter the threat posed by Iran, signified the shifting dynamics at play. Unsatisfied with imperfect deterrence, the UAE was exploring ways to entice Iran into a different relationship, one that would end the latter's acts of aggression, and secure the UAE's economy and business climate.[9] Reducing its defense cooperation with the United States, at least in regard to maritime security, was a step in that direction. America's mission to defend its partners persevered nonetheless, and as Iranian piracy intensified with the summer heat, the Pentagon deployed reinforcements to the region, including warships, A-10 and F-16 attack aircraft, and thousands of Marines.[10]

Yet, with Washington's regional relations under strain, and its own relations with neighbors improving, the circumstances necessary for Iran to achieve a fundamental change in regional security were perhaps developing. Iran's ambitions to that end were clear, and the news about the UAE's departure from the CMF squarely fit its agenda. Using Abu Dhabi's distancing act from Washington as a backdrop, the commander of Iran's regular navy, Rear Admiral Shahram Irani, announced in June a plan to form a joint maritime naval alliance that would include Iran, Saudi Arabia, the UAE, Pakistan, and India. The participation of the latter two countries, who remained intractable enemies, made the announcement unconvincing, but without denials from Arab states, it seemed that Iran's initiatives with its neighbors could, at some point, expand into military cooperation, at least to a limited extent. Whether such an initiative would amount to anything of substance was unclear. More likely, such pronouncements were a reflection of the shared Saudi and Emirati desire to placate Iran, rather than meaningfully embrace it. In that way, improving relations and engagement with Iran was perhaps as much about keeping their enemy close as anything else.

More so, however, for both the UAE and Saudi Arabia, addressing tensions with Iran was about business. Regional disruption served Iran's agenda but it no longer served theirs. They needed stability and security for their economies to flourish and for foreign investment and trade to grow. As the UAE sought to safeguard its role as a logistics and commercial hub linking Europe, Asia, and

Africa, Saudi Arabia aimed at transforming its place in the world by investing deeply in things that regular people across the globe cared about, and reforming its social and economic sectors. To that end, the Saudi Private Investment Fund (PIF), a sovereign wealth fund valued at $700 billion controlled by MBS, expanded its interests into sporting leagues. By creating a competitor to the PGA Tour in LIV Golf, Saudi Arabia ignited controversy, but ultimately prevailed in compelling the former into forging a partnership that would reshape the sport. Similarly, in first purchasing Newcastle United Football Club in the English Premier League in 2021, and then by funding the transfers of numerous high-level soccer players during the 2023 summer window, such as Karim Benzama from Real Madrid, N'Golo Kante from Chelsea, and longtime Liverpool captain Jordan Henderson, and incentivizing them to join the Saudi Pro League through extremely lucrative contracts they could not have gotten elsewhere, Saudi Arabia was similarly facilitating a revolution in the sport of international soccer. Combined with his ambitious plans outlined in Vision 2030, those inroads into professional sports put a spotlight on MBS's aspirations and his desire to both transform his country and resuscitate its image. In that way, Saudi Arabia and the UAE were now playing a different game than Iran—and in that contest, where money and international integration proved decisive, Iran was not only not a threat, it presented no competition at all.

As the rivalry in the Persian Gulf was cooling, Israel's domestic political situation was heating up. In order to secure his re-election as prime minister in November 2022, Benjamin Netanyahu put together a coalition of far-right and ultra-conservative parties. Netanyahu's cabinet was marked by its inclusion of a veteran settler extremist, Itamar Ben-Gvir, the leader of the Jewish Power party. The latter was an unconventional politician, and possessed a rap sheet that included convictions for "supporting a terrorist organization and incitement to racism," among other offenses. He was also the new minister of national security and charged with some of the most sensitive issues in the country. Bringing the far right to power tested Israel's foreign relations, especially with Washington.[11] Whereas America's support for Israel was not at immediate risk, the inclusion of politicians such as Ben-Gvir and Minister of Finance Bezalel Yoel Smotrich, the leader of the Religious Zionism Party, who both openly touted racist and anti-LBGTQ views, heightened tensions and provoked criticism from the U.S. Congress.[12]

The Israeli government's extremist turn coincided with increasing violence in the West Bank and vigilantism by Palestinian militants and fanatical settlers. In response to the murders of two Jewish settlers near the village of Huwara by a Palestinian gunman in late February 2023, an angry mob from neighboring settlements rampaged through Huwara and nearby towns, expelling Arab residents from dozens of homes and burning their structures to the ground.[13]

Smotrich voiced support for the aims of the vigilantes but not their methods, telling reporters: "I think that Huwara needs to be wiped out, but the State of Israel needs to do it." That statement earned a rare rebuke from the U.S. State Department, with its spokesperson, Ned Price, calling Smotrich's words "repugnant" and "disgusting." Price added: "Just as we condemn Palestinian incitement to violence, we condemn these provocative remarks that also amount to incitement to violence. We call on Prime Minister Netanyahu and other senior officials to publicly and clearly reject and disavow these comments."[14] The vigilantism was part of a larger wave of violence spreading across the West Bank, especially in the city of Jenin, with which the Israeli military struggled to deal. In one episode, militants launched rockets from the Jenin area, the first time Palestinian factions had used such weapons in the West Bank in almost two decades. The rockets were crude and failed to hit Israeli targets, but suggested that the groups in the West Bank were seeking to mimic the tactics of their Gazan counterparts, as well as learning from them.[15]

Spiraling violence threatened to return Israel to a period reminiscent of the Second Intifada. But more unsettling to its security was the political factionalism that was eroding the social cohesion of the Jewish state. Netanyahu and coalition partners did not agree on all aspects of policy, but one area where they were in firm agreement was in their desire to reform Israel's system of checks and balances by reducing the power of the country's supreme court. Judicial oversight was the main curb to populism within Israel's democracy, and Netanyahu sought to push through a law that would give the Knesset the ability to override rulings by the court through a simple majority vote. The threat of diluting Israeli democracy, and of potentially giving extremist coalitions unchecked power, provoked a rare and impassioned protest movement from Israeli citizens and military reservists. Initial demonstrations began in early January 2023, and culminated in late March after Israel's defense minister, Yoav Gallant, was fired for calling for a halt to Netanyahu's planned judicial overhaul. Gallant, a fellow member of the prime minister's Likud Party, said that the controversial plan had "created an internal rift that poses a clear and immediate threat for Israel's national security."[16] Gallant's censure, and mounting pressure from reservists, including by hundreds of highly trained pilots, prompted Netanyahu to temporarily pause the issue. However, in July, the prime minister pressed forward with the new law. Despite massive protests against the proposed reforms, including by the tens of thousands of Israelis who took part in a five-day march from Tel Aviv to Jerusalem to voice objection to the impending vote, Netanyahu's allies in parliament passed the first part of their plan for judicial reform on July 24.[17] In a phone call the week before, President Joe Biden had also counseled Netanyahu to not rush the bill, and instead seek a broader consensus, but such sentiments from Israel's most stalwart ally had no impact.[18] As Ben-Gvir told reporters after the law was passed: "From today, Israel will be a little more democratic, a little more Jewish. . . . With God's help, this will be just the beginning."[19] As much as he was speaking about political reforms, the national security minister's comments, perhaps intentionally, also spoke to Israel's deepening divide and the internal struggle for the soul of the country that promised to follow.

Observing Israel's turmoil unfold pleased Iranian officials. As protests against the judicial overhaul and West Bank violence spiked in mid-June, Iran's supreme leader, Ali Khamenei, commented in a speech: "Now the conditions for the Zionist regime have changed compared to 70 years ago. The Zionist leaders are correct to worry about their regime not seeing its 80th anniversary." For Khamenei, Israel's eventual end as a Jewish entity was a certainty, and the unraveling of the nation's social fabric portended that demise. Iran's support to the Gaza factions was also working, and the latter's increasing expansion into the West Bank was making their cause even more difficult for Israel to overcome.[20] Iran had designs in the West Bank, too, and was accelerating its efforts to traffic weapons to clients through a complex of routes crossing through Syria and Jordan. Much of what made it into the West Bank—from Iranian manufactured automatic rifles to anti-personnel mines—was destined for Iran-backed Palestinian Islamic Jihad cells, but other weapons ended up in the hands of dealers, who controlled a clandestine arms bazaar that sold the weapons at a premium.[21] Just as Iran had done in Gaza, it was seeking to further complicate Israel's ability to manage security in the West Bank, and was beginning to see signs of success.

Strengthening the enemies of Israel in order to keep the latter ensnared in unwinnable conflicts was a direct goal of Iran's regional strategy. And from the perspective of Iran's leaders, that strategy was working. Even though the United States continued to make strides in bringing Saudi Arabia and Israel together, making a normalization of ties between the two appear to be an eventual likelihood, Israel's integration into the region was counteracted by its mounting internal strife.[22]

China's expanding role in the Middle East similarly suited Iran. Where China's influence deepened, America's sway would loosen. But such a zero-sum contest did not entirely benefit Iran. Even though China reflexively shielded Iran from Western pressure, Iran was only part of Beijing's extensive interests in the Middle East. Gulf Arab states had more to offer China economically, and peeling them away from the United States provided more strategic upside than doubling down on ties with Iran. It was unsurprising, then, when following the first China-GCC Summit in December 2022, China signed a joint statement that affirmed the UAE's position on the contested status of the Persian Gulf islands of Abu Musa and the Greater and Lesser Tunbs—islands that Iran considered an unquestionable and inseparable part of its territory.[23] That angered Iranian commentators, but provoked a muted official response because Iran was in no position to esca-late the issue.[24] China's promises made to Iran in March 2021, as part of their 25-year strategic agreement, were also not being fulfilled. When President Ebrahim Raisi visited Beijing in February 2023, the first visit to China by an Iranian pres-ident in two decades, he commented on the slow pace of China's economic in-vestment in Iran, signaling annoyance. That did not prevent Raisi from signing numerous additional bilateral deals during his visit, but it perhaps heralded that those too might go unfulfilled and never meet Tehran's expectations.[25]

China was not alone in treating Iran in such a way; Russia was also balancing its interests in the Middle East, to Iran's frustration. Despite Iran's unswaying support, Russia continued to deepen ties with Gulf Arab rivals. Following the sixth iteration of the Russia-GCC strategic dialogue in July 2023, wherein Moscow hosted the council's foreign ministers, the participants issued a joint statement that again sided with the UAE's position on the disputed islands.[26] The spokesman for Iran's foreign ministry, Nasser Kanaani, quickly released a counter declaration, reminding Russia and its Arab neighbors that the issue was not up for debate: "These islands belong to Iran forever and issuing such statements is in contradiction with the friendly relations between Iran and its neighbors." Tehran further summoned Moscow's ambassador and issued a formal protest, not that it would matter.[27] Similar to China, Russia was dragging its feet in its commitments to Iran, and through late 2023, had failed to make good on the delivery of the Su-35s that Iran had purchased and had been long expecting—an inconvenient affair that Iran's military leadership was forced to acknowledge.[28]

Iran's partnerships with China and Russia had found their limits. Neither foreign power would back Iran to the extent that it harmed their relations else-where in the region, and their ties to Tehran would continue to be offset by their interests in the other side of the Gulf. Iranian officials were likely cognizant of that fact, but probably also understood that while China and Russia's balancing did not give them an advantage, it did not give their rivals an advantage either. China's growing regional influence was important because it reduced that of the United States.[29] Iran was prepared to navigate the region's shifting order, and saw more opportunity than peril.

October 7 and Ineluctable Conflict

Iran's regional strategy had given it many cards to play against its enemies, and the threat of conflict was its most salient. The Islamic Republic's leadership was banking on the idea that fueling turmoil would somehow bring about the real-ization of their strategic goals and political dreams. Even if they believed that the ends they sought would be attained, the pathway toward those ends was unmarked and unclear. It was only through effort, experimentation, risk-taking, and learning that the way forward could be delineated and progress achieved. With its Arab rivals bested, Israel was the main impediment to Iran's aspirations in the Middle East. And the events of October 7, 2023, and what would follow, presented Iran with new opportunities to advance its agenda—an agenda that was forcing the region down a volatile and dangerous course.

The attacks of October 7 began around 6:30 a.m., just before sunrise, with a rocket barrage fired from Gaza toward southern Israel. As Israel's national alert system notified citizens of the attack, advising them to seek shelter in bunkers and basements, Hamas's audacious operation, code-named "Al-Aqsa Storm," commenced. The aerial barrage had been a diversionary tactic aimed at disguising a massive ground infiltration. Within minutes, as Iron Dome missiles intercepted rockets with deafening blasts overhead, Hamas militants targeted the detection network that Israel relied on to monitor the Gaza border. Automated and remote-controlled cameras, sensors, and machine-gun towers were destroyed by snipers and explosives delivered by multirotor drones. With Israel's military in the dark, Hamas units used bombs and bulldozers to swiftly break through walls and security barriers in at least 30 points along the Gaza-Israeli border. Hundreds of militants rushed through the openings with motorcycles and pickup trucks, with each unit on a specific mission to hit preordained targets. The first militants through targeted nearby Israeli military positions, systematically destroying communication towers along the way. The corresponding internet, phone, and radio service outage disconnected Israeli Defense Forces (IDF) units from one another, headquarters, and potential reinforcements. Hamas's special forces division, Nukhba, rapidly overran at least seven IDF outposts, in some places coming upon their targets with complete surprise, with Israeli soldiers still sheltering in bunkers from the earlier rocket strikes. Militants killed many of the soldiers, and detained others, hauling them back into Gaza as the first of what would become hundreds of hostages.[30]

With local military forces besieged or defeated, other militant cells targeted civilian populations, ultimately rampaging through at least 20 residential communities. Each Hamas unit had simple instructions: to kill or capture the Israelis they encountered. As the militants entered towns and villages near the Gazan border, they set about the mission with cold-blooded efficiency. Men, women, and children, many still sheltering in bunkers, were killed with wanton abandon. Children were killed in front of their parents, and entire families were burned alive as militants set their houses on fire. When militants entered the Supernova music festival—an outdoor weekend rave that brought together a devoted following of electronic music enthusiasts and peace activists—they caught the crowd, who had been dancing through the night, unawares. Hamas militants using motorized paragliders to vault over the Gaza border wall also entered the fray, creating a frantic scene of mayhem that resulted in the murder of at least 260 concertgoers.[31]

As reports of the carnage began to emerge, the scale of what was unfolding was difficult to comprehend. Hamas had achieved an unprecedented and stunningly effective ground assault inside Israel. Israeli security forces nearby had been defeated and the government was slow to respond. Whereas some Hamas cells returned to Gaza with hostages, others stayed in Israel, killing every civilian, police officer, and soldier they could find. Militants even stormed a strategic military instillation around 10 miles from the Gaza border operated by the IDF's vaunted Unit 8200—a unit responsible for highly classified signals intelligence operations against all of Israel's enemies at home and abroad, undoubtedly including Iran. As Lieutenant Colonel Alon Eviatar, an IDF reservist and former member of Unit 8200, described the building: "It is the largest and most significant intelligence base in Israel, one of the country's greatest assets." "It was a top priority for them," Eviatar said of the Hamas attackers.[32]

Military reinforcements did not arrive for hours, and neutralizing the remaining militant cells took over 26 hours to complete.[33] When the dust settled, almost 1,200 people had been killed, including at least 350 IDF soldiers. An additional 250 people were taken hostage, including women, children, the elderly, and soldiers. Israeli leaders were forced to reckon with the grim reality that more Jews had been killed on October 7 than on any day since the Holocaust. Israel had lived through major wars with neighboring Arab states and decades of terrorist violence, but it had never experienced such a gruesome day. It was the deadliest attack on Israelis in history—and the country's greatest intelligence failure. Israeli officials immediately likened the attacks to 9/11, and in many ways, the comparison was apt. But in contrast to 9/11, which was a relatively crude plot, October 7 was carried out with sophisticated military tactics and efficiency. And the terrorists did not die on a suicide mission, they returned home with captives.

The operation's complexity suggested that it had been long in development and had benefited from outside support. Hamas took responsibility for the attack, and its leading military backer, Iran, was an obvious suspect. Iran denied any involvement, even as its leadership hailed Hamas's achievement as a victory for the resistance.[34] Reporting on the issue was uneven and painted a murky picture. Unnamed officials from Hezbollah, Hamas, and Iran told the *Wall Street Journal* and *New York Times* details that confirmed Iran's involvement. In those reports, IRGC officials oversaw the planning, trained Hamas fighters inside Iranian military bases, and greenlit the operation. Some Hamas officials also publicly claimed that Iran had been involved. U.S. and Israeli officials were less declarative. Iran was undoubtedly complicit in their view, but a common line shared by both was that they had not yet found a "smoking gun" directly tying Iran to the attacks.[35] As Prime Minister Benjamin Netanyahu told reporters when asked about the Iranian connection: "Iran supports Hamas [and] provides over 90% of Hamas's budget. It finances, it organizes, it directs, it guides. [But] I cannot tell you for certain that in this specific operation, at this particular moment, they were involved in the micro-planning."[36]

Pointing the finger at Iran was not a straightforward proposition. Hamas had provoked Israel into a war. Were Iran to be held equally responsible by either Israel or the United States, then a reaction to Iran would be necessary. Israel could not fight a war on multiple fronts, and the Biden administration—already occupied with the war against Russia in Ukraine and competition with China—had no desire to seek conflict with Iran, much less enter into another war in the Middle East. Even were Israeli and American officials to be convinced of Iranian involvement, there were good reasons to not rush a response.

The circumstantial evidence against Iran was strong: it was the leading supplier and financier of Hamas's military wing: the Izz al-Din al-Qassam Brigades. The rockets used at the outset of the attack, and much of the weaponry used by Hamas militants in the violence that followed, were a direct product of Iran's assistance. The high degree of planning, which included detailed maps and mockups of the military installations and towns that Hamas targeted, mirrored the type of planning the IRGC had honed in its campaign against U.S. forces in Iraq. The 2007 attack on the Provisional Joint Command Center base in Karbala, which resulted in the kidnapping and murder of five U.S. servicemen, was much smaller in scale but was carried out with similar precision and even, perhaps, aimed toward similar ends. Al-Aqsa Storm also fit squarely within Iran's larger strategy against Israel. Hamas had realized the very type of success that the IRGC had been working toward through its decades of support to its anti-Israel clients. Israel's vulnerability and weaknesses were exposed. Iran's ability to harm Israel by proxy was equally demonstrated. The upswelling of solidarity with the Palestinian cause, the corresponding spikes in both anti-Semitism and Islamophobia, and the brutality of Israel's rejoinder that was sure to come would all in some way advance Iran's agenda. Whether it was merely complicit through general support, or involved in the actual planning, the attack of October 7 was as much an achievement for the Islamic Republic as it was for Hamas.

Israel was obligated to respond to Hamas and restore security for its citizens. But the scale of depravity perpetrated against innocent civilians, some of which was documented with body cameras and smart phones by Hamas's own shock troops, also forced Israel's hand. Israel was compelled to retaliate to the unprecedented attacks with unprecedented force. And when Israel's retaliatory operations began, and ignited another Gaza war, the goal was unequivocal: the total annihilation of Hamas. In the words of IDF spokesman, Rear Admiral Daniel

Hagari: "the objectives of the war [are] the rout of Hamas and the elimination of its leaders. . . . This organization will not rule Gaza military and politically."[37] Such a goal was unsurprising and reasonable, but achieving it appeared nearly impossible. Hamas's military installations, stockpiles, launch sites, and militant cells were interwoven throughout and beneath the byzantine urban landscape of Gaza. Co-located in residential buildings, schools, and hospitals, and in networked tunnels under densely populated areas, Hamas's positions could not be targeted in isolation. Hamas knew that no war against it could be conducted without innocent civilians getting killed in large numbers. That was Hamas's advantage, and Israel's trap.

Israel entered into the war with a vast upwelling of sympathy, especially from Western states and eastern democracies such as India. Attitudes among Muslim states, including from Israel's newfound Arab friends, were more mixed and tempered by solidarity with the Palestinians.[38] Qatar and Turkey, both of which had strong relations with Hamas, were far more critical and blamed the attacks on Israel's decades of oppression of the Palestinian population.[39] A statement released by Qatar's Foreign Ministry in the midst of the October 7 attacks said that Israel was "solely responsible for the ongoing escalation due to its continuous violations of the rights of the Palestinian people, including the recent repeated incursions into the Al-Aqsa Mosque under the protection of the Israeli police."[40] Qatar was the main financier of the Hamas government in Gaza and home to much of the group's exiled leadership, and its *Aljazeera* satellite network covered the conflict in Gaza closely. The focus of international sentiment was primed to shift from Israel's suffering to that of the Palestinians, and Israel's approach to the war made that shift swift.

Israel's war against Hamas began with massive, daily bombardments of Gaza—strikes that were flattening buildings and killing thousands of innocent Palestinian civilians of all ages alongside uncertain numbers of Hamas fighters. Israel had also cut off electricity, fuel, and water to Gaza, seeking to starve Hamas of resources necessary for the fight, but inescapably also inflicting additional suffering on the civilians caught in the middle. With Israel insisting that civilians evacuate densely populated areas, the people of Gaza, who had little place to go and could not leave their territory, were stuck between an anvil and a hammer. Israel's bombardments ostensibly were aimed at Hamas positions, but the photographs coming out of Gaza suggested widespread destruction of entire urban areas. In an assessment of satellite imagery from the first weeks of the war, the *Economist* found that "around 24,000 buildings" had been damaged, which amounted to around 9 percent "of the building stock of the Gaza Strip."[41] With every image of a small child being pulled lifeless from the rubble of a Gazan apartment building, and every report of an entire family being killed in an Israeli strike, the massacre of October 7 lost salience in the news cycle, and Israel lost more of the moral high ground in the war.[42] International criticism against Israel correspondingly intensified—a dynamic that benefited Iran and its allies, whose uncompromising stance on the Israeli-Palestinian issue was gaining popularity and adherents.

An early casualty of Israel's Gaza campaign was its burgeoning relations with Saudi Arabia. On September 11, 2023, an Israeli delegation made history by traveling to Riyadh to attend a meeting of UNESCO's World Heritage Committee.[43] A month later, and four days into the Gazan conflict, Saudi crown prince MBS held a phone call with his Iranian counterpart, President Ebrahim Raisi, to discuss the war—the first direct communication between the two since the Saudi-Iranian rapprochement. In the official Saudi readout of the conversation, MBS "emphasized" to the Iranian president "that the Kingdom is exerting maximum effort to engage with all international and regional parties to halt the ongoing escalation, and [asserting its] opposition to any form of civilian targeting and the loss of innocent lives." MBS "also underscored the Kingdom's unwavering stance in standing up for the Palestinian Cause and supporting efforts aimed at achieving comprehensive and fair peace that ensures the Palestinian people's legitimate rights."[44] The prospects of Saudi-Israeli normalization were cloudy once again, and MBS, in an effort to associate himself with the plight of the Palestinians, saw advantage in aligning with Iran—at least symbolically—on the issue.

The call with MBS was a boon to Iran's position, and helped the regime escape culpability for honing Hamas's lethal capabilities and stoking conflict across the region. Although Iran denied a connection to October 7, it would not be denied involvement in the battle that followed. The United States had hurriedly moved to support Israel both politically and militarily after the October 7 attacks, redirecting the USS *Gerald R. Ford* Carrier Strike Group to the eastern Mediterranean in a signal of assurance to Israel and to deter Iran-backed proxies from joining the fray. In opposition, Iranian officials, IRGC officers, and the commanders of regional militias all pledged to join the fight against Israel should the war in Gaza continue or against the United States should its forces intervene.[45] As Hossein Amir-Abdollahian, Iran's foreign minister, warned in the first week of the war: "If the measures aimed at immediately stopping the Israeli attacks that are killing children in the Gaza Strip end in a deadlock, it is highly probable that many other fronts will be opened. This option is not ruled out and this is becoming increasingly more probable." He added: "If the Zionist entity [Israel] decides to enter Gaza, the resistance leaders will turn it into a graveyard of the occupation soldiers."[46] Such threats were being backed by action from Iran's clients. Through the first weeks of the war, Hezbollah engaged in daily sporadic attacks on northern Israel, threatening to open a second front. From Yemen, the Houthis, whose official mantra includes the line "death to America, death to Israel, curse upon the Jews," launched a series of strikes aimed at Israel for the first time. In one barrage, fired across the span of nine hours on October 19, the Houthis launched 15 drones and 4 cruise missiles, all of which were intercepted by the USS *Carney*, an Arleigh-Burke class destroyer that was traveling southward in the Red Sea at the time.[47]

Militias in Syria and Iraq engaged in equally provocative attacks against U.S. forces stationed in both countries. Across a 10-day span beginning on October 17, Iranian-backed militias launched at least 20 rocket and drone attacks against American forces in Syria and Iraq. The attacks were mostly unsuccessful; however, one U.S. contractor died of a heart attack while sheltering during a suspected assault on Ayn al-Assad base in Iraq, and at least 19 American personnel suffered traumatic brain injuries from the percussive explosive impacts in other attacks.[48] In response to Iran's provocations, the Pentagon announced the deployment of additional forces to the region, including a Terminal High Altitude Area Defense (THAAD) battery and Patriot missile battalions, and that further troops had been put on "prepare to deploy" orders. The USS *Dwight D. Eisenhower* Carrier Strike Group was also rerouted to the Gulf of Oman.[49]

As attacks persisted, President Biden sent a message to Iran's supreme leader that the United States would hold the regime responsible for attacks by its proxies. Speaking to a joint news conference on October 25, Biden said: "My warning to the Ayatollah was that if they continue to move against those troops, we will respond. And he should be prepared."[50] The next day, after additional attacks, the U.S. military struck two weapons storage facilities associated with the IRGC and its militia clients in Al Bukamal near Syria's border with Iraq. In announcing the strikes, Secretary of Defense Lloyd Austin released a statement aimed at Iran's leadership:

> The United States does not seek conflict and has no intention nor desire to engage in further hostilities, but these Iranian-backed attacks against U.S. forces are unacceptable and must stop. Iran wants to hide its hand and deny its role in these attacks against our forces. We will not let them. If attacks by Iran's proxies against U.S. forces continue, we will not hesitate to take further necessary measures to protect our people.[51]

Hours later, Iraqi militias launched another round of attacks against U.S. forces in Syria and Iraq—a signal of more to come.[52]

Iran also sought to send a message, one independent of its proxies, and Foreign Minister Hossein Amir-Abdollahian's trip to the UN General Assembly was a fitting venue. In his address to the gathering, Amir-Abdollahian said:

The world knows that the Islamic Republic of Iran plays the most constructive role in helping peace and security in West Asia and the whole world as well as fighting terrorism and ISIS. . . . But, today in New York and from the headquarters of the United Nations I say frankly to the American statesmen and military forces who are now managing the genocide in Palestine, that we do not welcome the expansion and scope of the war in the region, but I warn if the genocide in Gaza continues, they will not be spared from this fire.[53]

Iran and its allies were undeterred, and threatening a region-wide war.[54] With its proxies walking in lockstep, Iran was showcasing the degree to which it could pull the strings of a transnational movement. The specter of regional war highlighted Iran's wide geographic clout and strength, but it also betrayed certain constraints. Iran's Axis of Resistance could not defeat Israel militarily. They could stoke unrest, harass, and inflict damage, but they were unable to bring the fight to Israel. Iran's rapprochements with Saudi Arabia and the UAE had also decreased its coercive leverage with the United States. Unless it sought to sever those newly repaired relationships, and set back the regional order it aimed to establish, Iran could no longer credibly intimidate the United States by threatening to strike the cities of its Arab neighbors or U.S. forces stationed in Qatar or Bahrain. That left targeting the small numbers of U.S. forces in Iraq and Syria as Iran's main pressure point, which was of limited strategic value, in large part because if pushed too far, the escalation cycle would favor the United States.

Beyond what it meant for Israel and the Palestinians, October 7 was as revealing of the impediments to regional peace as it was for the propensity of conflict to break through. The Middle East was a tinder box, and Iran had spent decades passing out matches. Israel's pathway to security was a minefield, and Iran's campaign against it was insulated with layers of political, material, and ethical obstacles that Israel could not easily overcome. Yet, Israel would not be free from the persistent threat of war, and the Palestinian people would not be liberated from the terrorist groups that undermined their rightful cause for self-determination, until Iran's support to rejectionist factions in Gaza, the West Bank, and Lebanon ceased. Israel's attempts to discourage Iran's behavior in the shadow war had proved ineffective, suggesting that a replay of that covert tit-for-tat conflict would not fundamentally change the game. Israel would have to do more, and that necessity made further hostility between Iran and Israel inescapable. Israel's war began in Gaza, but it was unlikely to end there.

The United States would be inextricable from what would come. Iran viewed America and Israel as two halves of the same problem, and its desire to take on both was resolute. Although successive administrations had tried to shift U.S. resources away from the Middle East, Iran's determination routinely undercut those efforts. With the war in Ukraine, and mounting tensions with China over Taiwan, U.S. involvement in the Middle East could not be isolated from its strategic priorities elsewhere. The sense that tensions in Europe and Asia were coalescing into something larger and more dangerous was unavoidable. A storm was brewing, and the Middle East was once again a point of global convergence.

17

Conclusion

This book has explored the major conflicts that have ebbed and flowed across an almost quarter-century in the Middle East. That period is a snapshot of the region's modern history, yet, I would suggest, one that will prove to be a defining juncture in later considerations. War and conflict have shaped much of the Middle East's 21st-century experience, and will continue to do so. Fires across the region are still burning, and while some decline in intensity, others are growing stronger. The environment is permissive to such conflagrations, and the ambitions of regional states and non-state actors fuel them. Societal discontent, widespread and interwoven in the region's contentious politics, also remains a wellspring of instability and upheaval. Whether from the top or below, latent sources of tumult promise that episodic crises will be a recurrent theme in the region. With foreign and regional powers prone to intervention and involvement, each crisis will be considered by some an opportunity for gain, causing even localized convulsions to reverberate beyond national borders.

What has been a story of seemingly endless and intractable conflict has also been a story of change. The experiences of the various actors at play in this narrative have prompted re-evaluations of policy, interests, and goals. For some, approaches have been confirmed; for others, undesired results have prompted shifts in behavior and focus. Iran and the United States have been the central characters because they have been the most involved in the region's wars and, at different times and in different ways, the most disruptive. More consequential than their individual actions has been the impact of their clashing agendas, which set the tone for the region's dynamics and contributed to a period of intense interstate competition beginning with the Iraq War and continuing through the conflicts that followed the Arab Spring.

In this concluding chapter, I would like to recenter the focus on Iran and reflect on how its strategy has reshaped the region. To begin, however, it is important to reconsider where the heart of this story began: the Iraq War. It is evident that the Bush administration's decision to invade Iraq upended the Middle East's political trajectory. Its elective war aimed to not only topple a tenacious tyrant, but, more audaciously, to transmute an authoritarian state into a democratic one friendly to the West and amenable to its interests. Had the Iraq War gone according to plan, the country could have become a beacon of progress in a sea of regressive and repressive regimes. The war's architects envisioned a democratic Iraq at peace with itself, the West, and Israel, both economically strong and forward-looking. Such an Iraq, they imagined, would be transformative—a change agent that would one day inspire the Middle East's people to demand justice from their rulers and bring forth the social, cultural, and political revolution that many believed the region required to save it from the enmity and myopia that had stunted its development and had kept states, such as Syria and Iran, from moving past their bankrupting, incalcitrant ideologies. Achieving that turned out to be more difficult than optimists within the administration, and those cheering it along in the commentariat, appreciated. The war succeeded in part: it ousted a dictator, established a democracy, and flipped a hostile state into one that held positive relations with the United States and the international community. Those achievements came at an incalculable cost, foremost in terms of the lives lost and suffering endured by the millions of Iraqi civilians caught in the middle of the occupation and the turmoil that followed its end; but also in the thousands of U.S. and Coalition troops killed and injured in the war.

In terms of foreign policy, where the Bush administration fell shortest of its aspirations was in developing Iraq into a catalyst for a reorientation of the region—that is, one that would suit American interests rather than those of its adversaries. Though its architects had envisioned that the war would lead to a Middle East more inclined toward Western perspectives, the forces it set in motion pushed the region in a different direction. That outcome was brought about by many things, but nothing was more instrumental than the Islamic Republic of Iran's countervailing campaign. Iran's ambitions for the region were opposite those of the Bush administration, and focused foremost on overturning U.S. dominance. What had been the pipe dream of Iran's aging revolutionaries was given new life with the removal of Saddam Hussein. Occupied Iraq provided Iran both an opportunity to expand and an arena to challenge American hegemony. In the early days of the conflict, Iran's advantages were underestimated and discounted by the Bush administration. That allowed the IRGC and Iranian intelligence to weave a web of clandestine networks throughout the country with little interference, which they then used to gradually increase the temperature on the occupation through violence. By the end of President George W. Bush's second term, Iran's approach had proven effective—the IRGC and its proxies, along with Iraqi politicians susceptible to pressure from Tehran or on its payroll, were ascendant. After the withdrawal of U.S. combat forces from Iraq in 2011, Iran-backed militias operated with impunity and their allies held a broad share of the power in the capital. Protecting working relations with Washington remained important to the Iraqi government, but Iran's sway on the ground was unparalleled.

The war transformed Iraq and precipitated change in the region. But those changes favored Iran more than the United States. With its expansion of influence in Iraq, Iran gained confidence in its grand strategy. From the perspective of regime officials in Tehran, they had defeated the United States by making the occupation unwinnable. They understood their adversary's weaknesses and developed ways to exploit them through subterfuge, sleight of hand, and proxies. Gaining ascendancy in Iraq gave Iran a forward position in which to deal with the Arab Spring; and its actions in Syria and Yemen enabled it to strengthen its clients, expand its influence, deepen its encirclement of Israel, defeat its Arab rivals, and gain momentum in its showdown with the United States. Iraq was not a destination for the Islamic Republic; rather, it was a staging ground for the enlargement of its ambitions.

The reasons for Iran's successes are not complicated. It benefited foremost by its commitment to its cause and consistency in its policies. The regime's willingness to sacrifice the needs of its people for its political aspirations made it resilient to international pressure and sanctions. Iran risked more, suffered more, and remained more stalwart in its approach than its competitors. Iran also perfected the art of leverage and diversionary fires—issues that consumed the attentions of its adversaries and shielded its strategic activities. Iran's early strategy in the Syrian war, which allowed for the development of jihadist groups such as Nusra and ISIS, its stoking of the conflict in Yemen, and its piracy at sea are examples of the latter. Even more, the nuclear enrichment program was a compelling distractor for the West, and trying to solve that issue siphoned attention from, and diminished resolve for, addressing Iran's other destabilizing behavior. As Washington and its allies focused on curbing nuclear enrichment, Tehran, unswayed by sanctions and sabotage, steadily advanced that program anyway, establishing a hardened industrial capacity and a nuclear stockpile difficult to roll back or destroy. Iran's ability and willingness to strike U.S. forces in the region and escalate against its neighbors, both directly and through proxies, likewise served as leverage points with its adversaries. More importantly, that approach forestalled direct military action against Iran, giving the regime a strong belief that its matrix of capabilities and diversions, combined with its regional presence, could succeed in deterring its enemies from employing their core advantage: brute military force.

Honing such a strategy enabled Iran to succeed in contests where the stakes were viewed as zero-sum by its adversaries. Iran did not need a total victory in Iraq to prevail, it simply needed to deny victory to the United States. Likewise in Syria and Yemen, as well as in its bilateral feuds, Iran succeeded when its enemies failed to reach their objectives. Being able to operate in foreign countries below the threshold of state governments, such as in Lebanon, or at various levels of a state, such as in Syria, Iraq, Yemen, and to a lesser extent Gaza, differentiated Iran's approach from many of its competitors and allowed it to advance its agenda without securing outright victories in the conflicts it fought. Wherever the fight took place—at the political level, on the ground, or in the shadows—Iran had pieces to play.

Whereas that approach gave Iran an edge over its adversaries in the region's wars, it was less effective in its conflict with Israel. Although Iran cultivated an archipelago of heavily armed proxies to threaten Israel's security, Israel was not discouraged from using direct military force against the IRGC and its clients in Syria and Iraq, or from conducting covert operations inside Iran to kill and capture officials and sabotage strategic facilities. Instead of creating a deterrent, Iran's actions provoked Israel into responding. Moreover, Israel's ability to infiltrate Iranian territory to those ends exposed the porosity of Iran's internal security and its susceptibility to foreign aggression. That dynamic, wherein both sides engaged indirectly while seeking to avoid open war, gradually routinized into a dangerous game that had no easy off-ramps. Given the attacks of October 7, a new chapter in the Iranian-Israeli conflict is likely to unfold. With the possibility of direct escalation and the outbreak of a shooting war ever-present, Iran's elective campaign against Israel will remain pregnant with catastrophic potential, and because of the wide geography it encompasses, the single most destabilizing conflict in the Middle East.

Although Iran has been the most front-footed actor in the region, it has not been alone in its assertiveness or ambition. Its neighbors, Gulf Arab states and Turkey in particular, also have aspirations for themselves and for the region, and have pursued those goals through similar behavior, such as by backing proxies in Syria. Turkey stands out in its use of direct military force, both in its occupation of northern Syria and in its intervention in Libya, places where it succeeded in advancing its interests through determined, forceful policies. Saudi Arabia and the UAE pursued bold military action as well, albeit with less success. Their intervention in Yemen achieved the initial goal of reversing the Houthi advance on Aden, but struggled to make substantial gains thereafter, and failed to weaken the Houthis' hold of the north. The achievements in the south owed more to the UAE's approach than to Saudi Arabia's involvement, and also exposed their diverging aims. Where both Saudi Arabia and the UAE clearly failed, however, was in their goal of uprooting Iran's influence in Yemen. Instead, they achieved the opposite. By transforming a civil war into a regional one, they set the conditions for increased outside involvement while motivating the Houthis to draw closer to Iran as a patron. Unlike Iran, and to lesser extent Turkey, Saudi Arabia and the UAE proved less resilient to international pressure. And once Iran honed the

Houthis' missile and drone capabilities, the resulting attacks exposed a glaring liability. Neither Gulf Arab state could tolerate being the victim of war, and feared the damage that such incidents could inflict on their globally connected economies. The UAE's effort to establish Khalifa Haftar as Libya's strongman was another demonstration of its striving attempts to shape regional conflicts, though due to Qatar and Turkey's counter-effort, it was also unsuccessful.

When faced with uncertain or unwelcome outcomes, Turkey and Gulf Arab states were willing to recalibrate and adjust their aims. That sort of pragmatism, although more born out of struggling campaigns than promising ones, is something that separated their approaches from Iran's. The Islamic Republic's conviction in its objectives and strategy, combined with its alacrity to suffer long-term economic privation, differentiates it from its peers, and is largely why it has outlasted its rivals in regional competition. From a critical perspective, that confidence would appear misplaced. As its Gulf Arab rivals disentangle themselves from unproductive conflicts, seek greater integration with the global economy, gain more influence in foreign capitals, and get richer as a result, Iran's economy continues to suffer under the weight of sanctions, mismanagement, and international estrangement. As the regime privileges its pet projects abroad over improving social and economic conditions at home, the Iranian people grow increasingly desperate, discontent, and antagonistic to the ruling system. Israel is able to strike Iranian targets across the region and conduct operations inside Iran at will. Israel has also become more integrated into the region and has developed strategic ties with Gulf Arab monarchies—ties based in large part on a mutual desire to counter Iran. And while Iran has expanded its influence, everywhere that its influence has spread is either a failing or failed state. Iran's regional gains, so much as they can be considered as such, are a long way from being secured. Further, although Iran's relations with Russia and China are strong, they are offset by Russia and China's stronger and more lucrative relations with Gulf Arab states. Moscow and Beijing treat Iran not as an ally, but as a point of leverage in regional relations and a tool directed against the West. Iran is as used as it is useful, and has failed to make a case for the value of its partnership beyond its inclination to send arms into an unpopular war and sell sanctioned hydrocarbons at a discount.

From another perspective, however, and one held by the leadership in Tehran, the regime's strategy is steadily paying dividends and transforming the region along its desired lines. First and foremost, American influence in the Middle East has declined, and Iran's has increased. Iran's allies are ascendant in Iraq, Syria, and Yemen—places where its regional rivals have mostly lost out; and American partnerships are continually close to crisis. Iran's nuclear enrichment program has advanced despite Western pressure and threats. Its domestic missile and drone industries are among the region's most advanced, and have provided Iran not only an effective deterrent but also a coercive edge over its Arab neighbors. Because of the threat that its weapons and proxies pose, Gulf Arab states have lost the will to challenge Iran, and have instead capitulated while securing no change in Iran's strategic behavior. Iran's ability to wage aggression against its neighbors has also been a wedge that has driven the United States and its Gulf Arab partners further apart. By aiding Russia in Ukraine, the former has become indebted to Tehran, which has given it more leverage with Moscow and access to superior Russian military technology and platforms. Russia and China have both shielded Iran from Western pressure, and China has helped Iran stabilize its economy and circumnavigate sanctions. While Israeli aggression has not been fully deterred, the IRGC's effort to arm Hezbollah and Palestinian factions has not slowed. The October 7 attacks illustrated the brutal effectiveness of Iran's campaign, and Israel's war in Gaza resurrected the Palestinian issue as a focal point for the region. Beyond Israel's vulnerability to aggression by Iran's proxies, Israeli society is also strained by political divisions and an unending security crisis. Turmoil inside Israel is seen as a signal of its inevitable demise, and clear evidence that the regime's hostile policies toward Israel, and across the region, are working. Iran does not need to go to war with Israel to defeat it; rather, it simply needs to keep fostering insecurity within and around Israel, and allow Israelis—through their social divisions, political factionalism, and inability to solve the Palestinian issue—to do the rest.

The point here is not that Iran has won or lost, but rather that winning and losing in this contest is as much a matter of perspective as anything material. In the period under consideration, Iran's trajectory ascended in the Middle East, and U.S. influence declined. Those are relative measurements. In a broad sense, and for innumerable reasons, the United States will remain far more influential in the region and more important to its partners than Iran. And Iran, for all of its victories, will remain largely alienated, permeated with insecurity, and a hair's breadth away from a hot war with Israel, if not also with the United States. Yet, the region's shifting order has benefited Tehran more than Washington. Iran has become more influential, and its neighboring competitors have grown disinclined to challenge its push for regional supremacy. Iran's rise has also benefited Russia and China, which in different ways and to different extents have capitalized on the discontentment it has caused. Even though both Moscow and Beijing have facilitated Iran's advancements more than any other, regional states do not blame them for Iran's aggression. Their frustration is instead reserved for the United States, whom they blame, not for enabling Iran, but for not doing enough to stop it. China's political integration with the region has grown as a result, as has its clout as an alternative to the United States. Whereas the Abraham Accords were an outward success for U.S. foreign policy, the region's broader geopolitical reorientation was not.

Uncertain Prospects in a Changing Region

So, where is it going? The attacks on Israel, the Gaza war, and Iran's flirtation with a wider regional confrontation are all pushing the region down an unpredictable and perilous path. Should October 7 constitute a turning point in the region such as 9/11 proved to be, its impact and reverberations are likely to play out for years, if not decades. Nonetheless, and without seeking to be predictive, it is worth thinking through how the emerging order in the Middle East might take shape, and what it might mean for the interests of the United States and Iran. There are a multitude of possible angles to this, but in these final pages, I would like to explore where the trendlines of a few interrelated issues might be headed—Iran's regional influence; the potential for direct war between Iran and its adversaries; U.S. relations with Gulf Arab partners; and the growing role of China—and how they might further impact the Middle East.

In terms of advancing its strategic goals, no state has been more successful in the Middle East since the turn of the 21st century than the Islamic Republic of Iran. Iran's ability to shape the region has been made possible by its layered architecture of coercion, which is composed of three primary elements: its network of armed clients, proliferation of advanced weapons, and use of aggression. Militant clients are the bedrock of Iran's influence, and while those groups are effective coercive tools, their empowerment also keeps their states weak. Iran's approach has kept allied militias in Syria and Iraq divided and contending with each other for finite resources. Such a strategy has given Iran more leverage over individual groups, and proved effective in fighting the occupation in Iraq and the rebellion in Syria, but it has also retarded the development of client militias and has encouraged competition and avarice. By prioritizing their self-interests, militias regularly vie with their host governments, and their need to supplement their revenue streams has made them operate like organized criminal cartels. These groups have little support in the broad societies they operate in, and their reflexive interference in government affairs undermines both the ability of their governments to function and trust among their fellow citizens. Although Iran's proxies have proven formidable in war, their greatest vulnerability is democratic reform and strong central governments within their own countries.

Proliferating advanced weapons to clients has brought strategic benefit to Iran by providing it forward staging for retaliation and aggression against state adversaries. Such proliferation has made the region's conflicts more intractable, has intensified their destructiveness, and has empowered non-state actors beyond their government's control. It is Iran's single most destabilizing activity and, as October 7 and its aftermath exemplify, can trigger war. By outfitting Hezbollah, Syrian militias, Palestinian factions, and the Houthis with missiles, drones, and rockets, Iran has gained the ability to threaten Israel from the north and south, and to threaten Saudi Arabia and the UAE from Yemen. Israel cannot easily destroy the capabilities of Iran's clients, and as the destruction in Gaza bears out, cannot meaningfully degrade their stockpiles without using extensive and costly military force. That has made the danger those weapons pose significant, and has made the wars involving them more devastating. Likewise, neither Saudi Arabia nor the UAE has had any military answer to the Houthis' over-the-horizon capabilities. Instead, in response to the Houthis' ability to strike their territory, Riyadh and Abu Dhabi reversed their approach toward Iran and looked for ways to reduce their roles in the war.

Outwardly, then, proliferation has been a success for Iran. Yet, that is only because Iran's adversaries have not held it fully responsible for proxy attacks, even when there is clear evidence that the weaponry or technology used was supplied or operated by Iran. The attacks of October 7 could alter that approach. Prior to those attacks, Israel had not employed direct military force against Iranian territory. Israel had retailed against Iran in numerous other ways, including through lethal operations inside Iran, but not overtly. That element of restraint might have suggested to Iran's leaders that Israel had been partially deterred. Similarly, the United States military generally did not respond to Iranian-backed proxy attacks against its forces in Syria and Iraq unless those attacks crossed a certain threshold of violence or killed Americans. Iran could risk such behavior because it could reliably anticipate the American response, and have confidence that the response would be limited to discrete retaliation in another country. However, the longer Iran proceeds with such aggression, the more likely there is to be direct blowback against it. At some point, Iran's enemies might hold it directly responsible for the attacks of its proxies, and if they do, military action against Iran would be both possible and warranted. Iran's proxies are also not immune to degradation or destruction. A war against Iran's proxies by a greater power could prove devastating to those organizations. Israel's war against Hamas will be illustrative to that end. If Hamas can be defeated or neutralized, Iran will have lost a tool in its elective war against Israel. The challenge for Israel is that Iran will still retain other assets. It is that layered approach that makes Iran's proxy network so effective and difficult to overcome.

Proxies are one part of Iran's aggression architecture; the other is direct action by Iran. The most blatant acts of belligerence by Iran have been its missile and drone attacks against neighboring states. The strikes on Saudi Arabia and on U.S. forces stationed in Iraq were both acts of war that could have easily led to direct escalation. Less dangerous, but equally fraught, has been Iran's bellicosity at sea. Lethal attacks against Israeli-linked shipping, the commandeering of tankers, and acts of sabotage by Iranian military forces have not only triggered retaliation by Israel, they have also compelled the United States to increase its force posture in the Persian Gulf. As with proxy attacks, Iran's aggression has not led to direct military retaliation against Iranian territory, which has assuredly emboldened its sense of deterrence and confidence in engaging in such behavior. For similar reasons as mentioned above, Iran's ability to engage in aggression without sparking escalation should not be taken as natural law. Each new attack tests the tolerance and red lines of its adversaries. At some point, that well of tolerance might run dry, and those red lines, if crossed, could spark a more serious conflagration.

Beyond the potentially escalatory dynamics related to Iran's coercive activities, the issue most charged with the potential to trigger a future war is its nuclear program. Since Iran's secret program was revealed, successive administrations in Washington have made addressing the issue the center of their Iran policy, and each one has maintained the line that Iran will be prevented from developing a nuclear weapon. The pressure of sanctions, along with Iran's nuclear advances, made the first attempt at addressing the problem possible in the signing of the JCPOA in 2015. Yet, the parameters of that agreement were never acceptable to Israel or Gulf Arab states, and their lobbying against it helped convince President Donald J. Trump to withdraw U.S. participation and seek something better through the maximum pressure campaign. That campaign failed to achieve anything beyond a return of sanctions, and Iran has steadily progressed its nuclear program since.

Using covert action, Israel responded to Iran's nuclear advancements in tandem with retaliation against the latter's other forms of aggression. Whereas incidents such as the assassination of Mohsen Fakhrizadeh or the bombing of Natanz could have been triggers for escalation, Iran seemed content to play by Israel's terms and keep their conflict in the shadows. Were the attacks of October 7 to have been Iran's doing, and the product of its own desire for revenge against Israel, then Tehran will have enunciated its decision to cross the Rubicon and change the game. Should Israel hold Iran accountable for those attacks, then at some point, it might feel both justified and compelled to launch an attack aimed at destroying Iran's nuclear program, or to pursue a broader conflict with Iran that could draw in the United States. Although less likely, the United States could also see October 7 as a bridge too far, and walk away from the idea of managing Iran's nuclear program through another multilateral agreement. That decision would leave the United States only one option if it wanted to seriously forestall Iran's nuclear development: military force.

Either way, absent a considerable military effort or a comprehensive nuclear agreement, Iran's nuclear program will continue to progress, and that advancement will lead in only one direction: a future nuclear weapons capability. Iran, of course, might never decide to cross the line of developing a nuclear device, and it may never need to. In many respects, the deterrent effect of its program

has been already partially achieved. Returning to a nuclear deal would help ensure that this effect would continue, at least in forestalling military action by the
United States. But eventually, if Iran's nuclear program's evolution is not paused
or reversed, the red line affirmed for decades by successive governments in
Washington and their boasts of "all options" being on the table will be tested.
Israel too—if it has not acted—will be at an inflection point. Both states will be
forced to decide whether to use a large-scale military campaign to destroy Iran's
program, which doubtless would lead to a costly and uncertain war that could
envelop the entire region, or to accept Iran as a nuclear-armed power. Given the
past testimonies of U.S. and Israeli administrations, there is only one decision
that could be made. Yet, given American hesitancy to return to war in the Middle
East, and strategic prioritization of Russia and China, and Israel's inability to
conduct such a war on its own, Iran might ultimately succeed in attaining the
very capability the world has tried to deny it.

Finally, it is worth considering what could change Iran's behavior and thereby
decrease the likelihood of future conflicts. Obviously, Iran's ruling regime could
simply choose to adopt different policies, step back from its feud with Israel—
such as by openly halting its proliferation of advanced weaponry to Lebanon,
Gaza, and Syria—and agree to a nuclear deal acceptable to Israel. Doing so would
reduce tensions, increase security, free the country from the fetters of sanctions,
expand its connectivity with the West and other major economies, increase foreign investment and tourism, improve the living standards of the Iranian people,
and likely dampen their desire to revolt. Taking such a path seems like an easy
decision. By doing so, Iran would retain most of its gains in the region, and address most of the crises that keep it treading water in a volatile sea. That the regime has not chosen such an approach is because its ambitions in foreign policy
trump its domestic concerns. The Islamic Republic is therefore unlikely to pivot
from the course it has pursued for decades. It might temper some of its activities,
such as by agreeing to another limited nuclear deal, but it is unlikely to reverse
behavior in all areas. Iran's need for economic aid gives its foreign backers a degree of leverage, and China, in its quest to deepen involvement in the region
and provide a return to its Gulf Arab partners, could seek ways to entice Iran to
change some aspects of its behavior. That is unlikely to include Iran's policies
toward Israel, but Beijing could play a part in encouraging nuclear compromise
and in maintaining a semblance of peace between Iran and Saudi Arabia. Such
would require carrots as well as sticks, and although it deems the Arab-Iranian
convergence to be in its interests, it is unclear if China will be willing or able to
play that role.

Although the Islamic Republic is unlikely to change stride, a new governing
system in Iran could. That is not to advocate for regime change by force—
if nothing else, this book should be read as a cautionary tale against such

reveries—but it is inescapable that a war against Iran could eventually achieve such an outcome. Perhaps more promising, however, is the prospect of change from below. Iranians are increasingly antagonistic to the regime, and the prospect of domestic transformation is not beyond the realm of possibility. For example, should a popular revolution spring forth from the country's growing anti-regime protest movement, and the Islamic Republic be replaced by a secular, democratic system self-consciously and deliberately designed to be the antithesis of what it replaced, then Iran's foreign policy could change considerably. The most important shifts would likely be to Iran's policies toward Israel. Most regional proxies would have little utility to an Iranian government that stood in opposition to the ideologies and politics they profess, and supporting Bashar al-Assad's repressive regime would also lose appeal. Were such a government to cut support to Hezbollah, Hamas, and others, and step back from its military role in Syria, much of its tensions with Israel would disappear. Such a government would also likely seek to normalize relations with the United States, and improve ties with Western Europe, which would reverse Iran's most costly foreign policy feud and resuscitate its economy. Whereas such changes would undo much of the regime's strategic approach, a post-theocratic Iran would have interests that would also carry over. Sustaining a strong military, maintaining influence in Iraq, defending territorial integrity (to include disputed islands in the Persian Gulf), and retaining its status as a regional power would be among those. A secular, democratic Iran would not be a shrinking violet, but were it to abandon the Islamic Republic's path, it could go a long way in reducing Iran's involvement in regional conflict, and by extension, bring greater stability to the Middle East.

There are, of course, other ways reform could occur. The Islamic Republic has been defined by two primary forces: the IRGC and the supreme leader, Ali Khamenei. Whereas the IRGC has institutional mechanisms that can help perpetuate its role within the regime, the supreme leader's office is far more defined by the individual who occupies it. Khamenei's rule will one day come to an end, and a restructuring of the regime could follow. Iran has only replaced a supreme leader once, and should it do so again, a succession crisis, in which different factions within the system, as well as people on the street, vie for control of the country's future, could occur. Although the most likely scenario is that the regime, having long anticipated Khamenei's eventual death, will have a smooth transition with a replacement candidate, suitable to all major factions, identified beforehand, the internal and external political contexts of that moment will invariably shape it, and could lead to a less expected result. For example, should Iran's leading factions seek to capitalize on Khamenei's death to shift the country's direction, they could choose a more forward-looking theocrat. Such a leader could see the world differently, and realize that the path of his predecessors had led Iran into a series of unnecessary conflicts and costly vendettas, while also antagonizing the Iranian people and reducing their support for the theocratic system. Were that the case, he could reset Iran's priorities, and focus on improving the country's economy and improving conditions for its citizens, while also seeking to ease tensions with foreign adversaries by making small shifts in regional behavior and striking compromise on the nuclear issue. Those changes could mollify Iran's opponents and safeguard most of its advancements without abandoning the regime's broader aims.

Such an outcome is possible, but not likely. That is because the IRGC is the institution best positioned to gain should Khamenei be replaced, and the strongest faction within the organization is also its least compromising. The IRGC has the power, influence, and coercive control necessary to get its way in domestic disputes. In such a scenario, the IRGC is unlikely to concede to popular appetites or abandon its deeply engrained aspirations in order to reduce tensions with foreign adversaries or ameliorate conditions at home. Rather, the IRGC is more likely to seek an expansion of its already outsized influence by either securing the succession of a favored candidate or by weakening the role of the supreme leader, such as by engaging in a political effort to turn it into a clerical committee (which was an option also explored after Ruhollah Khomeini's death in 1989). In either situation, an institutional enfeebling of the supreme leader's office would allow the symbolic heart of the Islamic system to be preserved, which is key to the IRGC's own legitimacy as the system's guardian, while also allowing the organization to more easily and more directly rule behind the scenes as a military junta. Should the Islamic Republic live on after Khamenei, the IRGC's influence within the regime is likely to grow and its imprint on strategic policy likely to intensify.

The United States' relationship with the Middle East is based on a multitude of concerns. The defense of Israel, fighting terrorism, and ensuring the free flow of oil have been key among them. But in the Persian Gulf, the overriding issue has been ensuring the security of its partners by deterring aggression from Iran. Although the United States has devoted more resources to countering Iran's behavior in the region than anyone else, its partners—Saudi Arabia and the UAE in particular—have not been satisfied with the results. That is because Iran's persistent aggression has sown doubt among America's partners regarding the value of its protection. Beyond that, the United States has also lost traction with Gulf Arab partners for two other core reasons: because the United States has chosen to prioritize competition with China and Russia over its commitments in the Middle East; and because its partners have chosen to distance themselves from Washington out of resentment, a desire to diversify their security relationships, and an evolving sense of what pursuing their individual self-interests means. Combined with an enduring frustration with American foreign policy and intermittent focus on human rights, its regional partners have lost trust.

In distancing themselves from the United States, Gulf Arab states have complicated efforts aimed at dealing with Iran. As Washington has maintained a consistent line toward Iran, its partners have lost their resolve. Through their shifting policies, Gulf Arab states have indicated that they no longer view direct confrontation with Iran as a possibility. They lost going head-to-head with their neighbor, and have been forced to come to terms with living in a region where Iran has become the dominant power. That transition invariably will be disruptive in their relations with the United States. On the one hand, they have recognized a need to de-escalate tensions with Iran in order to pursue alternative, economic-focused strategies. On the other hand, they remain vulnerable to Iranian aggression, unhappy with Iran's regional policies, and untrusting of its intentions. Given the current limits of their military strengths, safeguarding themselves from potential Iranian belligerence can only be achieved in two ways: by being protected by a foreign power, or by aligning themselves more fully with Iran.

Given their extensive differences and conflicting goals, a strategic alignment with Iran might appear unlikely, but there is an obvious scenario in which it could happen. Should Iran ever achieve a nuclear weapons capability, or perhaps even an ambiguous capability, any lingering hope by its neighbors of curbing its regional influence will evaporate. Armed with a nuclear deterrent, or the semblance of one, military threats against Iran by its adversaries will lose credibility. That could embolden Iran's regional behavior, which would be further insulated by a nuclear umbrella. With no way to stop Iran in the region, and no way to confront it directly, Gulf Arab states would have a choice to make: stay in Iran's crosshairs, step aside entirely, or draw closer. They might also seek to match Iran's capability, but until they have, they might perceive little choice but to seek stronger integration with their former adversary. That would likely mean a further separation from their ties to the United States, and a fundamentally different regional order. In some ways, that shift has already begun, albeit at a mostly superficial level.

Although a future Iran-led Middle East is possible, more likely is that Gulf Arab states will remain attached to a foreign protector. Maintaining their security arrangements with the United States is their easiest course of action, and the one that would most limit Iranian aggression. However, even if Gulf Arab states might require the type of foreign military assistance and protection that only the United States has been willing and able to provide, that need is contradicted by their inclination to buck their partner's broader strategic interests. That is, by expanding ties with Russia and encouraging China's deepening presence in the region, the foreign policies of Gulf Arab states have underscored their displeasure with the United States and have signaled their desire to align closer with its competitors. Whereas America's relationship with the region is predicated foremost on security, China's relationship is more broadly based. China's massive economy, need for oil, extensive trade relations, and disinterest in democratic development or human rights concerns, not to mention its permanent seat on the UN Security Council, make it an easy partner for Gulf states. And given strong relations with Iran, China also has an advantage over the United States in that it can work productively with both sides of the divide. For those reasons, it might seem only a matter of time before China replaces the United States as the foremost external power in the Persian Gulf, if not also in the wider Middle East.

As attractive as a post-American Middle East might be to some, it is unlikely to be fully realized. The inertia of American relationships and military presence in the Persian Gulf alone might be enough to perpetuate its security involvement in the region. That is especially so should the defense of Israel require a more robust, enduring military commitment, or were the aim of seriously reducing the U.S. force presence in the Persian Gulf begin to be seen in Washington as ceding ground to China. Further, as long as Iran continues to be viewed as a problem in Washington, it will remain politically expedient for future governments to devote resources to address it. As long as Iran's fixation on Israel and support to the United States' adversaries persist, a desire to counter Iran will remain on the agenda. The irony here is that while the Islamic Republic has devoted much of its energy to driving the United States out of the Middle East, it is that very behavior that keeps America tethered to the region.

The Middle East is undoubtedly changing, but the order that is emerging is hardly clear-cut or certain. Rather, it is marked by indecision and flux. Despite the United States' desire to move on from the region and devote its resources elsewhere, it remains tangled in a web of unsolvable predicaments, conflicts, and tempestuous relations. Israel's desire for security is counteracted by the lack of political will among its leaders to meaningfully address the Palestinian issue, leaving a smoldering fire for its enemies to stoke. Similarly, even as Gulf Arab states strive to free themselves from the fetters of their partnerships with the United States, they do not want to lose the security benefits, however imperfect, that the relationship brings. In such an ocean of vacillation and contradiction, Iran's decisiveness stands out. Were only Iran's actions beneficial to its people and to the region, its strategic coherence might well be worth applauding. Instead, Iran has the dubious distinction of gaining the upper hand in a contest that has brought only ruin and misery to every place it has touched.

NOTES

Chapter 1

1. Defense Intelligence Agency, "Iranian UAVs in Ukraine: A Visual Comparison." October 27, 2022; and Joby Warrick and Amy B. Wang, "Iran to Send Hundreds of Drones to Russia for Use in Ukraine, U.S. Says," *Washington Post*, July 11, 2022, https://www.washingtonpost.com/national-security/2022/07/11/iran-drones-russia-ukraine/.

2. "Ukraine War: Iranian Drone Experts 'on the Ground' in Crimea—U.S.," *BBC News*, October 20, 2022, https://www.bbc.com/news/world-europe-63329266.

3. "'Unprecedented' Power Cuts in Ukraine after Russian Strikes Damage Infrastructure," *RFE/RL*, October 29, 2022, https://www.rferl.org/a/ukraine-iran-drones-kuleba-russia-energy-infrastructure/32105876.html.

4. Ankushka Patil, "Russia and Iran Are Strengthening Their Defense Partnership, the Biden Administration Warns," *New York Times*, December 9, 2022, https://www.nytimes.com/2022/12/09/world/europe/russia-iran-military.html; Barak Ravid, "Iran Plans to Limit Range of Missiles Sent to Russia, Israeli Officials Say," December 12, 2022, https://www.axios.com/2022/12/12/ukraine-war-russia-missiles-iran-limit; Patrick Wintour, "Iran Agrees to Supply Missiles as Well as Drones to Russia," October 18, 2022, https://www.theguardian.com/world/2022/oct/18/iran-agrees-to-supply-missiles-as-well-as-drones-to-russia.

5. "We Stand, We Fight and We Will Win. Because We Are United. Ukraine, America and the Entire Free World—Address by Volodymyr Zelenskyy in a Joint Meeting of the US Congress," President of Ukraine, December 22, 2022, https://www.president.gov.ua/en/news/mi-stoyimo-boremos-i-vigrayemo-bo-mi-razom-ukrayina-amerika-80017.

6. John Irish, "France Says Iranian Drone Transfers to Russia Would Violate U.N. Nuclear Deal Resolution," *Reuters*, October 13, 2022, https://www.reuters.com/world/france-says-iranian-drone-sales-russia-would-violate-un-security-council-2022-10-13/.

7. Patrick Wintour and Jennifer Rankin, "Iran Breaching Nuclear Deal by Providing Russia with Armed Drones, Says UK," *Guardian*, October 17, 2022, https://www.theguardian.com/world/2022/oct/17/iran-breaching-nuclear-deal-by-providing-russia-with-armed-drones-says-uk.

8. Kylie Atwood, "UK, France and Germany Push for UN to Carry Out Investigation of Iranian Drones Used by Russia in Ukraine," *CNN*, October 21, 2022, https://www.cnn.com/2022/10/21/politics/un-drone-investigation/index.html; David E. Sanger, Julian E. Barnes, and Eric Schmitt, "U.S. Scrambles to Stop Iran from Providing Drones for Russia," *New York Times*, December 28, 2022, https://www.nytimes.com/2022/12/28/us/politics/iran-drones-russia-ukraine.html; "After Netanyahu Talks, Macron Warns of Iran Nuclear 'Consequences,'" *RFI*, February 3, 2023, https://www.rfi.fr/en/international/20230203-after-netanyahu-talks-macron-warns-of-iran-nuclear-consequences.

9. Umar Farooq, "The Drone Problem": How the U.S. Has Struggled to Curb Turkey, a Key Exporter of Armed Drones," *ProPublica*, July 12, 2022, https://www.propublica.org/article/bayraktar-tb2-drone-turkey-exports.

10. Fabian Hinz, "Missile Multinational: Iran's New Approach to Missile Proliferation," IISS, April 2021; Garett Nada, "Explainer: Iran's Drone Exports Worldwide," *The Iran Primer*, United States Institute of Peace, November 16, 2022, https://iranprimer.usip.org/blog/2022/nov/16/explainer-iran's-drone-exports-worldwide; and "Iran Opens Military Drone Factory in Tajikistan," *Tasnim News Agency*, May 17, 2022, https://www.tasnimnews.com/en/news/2022/05/17/2712404/iran-opens-military-drone-factory-in-tajikistan.

11. Ariel I. Ahram, *War and Conflict in the Middle East and North Africa* (Medford, MA: Polity, 2020), pp. 26–27.

12. See Ian S. Lustick on the historical conditions that inhibited great powers from arising in the Middle East: "The Absence of Middle Eastern Great Powers: Political 'Backwardness' in Historical Perspective," *International Organization* 51, no. 4 (1997): 653–83.

13. See, for example: Mehran Kamrava, *Troubled Waters: Insecurity in the Persian Gulf* (Ithaca, NY, and London: Cornell University Press, 2018), p. 12; Elaine K. Denny and Barbara F. Walter, "Ethnicity and Civil War," *Journal of Peace Research* 51, no. 2 (2014): 199–212; Andrew Glazzard, Sasha Jesperson, Thomas Maguire, and Emily Winterbotham, *Conflict, Violent Extremism and Development* (London: Palgrave Macmillan, 2018); Ahram, *War and Conflict in the Middle East and North Africa*, pp. 77–103; Mohammed M. Hafez, Emily Kalah Gade, and Michael Gabbay, "Ideology in Civil Wars," in *The Routledge Handbook of Ideology and International Relations*, ed. Jonathan Leader Maynard and Mark L. Haas (London: Routledge, 2022); Robert D. Kaplan, "The Revenge of Geography," *Foreign Policy*, no. 172 (May–June 2009): 96–105; Vali Nasr, *The Shia Revival: How Conflicts within Islam Will Shape the Future* (New York: W. W. Norton, 2006); Christopher Ward and Sandra Ruckstuhl, *Water Scarcity, Climate Change and Conflict in the Middle East: Securing Livelihoods, Building Peace* (London: I. B. Tauris, 2017); and Michael Mason, "Climate Change and Conflict in the Middle East," *International Journal of Middle East Studies* 51 (2019): 626–28.

14. Ahram, *War and Conflict in the Middle East and North Africa*, pp. 121–34.

15. Beverley Milton-Edwards and Peter Hinchcliffe, *Conflicts in the Middle East: Since 1945*, 2nd edition (London: Routledge), p. 2.

16. Rashid Khalidi, *Sowing Crisis: The Cold War and American Dominance in the Middle East* (Boston: Beacon Press, 2010), p. 1.

17. For example, see Rashid Khalidi, *Brokers of Deceit: How the U.S. Has Undermined Peace in the Middle East* (New York; Boston: Beacon Press, 2014); and *Resurrecting Empire: Western Footprints and America's Perilous Path in the Middle East* (Boston: Beacon Press, 2005); Christopher Davidson, *Shadow Wars: The Secret Struggle for the Middle East* (London: Oneworld, 2016); Mahmood Mamdani, *Good Muslim, Bad Muslim: America, the Cold War, and the Roots of Terror* (New York: Pantheon Books, 2004); Vali Nasr, *The Dispensable Nation: American Foreign Policy in Retreat* (New York: Anchor, 2014); Khalidi, *Brokers of Deceit*; Seyed Hossein Mousavian (with Shahir Shahidsaless), *Iran and the United States: An Insider's View on the Failed Past and the Road to Peace* (New York: Bloomsbury, 2014); Noam Chomsky, Gilbert Achcar, and Stephan R. Shalom, *Perilous Power: The Middle East and U.S. Foreign Policy Dialogues on Terror, Democracy, War, and Justice* (New York: Routledge, 2015); Kylie Baxter and Shahram Akbarzadeh, *US Foreign Policy in the Middle East: The Roots of Anti-Americanism* (New York: Routledge, 2008); Ben Rhodes, *After the Fall: Being American in the World We've Made* (New York: Random House, 2021); Dina Badie, *After Saddam: American Foreign Policy and the Destruction of Secularism in the Middle East* (Lanham: Lexington Books, 2017); Majid Sharifi, *Insecurity Communities of South Asia and the Middle East: Consequences of US Foreign Policy* (New York: Routledge, 2020); and Faysal Itani, "The Origins and Consequences of US Nonintervention in Syria," *Current History* 115, no. 785 (December 2016): 337–42.

18. Giacomo Luciani, "Oil and Political Economy in the International Relations of the Middle East," in *International Relations of the Middle East*, ed. Louise Fawcett (Oxford: Oxford University Press, 2016), pp. 106–7.

19. Michael Ross, *The Oil Curse: How Petroleum Wealth Shapes the Development of Nations* (Princeton, NJ: Princeton University Press, 2013), pp. 2–3.

20. Oliver Schulmberger, ed., *Debating Arab Authoritarianism: Dynamics and Durability in Non-Democratic Regimes* (Stanford, CA: Stanford University Press, 2007).

21. Ahram, *War and Conflict in the Middle East and North Africa*, pp. 62–67.

22. Emily Meierding, *The Oil Wars Myth: Petroleum and the Causes of International Conflict* (Ithaca, NY: Cornell University Press, 2020).

23. Jeff Colgan, *Petro-Aggression: When Oil Causes War* (New York: New York University Press, 2013); Cullen Hendrix, "Oil Prices and Interstate Conflict," *Conflict Management and Peace Science* 34, no. 6 (2017): 575–96; and Amy Myers Jaffe and Jareer Elass, "War and the Oil Price Cycle," *Journal of International Affairs* 69, no. 1 (2015): 121–37.

24. Paul Collier, "The Market for Civil War," *Foreign Policy*, November 2, 2009, https://foreig npolicy.com/2009/11/02/the-market-for-civil-war/.

25. Robert I. Rotberg, "Failed States, Collapsed States, Weak States: Causes and Indicators," in *When States Fail: Causes and Consequences*, ed. Robert I. Rotberg (Princeton, NJ: Princeton University Press, 2004), pp. 1–24; Lothar Brock, Hans-Henrick Holm, George Sørensen, and Michael Stohl, *Fragile States: Violence and the Failure of Intervention* (Cambridge: Polity, 2012); Edward Newman, "Weak States, State Failure, and Terrorism," *Terrorism and Political Violence* 19, no. 4 (2007): 463–88; Muhammaed Nuruzzam, "Revisiting the Category of Fragile and Failed States in International Relations," *International Studies* 46, no. 3 (2009): 271–94; and Olivier Nay, "Fragile and Failed States: Critical Perspectives on Conceptual Hybrids," *International Political Science Review* 34, no. 3 (2013): 326–41.

26. Patrick Stewart, *Weak Links: Fragile States, Global Threats, and International Security* (New York: Oxford University Press, 2011); also see Sonja Grimm, Nicolar Lemay-Hébert, and Olivier Nay, "'Fragile States': Introducing a Political Concept," *Third World Quarterly* 35, no. 2 (2014): 197–209. On fragile states in the Middle East, see Mehran Kamrava et al., *Fragile Politics: Weak States in the Greater Middle East*, Center for International and Regional Studies, Georgetown University School of Foreign Service in Qatar, Summary Report No. 11, 2014; Seth Kaplan, "Identifying Truly Fragile States," *Washington Quarterly* 37, no. 1 (Spring 2014): 49–63; James A. Plaza, "Draining the Swamp: Democracy Promotion, State Failure, and Terrorism in 19 Middle Eastern Countries," *Studies in Conflict & Terrorism* 30, no. 6 (2007): 521–39; and Elaheh Koolaee and Ziba Akbari, "Fragile State in Iraq and Women Security," *Contemporary Review of the Middle East* 4, no. 3 (2017): 235–53.

27. F. Gregory Gause, "The Price of Order: Settling for Less in the Middle East," *Foreign Affairs*, March–April, 2022, https://www.foreignaffairs.com/middle-east/price-order.

28. Marc Lynch, *The New Arab Wars: Uprisings and Anarchy in the Middle East* (New York: Public Affairs, 2016), xiii.

29. Joel S. Migdal has cautioned against exaggerating U.S. influence on Middle East states: *Shifting Sands: The United States in the Middle East* (New York: Columbia University Press, 2014), pp. ix–x; Mehran Kamrava has called attention to the issue of agency in the Persian Gulf in *Troubled Waters: Insecurity in the Persian Gulf*, pp. 3–4; and F. Gregory Gause has highlighted the independence of Gulf states in regional policy: *The International Relations of the Persian Gulf* (Cambridge: Cambridge University Press, 2010), p. 6.

30. Adham Saouli, "Middling or Meddling? Origins and Constraints of External Influence in the Middle East," in *Unfulfilled Aspirations: Middle Power Politics in the Middle East*, ed. Adham Saouli (Oxford: Oxford University Press, 2020), pp. 11–30.

31. Kenneth M. Pollack, *Armies of Sand: The Past, Present, and Future of Arab Military Effectiveness* (New York: Oxford University Press, 2019); and Zoltan Barany, *Armies of Arabia: Military Politics and Effectiveness in the Gulf* (New York: Oxford University Press, 2021).

32. Afshon Ostovar, "The Grand Strategy of Militant Clients: Iran's Way of War," *Security Studies* 28, no. 1 (2019): 168–72.

33. SIPRI Military Expenditure Database 2022, https://www.sipri.org/databases/milex.

34. Ostovar, "The Grand Strategy of Militant Clients."

35. "Open-Source Analysis of Iran's Missile and UAV Capabilities and Proliferation," IISS, April 2021, https://www.iiss.org/blogs/research-paper/2021/04/iran-missiles-uavs-proliferation; Hinz, "Missile Multinational"; Paulina Izewicz, "Iran's Ballistic Missile Programme: Its Status and the Way Forward," SIPRI, EU Non-proliferation Paper no. 57, April 2017; Assaf Orion, "Iran's Missiles: Military Strategy," *The Iran Primer*, United States Institute of Peace, February

17, 2021; Missile Defense Project, "Missiles of Iran," Missile Threat, Center for Strategic and International Studies, June 14, 2018, last modified August 10, 2021, https://missilethreat. csis.org/country/iran/; Michael Rubin, "A Short History of the Iranian Drone Program," American Enterprise Institute, August 26, 2020, https://www.aei.org/wp-content/uplo ads/2020/08/A-short-history-of-the-Iranian-drone-program.pdf; and Kamran Taremi, "Beyond the Axis of Evil: Ballistic Missiles in Iran's Military Thinking," *Security Dialogue* 36, no. 1 (March 2005): 93–108. Also Michael J. Boyle, "The Costs and Consequences of Drone Warfare," *International Affairs* 89, no. 1 (January 2013): 1–29.

36. Marc A. Tessler, *A History of the Israeli-Palestinian Conflict* (Bloomington: Indiana University Press, 1994); and Charles D. Smith, *Palestine and the Arab-Israeli Conflict: A History with Documents* (New York: Bedford/St. Martin's, 2016).

37. Michael J. Totten, "The New Arab-Israeli Alliance," *World Affairs* 179, no. 2 (2016): 28–36; Omar Rahman, "The Emergence of GCC-Israel Relations in a Changing Middle East," Brookings Institute, July 28, 2021, https://www.brookings.edu/research/the-emergence-of-gcc-israel-relations-in-a-changing-middle-east/; and Yoel Guzansky and Zachary A. Marshall, "The Abraham Accords: Immediate Significance and Long-Term Implications," *Israel Journal of Foreign Affairs* 14, no. 3 (2020): 379–89.

38. David Romano and Mehmet Gurses, eds., *Conflict, Democratization, and the Kurds in the Middle East: Turkey, Iran, Iraq, and Syria* (New York: Palgrave Macmillan, 2014); Gareth Stansfield and Mohammed Shareef, eds., *The Kurdish Question Revisited* (London: Hurst, 2017); Fred H. Lawson, "Syria's Mutating Civil War and Its Impact on Turkey, Iraq and Iran," *International Affairs* 90, no. 6 (2014): 1351–65; H. Akın Ünver, "Schrödinger's Kurds: Transnational Kurdish Geopolitics in the Age of Shifting Borders," *Journal of International Affairs* 69, no. 2 (2016): 65–100; and Henri J. Barkey, "The Kurdish Awakening: Unity, Betrayal, and the Future of the Middle East," *Foreign Affairs* 98, no. 2 (2019): 107–22.

39. Jihan A. Mohammed and Abdullah F. Alrebh, "Iraqi Kurds: The Dream of Nation State," *Digest of Middle East Studies* 29, no. 2 (2020): 215–29; Michael B. Bishku, "Israel and the Kurds: A Pragmatic Relationship in Middle Eastern Politics," *Journal of South Asian and Middle Eastern Studies* 41, no. 2 (2018): 52–72; and Hawre Hasan Hama, "The Securitization and De-Securitization of Kurdish Societal Security in Turkey, Iraq, Iran, and Syria," *World Affairs* 183, no. 4 (Winter 2020): 291–314.

40. Eric Brewer, "Iran's Evolving Nuclear Program and Implications for U.S. Policy," Center for Strategic & International Studies, October 15, 2021, https://www.csis.org/analysis/irans-evolving-nuclear-program-and-implications-us-policy; Job Warrick, "Papers Stolen in a Daring Israeli Raid on Tehran Archive Reveal the Extent of Iran's Past Weapons Research," *Washington Post*, July 15, 2018, https://www.washingtonpost.com/world/national-security/papers-stolen-in-a-daring-israeli-raid-on-tehran-archive-reveal-the-extent-of-irans-past-weap ons-research/2018/07/15/0f7911c8-877c-11e8-8553-a3ce89036c78_story.html.

41. Steven Cook, "A New Iran Deal Means Old Chaos," *Foreign Policy*, February 17, 2022, https://foreignpolicy.com/2022/02/17/iran-deal-jcpoa-israel-saudi-emirates-houthis/; Nahal Toosi, "Arab States, Israel Say They Want in on Biden's Future Iran Talks," *Politico*, December 22, 2020, https://www.politico.com/news/2020/12/22/arab-states-israel-say-they-want-in-on-future-iran-talks-449763; and Zainab Fattah, Ben Bartenstein, and Daniel Avis, "UAE, Israel Pressure U.S. for Iran Security Guarantees," *Bloomberg*, March 14, 2022, https://www.bloomberg.com/news/articles/2022-03-14/uae-israel-pressure-u-s-for-iran-security-guarantees.

42. Michael Singh, "Axis of Abraham: Arab-Israeli Normalization Could Remake the Middle East," *Foreign Affairs*, March–April 2022, 40–50.

43. Summer Said, Dion Nissenbaum, Stephen Kalin, and Saleh al-Batati, "The Best of Frenemies: Saudi Crown Prince Clashes with U.A.E. President," *Wall Street Journal*, July 18, 2023, https://www.wsj.com/articles/frenemies-saudi-crown-prince-mbs-clashes-uae-presid ent-mbz-c500f9b1; Summer Said and Stephen Kalin, "Saudi Arabia and U.A.E. Clash over Oil, Yemen as Rift Grows," *Wall Street Journal*, March 3, 2023, https://www.wsj.com/artic les/saudi-arabia-and-u-a-e-clash-over-oil-yemen-as-rift-grows-ff286ff9; and Natasha Turak, "'Dramatic and Risky'—and a Shot at Dubai? Saudi Arabia Issues Bold Business Ultimatum to Pull Regional HQ Offices into the Kingdom," *CNBC*, February 16, 2021, https://www.

cnbc.com/2021/02/16/targeting-dubai-saudi-arabias-ultimatum-to-pull-hq-offices-to-king
dom.html.

44. Elizabeth N. Saunders, *Leaders at War: How President's Shape Military Interventions* (Ithaca, NY: Cornell University Press, 2014); Daniel Byman and Kenneth M. Pollack, "Let Us Now Praise Great Men: Bringing the Statesman Back In," *International Security* 25, no. 4 (Spring 2001): 107–46; Michael Horowitz, Rose McDermott, and Allan C. Stam, "Leader Age, Regime Type, and Violent International Relations," *Journal of Conflict Resolution* 49, no. 5 (October 2005): 661–85; Lene Hansen, "Discourse Analysis, Post-Structuralism, and Foreign Policy," in *Foreign Policy: Theories, Actors, Cases*, 3rd edition, ed. Steve Smith, Amelia Hadfield, and Timothy Dunne (New York: Oxford University Press, 2016), pp. 95–112; Janice Gross Stein, "Foreign Policy Decision Making: Rational, Psychological, and Neurological Models," in *Foreign Policy: Theories, Actors, Cases*, 3rd edition, ed. Steve Smith, Amelia Hadfield, and Timothy Dunne (New York: Oxford University Press, 2016), pp. 130–46; and Stephen B. Dyson and Thomas Briggs, "Leaders and Foreign Policy: Surveying the Evidence," in *The Oxford Encyclopedia of Empirical International Relations Theory*, ed. William R. Thompson (New York: Oxford University Press, 2017), https://doi.org/10.1093/acref ore/9780190228637.013.281.

45. Kamrava, *Troubled Waters*, p. 13.

46. Fouad Ajami, *The Vanished Imam: Musa al-Sadr and the Shia of Southern Lebanon* (Ithaca, NY: Cornell University Press, 2012), p. 163.

47. See Roschanack Shaery-Eisenlohr, *Shi'ite Lebanon: Transnational Religion and the Making of National Identities* (New York: Columbia University Press, 2008).

48. Shimon Shapira, "Who Was Behind the Killing of Iman Musa Sadr?," *Jewish Studies Political Review* 31, no. 1–2 (2020): 160–70.

49. Abbas Milani, *The Shah* (New York: St. Martin's Griffin, 2012).

50. Peter Mandaville and Shadi Hamid, "Islam as Statecraft: How Governments Use Religion in Foreign Policy," (Washington, D.C.: Brookings, 2018); ; Carol E. B. Choksy and Jamsheed K. Choksy, "The Saudi Connection: Wahhabism and Global Jihad," *World Affairs* 178, no. 1 (May–June 2015): 23–34; Scott Shane, "Saudis and Extremism: 'Both the Arsonists and the Firefighters,'" *New York Times*, August 25, 2016, https://www.nytimes.com/2016/08/26/world/middleeast/saudi-arabia-islam.html.

51. Afshon Ostovar, *Vanguard of the Imam: Religion, Politics, and Iran's Revolutionary Guards* (New York: Oxford University Press, 2016), pp. 134–35.

52. Seth Anziska, "Sabra and Shatila: New Revelations," *New York Review*, September 17, 2018, https://www.nybooks.com/daily/2018/09/17/sabra-and-shatila-new-revelations/; Leila Shahid, "The Sabra and Shatila Massacres: Eye-Witness Reports," *Journal of Palestine Studies* 32, no. 1 (2002): 36–58; Signoles Aude, "Sabra and Chatila," *Sciences Po*, March 14, 2008, https://www.sciencespo.fr/mass-violence-war-massacre-resistance/fr/document/sabra-and-chatila.html.

53. Matthew Levitt, *Hezbollah: The Global Footprint of Lebanon's Party of God* (Washington, D.C.: Georgetown University Press, 2015), pp. 22–24.

54. Trita Parsi, *Treacherous Alliance: The Secret Dealings of Israel, Iran, and the United States* (New Haven, CT: Yale University Press, 2007), pp. 124–26.

55. Colum Lynch, "Anatomy of an Accidental Shootdown," *Foreign Policy*, January 17, 2020, https://foreignpolicy.com/2020/01/17/accidental-shootdown-iran-united-states-ukraine/.

56. Norman Kempster, "U.S. Rejects Kurds' Plea for Help in Rebellion: Iraq: The Issue Poses a Moral and Political Dilemma for Bush, Who Has Urged the Overthrow of Hussein," *Los Angeles Times*, March 30, 1991, https://www.latimes.com/archives/la-xpm-1991-03-30-mn-845-story.html; and Faleh A. Jabar, *The Shi'ite Movement in Iraq* (London: Saqi, 2003), pp. 269–71.

57. Afshon Ostovar, "Iran, Its Clients, and the Future of the Middle East: The Limits of Religion," *International Affairs* 94, no. 6 (November 1, 2018): 1237–55.

58. Avraham Sela and P. R. Kumaraswamy, "The Perils of Israeli-Syrian Diplomatic Stalemate," *Security Dialogue* 32, no. 1 (March 2001): 11–25.

59. Volker Perthes, "Syrian Regional Policy under Bashar al-Asad," *MERIP*, no. 220 (Fall 2001), https://merip.org/2001/09/syrian-regional-policy-under-bashar-al-asad/.

60. Aliza Marcus, *Blood and Belief: The PKK and the Kurdish Fight for Independence* (New York: New York University Press, 2007); and Aytac Kadioglu, "Not Our War: Iraq, Iran and Syria's Approaches towards the PKK," *The Rest: Journal of Politics and Development* 9, no. 1 (Winter 2019): 44–57..

61. Henri J. Barkey and Ömer Taşpınar, "Turkey: On Europe's Verge?," Brookings, February 7, 2006, https://www.brookings.edu/articles/turkey-on-europes-verge/; and William Park, "Turkey's European Union Candidacy: From Luxembourg to Helsinki—to Ankara?," *Mediterranean Politics* 5, no. 3 (2000): 31–53; Alan Makovsky, "Defusing the Turkey-Syrian Crisis: Whose Triumph?," *WINEP*, February 1, 1999, https://www.washingtoninstitute.org/policy-analysis/defusing-turkish-syrian-crisis-whose-triumph.

Chapter 2

1. George W. Bush, *Decision Points* (New York: Crown, 2010), p. 127.

2. A spelling error in the original transcription was corrected by the author for the sake of clarity. "Text: President Bush Addresses the Nation," *Washington Post*, September 20, 2001, https://www.washingtonpost.com/wp-srv/nation/specials/attacked/transcripts/bushaddress_092001.html.

3. "Text: Bush Announces Strikes against Taliban," *Washington Post*, October 7, 2001, https://www.washingtonpost.com/wp-srv/nation/specials/attacked/transcripts/bushaddress_100801.htm.

4. "The Bush Doctrine," *Frontpage Magazine*, October 7, 2002, reposted by Carnegie Endowment for International Peace, https://carnegieendowment.org/2002/10/07/bush-doctrine-pub-1088.

5. Ryan Crocker Interview, George W. Bush Oral History Project, Miller Center, University of Virginia, September 2010.

6. David Crist, *The Twilight War: The Secret History of America's Thirty-Year Conflict with Iran* (New York: Penguin Press, 2012), pp. 432–33

7. Mousavian, *Iran and the United States*, pp. 169–70.

8. Ibid., pp. 168–69; and Crist, *Twilight War*, pp. 433–36.

9. "Text of President Bush's 2002 State of the Union Address," *Washington Post*, January 29, 2002, https://www.washingtonpost.com/wp-srv/onpolitics/transcripts/sou012902.htm.

10. Bush, *Decision Points*, p. 233; cf. Condoleezza Rice, *No Higher Honor: A Memoir of My Years in Washington* (New York: Crown, 2011), pp. 150–51. See also Crist, *Twilight War*, p. 441.

11. Mousavian, *Iran and the United States*, pp. 169–70.

12. George Tenet with Bill Harlow, *At the Center of the Storm: My Years at the CIA* (New York: HarperCollins, 2007), p. 315.

13. Tenet, *At the Center of the Storm*, p. 341.

14. Peter J. Boyer, "The Believer," October 24, 2004, https://www.newyorker.com/magazine/2004/11/01/the-believer.

15. Tenet, *At the Center of the Storm*, p. 301.

16. Bush, *Decision Points*, pp. 189–90.

17. "President Bush Outlines Iraqi Threat," Office of the Press Secretary, October 7, 2002, https://georgewbush-whitehouse.archives.gov/news/releases/2002/10/20021007-8.html.

18. Thomas L. Friedman, "Thinking about Iraq (I)," *New York Times*, January 22, 2003, https://www.nytimes.com/2003/01/22/opinion/thinking-about-iraq-i.html.

19. A spelling error in the original transcription was corrected by the author for the sake of clarity. "Transcript: Interview with Condoleezza Rice," *CNN*, September 8, 2002, https://transcripts.cnn.com/show/le/date/2002-09-08/segment/00.

20. Ibid.

21. Caroll Doherty and Jocelyn Kiley, "A Look Back at How Fear and False Beliefs Bolstered U.S. Public Support for War in Iraq," Pew Research Center, March 14, 2023; and "Americans Favor Force in Iraq, Somalia, Sudan and . . . ," Pew Research Center, January 22, 2002, https://www.pewresearch.org/politics/2002/01/22/americans-favor-force-in-iraq-somalia-sudan-and/.

22. "Senate Approves Iraq War Resolution," *CNN*, October 11, 2002, https://www.cnn.com/2002/ALLPOLITICS/10/11/iraq.us/; also "Roll Call Vote 107th Congress—2nd Session,

On the Joint Resolution (H.J.Res. 114)," United States Senate, https://www.senate.gov/legi slative/LIS/roll_call_votes/vote1072/vote_107_2_00237.htm.

23. Sue Chan, "Massive Anti-War Outpouring," *CBS News*, February 16, 2003, https://www. cbsnews.com/news/massive-anti-war-outpouring/.

24. "France and Germany United against Iraq War," *The Guardian*, January 22, 2003, https:// www.theguardian.com/world/2003/jan/22/germany.france

25. Joseph Fiorino, "Why Canada Really Didn't Go to Iraq in 2003," NATO Association of Canada, June 9, 2015, http://natoassociation.ca/why-canada-really-didnt-go-to-iraq-in-2003/.

26. Raymond Hinnebusch, "Syria-Iraq Relations: State Construction and Deconstruction and the MENA States System." London: LSE Middle East Centre Paper Series no. 4, 2014, p. 19.

27. Curtis Ryan, "Between Iraq and a Hard Place: Jordanian-Iraqi Relations," *Middle East Report*, no. 215 (Summer 2000): 40–42; Alan Sipress, "Jordan Breathes a Sigh of Relief after Iraq War," *Washington Post*, May 6, 2003, https://www.washingtonpost.com/archive/politics/2003/05/06/jordan-breathes-sigh-of-relief-after-iraq-war/bd0793fe-9d7b-4e72-8b33-8c82f9dc77ae/.

28. Richard Beeston, "Turks Start Diplomatic Campaign to Avert War," *The Times* (London), January 17, 2003, p. 19.

29. "Threats and Responses: Turkey; Turkish Leader Arrives in Saudi Arabia for Talks on Iraq Crisis," *New York Times*, January 12, 2003, p. 11.

30. Steven Lee Myers, "Threats and Responses: Persian Gulf; United Arab Emirates Urge Hussein to Give Up Power," *New York Times*, March 2, 2003, p. 11.

31. Richard Beeston, "Leaders of Arab States Call for a Deal but Prepare for War," *The Times* (London), March 1, 2003, p. 20.

32. Anthony Shadid, "UAE Urges Hussein to Go into Exile; Proposal Is Kept off Arab League's Agenda at Bitterly Divided Summit," *Washington Post*, March 2, 2003, p. A17.

33. Jane Perlez, "Threats and Responses: Muslims Meeting; Conference in Qatar, Called to Consider Exile for Hussein, Erupts in a Shouting Match," *New York Times*, March 6, 2003, p. 16.

34. Myers, "Threats and Responses: Persian Gulf; United Arab Emirates Urge Hussein to Give Up Power," p. 11.

35. An American official told the *New York Times* that Powell's statement and the UAE proposal were unrelated, and any apparent relation was coincidental. See Perlez, "Threats and Responses: Muslims Meeting; Conference in Qatar," p. 16.

36. Shadid, "UAE Urges Hussein to Go into Exile," p. A17.

37. Ibid.

38. Ibid.

39. Ibid.

40. Myers, "Threats and Responses: Persian Gulf; United Arab Emirates Urge Hussein to Give Up Power," p. 11.

41. Ibid.

42. Geoffrey York, "Veil of Arab Unity Lifted at Bitter Summit; Third Vicious Clash Erupts at Islamic Talks under Pressure of the Looming War in Iraq," *Globe and Mail*, March 6, 2003, p. A12.

43. Ibid.

44. David Hirst, "Threat of War: Analysis: Arab States Paralysed by Fear of Their People and the US," *The Guardian*, March 1, 2003, p. 6.

45. Dexter Filkins with Eric Schmitt, "Threats and Responses: Bargaining; Turkey Demands $32 Billion U.S. Aid Package if It Is to Take Part in a War on Iraq," February 19, 2003, *New York Times*, https://www.nytimes.com/2003/02/19/world/threats-responses-bargaining-turkey-demands-32-billion-us-aid-package-if-it-take.html.

46. Richard Boudreaux and Amberin Zaman, "Turkey Rejects U.S. Troop Deployment," March 2, 2003, *Los Angeles Times*, https://www.latimes.com/archives/la-xpm-2003-mar-02-fg-iraq2-story.html.

47. Bush, *Decision Points*, p. 250.

48. Donald Rumsfeld, *Known and Unknown: A Memoir* (New York: Sentinel, 2011), pp. 479–92, passim, and 516–17.
49. Ibid., p. 15. See also James P. Pfiffner, "U.S. Blunders in Iraq: De-Baathification and Disbanding the Army," *Intelligence and National Security* 25, no. 1 (February 2010): 76–85, at 78.
50. Rumsfeld, *Known and Unknown*, pp. 514–15; cf. Bush, *Decision Points*, pp. 259–60.
51. Pfiffner, "U.S. Blunders in Iraq," p. 79.
52. Michael Eisenstadt and Jeffrey White, "Assessing Iraq's Sunni Arab Insurgency," Washington Institute for Near East Policy, Policy Focus no. 50, December 2005, p. 8; see also United Nations Development Program, Iraq Living Conditions Survey 2004, Vol. III: Socio-economic Atlas of Iraq (Baghdad: Central Organization for Statistics and Information Technology, Ministry of Planning and Development Cooperation, 2005), pp. 15–19.
53. Florence Gaub, "Meet Iraq's Sunni Arabs: A Strategic Profile." European Union Institute for Strategic Studies, October 2017, p. 2, https://www.iss.europa.eu/sites/default/files/EUI SSFiles/Brief%2026%20Iraq%27s%20Sunnis_0.pdf.
54. William McCants, *The ISIS Apocalypse: The History, Strategy, and Doomsday Vision of the Islamic State* (New York: St. Martin's Press, 2015), pp. 8–9.
55. Ibid., pp. 31–32.
56. Ibid., p. 11.
57. International Crisis Group, "In Their Own Words: Reading the Iraqi Insurgency," *Middle East Report* no. 50, February 15, 2006.
58. Eisenstadt and White, "Assessing Iraq's Sunni Arab Insurgency," p. 7.
59. Ian Fisher and Edward Wong, "The Reach of War: The Insurgency; Iraq's Rebellion Develops Signs of Internal Rifts," *New York Times*, July 11, 2004, https://www.nytimes.com/2004/07/11/world/the-reach-of-war-the-insurgency-iraq-s-rebellion-develops-signs-of-internal-rift.html.
60. Nicholas Krohley, *The Death of the Mahdi Army: The Rise, Fall, and Revival of Iraq's Most Powerful Militia* (New York: Oxford University Press, 2015), pp. 60–62.
61. Patrick Cockburn, *Muqtada: Muqtada al-Sadr, the Shia Revival, and the Struggle for Iraq* (New York: Scribner, 2008), pp. 135–36.
62. Scott Wilson, "Over 60 Days, Troops Suppressed an Uprising," *Washington Post*, June 26, 2004, https://www.washingtonpost.com/archive/politics/2004/06/26/over-60-days-troops-sup pressed-an-uprising/1785b3d6-79cc-40cd-9ba9-50575d5a4d92/.
63. Francis X. Kozlowski, *U.S. Marines in Battle An-Najaf* (Washington, D.C.: United States Marine Corps History Division, 2009), pp. 12–14.
64. Wilson, "Over 60 Days, Troops Suppressed an Uprising."
65. Kozlowski, *U.S. Marines in Battle An-Najaf*, pp. 39–40.
66. Michael Gordon and Bernard E. Trainor, *Endgame: The Inside Story of the Struggle for Iraq, from George W. Bush to Barack Obama* (New York: Vintage Books, 2021), pp. 104–5; Kozlowski, *U.S. Marines in Battle An-Najaf*, pp. 41–42.
67. Wilson, "Over 60 Days, Troops Suppressed an Uprising."

Chapter 3

1. James Bennet with Joel Greenberg, "Israel Seizes Ship It Says Was Arming Palestinians," *New York Times*, January 5, 2002, https://www.nytimes.com/2002/01/05/world/israel-sei zes-ship-it-says-was-arming-palestinians.html.
2. Douglas Frantz and James Risen, "A Secret Iran-Arafat Connection Is Seen Fueling the Mideast Fire," *New York Times*, March 24, 2002, https://www.nytimes.com/2002/03/24/world/nation-challenged-terrorism-secret-iran-arafat-connection-seen-fueling-mideast.html; Yonah Jeremy Bob, "The PA, Iran's 'Karine A' Rockets vs Hamas' Boat," *Jerusalem Post*, February 8, 2020, https://www.jpost.com/middle-east/the-pa-irans-karine-a-rockets-vs-hamas-boat-of-naval-commando-weapons-616809; and Crist, *Twilight War*, p. 436.
3. Bush, *Decision Points*, p. 233.
4. Rice, *No Higher Honor*, p. 136.
5. Tenet, *At the Center of the Storm*, p. 244.

6. See, Adrian Levy and Cathy Scott Clark, *The Exile: The Stunning Inside Story of Osama bin Laden and Al Qaeda in Flight* (New York: Bloomsbury Publishing, 2017).

7. Crist, *Twilight War*, pp. 437–38.

8. Rice, *No Higher Honor*, pp. 164–65.

9. Director of National Intelligence, "Iran: Nuclear Intentions and Capabilities," *National Intelligence Estimate*, November 2007, https://www.dni.gov/files/documents/Newsroom/ Reports%20and%20Pubs/20071203_release.pdf. Also, David Albright and Andrea Stricker, "Iran's Nuclear Program," *The Iran Primer*, United States Institute of Peace, October 6, 2010, https://iranprimer.usip.org/resource/irans-nuclear-program.

10. Crist, *Twilight War*, p. 453.

11. Crist, *Twilight War*, pp. 454–55.

12. Tenet, *At the Center of the Storm*, p. 391.

13. Crist, *Twilight War*, pp. 463–65.

14. L. Paul Bremer, *My Year in Iraq: The Struggle to Build a Future of Hope* (New York: Simon & Schuster, 2006), p. 59.

15. "IRIDIUM INDEX—IRGC-QF Intelligence Officers and Operations in Iraq (U)," U.S. Department of Defense, December 26, 2006, USCENTCOM FOIA 18-0555, April 29, 2015.

16. Crist, *Twilight War*, p. 484.

17. Details on Shahlai's many aliases were confirmed by the U.S. Treasury Department designations. See, e.g., "Anti-Terrorism Designations; Iran Revolutionary Guard Corps Related Designations," U.S. Department of the Treasury, October 11, 2011, https://home. treasury.gov/policy-issues/financial-sanctions/recent-actions/20111011.

18. "IRIDIUM INDEX—IRGC-QF Intelligence Officers."

19. "IRIDIUM INDEX—IRGC-QF Intelligence Officers"; and "IRIDIUM INDEX—Iranian Revolution Guards Corps—Ramazan Corps Responsible for Infiltration to Support Iraqi Insurgents (U)," U.S. Department of Defense, October 19, 2006, USCENTCOM FOIA 18-0555, September 4, 2018. See also Adam Rawnsely, "Meet the General Who Ran Soleimani's Spies, Guns and Assassins," *Daily Beast*, January 21, 2020, https://www.thedailybeast.com/ meet-the-general-who-ran-qassem-soleimanis-spies-guns-and-assassins; and Bill Roggio, "Iran's Ramazan Corps and the Ratlines into Iraq," *Long War Journal*, December 5, 2007, https://www.longwarjournal.org/archives/2007/12/irans_ramazan_corps.php.

20. "Shi'a SDE Tactical Interrogation Report," USCENTOM, July 18, 2007, J-2A 00368-18, pp. 54–55; and July 20, 2007, pp. 56–57 (declassified on February 23, 2018).

21. "Shi'a SDE Tactical Interrogation Report," July 18, 2007, pp. 54–55.

22. "Shi'a SDE Tactical Interrogation Report," USCENTOM, July 4, 2007, J-2A 00368-18, p. 44; and July 24, 2007, p. 60 (declassified on February 23, 2018).

23. "IRIDIUM INDEX—Iranian Revolution Guards Corps."

24. Ibid.

25. "IRIDIUM INDEX—IRGC-QF Intelligence Officers," p. 8.

26. "Shi'a SDE Tactical Interrogation Report," USCENTOM, November 25, 2007, J-2A 00368-18, p. 87 (declassified on February 23, 2018).

27. "Shi'a SDE Tactical Interrogation Report," USCENTOM, November 14, 2007, J-2A 00368-18, p. 92; and May 30, 2008, p. 160 (declassified on February 23, 2018).

28. "Shi'a SDE Tactical Interrogation Report," USCENTOM, November 28, 2007, J-2A 00368-18, pp. 96–97 (declassified on February 23, 2018).

29. John F. Burns and Michael R. Gordon, "U.S. Says Iran Helped Iraqis Kill Five G.I.'s," *New York Times*, July 3, 2007, https://www.nytimes.com/2007/07/03/world/middleeast/ 03iraq.html; Also see Brian Fishman and Joseph Felter, "Iranian Strategy in Iraq: Politics and 'Other Means,'" Combating Terrorism Center at West Point, October 13, 2008, p. 56 and passim, https://ctc.westpoint.edu/wp-content/uploads/2010/06/Iranian-Strategy-in-Iraq.pdf.

30. "Shi'a SDE Tactical Interrogation Report," USCENTOM, November 29, 2007, J-2A 00368-18, pp. 101–2 (declassified on February 23, 2018).

31. "Shi'a SDE Tactical Interrogation Report," USCENTOM, May 8, 2007, J-2A 00368-18, p. 208 (declassified on February 23, 2018).

32. "Shi'a SDE Tactical Interrogation Report," USCENTOM, November 27, 2007, J-2A 00368-18, pp. 96–97 (declassified on February 23, 2018).

33. "Shi'a SDE Tactical Interrogation Report," USCENTOM, December 26, 2007, J-2A 00368-18, p. 108 (declassified on February 23, 2018).

34. "Goftogu-ye tafsili-e fars ba namayandeh-ye 'asa'ib ahl al-haq' dar iran" ["Detailed Fars interview with 'Asaib Ahl al-Haq's' representative in Iran"], Fars News, November 16, 2014, https://web.archive.org/web/20141128173220/http://www.farsnews.com/newstext.php?nn=13930824000516; and "Taht-e za'amat-e marja'iyyat va velayat-e faqih az eslam-e asil siyanat konim" ["Under the leadership of the Marja'iyyat and Velayat-e Faqih we safeguard true Islam"], Mehr News, January 20, 2017, https://www.mehrnews.com/news/3882102.

35. "Shi'a SDE Tactical Interrogation Report," USCENTOM, June 18, 2007, J-2A 00368-18, pp. 21–22 (declassified on February 23, 2018); and "IRIDIUM INDEX—Iranian Revolution Guards Corps."

36. Crist, Twilight War, p. 518.

37. Dexter Filkins, "Sunnis Accuse Iraqi Military of Kidnappings and Slayings," New York Times, November 29, 2005, https://www.nytimes.com/2005/11/29/world/middleeast/sunnis-accuse-iraqi-military-of-kidnappings-and-slayings.html.

38. "Shi'a SDE Tactical Interrogation Report," USCENTOM, June 30, 2007, J-2A 00368-18, pp. 21–22 (declassified on February 23, 2018).

39. "Continuation Sheet—MC Form 458 Jan 07, Block II Charges and Specifications in the case of United States of America v. Ali Musa Daqduq al Musawi," January 2007, https://web.archive.org/web/20170521014002/http://lawfare.s3-us-west-2.amazonaws.com/staging/s3fs-public/uploads/2012/02/daqduq-tribunal-chargesheet.pdf. Also, John F. Burns and Michael R. Gordon, "U.S. Says Iran Helped Iraqis Kill Five G.I.'s," New York Times, July 3, 2007, https://www.nytimes.com/2007/07/03/world/middleeast/03iraq.html

40. "Shi'a SDE Tactical Interrogation Report," USCENTOM, January 10, 2008, J-2A 00368-18, p. 120 (declassified on February 23, 2018).

41. Crist, Twilight War, pp. 520–21.

42. "Shi'a SDE Tactical Interrogation Report," USCENTOM, June 18, 2007, J-2A 00368-18, pp. 21–22 (declassified on February 23, 2018).

43. "Tactical Interrogation Report," USCENTOM, April 18, 2007, J-2A 00368-18, pp. 351–52 (declassified on April 6, 2018).

Chapter 4

1. "President Bush Discusses Importance of Democracy in Middle East," Office of the Press Secretary, February 4, 2004, https://georgewbush-whitehouse.archives.gov/news/releases/2004/02/20040204-4.html.

2. The spelling of Tehran was changed from the original transcript for consistency. "President Bush Discusses Freedom in Iraq and Middle East," Office of the Press Secretary, November 6, 2003, https://georgewbush-whitehouse.archives.gov/news/releases/2003/11/20031106-2.html.

3. Rumsfeld, Known and Unknown, p. 676; Ahmed Twaij, "For Iraqis, War Is Not a Game," Foreign Policy, May 30, 2021, https://foreignpolicy.com/2021/05/30/united-states-iraq-war-six-days-in-fallujah-video-game/; Rory McCarthy and Peter Beaumont, "Civilian Cost of Battle for Falluja Emerges," The Guardian, November 13, 2004, https://www.theguardian.com/world/2004/nov/14/iraq.iraq3; Dan Lamothe, "Remembering the Iraq War's Bloodiest Battle, 10 Years Later," Washington Post, November 4, 2014, https://www.washingtonpost.com/news/checkpoint/wp/2014/11/04/remembering-the-iraq-wars-bloodiest-battle-10-years-later/; and Andrea Scott, "The Second Battle of Fallujah: 15 Years Later," Military Times, November 27, 2019, https://www.marinecorpstimes.com/news/your-marine-corps/2019/11/28/the-second-battle-of-fallujah-15-years-later/.

4. For example, Timothy S. McWilliams with Nicholar J. Schlosser, Fallujah: U.S. Marines in Battle (Quantico, VA: History Division, United States Marines Corps, 2014); John Spencer and Jayson Geroux, "Urban Warfare Project Case Study Series: Case Study #6—Fallujah I," West Point, NY: Modern Institute of War, February 2022.

5. "Transcript of Bush Address on Iraq Election," *CNN*, January 30, 2005, http://www.cnn.com/2005/ALLPOLITICS/01/30/bush.transcript/.
6. See Iraq's 2005 constitution: https://www.constituteproject.org/constitution/Iraq_2005.pdf?lang=en.
7. Herb Keinon, "Rejected once, Turks still keen for Israel-Syria mediation role," *The Jerusalem Post*, January 4, 2005, p. 2.
8. Karl Vick, "In Turkey, New Fears That Peace Has Passed; Army Takes Offensive as Kurdish Rebels Return from Iraq," *Washington Post*, May 10, 2005, p. A12.
9. Ibid.
10. Mohammed Ihsan, "Arabization as Genocide: The Case of the Disputed Territories of Iraq," in *The Kurdish Question Revisited*, ed. Gareth Stansfield and Mohammed Shareef (New York: Oxford University Press, 2017), pp. 381–83; also Arbella Bet-Shlimon, *City of Black Gold: Oil, Ethnicity, and the Making of Modern Kirkuk* (Palo Alto, CA: Stanford University Press, 2019).
11. Simon Tisdall, "Poll Success Fuels Turkish Fear of Kurdish Independence: World Briefing," *The Guardian*, February 15, 2005, p. 13.
12. Ibid.
13. Joel Brinkley, "Saudi Minister Warns U.S. Iraq May Face Disintegration," *New York Times*, September 23, 2005, https://www.nytimes.com/2005/09/23/world/saudi-minister-warns-us-iraq-may-face-disintegration.html.
14. The spelling of Baathist was changed from the original for consistency. "Iraq Crisis: Country Is Hurtling toward Disintegration, Saudis Warn," *The Guardian*, September 24, 2005, p. 10.
15. "Bush Didn't Listen over Iraq, Say the Saudis," *Daily Mail* (London), September 24, 2005, p. 10.
16. Richard Beeston, "Two Years on, Iran Is the Only Clear Winner of War on Saddam," *The Times* (London), September 23, 2005, p. 46.
17. Peter Baker, "History Likely to Link Bush, Mideast Elections," *NBC News*, January 8, 2005, https://www.nbcnews.com/id/wbna6803688.
18. United Nations Security Council Resolution 1559, September 2, 2004, https://www.un.org/press/en/2004/sc8181.doc.htm.
19. Ronen Bergman, "The Hezbollah Connection," *New York Times Magazine*, February 10, 2010, https://www.nytimes.com/2015/02/15/magazine/the-hezbollah-connection.html.
20. Paula J. Dobriansky, "Remarks on Release of Country Reports on Human Rights Practices for 2004," U.S. Department of State, February 28, 2005, https://2001-2009.state.gov/g/rls/rm/2005/42793.htm.
21. Nicholas Blanford, *Killing Mr. Lebanon: The Assassination of Rafik Hariri and Its Impact on the Middle East* (London: I. B. Tauris, 2006), p. 158.
22. Ibid., p. 159.
23. "Hezbollah Leads Huge Pro-Syrian Protest in Central Beirut," March 8, 2005, *New York Times*, https://www.nytimes.com/2005/03/08/international/middleeast/hezbollah-leads-huge-prosyrian-protest-in-central.html.
24. "Transcript of Bush Speech on Terrorism," CNN, March 8, 2005, http://www.cnn.com/2005/ALLPOLITICS/03/08/bush.transcript/
25. Ibid.
26. Blanford, *Killing Mr. Lebanon*, pp. 160–61.
27. "Ariel Sharon Administration: Speech First Describing Gaza 'Disengagement Plan,'" December 18, 2003, https://www.jewishvirtuallibrary.org/prime-minister-sharon-speech-first-describing-gaza-ldquo-disengagement-plan-rdquo-december-2003.
28. David Landau, "'Maximum Jews, Minimum Palestinians,'" *Ha'aretz*, November 2003, https://www.haaretz.com/1.4759973.
29. "Letter from President Bush to Prime Minister Sharon," Office of the Press Secretary, April 14, 2005, https://georgewbush-whitehouse.archives.gov/news/releases/2004/04/20040414-3.html.
30. Conal Urquhart, "Netanyahu Quits over Withdrawal from Gaza," *The Guardian*, August 8, 2005, https://www.theguardian.com/world/2005/aug/08/israel.
31. "The Gaza Disengagement: Palestinian Perceptions and Expectations?," *Palestine-Israel Journal* 12, no. 2 (2005): https://pij.org/articles/358/the-gaza-disengagement-palestinian-perceptions-and-expectations.

32. "President Bush Discusses Freedom in Iraq and Middle East," Office of the Press Secretary, November 6, 2003, https://georgewbush-whitehouse.archives.gov/news/releases/2003/11/20031106-2.html.
33. "President Bush Calls for New Palestinian Leadership," Office of the Press Secretary, June 24, 2002, https://georgewbush-whitehouse.archives.gov/news/releases/2002/06/20020624-3.html.
34. Nedra Pickler, "Bush Opposes Palestinian Gov't with Hamas," *Associated Press*, January 30, 2006; also, Weekly Compilation of Presidential Documents. Office of the Federal Register, National Archives and Records Administration, Monday, February 6, 2006, Vol. 42, No. 5, P. 143, https://www.govinfo.gov/content/pkg/WCPD-2006-02-06/pdf/WCPD-2006-02-06.pdf
35. Shira Efron and Ilan Goldenberg, "United States Policy toward the Gaza Strip," in *The Crisis of the Gaza Strip: A Way Out*, ed. Anat Kurtz, Udi Dekel, and Benedetta Berti (Tel Aviv: International Institute for Security Studies, 2018), p. 167.
36. The Bush administration's efforts, along with Israel, to isolate and undermine Hamas were extensive and began in the early weeks after January election. See Steve Erlanger, "U.S. and Israel Are Said to Talk of Hamas Ouster," *New York Times*, February 14, 2018, https://www.nytimes.com/2006/02/14/world/middleeast/us-and-israelis-are-said-to-talk-of-hamas-ouster.html; see also David Rose, "The Gaza Bombshell," *Vanity Fair*, March 3, 2008, https://www.vanityfair.com/news/2008/04/gaza200804.
37. Efron and Goldenberg, "United States Policy toward the Gaza Strip," pp. 167–68.
38. https://inflationdata.com/articles/inflation-adjusted-prices/historical-crude-oil-prices-table/.
39. Sarah El Deeb, "Haniyeh: Iran Pledges $250M in Aid," *Associated Press*, December 11, 2006, https://www.iranfocus.com/en/terrorism-mainmenu-31/9475-haniyeh-iran-pledges-250m-in-aid.
40. Sima Shine and Anna Catran, "Iran's Policy on the Gaza Strip," in *The Crisis of the Gaza Strip: A Way Out*, ed. Anat Kurtz, Udi Dekel, and Benedetta Berti (Tel Aviv: International Institute for Security Studies, 2018), pp. 151–52.

Chapter 5

1. Ostovar, *Vanguard of the Imam*, pp. 121–40.
2. *Payam-e Enqelab*, no. 59, May 29, 1982, p. 28.
3. Marcus Weisgerber, "How Many US Troops Were Killed by Iranian IEDs in Iraq?," *Defense One*, September 8, 2015, https://www.defenseone.com/threats/2015/09/how-many-us-troops-were-killed-iranian-ieds-iraq/120524/.
4. Crist, *Twilight War*, p. 521.
5. Crist, *Twilight War*, pp. 521–22.
6. Michael Howard, "Sectarian Violence Explodes after Attack on Mosque," *The Guardian*, February 24, 2006, https://www.theguardian.com/world/2006/feb/24/iraq.topstories3.
7. Dexter Filkins, "Sunnis Accuse Iraqi Military of Kidnappings and Slayings," *New York Times*, November 29, 2005, https://www.nytimes.com/2005/11/29/world/middleeast/sunnis-accuse-iraqi-military-of-kidnappings-and-slayings.html.
8. Crist, *Twilight War*, p. 524.
9. Rumsfeld, *Known and Unknown*, p. 638; cf. Crist, *Twilight War*, p. 525.
10. Steven Erlanger and Richard A. Oppel Jr., "A Disciplined Hezbollah Surprises Israel with Its Training, Tactics and Weapons," *New York Times*, August 7, 2006, https://www.nytimes.com/2006/08/07/world/middleeast/07hezbollah.html.
11. Amos Harel and Avi Issacharoff, *34 Days: Israel, Hezbollah, and the War in Lebanon* (New York: Palgrave-Macmillan, 2008), p. 7.
12. Ibid., pp. 8–13.
13. Greg Myre and Steven Erlanger, "Israelis Enter Lebanon after Attack," *New York Times*, July 13, 2006, https://www.nytimes.com/2006/07/13/world/middleeast/13mideast.html.
14. Gil Merom, "The Second Lebanon War: Democratic Lessons Imperfectly Applied," *Democracy and Security* 4, no. 1 (2008): 7.

15. "Factbox: Costs of War and Recovery in Lebanon and Israel," *Reuters*, July 9, 2007, https://www.reuters.com/article/us-lebanon-war-cost/factbox-costs-of-war-and-recovery-in-leba non-and-israel-idUSL0822571220070709; "Second Lebanon War," Knesset Lexicon of Terms, https://www.knesset.gov.il/lexicon/eng/Lebanon_war2_eng.htm; and Merom, "The Second Lebanon War," p. 12.

16. "Untold Facts on Israel-Hezbollah War in an Interview with Major General Qassem Soleimani," *Khamenei.ir*, October 1, 2019, http://english.khamenei.ir/news/7074/Untold-facts-on-Israel-Hezbollah-war-in-an-interview-with-Major.

17. See Nasrallah's February 2020 interview, originally broadcast on Hezbollah's satellite network *Al-Manar*, https://www.youtube.com/watch?time_continue=43&v=ZgHYqVtfXyM&feat ure=emb_title. A translation of Nasrallah's comments was posted by the Lebanon analyst David A. Daoud here: https://twitter.com/DavidADaoud/status/1228049575132508161.

18. Ibid.

19. Merom, "The Second Lebanon War," p. 12; "Second Lebanon War," Knesset Lexicon of Terms, https://www.knesset.gov.il/lexicon/eng/Lebanon_war2_eng.htm; Human Rights Watch, "Civilians under Assault: Hezbollah's Rocket Attacks on Israel in the 2006 War," August 28, 2007, https://www.hrw.org/report/2007/08/28/civilians-under-assault/hezbollahs-rocket-attacks-israel-2006-war; and "Factbox: Costs of War and Recovery in Lebanon and Israel."

20. Erlanger and Oppel Jr., "A Disciplined Hezbollah Surprises Israel with Its Training, Tactics and Weapons."

21. See Russell W. Glenn, "All Glory Is Fleeting: Insights from the Second Lebanon War," Rand Corporation, 2012, https://www.rand.org/content/dam/rand/pubs/monographs/2012/RAND_MG708-1.pdf; William M. Arkin, *Divining Victory: Airpower in the 2006 Israel-Hezbollah War* (Maxwell Airforce Base, AL: Air University Press, August 2007), https://www.airuniversity.af.edu/Portals/10/AUPress/Books/B_0109_ARKIN_DIVINING_VICT ORY.pdf; and "Second Lebanon War," Knesset Lexicon of Terms, https://www.knesset.gov.il/lexicon/eng/Lebanon_war2_eng.htm.

22. Steven Simon, "Won't You Be My Neighbor: Syria, Iraq and the Changing Strategic Context in the Middle East." United States Institute for Peace, March 2009, pp. 11–12.

23. Crist, *Twilight War*, p. 526.

24. Ibid., p. 527.

25. James Glanz and Sabrina Tavernise, "U.S. Is Holding Iranians Seized in Raids in Iraq," *New York Times*, December 25, 2006, https://www.nytimes.com/2006/12/25/world/mid dleeast/25iraq.html.

26. "President's Address to the Nation," Office of the Press Secretary, January 10, 2007, https://web.archive.org/web/20090113232546/https://www.whitehouse.gov/news/releases/2007/01/20070110-7.html.

27. James Glanz, "G.I.'s in Iraq Raid Iranians' Offices," *New York Times*, January 11, 2007, https://www.nytimes.com/2007/01/12/world/middleeast/12raid.html.

28. Ostovar, *Vanguard of the Imam*, p. 172.

29. Glanz, "G.I.'s in Iraq Raid Iranians' Offices."

30. "Kurdish Leader: US Sought to Capture Iranian Revolutionary Guard Officials in Irbil Raid," *Associated Press*, April 6, 2007, https://web.archive.org/web/20071016061620/http://www.iht.com/articles/ap/2007/04/07/africa/ME-GEN-Iraq-US-Iran-Prisoners.php.

31. "Vazir-e kharejeh-ye 'eraq: Diplomat-haye Irani khordad-e mah azad mi-shavand" ["Foreign Minister of Iraq: The Iranian Diplomats Will Be Released in the Month of Khordad"], *Asr-e Iran*, May 9, 2007, https://www.asriran.com/fa/news/17101.

32. Patrick Cockburn, "The Botched US Raid That Led to the Hostage Crisis," *The Independent*, April 3, 2007, https://web.archive.org/web/20070406172103/http://news.independent.co.uk/world/middle_east/article2414760.ece.

33. "Kurdish Leader: US Sought to Capture Iranian Revolutionary Guard Officials in Irbil Raid."

34. Chad Garland, "US Offers Multi-Million Dollar Bounty for Info on Iranian Planner of Deadly 2007 Attack," *Stars and Stripes*, December 6, 2019, https://www.stripes.com/news/us-off

ers-multi-million-dollar-bounty-for-info-on-iranian-planner-of-deadly-2007-attack-1.610080. See also Ostovar, *Vanguard of the Imam*, p. 173.

35. Robert M. Gates, *Duty: Memoirs of a Secretary at War* (New York: Alfred A. Knopf, 2014), pp. 225–26.
36. Bill Roggio, "U.S. Finds Karbala PJCC Mockup Inside Iran," *Weekly Standard*, June 9, 2007, https://www.washingtonexaminer.com/weekly-standard/us-finds-karbala-pjcc-mockup-inside-iran.
37. "Third-Deadliest Day of War for U.S. Troops," *Associated Press*, January 21, 2007, http://www.nbcnews.com/id/16722042#.XjsRexNKg8Y.
38. Crist, *Twilight War*, p. 529.
39. Bill Roggio, "The Karbala Attack and the IRGC," *Longwar Journal*, January 26, 2007, https://www.longwarjournal.org/archives/2007/01/the_karbala_attack_a.php.
40. Ibid.
41. Michael Gordon, "U.S. Ties Iran to Deadly Iraq Attack," *New York Times*, July 2, 2007, https://www.nytimes.com/2007/07/02/world/middleeast/02cnd-iran.html; and, Operation Iraqi Freedom, Multi-National Force–Iraq, Press Briefing, July 2, 2007, https://web.archive.org/web/20081016013840/; http://www.mnf-iraq.com/index.php?option=com_content&task=view&id=12641&Itemid=131
42. Ostovar, *Vanguard of the Imam*, p. 172.
43. Marissa Cochrane, "The Battle for Basra," Institute for the Study of War, June 23, 2008, http://www.understandingwar.org/report/battle-basra.
44. Ibid.; see also Mary Kaldor, "The Paradox of Basra," *Open Democracy*, January 13, 2009, https://www.opendemocracy.net/en/kaldor-in-basra/.
45. Michael Kamber and James Glanz, "Iraqi Crackdown on Shiite Forces Sets Off Fighting," *New York Times*, March 26, 2008, https://www.nytimes.com/2008/03/26/world/middleeast/26iraq.html.
46. Sudarsan Raghavan and Sholnn Freeman, "U.S. Appears to Take Lead in Fighting in Baghdad," *Washington Post*, April 1, 2008, https://www.washingtonpost.com/wp-dyn/content/article/2008/04/01/AR2008040100833.html.
47. Matthew Weaver, "Sadr Urges 'Civil Revolt' as Battles Erupt in Basra," *The Guardian*, March 25, 2008, https://www.theguardian.com/world/2008/mar/25/iraq.
48. Kamber and Glanz, "Iraqi Crackdown on Shiite Forces Sets Off Fighting."
49. Leila Fadel, "Iranian General Played Key Role in Iraq Cease-Fire," *McClatchy*, March 30, 2008, https://www.mcclatchydc.com/news/nation-world/world/article24479815.html. See also "Aide: Iraq's al-Sadr May Stay in Iran for Years," *Associated Press*, August 22, 2008, http://www.nbcnews.com/id/26351543/ns/world_news-mideast_n_africa/t/aide-iraqs-al-sadr-may-stay-iran-years/#.Xkcs9xNKg8Y.
50. Fadel, "Iranian General Played Key Role in Iraq Cease-Fire."
51. Hannah Allam, Jonathan S. Landay, and Warren P. Strobel, "Iranian Outmaneuvers U.S. in Iraq," *McClatchy*, April 28, 2008, https://www.mcclatchydc.com/news/nation-world/world/article24482134.html.
52. Rumsfeld, *Known and Unknown*, pp. 638–39.
53. Ewan MacAskill, "Iran and US See 'Positive' Steps in First Formal Talks since Hostage Crisis of 1980," *The Guardian*, May 28, 2007, https://www.theguardian.com/world/2007/may/29/iraq.topstories3; and "U.S., Iranian Ambassadors Meet in Baghdad," *RFERL*, May 28, 2007, https://www.rferl.org/a/1076745.html.
54. Thomas Erdbrink and Amit R. Paley, "Iran Urges Closer Defense Ties with Iraq," *Washington Post*, June 9, 2008, https://www.washingtonpost.com/wp-dyn/content/article/2008/06/08/AR2008060801897.html.
55. "Razmandegan-e bedun-e marz beshnasid / niru-ye qods-e sepah shekl gereft?" ["Better Know the Warriors Without Borders, How Did the Corps' Quds Force Come to Be?"], *Fars News Agency*, January 25, 2020, https://www.farsnews.ir/news/13981105000470.
56. Ernesto Londoño, "Iran Interfering in U.S.-Iraq Security Pact, General Says," *Washington Post*, October 13, 2008, https://www.washingtonpost.com/wp-dyn/content/article/2008/10/12/AR2008101201871.html.
57. Gates, *Duty*, p. 236.

58. Ernesto Londoño and Dan Eggen, "Iraq Wants Withdrawal Timetable in U.S. Pact," *Washington Post*, July 9, 2008, https://www.washingtonpost.com/wp-dyn/content/article/2008/07/08/AR2008070801311.html.

59. Gates, *Duty*, pp. 235–38.

60. Jim Mattis and Bing West, *Call Sign Chaos* (New York: Random House, 2019), p. 203.

61. Tim Craig and Ed O'Keefe, "U.S. Military Says Iran Behind Rising Deaths," *Washington Post*, June 30, 2011, https://www.washingtonpost.com/world/3-us-troops-killed-in-iraq-adding-to-deadly-month/2011/06/30/AGrDQprH_story.html.

62. James F. Jeffrey, "The Iraq Troop-Basing Question and the New Middle East," Policy Notes no. 21, The Washington Institute for Near East Policy, November 2014, p. 5, https://www.washingtoninstitute.org/uploads/Documents/pubs/PolicyNote21_Jeffrey2.pdf

63. Mattis and West, *Call Sign Chaos*, p. 208.

64. Ibid., p. 207.

65. Joseph Logan, "Last U.S. Troops Leave Iraq, Ending War," *Reuters*, December 17, 2011, https://www.reuters.com/article/us-iraq-withdrawal/last-u-s-troops-leave-iraq-ending-war-idUSTRE7BH03320111218.

66. Jeffrey, "The Iraq Troop-Basing Question and the New Middle East," pp. 5–6; Mattis and West, *Call Sign Chaos*, pp. 208–10.

Chapter 6

1. On the Green Movement's rise and fall, see Pouya Alimagham, *Contesting the Iranian Revolution: The Green Uprisings* (Cambridge: Cambridge University Press, 2020).

2. Barack Obama, *A Promised Land* (New York: Viking, 2020), p. 454.

3. "President Barack Obama's Inaugural Address," The White House, President Barack Obama, January 21, 2009, https://obamawhitehouse.archives.gov/blog/2009/01/21/president-Barack-obamas-inaugural-address.

4. Obama, *A Promised Land*, p. 454.

5. "Videotaped Remarks by the President in Celebration of Nowruz," The White House, Office of the Press Secretary, March 20, 2009, https://obamawhitehouse.archives.gov/the-press-office/videotaped-remarks-president-celebration-nowruz.

6. "Remarks by the President at Cairo University," The White House, Office of the Press Secretary, June 4, 2009, https://obamawhitehouse.archives.gov/the-press-office/remarks-president-cairo-university-6-04-09.

7. Obama, *A Promised Land*, p. 455; and Hillary Rodham Clinton, *Hard Choices: A Memoir* (New York: Simon & Schuster, 2014), p. 423.

8. Obama, *A Promised Land*, pp. 454–56.

9. Clinton, *Hard Choices*, pp. 343–45; and Gates, *Duty*, pp. 504–7. See also Hilary Leila Krieger, "US Condemns Violence against Egyptian Protesters," *Jerusalem Post*, February 2, 2011, https://www.jpost.com/international/us-condemns-violence-against-egyptian-protesters.

10. Clinton, *Hard Choices*, p. 343; and Laura Rozen and Glenn Thrush, "Obama: Transition in Egypt 'Must Begin Now,'" *Politico*, February 1, 2011, https://www.politico.com/story/2011/02/obama-transition-in-egypt-must-begin-now-048613.

11. Gates, *Duty*, p. 507.

12. Christopher Phillips, *The Battle for Syria: International Rivalry in the New Middle East* (New Haven, CT, and London: Yale University Press, 2016), p. 61.

13. Gates, *Duty*, pp. 506–9.

14. Ibid., p. 507.

15. *Fars News Agency*, February 19, 2011, http://english2.farsnews.com/newstext.php?nn=8911300865.

16. Ibon Villelabeitia and Pinar Aydinli, "Turkey Tells Mubarak to Listen to the People," *Reuters*, February 1, 2011, https://www.reuters.com/article/us-egypt-turkey/turkey-tells-mubarak-to-listen-to-the-people-idUSTRE71047Y20110201.

17. Kristian Coates Ulrichsen, *Qatar and the Arab Spring* (New York: Oxford University Press, 2014), pp. 110–11.

18. Kristian Coates Ulrichsen, "Qatar and the Arab Spring: Policy Drivers and Regional Implications." Carnegie Endowment for International Peace, September 2014, p. 9.

19. Målfrid Braut-Hegghammer, "Giving Up on the Bomb: Revisiting Libya's Decision to Dismantle Its Nuclear Program," *Sources and Methods*, October 23, 2017, https://www.wilso ncenter.org/blog-post/giving-the-bomb-revisiting-libyas-decision-to-dismantle-its-nuclear-program.

20. "Security Council Approves 'No-Fly Zone' over Libya, Authorizing 'All Necessary Measures' to Protect Civilians, by Vote of 10 in Favour with 5 Abstentions," U.N. Security Council, March 17, 2011, https://www.un.org/press/en/2011/sc10200.doc.htm.

21. Obama, *A Promised Land*, p. 657; and, Gates, *Duty*, pp. 511–12.

22. Clinton, *Hard Choices*, pp. 370–71.

23. Obama, *A Promised Land*, pp. 658–60.

24. Bruce R. Nardulli, "The Arab States' Experiences," in *Precision and Purpose: Airpower in the Libyan Civil War*, ed. Karl P. Mueller (Santa Monica, CA: RAND), pp. 344–58.

25. Todd R. Phinney, "Reflections on Operation Unified Protector," *Joint Force Quarterly* 73 (April 2014): 90.

26. Robin Pomeroy, "Don't Bomb Libya, Arm Rebels, Says Iran's Khamenei," *Reuters*, March 21, 2011, https://www.reuters.com/article/us-iran-khamenei/dont-bomb-libya-arm-rebels-says-irans-khamenei-idUSTRE72K50L20110321.

27. Tim Gaynor and Taha Zargoun, "Qaddafi Caught like 'Rat' in a Drain, Humiliated and Shot," *Reuters*, October 21, 2011, https://www.reuters.com/article/us-libya-Qaddafi-finalhours/Qaddafi-caught-like-rat-in-a-drain-humiliated-and-shot-idUSTRE79K43S20111021; and Tracy Shelton, "Qaddafi Sodomized: Video Shows Abuse Frame by Frame," *PRI: The World*, October 24, 2011, https://www.pri.org/stories/2011-10-24/Qaddafi-sodomized-video-shows-abuse-frame-frame-graphic.

28. Clinton, *Hard Choices*, pp. 355–57; and Obama, *A Promised Land*, pp. 652–53.

29. Toby Matthiesen, *Sectarian Gulf: Bahrain, Saudi Arabia, and the Arab Spring That Wasn't* (Stanford, CA: Stanford Briefs, 2013), p. 3.

30. Toby Matthiesen, *The Other Saudis: Shiism, Dissent, and Sectarianism* (Cambridge: Cambridge University Press, 2015), pp. 162–63.

31. "Bahrain Hints at Iranian Role over Country's Shia Uprising," *Associated Press*, March 21, 2011, https://www.theguardian.com/world/2011/mar/21/bahrain-iran-role-uprising-shia.

32. Michael Slackman, "The Proxy Battle in Bahrain," *New York Times*, March 19, 2011, https://www.nytimes.com/2011/03/20/weekinreview/20proxy.html.

33. Ethan Bronner and Michael Slackman, "Saudi Troops Enter Bahrain to Help Put Down Unrest," *New York Times*, March 14, 2011, https://www.nytimes.com/2011/03/15/world/middleeast/15bahrain.html.

34. Ethan Bronner, "Forces Rout Protesters from Bahrain Square," *New York Times*, March 16, 2011, https://www.nytimes.com/2011/03/17/world/middleeast/17bahrain.html.

35. *Fars News Agency*, April 26, 2011, https://www.farsnews.ir/news/9002031362.

36. Amnesty International, "Saudi Arabia: Repression in the Name of Security," December 2011, p. 41.

37. On the protests, see: Frederic Wehrey, "The Forgotten Uprising in Eastern Saudi Arabia," Carnegie Endowment for International Peace, June 14, 2013, https://carnegieendowment.org/2013/06/14/forgotten-uprising-in-eastern-saudi-arabia-pub-52093; also, Toby Matthiesen, "A "Saudi Spring?": The Shi'a Protest Movement in the Eastern Province 2011–2012," *Middle East Journal* 66, no. 4 (Autumn 2012): 628–59.

38. "Saudi Arabia Blames Riots on 'Outside Forces,'" *Al Jazeera*, October 4, 2011, https://www.aljazeera.com/news/middleeast/2011/10/2011104154541907192.html.

39. Ian Black, "Saudis Crush Dissent and Point Finger at Iran for Trouble in Eastern Province," *The Guardian*, October 6, 2011, https://www.theguardian.com/world/2011/oct/06/saudi-crush-protests-iran.

40. Nada Bakri and J. David Goodman, "Thousands in Yemen Protest against the Government," *New York Times*, January 27, 2011, https://www.nytimes.com/2011/01/28/world/middlee ast/28yemen.html.

41. Ernesto Londono and Greg Miller, "Yemen's Saleh Refuses to Sign Deal to Quit," *Washington Post*, May 23, 2011, https://www.washingtonpost.com/world/middle-east/yemens-saleh-refuses-to-sign-deal-to-quit/2011/05/22/AFR4iS9G_story.html.

42. "Yemen Leader Refuses to Exit; Violence Erupts," *Associated Press*, May 23, 2011, https://www.cbsnews.com/news/yemen-leader-refuses-to-exit-violence-erupts/.

43. "Yemen's President Ali Abdullah Saleh Cedes Power," *BBC News*, February 27, 2012, https://www.bbc.com/news/world-middle-east-17177720.

44. Mohammed Jamjoom, "Yemen Holds Presidential Election with One Candidate," *CNN*, February 22, 2012, https://www.cnn.com/2012/02/21/world/meast/yemen-elections/index.html.

45. Ostovar, *Vanguard of the Imam*, pp. 197–200.

46. David E. Sanger, "Obama Order Sped Up Wave of Cyberattacks against Iran," *New York Times*, June 1, 2012, https://www.nytimes.com/2012/06/01/world/middleeast/obama-ordered-wave-of-cyberattacks-against-iran.html.

47. Phoebe Greenwood, "Israeli Secret Service the Mossad Linked to Iran Military Blast," *The Guardian*, November 14, 2011, https://www.theguardian.com/world/2011/nov/14/israel-mossad-iran-blast.

48. Ostovar, *Vanguard of the Imam*, p. 200.

49. *Fars News Agency*, April 26, 2011, http://www.farsnews.com/newstext.php?nn=9002031362.

50. "Manssor Arbabsiar Sentenced in New York City Federal Court to 25 Years in Prison for Conspiring with Iranian Military Officials to Assassinate the Saudi Arabian Ambassador to the United States," U.S. Department of Justice, Office of Public Affairs, May 30, 2013, http://www.justice.gov/opa/pr/manssor-arbabsiar-sentenced-new-york-city-federal-court-25-years-prison-conspiring-iranian.

51. Clinton, *Hard Choices*, pp. 436–38.

52. Randy Kreider, "Iranians Planned to Attack US, Israeli Targets in Kenya: Officials," *ABC News*, July 2, 2012, https://abcnews.go.com/Blotter/iranians-planned-attack-us-israeli-targets-kenya-officials/story?id=16699615.

53. "Bulgaria Court Convicts Two over 2012 Burgas Bus Attack on Israelis," *BBC News*, September 21, 2020, https://www.bbc.com/news/world-europe-54240101; see also Matthew Levitt, *Hezbollah: The Global Footprint of Lebanon's Party of God* (Washington, D.C.: Georgetown University Press, 2013), pp. 354–55.

54. Jason Burke, "Iran Was Behind Bomb Plot against Israeli Diplomats, Investigators Find," *The Guardian*, June 17, 2012, http://www.theguardian.com/world/2012/jun/17/iran-bomb-plot-israel-nuclear-talks.

55. Kate Hodal, "Iranians Convicted over Bangkok Bomb Plot," *The Guardian*, August 22, 2013, http://www.theguardian.com/world/2013/aug/22/thai-court-convicts-iranians-bomb-plot.

Chapter 7

1. Phillips, *The Battle for Syria*, p. 43.

2. Ibid., pp. 46–47.

3. Ibid., pp. 66–67; see also Stephanie van den Berg and Maya Gebeily, "Exclusive: Syrian Regime Organised Feared Ghost Militias, War Crimes Researchers Say," *Reuters*, July 4, 2023, https://www.reuters.com/world/middle-east/syrian-regime-organised-feared-ghost-militias-war-crimes-researchers-say-2023-07-04/.

4. "Syrian Opposition Moves towards Setting Up National Council," *The Guardian*, August 23, 2011, https://www.theguardian.com/world/2011/aug/23/syrian-opposition-national-council.

5. Leila Fadel, "Syria's Assad Moves to Allay Fury after Security Forces Fire on Protesters," *Washington Post*, March 26, 2011, https://www.washingtonpost.com/world/syrias-assad-moves-to-allay-fury-after-security-forces-fire-on-protesters/2011/03/26/AFFoZDdB_story.html.

6. George Kadar, "The Last Friends of Sednaya Prison," *The Syrian Observer*, January 4, 2016, https://syrianobserver.com/EN/features/27958/the_last_friends_sednaya_prison.html.

7. Ali El Yassir, "The Ahrar al Sham Movement: Syria's Local Salafists," The Wilson Center, August 23, 2016, https://www.wilsoncenter.org/article/the-ahrar-al-sham-movement-syrias-local-salafists-0.

8. Charles Lister, "Profiling Jabhat al-Nusra," The Brookings Project on U.S. Relations with the Islamic World, no. 24, July 2016, pp. 9–10, https://www.brookings.edu/wp-content/uploads/2016/07/iwr_20160728_profiling_nusra.pdf

9. Phillips, The Battle for Syria, p. 65.

10. Clinton, Hard Choices, pp. 460–61.

11. Jason Ukman and Liz Sly, "Obama: Syrian President Assad Must Step Down," Washington Post, August 18, 2011, https://www.washingtonpost.com/blogs/checkpoint-washington/post/obama-syrian-president-assad-must-step-down/2011/08/18/gIQAM75UNJ_blog.html.

12. Scott Wilson and Joby Warrick, "Assad Must Go, Obama Says," Washington Post, August 18, 2011, https://www.washingtonpost.com/politics/assad-must-go-obama-says/2011/08/18/gIQAelheOJ_story.html.

13. Ukman and Sly, "Obama: Syrian President Assad Must Step Down."

14. Nicholas Blanford, "Why Syria and Saudi Arabia Are Talking Again," Christian Science Monitor, March 12, 2009, https://www.csmonitor.com/World/Middle-East/2009/0312/p07s04-wome.html.

15. Phillips, The Battle for Syria, pp. 34–35.

16. "Qatari Ambassador Closes Embassy, Leaves Damascus," France 24, July 18, 2011, https://www.france24.com/en/20110718-qatar-ambassador-suspends-embassy-operations-leaves-damascus-khayarine-syria.

17. Jonathon Burch, "Turkish PM Calls on Syria's Assad to Quit," Reuters, November 22, 2011, https://www.reuters.com/article/us-turkey-syria/turkish-pm-calls-on-syrias-assad-to-quit-idUSTRE7AL0WJ20111122.

18. "Saudi Arabia Shuts Embassy in Syria, Withdraws Staff as Deaths Mount," Al Arabiya, March 14, 2012, https://www.alarabiya.net/articles/2012/03/14/200762.html.

19. "Security Council Fails to Adopt Draft Resolution on Syria as Russian Federation, China Veto Text Supporting Arab League's Proposed Peace Plan," UNSC Department of Public Information, February 4, 2011, https://www.un.org/press/en/2012/sc10536.doc.htm.

20. Thomas Grove and Erika Solomon, "Russia Boosts Arms Sales to Syria despite World Pressure," Reuters, February 21, 2012, https://www.reuters.com/article/us-syria-russia-arms/russia-boosts-arms-sales-to-syria-despite-world-pressure-idUSTRE81K13420102221.

21. Phillips, The Battle for Syria, pp. 29–30.

22. Chris Buckley, "China Defends Syria Veto, Doubts West's Intentions," Reuters, February 6, 2012, https://www.reuters.com/article/us-china-syria-un-idUSTRE8150NY20120206.

23. Roy Allison, "Russia and Syria: Explaining Alignment with a Regime in Crisis," International Affairs 89, no. 4 (2013): 796.

24. Clinton, Hard Choices, p. 460; Phillips, The Battle for Syria, pp. 75–76.

25. Katherine Zimmerman, "Arming Hezbollah: Syria's Alleged Scud Missile Transfer," Critical Threats, May 11, 2010, https://www.criticalthreats.org/analysis/estimates-for-hezbollahs-arsenal; see also Andrew Tabler, "Inside the Syrian Missile Crisis," Foreign Policy, April 14, 2010, https://foreignpolicy.com/2010/04/14/inside-the-syrian-missile-crisis-2/.

26. Ostovar, Vanguard of the Imam, p. 208.

27. Louis Charbonneau, "Exclusive: Iran Steps Up Weapons Lifeline to Assad," Reuters, March 13, 2013, https://www.reuters.com/article/us-syria-crisis-iran/exclusive-iran-steps-up-weapons-lifeline-to-assad-idUSBRE92D05U20130314; Alaa Shahine and Donna Abu-Nasr, "Syria Counts on $1 Billion Iran Fund to Support Pound," Bloomberg, June 18, 2013, https://www.bloomberg.com/news/articles/2013-06-18/syria-counts-on-1-billion-iran-fund-to-support-pound; Suleiman Al-Khalidi, "Iran Grants Syria $3.6 Billion Credit to Buy Oil Products," Reuters, July 31, 2013, https://www.reuters.com/article/us-syria-crisis-iran/iran-grants-syria-3-6-billion-credit-to-buy-oil-products-idUSBRE96U0XN20130731.

28. "Sardar qaani: jelo-ye koshtar-haye bozorg dar suriyeh ra gereftim," Quds Online, May 25, 2012, http://qudsonline.ir/detail/News/50685.

29. "Jafari: hamleh pish dastaneh ne-mikonim," *Iranian Students News Agency*, September 16, 2012, http://isna.ir/fa/news/0000178343.

30. "Insight: Syrian Government Guerilla Fighters Being Sent to Iran for Training," *Reuters*, April 4, 2013, http://www.reuters.com/article/2013/04/04/us-syria-iran-training-insight-idUSBRE9330DW20130404.

31. Ostovar, *Vanguard of the Imam*, p. 216.

32. Ibid., pp. 217–18.

33. Gabe Fisher, "'Israel's Strike on Syria Last Month Killed Top Iranian General,'" *Times of Israel*, February 22, 2013, https://www.timesofisrael.com/top-iranian-general-said-target-of-isra eli-strike-in-syria/.

34. See the September 2013 BBC documentary "Iran's Secret Army," https://www.youtube.com/watch?v=ZI_88ChjQtU.

35. "Assad Pressures Syria's 'Neutral' Druze to Join His Conscripts," *Al-Araby Al-Jadeed*, November 15, 2018, https://syrianobserver.com/EN/news/46880/assad_pressures_syria_neutral_dr uze_join_his_conscripts.html.

36. Afshon Ostovar and William McCants, "The Rebel Alliance: Why Syria's Armed Opposition Has Failed to Unify," Alexandria: CNA, March 2013, pp. 1–3.

37. Justin Vela, "Exclusive: Arab States Arm Rebels as UN Talks of Syrian Civil War," June 13, 2012, https://www.independent.co.uk/news/world/middle-east/exclusive-arab-states-arm-rebels-as-un-talks-of-syrian-civil-war-7845026.html.

38. Ostovar and McCants, "The Rebel Alliance," p. 19.

39. "National Coalition for Syrian Revolutionary and Opposition Forces," Carnegie Endowment for International Peace, January 11, 2013, https://carnegie-mec.org/diwan/50628?lang=en.

40. Mark Hosenball, "Exclusive: Obama Authorizes Secret U.S. Support for Syrian Rebels," *Reuters*, August 1, 2012, https://www.reuters.com/article/us-usa-syria-obama-order/exclus ive-obama-authorizes-secret-u-s-support-for-syrian-rebels-idUSBRE8701OK20120801.

41. Mark Mazzetti and Matt Apuzzo, "U.S. Relies Heavily on Saudi Money to Support Syrian Rebels," *New York Times*, January 23, 2016, https://www.nytimes.com/2016/01/24/world/middleeast/us-relies-heavily-on-saudi-money-to-support-syrian-rebels.html.

42. David S. Cloud and Raja Abdulrahim, "U.S. Has Secretly Provided Arms Training to Syria Rebels since 2012," *Los Angeles Times*, June 21, 2013, https://www.latimes.com/world/mid dleeast/la-xpm-2013-jun-21-la-fg-cia-syria-20130622-story.html.

43. Julian Borger, "West Seeks New Syrians to Back," *Australian Financial Review*, August 15, 2012. Cited in Ostovar and McCants, "The Rebel Alliance," p. 23.

44. Mazzetti and Apuzzo, "U.S. Relies Heavily on Saudi Money to Support Syrian Rebels."

45. Cloud and Abdulrahim, "U.S. Has Secretly Provided Arms Training to Syria Rebels since 2012."

46. Clinton, *Hard Choices*, pp. 463–64.

47. Ostovar and McCants, "The Rebel Alliance," pp. 23–24.

48. Anne Marie Baylouny and Creighton A. Mullens, "Cash Is King: Financial Sponsorship and Changing Priorities in the Syrian Civil War," *Studies in Conflict & Terrorism* 41, no. 12 (2017): 9. doi:10.1080/1057610X.2017.1366621

49. William McCants, *ISIS Apocalypse: The History, Strategy, and Doomsday Vision of the Islamic State* (New York: St. Martin's Press, 2015), p. 91.

50. Ibid., pp. 91–92.

51. Ibid., p. 92.

52. Lister, "Profiling Jabhat al-Nusra," pp. 12–13.

53. See, for example, Mariam Karouny, "Insight: Syria's Opposition Considers National Rebel Army, Islamists Angered," *Reuters*, August 25, 2013, https://www.reuters.com/article/us-syria-rebels/insight-syrias-opposition-considers-national-rebel-army-islamists-angered-idUSBRE97O07I20130825.

54. Ben Hubbard, "Syrian Rebels Seize Base, Arms Trove," *Times of Israel*, November 21, 2012, https://www.timesofisrael.com/syrian-rebels-seize-base-arms-trove/.

55. David Enders, "Rebels Flying Black Islamist Flag Seize Artillery Base in Syria's Deir al Zour Province," *McClatchy*, November 22, 2012, https://www.mcclatchydc.com/news/nation-world/world/article24740659.html.

56. Anne Barnard, "Savvier, Rebels Shift Tactics in Syria," *New York Times*, November 26, 2012, https://www.nytimes.com/2012/11/27/world/middleeast/rebels-claim-they-seized-air-bases-and-a-dam-in-syria.html; see also "Activists: Syrian Rebels Seize Major Dam in North," *Associated Press*, November 26, 2012, https://www.usatoday.com/story/news/world/2012/11/26/syrian-rebels/1726523/.

57. Ben Hubbard, "Captured Syrian City a Test for Rebel Forces," *Associated Press*, March 10, 2013, https://apnews.com/d5461b54f7564c8781663e31c198dadd.

58. Anne Barnard and Hwaida Saad, "Syrian Rebel Infighting Undermines Anti-Assad Effort," *New York Times*, July 12, 2013, https://www.nytimes.com/2013/07/13/world/middleeast/syrian-rebel-infighting-undermines-anti-assad-effort.html.

59. Martin Chulov, "Syrian Town of Qusair Falls to Hezbollah in Breakthrough for Assad," *The Guardian*, June 5, 2013, https://www.theguardian.com/world/2013/jun/05/syria-army-seizes-qusair.

60. Nicholas Blanford, "The Battle for Qusayr: How the Syrian Regime and Hizb Allah Tipped the Balance," *CTC Sentinel* 6, no. 8 (August 2013): https://ctc.usma.edu/the-battle-for-qusayr-how-the-syrian-regime-and-hizb-allah-tipped-the-balance/; and Anne Barnard, "In Syrian Victory, Hezbollah Risks Broader Fight," *New York Times*, June 5, 2013, https://www.nytimes.com/2013/06/06/world/middleeast/syria.html.

61. On the Assad regime's use of chemical weapons and chemical agents in the conflict, see Arms Control Association, "Timeline of Syrian Chemical Weapons Activity, 2012–2020," https://www.armscontrol.org/factsheets/Timeline-of-Syrian-Chemical-Weapons-Activity.

62. Human Rights Watch, "Attacks on Ghouta: Analysis of Alleged Use of Chemical Weapons in Syria," September 10, 2013, https://www.hrw.org/report/2013/09/10/attacks-ghouta/analysis-alleged-use-chemical-weapons-syria#.

63. "Government Assessment of the Syrian Government's Use of Chemical Weapons on August 21, 2013," The White House, Office of the Press Secretary, August 30, 2013, https://obamawhitehouse.archives.gov/the-press-office/2013/08/30/government-assessment-syrian-government-s-use-chemical-weapons-august-21.

64. "Remarks by the President to the White House Press Corps," The White House, Office of the Press Secretary, August 20, 2012, https://obamawhitehouse.archives.gov/the-press-office/2012/08/20/remarks-president-white-house-press-corps.

65. Peter Baker, Mark Landler, David E. Sanger, and Anne Barnard, "Off-the-Cuff Obama Line Put U.S. in Bind on Syria," *New York Times*, May 4, 2013, https://www.nytimes.com/2013/05/05/world/middleeast/obamas-vow-on-chemical-weapons-puts-him-in-tough-spot.html.

66. John Kerry, *Every Day Is Extra* (New York: Simon & Schuster, 2018), pp. 526–27.

67. Ibid., pp. 527–29.

68. Jeffrey Goldberg, "The Obama Doctrine," *The Atlantic*, April 2016, https://www.theatlantic.com/magazine/archive/2016/04/the-obama-doctrine/471525/.

69. Kerry, *Every Day Is Extra*, pp. 532–36.

70. Ibid., pp. 536–37; Goldberg, "The Obama Doctrine"; Dexter Filkins, "The Thin Red Line," *The New Yorker*, May 6, 2013, https://www.newyorker.com/magazine/2013/05/13/the-thin-red-line-2; Anne Gearan and Scott Wilson, "U.S., Russia Reach Agreement on Seizure of Syrian Chemical Weapons Arsenal," *Washington Post*, September 14, 2013, https://www.washingtonpost.com/world/us-russia-reach-agreement-on-seizure-of-syrian-chemical-weapons-arsenal/2013/09/14/69e39b5c-1d36-11e3-8685-5021e0c41964_story.html.

71. "Remarks by the President in Address to the Nation on Syria," The White House, Office of the Press Secretary, September 10, 2013, https://obamawhitehouse.archives.gov/the-press-office/2013/09/10/remarks-president-address-nation-syria.

72. "Timeline of Syrian Chemical Weapons Activity, 2012–2022," Arms Control Association, https://www.armscontrol.org/factsheets/Timeline-of-Syrian-Chemical-Weapons-Activity.

73. Greg Jaffe, "The Problem with Obama's Account of the Syrian Red-Line Incident," *Washington Post*, October 4, 2016, https://www.washingtonpost.com/news/post-politics/wp/2016/10/04/the-problem-with-obamas-account-of-the-syrian-red-line-incident/; also see Jonathan Chait, "Five Days That Shaped a Presidency," *New York Magazine*, October 3, 2016, https://nymag.com/intelligencer/2016/10/barack-obama-on-5-days-that-shaped-his-presidency.html.

74. Goldberg, "The Obama Doctrine."

75. For example, Justin Sink, "Panetta: Obama's 'Red Line' on Syria Damaged US Credibility," *The Hill*, October 7, 2014, https://thehill.com/policy/international/219984-panetta-oba mas-red-line-on-syria-damaged-us-credibility.
76. Goldberg, "The Obama Doctrine."
77. Oren Dorrell, "Canceled Syria Talks May Get New Start in Moscow," *USA Today*, November 7, 2013, https://www.usatoday.com/story/news/world/2013/11/07/syria-peace-talks-chemi cal-weapons/3464091/.

Chapter 8

1. Wladimir van Wilgenburg, "Iraqi Kurdistan Hit by First Suicide Bombing in Six Years," *Al-Monitor*, September 30, 2013, https://www.al-monitor.com/pulse/originals/2013/09/iraq-erbil-bombing-suicide.html.; "Kurds, al-Nusra Clash at Turkey's Syrian Border," *Hurriyet Daily*, July 17, 2013, https://www.hurriyetdailynews.com/kurds-al-nusra-clash-at-turkeys-syrian-border-50864; Aymenn Jawad Al-Tamimi and Fadel al-Kifa'ee, "The Fall of Yaroubiya to the YPG in Context," *NewsDeeply*, November 6, 2013, https://www.newsdeeply.com/syria/community/2013/11/06/the-fall-of-yaroubiya-to-the-ypg-in-context.
2. https://www.hrw.org/news/2014/01/03/iraq-investigate-violence-protest-camp.
3. Ned Parker, Ahmed Rasheed, and Raheem Salman, "Before Iraq Election, Shi'ite Militias Unleashed in War on Sunni Insurgents," *Reuters*, April 27, 2014, https://uk.reuters.com/article/uk-iraq-strife/before-iraq-election-shiite-militias-unleashed-in-war-on-sunni-insurge nts-idUKBREA3Q0FO20140427; Philip 'PJ' Dermer, "The 'Sons of Iraq,' Abandoned by Their American Allies," *Wall Street Journal*, July 1, 2014, https://www.wsj.com/articles/phi lip-dermer-the-sons-of-iraq-abandoned-by-their-american-allies-1404253303.
4. "Iraq: Pro-Government Militias' Trail of Death," Human Rights Watch, July 31, 2014, https://www.hrw.org/news/2014/07/31/iraq-pro-government-militias-trail-death.
5. Yasir Abbas and Dan Trombly, "Inside the Collapse of the Iraqi Army's 2nd Division," *War on the Rocks*, July 1, 2014, https://warontherocks.com/2014/07/inside-the-collapse-of-the-iraqi-armys-2nd-division/; Kareem Fahim and Suadad Al-Salhy, "Exhausted and Bereft, Iraqi Soldiers Quit Fight," *New York Times*, June 10, 2014, https://www.nytimes.com/2014/06/11/world/middleeast/exhausted-and-bereft-iraqi-soldiers-quit-fight.html; and Ned Parker, Isabel Coles, and Raheem Salman, "Special Report: How Mosul Fell: An Iraqi General Disputes Baghdad's Story," *Reuters*, October 14, 2014, https://www.reuters.com/article/us-mideast-crisis-gharawi-special-report/special-report-how-mosul-fell-an-iraqi-general-dispu tes-baghdads-story-idUSKCN0I30Z820141014.
6. Patrick Cockburn, "Camp Speicher Massacre: Retracing the Steps of ISIS's Worst-Ever Atrocity," *The Independent*, November 6, 2017, https://www.independent.co.uk/news/world/middle-east/camp-speicher-massacre-isis-islamic-state-tikrit-air-academy-iraq-a8040 576.html; and Mina Aldroubi, "UN War Probe Says ISIS Committed 7 International Crimes in Camp Speicher Massacre," *The National*, June 15, 2020, https://www.thenational.ae/world/mena/un-war-probe-says-isis-committed-7-international-crimes-in-camp-speicher-massacre-1.1034082.
7. Alissa J. Rubin, "Militant Leader in Rare Appearance in Iraq," *New York Times*, July 5, 2014, https://www.nytimes.com/2014/07/06/world/asia/iraq-abu-bakr-al-baghdadi-sermon-video.html.
8. "Islamic State Group Defeated as Final Territory Lost, US-Backed Forces Say," *BBC News*, March 23, 2019, https://www.bbc.com/news/world-middle-east-47678157.
9. "Barzani Says Turkey Sent Arms to KRG, PYD Members Treated in Turkey," *Hurriyet Daily News*, October 13, 2014, https://www.hurriyetdailynews.com/barzani-says-turkey-sent-arms-to-krg-pyd-members-treated-in-turkey--72924.
10. Sistani's fatwa was given on July 11, 2014, through his representative Shaykh Abd al-Mahdi al-Karbalai. The text can be found here: http://www.sistani.org/arabic/archive/24925/.
11. Kerry, *Every Day Is Extra*, pp. 543–45. See also Helene Cooper, Mark Landler, and Alissa J. Rubin, "Obama Allows Limited Airstrikes on ISIS," *New York Times*, August 7, 2014, https://www.nytimes.com/2014/08/08/world/middleeast/obama-weighs-military-strikes-to-aid-trapped-iraqis-officials-say.html.

12. Ahmed Rasheed, "Exclusive: Iraq Says Islamic State Killed 500 Yazidis, Buried Some Victims Alive," *Reuters*, August 10, 2014, https://www.reuters.com/article/us-iraq-security-yazidis-killings/exclusive-iraq-says-islamic-state-killed-500-yazidis-buried-some-victims-alive-idUSKBN0GA0FF20140810.

13. Chelsea J. Carter, Mohammed Tawfeeq, and Barbara Starr, "Officials: U.S. Airstrikes Pound ISIS Militants Firing at Iraq's Yazidis," *CNN*, August 10, 2014, https://www.cnn.com/2014/08/09/world/meast/iraq-crisis.

14. President Obama provided the initial scope of U.S. intervention in a public address: "Statement by the President," The White House, Office of the Press Secretary, August 7, 2014, https://obamawhitehouse.archives.gov/the-press-office/2014/08/07/statement-president.

15. Kerry, *Every Day Is Extra*, p. 544.

16. Loveday Morris and Greg Jaffe, "Iraq Approves New Government, Opens Way for Expanded U.S. Role," *Washington Post*, September 8, 2014, https://www.washingtonpost.com/world/middle_east/un-human-rights-chief-calls-on-world-to-protect-women-children-from-islamic-state/2014/09/08/300ac70e-84a6-41e8-9cc3-9e8f9dca8ac4_story.html.

17. Kerry, *Every Day Is Extra*, pp. 546–48.

18. "Remarks by President Obama at the Leaders' Summit on Countering ISIL and Violent Extremism," The White House, Office of the Press Secretary, September 29, 2015, https://obamawhitehouse.archives.gov/the-press-office/2015/09/29/remarks-president-obama-leaders-summit-countering-isil-and-violent.

19. "Statement by the President on ISIL," The White House, Office of the Press Secretary, September 10, 2014, https://obamawhitehouse.archives.gov/the-press-office/2014/09/10/statement-president-isil-1.

20. The Soviet-era aircraft had originally been purchased by Saddam Hussein, who moved them to Iran in 1991 to spare them during the U.S.-led Gulf War. Iran kept the aircraft as reparations for Saddam having initiated the Iran-Iraq War, and they became the core of the IRGC's small combat air fleet. Iran denied that its pilots were flying missions over Iraq, but it was unlikely that the Iraqi military retained pilots with the knowhow to operate the aircraft.

21. "Iran Jets Bomb Islamic State Targets in Iraq—Pentagon," *BBC News*, December 3, 2014, https://www.bbc.com/news/world-middle-east-30304723.

22. Cassandra Vinograd and Ammar Cheikh Omar, "Syria, ISIS Have Been 'Ignoring' Each Other on Battlefield, Data Suggests," *NBC News*, December 11, 2014, https://www.nbcnews.com/storyline/isis-uncovered/syria-isis-have-been-ignoring-each-other-battlefield-data-suggests-n264551.

23. Gaith Abdul-Ahad, "Yemen's Dream of a Civil Society Suffocated by Religion and Tribalism," *The Guardian*, February 6, 2014, https://www.theguardian.com/world/2014/feb/06/yemen-civil-society-religion-tribalism.

24. David Arnold, "President Sacks Generals, Renews National Dialogue in Divided Yemen," *VOA News*, April 29, 2013, https://www.voanews.com/world-news/middle-east-dont-use/president-sacks-generals-renews-national-dialogue-divided-yemen.

25. Ginny Hill, *Yemen Endures: Civil War, Saudi Adventurism, and the Future of Arabia* (New York: Oxford University Press, 2017), p. 263.

26. "Al Qaeda in Yemen Seeks More Western Recruits," *CBS News*, November 1, 2010, https://www.cbsnews.com/news/al-qaeda-in-yemen-seeks-more-western-recruits/.

27. Marieke Brandt, *Tribes and Politics in Yemen: A History of the Houthi Conflict* (New York: Oxford University Press, 2017), pp. 106–9.

28. Hill, *Yemen Endures*, p. 269.

29. "Saudi Arabia Declares Muslim Brotherhood 'Terrorist Group,'" *BBC News*, March 7, 2014, https://www.bbc.com/news/world-middle-east-26487092.

30. "UAE Lists Muslim Brotherhood as Terrorist Group," *Reuters*, November 15, 2014, https://www.reuters.com/article/us-emirates-politics-brotherhood/uae-lists-muslim-brotherhood-as-terrorist-group-idUSKCN0IZ0OM20141115.

31. Angus McDowell, "Analysis: Egypt's Rulers Can Count on Gulf Aid Despite Bloodshed," *Reuters*, August 19, 2013, https://www.reuters.com/article/us-egypt-protests-saudi-analysis/analysis-egypts-rulers-can-count-on-gulf-aid-despite-bloodshed-idUSBRE97I0GG20130819.

32. Laura King, "Saudi King's Visit Key Show of Support for Egypt and Its New President," *Los Angeles Times*, June 21, 2014, https://www.latimes.com/world/middleeast/la-fg-egypt-saudi-arabia-20140622-story.html.

33. Scott Shane, "Saudis and Extremism: Both the Arsonists and the Firefighters," *New York Times*, August 25, 2016, https://www.nytimes.com/2016/08/26/world/middleeast/saudi-arabia-islam.html.

34. Robert F. Worth, "Egypt Is Arena for Influence of Arab Rivals," *New York Times*, July 9, 2013, https://www.nytimes.com/2013/07/10/world/middleeast/aid-to-egypt-from-saudis-and-emiratis-is-part-of-struggle-with-qatar-for-influence.html.

35. Hill, *Yemen Endures*, p. 269.

36. Saeed Al-Batati, "Violence Erupts in Yemen Capital after Weeks of Rallies," *New York Times*, September 9, 2014, https://www.nytimes.com/2014/09/10/world/middleeast/violence-erupts-in-yemen-capital-after-weeks-of-rallies.html.

37. "How Yemen's Capital Sanaa Was Seized by Houthi Rebels," *BBC News*, September 27, 2014, https://www.bbc.com/news/world-29380668.

38. "Yemen: Deal to End Political Crisis Signed," *BBC News*, September 21, 2014, https://www.bbc.com/news/world-middle-east-29302898.

39. Hill, *Yemen Endures*, p. 269.

40. Rod Nordland and Shuaib Almosawa, "U.S. Embassy Shuts in Yemen, Even as Militant Leader Reaches Out," *New York Times*, February 10, 2015, https://www.nytimes.com/2015/02/11/world/middleeast/yemen-houthi-leader-pledges-to-pursue-power-sharing-accord.html.

41. Ibid.

42. Hill, *Yemen Endures*, p. 271.

43. Nadwa Al-Dawsari, "Tribes and AQAP in South Yemen," Atlantic Council, June 5, 2014, https://www.atlanticcouncil.org/blogs/menasource/tribes-and-aqap-in-south-yemen/; "Yemen's al-Qaeda: Expanding the Base," International Crisis Group, Report 174, February 2, 2017, https://www.crisisgroup.org/middle-east-north-africa/gulf-and-arabian-peninsula/yemen/174-yemen-s-al-qaeda-expanding-base; Saeed Al-Batati and Kareem Fahim, "Affiliate of Al Qaeda Seizes Major Yemeni City, Driving Out the Military," *New York Times*, April 3, 2015, https://www.nytimes.com/2015/04/04/world/middleeast/al-qaeda-al-mukalla-yemen.html.

44. Mohammed Ghobari and Mohammed Mukhashaf, "Suicide Bombers Kill 137 in Yemen Mosque Attacks," *Reuters*, March 20, 2015, https://www.reuters.com/article/idUSKB N0MG11J/.

45. Brandt, *Tribes and Politics in Yemen*, p. 132.

46. See Bernard Haykel, *Revival and Reform in Islam: The Legacy of Muhammad al-Shawkani* (Cambridge: Cambridge University Press, 2003).

47. Brandt, *Tribes and Politics in Yemen*, pp. 206–8.

48. Erika Solomon, "Lebanon's Hizbollah and Yemen's Houthis Open Up on Links," *Financial Times*, May 8, 2015, https://www.ft.com/content/e1e6f750-f49b-11e4-9a58-00144feab7de; and Alex Vatanka, "Iran's Role in the Yemen Crisis," in *Global, Regional, and Local Dynamics in the Yemen Crisis*, ed. S. W. Day and N. Brehony (London: Palgrave Macmillan, 2020), pp. 157–60; Crist, *Twilight War*, p. 562; Katherine Zimmerman, "Iran's Man in Yemen and the al Houthis," *Critical Threats*, January 17, 2020, https://www.criticalthreats.org/analysis/irans-man-in-yemen-and-the-al-houthis.

Chapter 9

1. William J. Burns, *The Back Channel: A Memoir of American Diplomacy and the Case for Its Renewal* (New York: Random House, 2020), pp. 366–67.

2. Kerry, *Every Day Is Extra*, pp. 496–97.

3. Jeff Mason and Louis Charbonneau, "Obama, Iran's Rouhani Hold Historic Phone Call," *Reuters*, September 27, 2020, https://www.reuters.com/article/us-un-assembly-iran/obama-irans-rouhani-hold-historic-phone-call-idUSBRE98Q16S20130928.

4. Kerry, *Every Day Is Extra*, p. 486.

5. Resolution 2231 (2015) on Iran Nuclear Issue, United Nations Security Council, https://www.un.org/securitycouncil/content/2231/background.

6. Bruce Reidel, "Saudi Arabia's Role in the Yemen Crisis," in *Global, Regional, and Local Dynamics in the Yemen Crisis*, ed. S. W. Day and N. Brehony (London: Palgrave Macmillan, 2020), p. 122.

7. Baqir Sajjad Syed, "PM Holds Talks with King Salman, Meets Yemen President Hadi," *Dawn*, April 24, 2015, https://www.dawn.com/news/1177861.

8. Jon Boone and Saeed Kamali Dehgan, "Pakistan's Parliament Votes against Entering Yemen Conflict," *The Guardian*, April 10, 2015, https://www.theguardian.com/world/2015/apr/10/pakistans-parliament-votes-against-entering-yemen-conflict.

9. "Iran's Zarif Seeks Pakistan's Help in Yemen Crisis," *Aljazeera*, April 8, 2015, https://www.aljazeera.com/news/2015/04/08/irans-zarif-seeks-pakistans-help-in-yemen-crisis/.

10. Mateen Haider, "PM Nawaz Expresses 'Solidarity' with Saudi Arabia over Yemen," *Dawn*, April 23, 2015, https://www.dawn.com/news/1177731.

11. "America's Counterterrorism Wars: The War in Yemen," New America Foundation, https://www.newamerica.org/international-security/reports/americas-counterterrorism-wars/the-war-in-yemen/.

12. "Statement by Saudi Ambassador Al-Jubeir on Military Operations in Yemen," The Embassy of The Kingdom of Saudi Arabia, Washington, D.C., March 25, 2015, https://www.saudiembassy.net/press-release/statement-saudi-ambassador-al-jubeir-military-operations-yemen.

13. "Arabestan ba hamleh beh yaman darsadad ejra-ye eradeh-ye amrika va esra'il ast" ["With the attack on Yemen, Saudi Arabia aims to carry out the will of America and Israel"], *Tasnim News*, March 26, 2015, https://www.tasnimnews.com/fa/news/1394/01/06/695024.

14. "Ansar allah dar yaman ba manteq-e enqelab-e eslami amal mi-konad" ["Ansar Allah in Yemen uses the logic of the Islamic revolution"], *Tasnim News*, March 26, 2015, https://www.tasnimnews.com/fa/news/1394/01/06/695014.

15. "Security Council Demands End to Yemen Violence, Adopting Resolution 2216 (2015), with Russian Federation Abstaining," United Nations Meetings Coverage and Press Releases, April 14, 2015, https://www.un.org/press/en/2015/sc11859.doc.htm.

16. Hill, *Yemen Endures*, p. 276.

17. Noel Brehony, "The UAE's Role in the Yemen Crisis," in *Global, Regional, and Local Dynamics in the Yemen Crisis*, ed. S. W. Day and N. Brehony (London: Palgrave Macmillan, 2020), p. 138.

18. Stephanie Nebehay and Mohammed Ghobari, "Yemen Peace Talks to Start December 15 Alongside Ceasefire: U.N.," *Reuters*, December 7, 2015, https://www.reuters.com/article/us-yemen-security-talks/yemen-peace-talks-to-start-december-15-alongside-ceasefire-u-n-idUSKBN0TQ0ZW20151207.

19. Hill, *Yemen Endures*, p. 276.

20. Paul Lewis, Martin Chulov, Julian Borger, and Nicholas Watt, "Iran Warns West against Military Intervention in Syria," *The Guardian*, August 27, 2013, https://www.theguardian.com/world/2013/aug/26/syria-us-un-inspection-kerry.

21. "The Latest American Provocation Will Lead to End with the Annihilation of Israel" ["Jang-afruzi-e jaded-e amrika behbaha-ye nabudi-ye esra'il tamam khahad shod"], *Tasnim News*, August 28, 2013, https://www.tasnimnews.com/fa/news/1392/06/06/128135.

22. "Statement by the President on ISIL," The White House, Office of the Press Secretary, September 10, 2014, https://obamawhitehouse.archives.gov/the-press-office/2014/09/10/statement-president-isil-1.

23. Karen DeYoung and Hugh Naylor, "Kurds Drive Islamic State Fighters from Strategic Town of Kobane," *Washington Post*, January 26, 2015, https://www.washingtonpost.com/world/assad-is-defiant-ahead-of-peace-discussion-scheduled-monday-in-moscow/2015/01/26/55d0ea22-a564-11e4-a2b2-776095f393b2_story.html.

24. Suleiman Al-Khalidi and Tom Perry, "New Syrian Rebel Alliance Formed, Says Weapons on the Way," *Reuters*, October 11, 2015, https://www.reuters.com/article/us-mideast-crisis-syria-kurds-iduskcn0s60bd20151012.

25. Aaron Stein, "The YPG-PKK Connection," The Atlantic Council, January 26, 2016, https://www.atlanticcouncil.org/blogs/menasource/the-ypg-pkk-connection/.

26. Aldar Khalil, "Syria's Kurds Are Not the PKK," *Foreign Policy*, May 15, 2017, https://foreignpolicy.com/2017/05/15/syrias-kurds-are-not-the-pkk-Erdoğan-pyd-ypg/.

27. Ben Hubbard, "ISIS Loses Control of Crucial Syrian Border Town," *New York Times*, June 16, 2015, https://www.nytimes.com/2015/06/17/world/middleeast/isis-loses-control-of-crucial-syrian-border-town.html.
28. Ayla Jean Yackley, "Erdoğan Says Turkey May Hit U.S.-Backed Syrian Kurds to Block Advance," *Reuters*, October 28, 2015, https://www.reuters.com/article/us-mideast-crisis-tur key-kurds/Erdoğan-says-turkey-may-hit-u-s-backed-syrian-kurds-to-block-advance-idUSKC N0SM2V620151028.
29. Liz Sly, "Syrian Rebels Take Strategic Town of Idlib," *Washington Post*, March 28, 2015, https://www.washingtonpost.com/world/middle_east/syrian-rebels-take-strategic-town-of-idlib/2015/03/28/59e33562-d55b-11e4-8b1e-274d670aa9c9_story.html.
30. Anne Barnard, "ISIS Speeds Up Destruction of Antiquities in Syria," August 24, 2015, https://www.nytimes.com/2015/08/25/world/isis-accelerates-destruction-of-antiquities-in-syria.html; Stuart Jeffries, "ISIS's Destruction of Palmyra: 'The Heart Has Been Ripped Out of the City,'" September 2, 2015, https://www.theguardian.com/world/2015/sep/02/isis-destruction-of-palmyra-syria-heart-been-ripped-out-of-the-city.
31. Ostovar, *Vanguard of the Imam*, p. 231.
32. Robert E. Hamilton, Chris Miller, and Aaron Stein, eds., *Russia's Way of War in Syria: Assessing Russian Military Capabilities and Lessons Learned* (Philadelphia: Foreign Policy Research Institute, 2020), p. 3.
33. Jack Stubbs, "Four-Fifths of Russia's Syria Strikes Don't Target Islamic State: Reuters Analysis," *Reuters*, October 21, 2015, https://www.reuters.com/article/us-mideast-crisis-syria-russia-strikes/four-fifths-of-russias-syria-strikes-dont-target-islamic-state-reuters-analysis-idUSKC N0SF24L20151021; Jack Stubbs and Humeyra Pamuk, "Russian Raids Repeatedly Hit Syrian Turkmen Areas, Moscow's Data Shows," *Reuters*, November 27, 2015, https://www.reuters.com/article/us-mideast-crisis-russia-turkey-airstrik/russian-raids-repeatedly-hit-syr ian-turkmen-areas-moscows-data-shows-idUSKBN0TG1YQ20151127.
34. Keith Bradsher, "Range of Frustrations Reached Boil as Turkey Shot Down Russian Jet," *New York Times*, November 25, 2015, https://www.nytimes.com/2015/11/26/world/eur ope/turkey-russia-fighter-jet.html.
35. Neil MacFarquhar and Tim Arango, "Putin and Erdoğan, Both Isolated, Reach Out to Each Other," August 8, 2016, https://www.nytimes.com/2016/08/09/world/europe/russia-putin-turkey-Erdoğan-syria.html.
36. Jamie Crawford and Jennifer Rizzo, "U.S. and Russia Sign Syria Memorandum," *CNN*, October 20, 2015, https://www.cnn.com/2015/10/20/politics/u-s-russia-sign-syrian-mem orandum/index.html; see also "Press Conference by the President," The White House, Office of the Press Secretary, October 2, 2015, https://obamawhitehouse.archives.gov/the-press-office/2015/10/02/press-conference-president.
37. "Security Council Unanimously Adopts Resolution 2254 (2015), Endorsing Road Map for Peace Process in Syria, Setting Timetable for Talks," United Nations Meetings Coverage and Press Releases, December 18, 2015, https://www.un.org/press/en/2015/sc12171.doc.htm.
38. Chris Kozakj, "Russian-Syrian-Iranian Coalition Seizes ISIS-Held Palmyra," Institute for the Study of War, May 27, 2016, http://www.understandingwar.org/backgrounder/russian-syr ian-iranian-coalition-seizes-isis-held-palmyra; and Richard Spencer, "Where Are the Syrians in Assad's Syrian Arab Army?," *The Telegraph*, April 9, 2016, https://www.telegraph.co.uk/news/2016/04/09/where-are-the-syrians-in-assads-syrian-arab-army/.
39. Hamilton, Miller, and Stein, *Russia's Way of War in Syria*, p. 5.
40. Ibid.
41. Anne Barnard, "Battle over Aleppo Is Over, Russia Says, as Evacuation Deal Reached," *New York Times*, December 13, 2016, https://www.nytimes.com/2016/12/13/world/mid dleeast/syria-aleppo-civilians.html.
42. Hugh Naylor, "Turkish-Backed Rebels in Syria Make Major Gains against Islamic State," *Washington Post*, April 8, 2016, https://www.washingtonpost.com/world/turkish-backed-rebels-in-syria-make-major-gains-against-islamic-state/2016/04/08/7560a314-91ff-47dd-9dc9-393570c0ddad_story.html.
43. Aaron Stein, "How Russia Beat Turkey in Syria," The Atlantic Council, March 27, 2017, https://www.atlanticcouncil.org/blogs/syriasource/how-russia-beat-turkey-in-syria/.

44. Anne Barnard and Hwaida Saad, "Iran, Russia and Turkey Agree to Enforce Syria Cease-Fire, but Don't Explain How," *New York Times*, January 24, 2017, https://www.nytimes.com/2017/01/24/world/middleeast/syria-war-iran-russia-turkey-cease-fire.html.

Chapter 10

1. The presence of Russian ambassador Kislyak led to some controversy: https://nationalinter est.org/feature/statement-regarding-president-trumps-april-27-2016-foreign-19715.
2. "Transcript: Donald Trump's Foreign Policy Speech," *New York Times*, April 16, 2016, https://www.nytimes.com/2016/04/28/us/politics/transcript-trump-foreign-policy.html; also see Donald J. Trump, "Trump on Foreign Policy," *National Interest*, April 27, 2016, https://natio nalinterest.org/feature/trump-foreign-policy-15960.
3. This section of the speech is quoted from the official publication in the *National Interest*: https://nationalinterest.org/feature/trump-foreign-policy-15960. The words in the speech as delivered are nearly exactly the same, although with added grammatical errors and awkward ad libs that cloud its readability.
4. "Turkey Ends 'Shield' Military Operation in Syria, PM Says," *Reuters*, March 29, 2017, https://www.reuters.com/article/us-mideast-crisis-syria-turkey/turkey-ends-shield-milit ary-operation-in-syria-pm-says-idUSKBN17030R.
5. "Battle for Mosul: Turkey Confirms Military Involvement," *Aljazeera*, October 24, 2016, https://www.aljazeera.com/news/2016/10/24/battle-for-mosul-turkey-confirms-military-involvement; Tulay Karadeniz and Ercan Gurses, "Turkey Says Its Troops to Stay in Iraq until Islamic State Cleared from Mosul," *Reuters*, October 11, 2016, https://www.reuters.com/arti cle/us-mideast-crisis-iraq-turkey/turkey-says-its-troops-to-stay-in-iraq-until-islamic-state-cleared-from-mosul-idUSKCN12C0KF.
6. Maher Chmaytelli and Tuvan Gumrukcu, "Baghdad Bridles at Turkey's Military Presence, Warns of 'Regional War,'" *Reuters*, October 5, 2016, https://www.reuters.com/article/us-mideast-crisis-iraq-turkey/baghdad-bridles-at-turkeys-military-presence-warns-of-regional-war-idUSKCN1250H9.
7. Aaron Stein, "Behind Erdoğan's Dismissive Statements to Iraq's Prime Minister," Atlantic Council, October 12, 2016, https://www.atlanticcouncil.org/blogs/menasource/behind-erdogan-s-dismissive-statements-to-iraq-s-prime-minister/.
8. Phil Stewart and Tuvan Gumrukcu, "Iraqi PM Declines Turkish Offer to Help in Mosul Battle," *Reuters*, October 22, 2016, https://www.reuters.com/article/idUSKCN12M0GQ/
9. Marc Lowen, "Battle for Mosul: A Row between Turkey and Iraq Could Derail the Offensive," *BBC News*, October 12, 2016, https://www.bbc.com/news/world-europe-37629577.
10. Tim Arango, "Tal Afar, West of Mosul, Becomes Center of Battle for Influence in Iraq," *New York Times*, October 29, 2016, https://www.nytimes.com/2016/10/30/world/middlee ast/tal-afar-iraq-isis.html.
11. Mustafa Saadoun, "Iran, Turkey Fight over Tal Afar," *Al-Monitor*, November 18, 2016, https://www.al-monitor.com/pulse/originals/2016/11/tal-afar-iraq-turkman-turkey-pmu-syria.html.
12. Ahmet Sait Akçay, "Erdoğan Warns of Shia Militia Entering Iraq's Tal Afar," *Anadolu Agency*, October 29, 2016, https://www.aa.com.tr/en/middle-east/erdogan-warns-of-shia-militia-entering-iraqs-tal-afar/674842.
13. Saadoun, "Iran, Turkey Fight over Tal Afar."
14. Siraj Wahab, "Erdoğan Calls Al-Hashd Al-Shaabi a 'Terror' Organization," *Arab News*, April 21, 2017, https://www.arabnews.com/node/1087911/amp.
15. Amos C. Fox, "The Mosul Study Group and the Lessons of the Battle of Mosul," The Association of the United States Army, Land Warfare Paper 130, February 2020, https://www.ausa.org/sites/default/files/publications/LWP-130-The-Mosul-Study-Group-and-the-Lessons-of-the-Battle-of-Mosul.pdf.
16. Thomas D. Arnold and Nicolas Fiore, "Five Operational Lessons from the Battle for Mosul," *Military Review*, January–February 2019, https://www.armyupress.army.mil/Journals/Milit ary-Review/English-Edition-Archives/Jan-Feb-2019/Arnold-Mosul/.

17. Becca Wasser, Stacie L. Pettyjohn, Jeffrey Martini, et al., *The Air War against the Islamic State: The Role of Airpower in Operation Inherent Resolve* (Santa Monica, CA: RAND, 2021), pp. 167–72.
18. Arnold and Fiore, "Five Operational Lessons from the Battle for Mosul."
19. Wasser, Pettyjohn, Martini, et al., *The Air War against the Islamic State*, p. 169.
20. Arnold and Fiore, "Five Operational Lessons from the Battle for Mosul."
21. Fox, "The Mosul Study Group and the Lessons of the Battle of Mosul," p. 3.
22. Karen DeYoung and Missy Ryan, "Turkish President Renews Threat to Launch Offensive against Kurds in U.S.-Controlled Territory in Syria," *Washington Post*, December 17, 2018, https://www.washingtonpost.com/world/national-security/turkish-president-renews-thr eat-to-launch-offensive-against-kurds-in-us-controlled-territory-in-syria/2018/12/17/ 34b41596-022e-11e9-b5df-5d3874f1ac36_story.html.
23. Karen DeYoung, Missy Ryan, Josh Dawsey, and Greg Jaffe, "A Tumultuous Week Began with a Phone Call between Trump and the Turkish President," *Washington Post*, December 21, 2018, https://www.washingtonpost.com/world/national-security/a-tumultuous-week-began-with-a-phone-call-between-trump-and-the-turkish-president/2018/12/21/8f49b562-0542-11e9-9122-82e98f91ee6f_story.html.
24. John Bolton, *The Room Where It Happened: A White House Memoir* (New York: Simon & Schuster, 2020), pp. 193–94.
25. DeYoung, Ryan, Dawsey and Jaffe, "A Tumultuous Week Began with a Phone Call between Trump and the Turkish President."
26. https://twitter.com/LindseyGrahamSC/status/1075578496733364226/photo/1.
27. Bolton, *The Room Where It Happened*, pp. 194–95.
28. Ibid., p. 192.
29. Aaron Mehta, "Turkey Officially Kicked Out of F-35 Program, Costing US Half a Billion Dollars," *Defense News*, July 17, 2019, https://www.defensenews.com/air/2019/07/17/tur key-officially-kicked-out-of-f-35-program/.
30. Bolton, *The Room Where It Happened*, pp. 207–13.
31. Adam Edelman and Elizabeth Janowski, "Republicans Slam Trump's Syria Pullout: 'Disaster,' 'Betrayal,' 'Mistake,'" *NBC News*, October 7, 2019, https://www.nbcnews.com/politics/ national-security/disaster-betrayal-mistake-republicans-slam-trump-s-syria-pull-out-n106 325.1.
32. "Turkey Launches Airstrikes on Northern Syria after Trump Pulls Back U.S. Troops," *CBS News*, October 9, 2019, https://www.cbsnews.com/news/turkey-invades-syria-turkish-president-erdogan-announces-military-operation-today-2019-10-09/.
33. Aaron Blake, "'They Didn't Help Us with Normandy': Trump Abandons the Kurds—Rhetorically if Not Literally," *Washington Post*, October 9, 2019, https://www.washingtonp ost.com/politics/2019/10/09/trump-has-abandoned-kurds-least-rhetorically/.
34. "Turkish Military Operation East Euphrates Kills More than 70 Civilians so Far and Forces Nearly 300 Thousand People to Displace from Their Areas," Syrian Observatory for Human Rights, October 16, 2019, https://www.syriahr.com/en/144078/.
35. Asli Aydıntaşbaş, "A New Gaza: Turkey's Border Policy in Northern Syria," European Council on Foreign Relations, May 28, 2020, https://ecfr.eu/publication/a_new_gaza_turkeys_border_policy_in_northern_syria/.
36. Jiyar Gol, "Syria Conflict: The 'War Crimes' Caught in Brutal Phone Footage," *BBC News*, November 3, 2019, https://www.bbc.com/news/world-middle-east-50250330; Dan Sabbagh, "Investigation into Alleged Use of White Phosphorus in Syria," *The Guardian*, October 18, 2018, https://www.theguardian.com/world/2019/oct/18/un-investigates-turkey-alleged-use-of-white-phosphorus-in-syria; and Robbie Gramer and Lara Seligman, "Lawmakers Demand Answers on Alleged War Crimes by Turkish-Backed Forces in Syria," *Foreign Policy*, October 25, 2019, https://foreignpolicy.com/2019/10/25/trump-syria-kurds-turkey-reported-war-crimes-lawmakers-press-pompeo-state-department-for-answers/. See also "Syria: Civilians Abused in 'Safe Zones': Summary Executions, Blocked Returns by Turkish-Backed Armed Groups," Human Rights Watch, November 27, 2019, https://www.hrw.org/news/2019/11/27/syria-civilians-abused-safe-zones#.

37. Robin Emmott, "EU Governments Limit Arms Sales to Turkey but Avoid Embargo," *Reuters*, October 13, 2021, https://www.reuters.com/article/us-syria-security-eu-france-idUSKB N1WT0M4.

38. Robin Emmott and John Irish, "Furious with Turkey, EU Threatens Sanctions, Arms Embargo," *Reuters*, October 11, 2019, https://www.reuters.com/article/us-syria-security-tur key-eu/furious-with-turkey-eu-threatens-sanctions-arms-embargo-idUSKBN1WQ1QE.

39. U.S. Department of Treasury, "Treasury Designates Turkish Ministries and Senior Officials in Response to Military Action in Syria," October 14, 2019, https://home.treasury.gov/news/ press-releases/sm792. See also "Turkey-Syria Offensive: US Sanctions Turkish Ministries," *BBC News*, October 15, 2019, https://www.bbc.com/news/world-middle-east-50050264.

40. "Text—S.2644—116th Congress (2019–2020): Countering Turkish Aggression Act of 2019," October 21, 2019, https://www.congress.gov/bill/116th-congress/senate-bill/2644/text; see also Alan Fram, "Bipartisan House OKs Bill Hitting Turkey for Syria Incursion," *Associated Press*, October 29, 2019, https://apnews.com/article/25a4f52cb21f4706923e93dc22f4faca.

Chapter 11

1. "Iran: Saudis Face 'Divine Revenge' for Executing al-Nimr," *BBC News*, January 3, 2016, https://www.bbc.com/news/world-middle-east-35216694.

2. Afshon Ostovar, "Sectarianism and Iranian Foreign Policy," in *Beyond Sunni and Shia: The Roots of Sectarianism in a Changing Middle East*, ed. Frederic Wehrey (London: Hurst, 2017), pp. 89–90.

3. Mohammad Javad Zarif, "Mohammad Javad Zarif: Saudi Arabia's Reckless Extremism," *New York Times*, January 10, 2016, https://www.nytimes.com/2016/01/11/opinion/moham mad-javad-zarif-saudi-arabias-reckless-extremism.html.

4. Adel Bin Ahmed Al-Jubeir, "Can Iran Change?," *New York Times*, January 19, 2016, https:// www.nytimes.com/2016/01/19/opinion/saudi-arabia-can-iran-change.html.

5. David B. Roberts, *Qatar: Securing the Global Ambitions of a City-State.* (London: Hurst, 2017), pp. 28–32; and Mehran Kamrava, *Troubled Waters: Insecurity in the Persian Gulf* (Ithaca, NY, and London: Cornell University Press, 2018), pp. 105–7.

6. Rebecca Savransky, "Trump: 'There Can No Longer Be Funding of Radical Ideology,'" *The Hill*, June 6, 2017, https://thehill.com/homenews/administration/336484-trump-there-can-no-longer-be-funding-of-radical-ideology.

7. Gardiner Harris, "State Dept. Lashes Out at Gulf Countries over Qatar Embargo," *New York Times*, June 20, 2017, https://www.nytimes.com/2017/06/20/world/middleeast/qatar-saudi-arabia-trump-tillerson.html; Lally Weymouth, "Qatar to Saudi Arabia: Quit Trying to Overthrow Our Government," *Washington Post*, February 2, 2018, https://www.washing tonpost.com/outlook/qatar-to-saudi-arabia-quit-trying-to-overthrow-our-government/ 2018/02/02/05a1a848-0759-11e8-8777-2a059f168dd2_story.html; and Alex Emmons, "Saudi Arabia Planned to Invade Qatar Last Summer. Rex Tillerson's Efforts to Stop It May Have Cost Him His Job," *The Intercept*, August 1, 2018, https://theintercept.com/2018/08/ 01/rex-tillerson-qatar-saudi-uae/.

8. "What Are the 13 Demands Given to Qatar?," *Gulf News*, June 23, 2017, https://gulfnews. com/world/gulf/qatar/what-are-the-13-demands-given-to-qatar-1.2048118.

9. Kathy Gilsinan and Jeffrey Goldberg, "Emirati Ambassador: Qatar Is a Destructive Force in the Region," *The Atlantic*, https://www.theatlantic.com/international/archive/2017/08/you sef-al-otaiba-qatar-gcc/538206/.

10. Robert F. Worth, "Kidnapped Royalty Become Pawns in Iran's Deadly Plot," *New York Times Magazine*, March 14, 2018, https://www.nytimes.com/2018/03/14/magazine/how-a-ran som-for-royal-falconers-reshaped-the-middle-east.html.

11. "Syria Conflict: Besieged Towns of Foah and Kefraya Evacuated," *BBC News*, July 19, 2018, https://www.bbc.com/news/world-middle-east-44870998.

12. Worth, "Kidnapped Royalty Become Pawns in Iran's Deadly Plot."

13. Tom Finn, "Turkey to Set Up Qatar Military Base to Face 'Common Enemies,'" *Reuters*, December 16, 2015, https://www.reuters.com/article/us-qatar-turkey-military/turkey-to-set-up-qatar-military-base-to-face-common-enemies-idUSKBN0TZ17V20151216.

14. "Saudi Official: Turkish Military Base in Qatar 'Complicates' the Situation," *Al Arabiya*, June 30, 2017, https://english.alarabiya.net/News/gulf/2017/06/30/Saudi-official-The-Turkish-military-base-in-Qatar-complicates-the-situation.

15. "Saudi Official Hints at Plan to Dig Canal on Qatar Border,'" *Reuters*, August 31, 2018, https://www.reuters.com/article/us-saudi-qatar-canal/saudi-official-hints-at-plan-to-dig-canal-on-qatar-border-idUSKCN1LG13H.

16. "Turkey Sends More Troops to Qatar," *Aljazeera*, December 27, 2017, https://www.aljazeera.com/news/2017/12/27/turkey-sends-more-troops-to-qatar.

17. Giorgio Cafiero and Daniel Wagner, "Turkey and Qatar's Burgeoning Strategic Alliance," Middle East Institute, June 8, 2016, https://www.mei.edu/publications/turkey-and-qatars-burgeoning-strategic-alliance.

18. Mustafa Kutlay and Ziya Öniş, "Turkish Foreign Policy in a Post-Western Order: Strategic Autonomy or New Forms of Dependence?," *International Affairs* 97, no. 4 (July 2021): 1085–1104.

19. Cafiero and Wagner, "Turkey and Qatar's Burgeoning Strategic Alliance."

20. Jamal Khashoggi, "Opinion: Saudi Arabia's Crown Prince Must Restore Dignity to His Country—by Ending Yemen's Cruel War," *Washington Post*, September 11, 2018, https://www.washingtonpost.com/news/global-opinions/wp/2018/09/11/saudi-arabias-crown-prince-must-restore-dignity-to-his-country-by-ending-yemens-cruel-war/.

21. Ian Pannell, "Though Khashoggi Never Suspected He Might Be in Mortal Danger, He Was Apprehensive about Visiting the Consulate," *ABC News*, October 30, 2018, https://abcnews.go.com/International/khashoggi-lured-back-saudi-consulate-warm-greeting-time/story?id=58857344.

22. Editorial Board, "Opinion: Jamal Khashoggi Was Brutally Murdered Four Weeks Ago. We're Still Waiting for Answers," *Washington Post*, October 30, 2018, https://www.washingtonpost.com/opinions/global-opinions/jamal-khashoggi-was-brutally-murdered-four-weeks-ago-were-still-waiting-for-answers/2018/10/30/e4469d58-dc63-11e8-85df-7a6b4d25cfbb_story.html.

23. "Jamal Khashoggi: Who's Who in Alleged Saudi 'Hit Squad,'" *BBC News*, October 19, 2018, https://www.bbc.com/news/world-middle-east-45906396.

24. Gul Tuysuz, Salma Abdelaziz, Ghazi Balkiz, Ingrid Formanek, and Clarissa Ward, "Surveillance Footage Shows Saudi 'Body Double' in Khashoggi's Clothes after He Was Killed, Turkish Source Says," *CNN*, October 23, 2018, https://www.cnn.com/2018/10/22/middleeast/saudi-operative-jamal-khashoggi-clothes/index.html.

25. Kareem Fahim and John Hudson, "How Turkey's President Pressured the Saudis to Account for Khashoggi's Death," *Washington Post*, October 19, 2018, https://www.washingtonpost.com/world/national-security/how-turkeys-president-became-a-pivotal-dealmaker-after-saudi-journalist-disappeared/2018/10/19/ba337b86-d30c-11e8-8c22-fa2ef74bd6d6_story.html.

26. Saphora Smith, "Saudi Arabia Now Admits Khashoggi Killing Was 'Premeditated,'" *CNBC*, October 25, 2018, https://www.nbcnews.com/news/world/saudi-arabia-now-admits-khashoggi-killing-was-premeditated-n924286.

27. Mark Landler, "In Extraordinary Statement, Trump Stands with Saudis despite Khashoggi Killing," *New York Times*, November 20, 2018, https://www.nytimes.com/2018/11/20/world/middleeast/trump-saudi-khashoggi.html.

28. Jonathan Franklin, "D.C. Council Renames the Street in Front of the Saudi Embassy after Jamal Khashoggi," *NPR*, December 8, 2021, https://www.npr.org/2021/12/08/1062469781/dc-council-renames-street-saudi-embassy-jamal-khashoggi.

29. Karoun Demirjian, "Senate Rebukes Trump with Vote Ordering U.S. Military to End Support for Saudi-Led War in Yemen," *Washington Post*, March 13, 2019, https://www.washingtonpost.com/powerpost/senate-rebukes-trump-with-vote-ordering-us-military-to-end-support-for-saudi-led-war-in-yemen/2019/03/13/da6a24a8-45c2-11e9-8aab-95b8d80a1e4f_story.html.

30. Mark Landler and Peter Baker, "Trump Vetoes Measure to Force End to U.S. Involvement in Yemen War," *New York Times*, April 16, 2019, https://www.nytimes.com/2019/04/16/us/politics/trump-veto-yemen.html.

31. Marianne Levine, "Senate Rebukes Trump with Vote to Block Arms Sales to Saudi Arabia, UAE," *Politico*, June 20, 2019, https://www.politico.com/story/2019/06/20/senate-votes-to-block-arms-sales-to-saudi-arabia-1373203.

32. Thomas Juneau, "The UAE and the War in Yemen: From Surge to Recalibration," *Survival 62*, no. 4 (2020): 190–92.

33. "How the UAE Extends Its Military Reach in Yemen and Somalia—With Deadly Results," *Haaretz*, May 13, 2018, https://www.haaretz.com/middle-east-news/how-uae-extends-milit ary-reach-in-yemen-and-somalia-1.6077658.

34. David Hearst, "Exclusive: Yemen President Says UAE Acting like Occupiers," *Middle East Eye*, May 12, 2018, https://www.middleeasteye.net/news/exclusive-yemen-president-says-uae-acting-occupiers; "UAE Forces 'Occupy' Sea and Airports on Yemen's Socotra," *Aljazeera*, May 4, 2018, https://www.aljazeera.com/news/2018/5/4/uae-forces-occupy-sea-and-airports-on-yemens-socotra. On the Saudi handover: "Saudi Forces Arrive in Socotra as Yemen, UAE Reach Deal," *Daily Sabah*, May 14, 2018, https://www.dailysabah.com/mide ast/2018/05/14/saudi-forces-arrive-in-socotra-as-yemen-uae-reach-deal.

35. Juneau, "UAE and the War in Yemen," pp. 188–89.

36. Ibid.

37. "250,000 People 'May Lose Everything—Even Their Lives' in Assault on Key Yemeni Port City: UN Humanitarian Coordinator," *UN News*, June 8, 2018, https://news.un.org/en/story/2018/06/1011701.

38. Bethan McKernan, "Battle Rages in Yemen's Vital Port as Showdown Looms," *The Guardian*, November 7, 2018, https://www.theguardian.com/world/2018/nov/07/yemen-hodeidah-airstrikes-saudi-led-coalition-ceasefire-calls.

39. Juneau, "UAE and the War in Yemen," p. 190.

40. Declan Walsh and David D. Kirkpatrick, "U.A.E. Pulls Most Forces from Yemen in Blow to Saudi War Effort," *New York Times*, July 11, 2019, https://www.nytimes.com/2019/07/11/world/middleeast/yemen-emirates-saudi-war.html; and Michael Knights, "Lessons from the UAE War in Yemen," *Lawfare*, August 18, 2019, https://www.lawfareblog.com/less ons-uae-war-yemen.

41. Juneau, "UAE and the War in Yemen," p. 196.

42. Ibrahim Jalal, "The UAE May Have Withdrawn from Yemen, but Its Influence Remains Strong," Middle East Institute, February 25, 2020, https://www.mei.edu/publications/uae-may-have-withdrawn-yemen-its-influence-remains-strong.

Chapter 12

1. "Libya's Islamist Militias Claim Control of Tripoli," *VOA*, August 24, 2014, https://www.voan ews.com/a/misrati-militia-calls-for-ouster-of-elected-libyan-parliament/2426301.html.

2. "Libya Faces Chaos as Top Court Rejects Elected Assembly," *Reuters*, November 6, 2014, https://www.reuters.com/article/us-libya-security-parliament/libya-faces-chaos-as-top-court-rejects-elected-assembly-idUSKBN0IQ0YF20141106.

3. Frederic Wehrey and Andrew Seger, "Can Libya's Divisions Be Healed?" Interview with the Council of Foreign Relations, August 15, 2018, https://carnegieendowment.org/2018/08/15/can-libya-s-divisions-be-healed-pub-77073.

4. "Unanimously Adopting Resolution 2259 (2015), Security Council Welcomes Signing of Libyan Political Agreement on New Government for Strife-Torn Country," United Nations Security Council, December 23, 2015, https://www.un.org/press/en/2015/sc12185.doc.htm.

5. Amro Hassan, "In Libya, Islamist Rebels Claim Control of Benghazi," *Los Angeles Times*, July 31, 2014, https://www.latimes.com/world/middleeast/la-fg-libya-benghazi-20140731-story.html.

6. Aaron Y. Zelin, "The Others: Foreign Fighters in Libya," Washington Institute for Near East Policy, Policy Note 45, 2018.

7. Inga Kristina Trauthig, "Islamic State in Libya: From Force to Farce?," *ICSR*, March 10, 2020, pp. 7–9.

8. Ruth Michaelson, "Turkey and UAE Openly Flouting UN Arms Embargo to Fuel War in Libya," *The Guardian*, October 7, 2020, https://www.theguardian.com/global-development/2020/oct/07/turkey-and-uae-openly-flouting-un-arms-embargo-to-fuel-war-in-libya.

9. Missy Ryan and Sudarsan Raghavan, "U.S. Special Operations Troops Aiding Libyan Forces in Major Battle against Islamic State," *Washington Post*, August 9, 2016, https://www.washing tonpost.com/news/checkpoint/wp/2016/08/09/u-s-special-operations-forces-are-provid ing-direct-on-the-ground-support-for-the-first-time-in-libya/.

10. Frederic Wehrey and Anouar Boukhars, *Salafism in the Maghreb* (New York: Oxford University Press, 2019), pp. 125–30.

11. Martin Chulov and Julian Borger, "Trump Officials Snub Strongman Khalifa Haftar as US Shifts Course on Libya," *The Guardian*, June 8, 2019, https://www.theguardian.com/us-news/2019/jun/08/libya-civil-war-khalifa-haftar.

12. "Chad to Send 1,500 Troops to Libya in Support of Marshal Haftar," *Atalayer*, June 12, 2020, https://atalayar.com/en/content/chad-send-1500-troops-libya-support-marshal-haftar; and United Nations Security Council, "Letter Dated 8 March 2021 from the Panel of Experts on Libya Established Pursuant to Resolution 1973 (2011) Addressed to the President of the Security Council," March 8, 2021.

13. "Libya Attack: French Soldiers Die in Helicopter Crash," *BBC News*, July 20, 2016, https://www.bbc.com/news/world-africa-36843186.

14. Jalel Harchaoui, "How France Is Making Libya Worse: Macron Is Strengthening Haftar," *Foreign Affairs*, September 21, 2017, https://www.foreignaffairs.com/articles/france/2017-09-21/how-france-making-libya-worse; see also Paul Taylor, "France's Double Game in Libya," *Politico*, April 17, 2019, https://www.politico.eu/article/frances-double-game-in-libya-nato-un-khalifa-haftar/.

15. Jared Malsin, "Russia Reinforces Foothold in Libya as Militia Leader Retreats," *Wall Street Journal*, June 29, 2020, https://www.wsj.com/articles/russia-reinforces-foothold-in-libya-as-militia-leader-retreats-11593453304.; Ilya Barabanov and Nader Ibrahim, "Wagner: Scale of Russian Mercenary Mission in Libya Exposed," *BBC News*, August 11, 2021, https://www.bbc.com/news/world-africa-58009514.

16. Samuel Ramani, "Russia's Strategy in Libya," *RUSI*, April 7, 2020, https://rusi.org/explore-our-research/publications/commentary/russias-strategy-libya; and Yuri Barman, "Russia Enters Libya's Conflict," Middle East Institute, May 2, 2017, https://www.mei.edu/publicati ons/russia-enters-libyas-conflict.

17. Jason Pack and Wolfgang Pusztai, "Turning the Tide: How Turkey Won the War for Tripoli," Middle East Institute, November 2020, pp. 2–4.

18. "The Berlin Conference on Libya—Conference Conclusions," January 19, 2020, https://reliefweb.int/report/libya/berlin-conference-libya-conference-conclusions-19-january-2020.

19. Amy Mackinnon and Jack Detsch, "Pentagon Says UAE Possibly Funding Russia's Shadowy Mercenaries in Libya," *Foreign Policy*, November 30, 2020, https://foreignpolicy.com/2020/11/30/pentagon-trump-russia-libya-uae/.

20. Declan Walsh, "Waves of Russian and Emirati Flights Fuel Libyan War, U.N. Finds," *New York Times*, September 3, 2020, https://www.nytimes.com/2020/09/03/world/middleeast/libya-russia-emirates-mercenaries.html.

21. Pack and Pusztai, "Turning the Tide: How Turkey Won the War for Tripoli," pp. 4–5.

22. United Nations Security Council, "United Nations Support Mission in Libya: Report of the Secretary-General," January 15, 2020, pp. 4–5.

23. Frederic Wehrey, "A Minister, a General, & the Militias: Libya's Shifting Balance of Power," *New York Review of Books*, March 19, 2019, https://www.nybooks.com/daily/2019/03/19/a-minister-a-general-militias-libyas-shifting-balance-of-power/.

24. Ryan Browne, "Trump Praises Libyan General as His Troops March on US Backed Government in Tripoli," *CNN*, April 19, 2019, https://www.cnn.com/2019/04/19/politics/us-libya-praise-haftar/index.html.

25. Pack and Pusztai, "Turning the Tide: How Turkey Won the War for Tripoli," pp. 5–9.

26. Frederic Wehrey, "Among the Syrian Militiamen of Turkey's Intervention in Libya," *New York Review of Books*, January 23, 2020, https://www.nybooks.com/daily/2020/01/23/

among-the-syrian-militiamen-of-turkeys-intervention-in-libya/; Sam Magdy, "US: Turkey-Sent Syrian Fighters Generate Backlash in Libya," *Associated Press*, September 2, 2020, https://apnews.com/article/middle-east-africa-679a6d6fc549bda59f8627d91d9a363c; and Matt Powers, "Making Sense of Sadat, Turkey's Private Military Company," *War on the Rocks*, October 8, 2021, https://warontherocks.com/2021/10/making-sense-of-sadat-turkeys-private-military-company./

27. Pack and Pusztai, "Turning the Tide: How Turkey Won the War for Tripoli," p. 10.

28. Kareem Fahim and Zakaria Zakaria, "These Syrian Militiamen Were Foes in Their Civil War. Now They Are Battling Each Other in Libya," *Washington Post*, June 25, 2020, https://www.washingtonpost.com/world/middle_east/these-syrian-militiamen-were-foes-in-their-civil-war-now-they-are-battling-each-other-in-libya/2020/06/25/c7ceff8c-affa-11ea-98b5-279a6479a1e4_story.html.

29. "Increased Turkish Seismic Research in Eastern Mediterranean Angers Cyprus and Greece," *Ahval*, January 3, 2019, https://ahvalnews.com/eastern-mediterranean/increased-turkish-seismic-research-eastern-mediterranean-angers-cyprus-and.

30. "Turkish Ships Escort Research Vessel to Avoid Greek Harassment," *Ahval*, December 10, 2018, https://ahvalnews.com/turkish-navy/turkish-ships-escort-research-vessel-avoid-greek-harassment-pro-govt-daily; Daren Butler and Angeliki Koutantou, "Turkey Extends East Med Survey, Greece Calls It an 'Illegal Move,'" *Reuters*, October 24, 2018, https://www.reuters.com/article/turkey-greece-ship/turkey-extends-east-med-survey-greece-calls-it-an-illegal-move-idUSKBN27A07B; Jamie Prentis, "US Condemns Turkey's Redeployment of Survey Ship Oruc Reis to Eastern Mediterranean," October 13, 2020, https://www.thenationalnews.com/world/europe/us-condemns-turkey-s-redeployment-of-survey-ship-oruc-reis-to-eastern-mediterranean-1.1092851; "Turkish Navy Orders Israeli Ship Out of Cyprus's Waters," *Aljazeera*, December 15, 2019, https://www.aljazeera.com/economy/2019/12/15/turkish-navy-orders-israeli-ship-out-of-cypruss-waters; "Eastern Mediterranean: Turkey Must Immediately End Illegal Drilling Activities," Aktuelles Europäisches Parlament, September 17, 2020, https://www.europarl.europa.eu/news/de/press-room/20200910IPR86828/eastern-mediterranean-turkey-must-immediately-end-illegal-drilling-activities.

31. Galip Dalay, "Turkey, Europe, and the Eastern Mediterranean: Charting a Way Out of the Current Deadlock," Brookings Institution, January 28, 2021, https://www.brookings.edu/articles/turkey-europe-and-the-eastern-mediterranean-charting-a-way-out-of-the-current-deadlock/.

32. "Turkey and Libya Sign Deal on Maritime Zones in the Mediterranean," *Reuters*, November 28, 2019, https://www.reuters.com/article/turkey-libya/turkey-and-libya-sign-deal-on-maritime-zones-in-the-mediterranean-idUSL8N2880W2.

33. "Turkey Flexes Muscle as Greece and EU Stick to International Law," *Aljazeera*, December 13, 2019, https://www.aljazeera.com/economy/2019/12/13/turkey-flexes-muscle-as-greece-and-eu-stick-to-international-law/.

34. Luke Baker, Tuvan Gumrukcu, and Michele Kambas, "Turkey-Libya Maritime Deal Rattles East Mediterranean," *Reuters*, December 25, 2019, https://www.reuters.com/article/us-turkey-libya-eastmed-tensions-explain/turkey-libya-maritime-deal-rattles-east-mediterranean-idUSKBN1YT0JK.

35. Pack and Pusztai, "Turning the Tide: How Turkey Won the War for Tripoli," pp. 5–6.

36. Hani Amara and Ulf Laessing, "Mortar Bombs Land on Tripoli Suburb as Two-Week Battle Rages On," *Reuters*, April 18, 2019, https://www.reuters.com/article/us-libya-security/mortar-bombs-land-on-tripoli-suburb-as-two-week-battle-rages-on-idUSKCN1RU11D.

37. Pack and Pusztai, "Turning the Tide: How Turkey Won the War for Tripoli," pp. 10–11.

38. Ibid., p. 12.

39. "Libya's UN-Recognised Government Announces Immediate Ceasefire," *Aljazeera*, August 22, 2020, https://www.aljazeera.com/news/2020/8/22/libyas-un-recognised-government-announces-immediate-ceasefire.

40. "Agreement for a Complete and Permanent Ceasefire in Libya (Unofficial Translation)," United Nations Support Mission in Libya, signed October 23, 2020, https://unsmil.unmissions.org/sites/default/files/ceasefire_agreement_between_libyan_parties_english.pdf.

41. Pack and Pusztai, "Turning the Tide: How Turkey Won the War for Tripoli," pp. 8–9, 11–13.

Chapter 13

1. David M. Halbfinger, David E. Sanger, and Ronen Bergman, "Israel Says Secret Files Detail Iran's Nuclear Subterfuge," *New York Times*, April 30, 2018, https://www.nytimes.com/2018/04/30/world/middleeast/israel-iran-nuclear-netanyahu.html.
2. Bolton, *The Room Where It Happened*, pp. 65–66.
3. Ibid., pp. 69–74, passim.
4. Michael R. Pompeo, "After the Deal: A New Iran Strategy," The Heritage Foundation, May 21, 2018, https://www.heritage.org/defense/event/after-the-deal-new-iran-strategy.
5. Ibid.
6. Ibid.
7. "Zarif Responds to Pompeo's Demands," Iran Primer, United States Institute of Peace, June 21, 2018, https://iranprimer.usip.org/blog/2018/jun/21/zarif-responds-pompeo%E2%80%99s-demands.
8. Tamer El-Ghobashy and Mustafa Salim, "U.S. Sanctions on Iran Hit an Unintended Target: Ordinary Iraqis," *Washington Post*, August 14, 2018, https://www.washingtonpost.com/world/us-sanctions-on-iran-hit-an-unintended-target-ordinary-iraqis/2018/08/13/fd72d22c-9e67-11e8-b562-1db4209bd992_story.html; Ahmed Twaij, "U.S. Sanctions on Iran Will Harm Iraq," *Foreign Policy*, December 21, 2018, https://foreignpolicy.com/2018/12/21/u-s-sanctions-on-iran-will-harm-iraq/
9. Mohammed Tawfeeq, "US Will Reduce Troop Levels in Iraq, Baghdad Says," *CNN*, February 6, 2018, https://www.cnn.com/2018/02/06/middleeast/american-troops-iraq-intl/index.html.
10. Ahmad Majidyar, "Iran-Backed Iraqi Militias Step Up Threat of Violence against US Forces in Iraq," Middle East Institute, February 7, 2018, https://www.mei.edu/publications/iran-backed-iraqi-militias-step-threat-violence-against-us-forces-iraq.
11. "Republic of Iraq," Election Guide, May 12, 2018, https://www.electionguide.org/elections/id/3060/.
12. Qassim Abdul-Zahra, "Iraqi Protesters Set Fire to Iran Consulate in Southern City," *Associated Press*, September 7, 2018, https://apnews.com/article/7bf62e4259464e90818cc8cf27915e69.
13. Isabel Coles and Ali Nabhan, "Rockets Fired toward U.S. Diplomatic Missions in Iraq," *Wall Street Journal*, September 8, 2018.
14. Bolton, *The Room Where It Happened*, pp. 194–96.
15. Thomas Gibbons-Neff, "How a 4-Hour Battle between Russian Mercenaries and U.S. Commandos Unfolded in Syria," *New York Times*, May 24, 2018, https://www.nytimes.com/2018/05/24/world/middleeast/american-commandos-russian-mercenaries-syria.html.
16. "Israeli Missiles Hit Military Post Near Damascus: Syrian State TV," *Reuters*, December 2, 2017, https://www.reuters.com/article/us-mideast-crisis-syria-attack/israeli-missiles-hit-military-post-near-damascus-syrian-state-tv-idUSKBN1DW081.
17. Judah Ari Gross, "IDF Says It Has Bombed over 200 Iranian Targets in Syria since 2017," *Times of Israel*, September 4, 2018, https://www.timesofisrael.com/idf-says-it-has-carried-out-over-200-strikes-in-syria-since-2017/
18. "Jangandeh moqabel-e pahpad: payami mohem baraay-e esra'il dar jonub-e suriyeh," ["Fighter jet Versus Drone: An Important Message for Israel in Southern Syria"], *Fars News*, February 10, 2018, https://www.farsnews.ir/news/13961121001445/.
19. Judah Ari Gross, "IDF: F-16 Appears to Have Been Downed by Shrapnel," *Times of Israel*, February 11, 2018, https://www.timesofisrael.com/idf-f-16-appears-to-have-been-downed-by-shrapnel/.
20. U.S. Department of the Treasury, "Treasury Designates the IRGC under Terrorism Authority and Targets IRGC and Military Supporters under Counter-Proliferation Authority," October 13, 2017, https://www.treasury.gov/press-center/press-releases/Pages/sm0177.aspx.
21. Mohammad Ali Shabani, "Protests in Iran Unlikely to Bring about Change," *Al-Monitor*, December 29, 2017, https://www.al-monitor.com/originals/2017/12/iran-protests-change-unlikely-mashhad-inflation-high-prices.html.
22. Thomas Erdbrink, "Scattered Protests Erupt in Iran over Economic Woes," *New York Times*, December 29, 2017, https://www.nytimes.com/2017/12/29/world/middleeast/scattered-protests-erupt-in-iran-over-economic-woes.html; and Marwa Eltagouri, "Tens of Thousands

of People Have Protested in Iran. Here's Why," *Washington Post*, January 3, 2019, https://www.washingtonpost.com/news/worldviews/wp/2018/01/03/tens-of-thousands-of-peo ple-protested-in-iran-this-week-heres-why/.

23. Saeid Golkar, "Protests and Regime Suppression in Post-Revolutionary Iran," Washington Institute for Near East Policy, Policy Notes 85, 2020, pp. 11–13.

24. "Six Charts That Show How Hard US Sanctions Have Hit Iran," *BBC News*, December 9, 2019, https://www.bbc.com/news/world-middle-east-48119109.

25. "'Maximum Pressure': US Economic Sanctions Harm Iranians' Right to Health," Human Rights Watch, October 29, 2019, https://www.hrw.org/report/2019/10/29/maximum-pressure/us-economic-sanctions-harm-iranians-right-health.

26. "Special Report: Iran's Leader Ordered Crackdown on Unrest: 'Do Whatever It Takes to End It,'" *Reuters*, December 23, 2019, https://www.reuters.com/article/us-iran-protests-specia lreport/special-report-irans-leader-ordered-crackdown-on-unrest-do-whatever-it-takes-to-end-it-idUSKBN1YR0QR.

27. Golkar, "Protests and Regime Suppression in Post-Revolutionary Iran," pp. 12–13.

28. Farnaz Fassihi and Rick Gladstone, "With Brutal Crackdown, Iran Is Convulsed by Worst Unrest in 40 Years," *New York Times*, December 1, 2019, https://www.nytimes.com/2019/12/01/world/middleeast/iran-protests-deaths.html.

29. "Special Report: Iran's Leader Ordered Crackdown on Unrest."

30. "Iran News: Iranian President Hassan Rouhani Announces Partial Withdrawal from 2015 Nuclear Deal," *CBS News*, May 8, 2019, https://www.cbsnews.com/news/nuclear-deal-iran-announces-partial-withdrawal-2015-pact/.

31. Ivana Kottasová, "Iran to Breach Uranium Enrichment Limits Set by Landmark Nuclear Deal," *CNN*, July 7, 2019, https://edition.cnn.com/2019/07/07/middleeast/iran-nuclear-agreement-intl/index.html.

32. David E. Sanger and Richard Pérez-Peña, "Iran Adds Advanced Centrifuges, Further Weakening Nuclear Deal," *New York Times*, November 4, 2019, https://www.nytimes.com/2019/11/04/world/middleeast/iran-nuclear-centrifuges-uranium.html; and Erin Cunningham, "Iran Takes New Step Away from Nuclear Deal by Activating Sensitive Enrichment Facility," *Washington Post*, November 5, 2019, https://www.washingtonpost.com/world/iran-takes-new-step-away-from-nuclear-deal-by-activating-sensitive-fordow-enrichment-facility/2019/11/05/f334d17e-ff9c-11e9-9518-1e76abc088b6_story.html.

33. Vivian Yee, "Claim of Attacks on 4 Oil Vessels Raises Tensions in Middle East," *New York Times*, May 13, 2019, https://www.nytimes.com/2019/05/13/world/middleeast/saudi-ara bia-oil-tanker-sabotage.html.

34. Barbara Starr, Devan Cole, Eliza Mackintosh, and Michelle Kosinski, "US Releases Video It Claims Shows Iran Removing Unexploded Mine from Gulf Tanker," *CNN*, June 14, 2019, https://www.cnn.com/2019/06/13/politics/us-images-iranian-boat-removing-mine/index.html.

35. "Strait of Hormuz: US Confirms Drone Shot Down by Iran," *BBC News*, June 20, 2019, https://www.bbc.com/news/world-middle-east-48700965.

36. Peter Baker, Eric Schmitt, and Michael Crowley, "An Abrupt Move That Stunned Aides: Inside Trump's Aborted Attack on Iran," *New York Times*, September 21, 2019, https://www.nyti mes.com/2019/09/21/us/politics/trump-iran-decision.html.

37. Bolton, *The Room Where It Happened*, pp. 398–400.

38. Ibid., p. 401.

39. Baker, Schmitt, and Crowley, "An Abrupt Move That Stunned Aides: Inside Trump's Aborted Attack on Iran." Bolton suggests that Trump's decision to abandon strike plans occurred almost two and a half hours before their scheduled commencement; *The Room Where It Happened*, p. 402–3.

40. Bill Chappell, "Trump Says He Called Off Strike on Iran Because He Didn't See It as 'Proportionate,'" *NPR*, June 21, 2019, https://www.npr.org/2019/06/21/734683701/trump-reportedly-orders-strike-on-iran-then-calls-off-attack-plan.

41. Bolton, *The Room Where It Happened*, pp. 403–4, 408.

42. Natasha Turak, "How Saudi Arabia Failed to Protect Itself from Drone and Missile Attacks despite Billions Spent on Defense Systems," *CNBC*, September 19, 2019, https://www.

cnbc.com/2019/09/19/how-saudi-arabia-failed-to-protect-itself-from-drones-missile-atta cks.html.

43. Michael Safi and Julian Borger, "How Did Oil Attack Breach Saudi Defences and What Will Happen Next?," *The Guardian*, September 18, 2019, https://www.theguardian.com/world/ 2019/sep/19/how-did-attack-breach-saudi-defences-and-what-will-happen-next.

44. Frederick W. Kagan, "Attribution, Intent, and Response in the Abqaiq Attack," *Critical Threats*, September 25, 2019, https://www.criticalthreats.org/analysis/attribution-intent-and-respo nse-in-the-abqaiq-attack.

45. "Timeline: Houthis' Drone and Missile Attacks on Saudi Targets," *Aljazeera*, September 14, 2019, https://www.aljazeera.com/news/2019/9/14/timeline-houthis-drone-and-missile- attacks-on-saudi-targets.

46. Kareem Fahim, Carol Morello, and John Wagner, "Pompeo Calls Attacks on Saudi Oil Facilities 'Act of War' as Trump Orders Increase in Sanctions on Iran," *Washington Post*, September 18, 2019, https://www.washingtonpost.com/world/middle_east/iran-warns- us-of-broad-retaliation-in-case-of-any-attack/2019/09/18/35a1275c-d99f-11e9-a1a5-162 b8a9c9ca2_story.html.

47. Humeyra Pamuk, "U.S. probe of Saudi Oil attack shows it came from north – report," *Reuters*, December 19, 2019, https://www.reuters.com/article/idUSL1N28T04F/.

48. Patrick Wintour and Julian Borger, "Saudi Offers 'Proof' of Iran's Role in Oil Attack and Urges US Response," *The Guardian*, September 18, 2019, https://www.theguardian.com/world/ 2019/sep/18/saudi-oil-attack-rouhani-dismisses-us-claims-of-iran-role-as-slander; and Tim Michetti, "Expediting Evidence of Iranian Attacks: The Aramco Case," Washington Institute of Near East Policy, Policy Watch 3244, January 21, 2020, https://www.washingtoninstitute. org/policy-analysis/expediting-evidence-iranian-attacks-aramco-case.

49. "Special Report: 'Time to Take Out Our Swords'—Inside Iran's Plot to Attack Saudi Arabia," *Reuters*, November 25, 2019, https://www.reuters.com/article/us-saudi-aramco-attacks- iran-special-rep/special-reporttime-to-take-out-our-swords-inside-irans-plot-to-attack- saudi-arabia-idUSKBN1XZ16H.

50. Wintour and Borger, "Saudi Offers 'Proof' of Iran's Role in Oil Attack and Urges US Response."

51. Julian Borger and Martin Chulov, "Trump Says US Response to Oil Attack Depends on Saudi Arabia's Assessment," *The Guardian*, September 16, 2019, https://www.theguardian.com/ world/2019/sep/16/iran-trump-saudi-arabia-oil-attack-assessment-latest

52. Elisha Fieldstadt, "U.S. Contractor Whose Killing in Iraq Was Cited by Trump Was Linguist with 2 Young Sons," *NBC News*, January 8, 2020, https://www.nbcnews.com/news/us- news/u-s-contractor-whose-killing-iraq-was-cited-trump-was-n1112266.

53. "Pompeo Hits Out at Iran after Deadly US Strikes in Iraq and Syria," *The Guardian*, December 29, 2019, https://www.theguardian.com/us-news/2019/dec/29/us-military-carries-out- defensive-strikes-in-iraq-and-syria.

54. Mustafa Salim and Liz Sly, "Militia Supporters Chanting 'Death to America' Break into U.S. Embassy Compound in Baghdad," *Washington Post*, December 31, 2019, https://www.was hingtonpost.com/world/iran-backed-militia-supporters-converge-on-us-embassy-in-bagh dad-shouting-death-to-america/2019/12/31/93f050b2-2bb1-11ea-bffe-020c88b3f120_st ory.html.

55. Alex Johnson, Abigail Williams, Mosheh Gains, and Dan De Luce, "U.S. Sends Hundreds of Troops to Mideast after Attack on Embassy Compound in Baghdad," *NBC News*, January 1, 2020, https://www.nbcnews.com/news/world/u-s-sending-hundreds-troops-mideast- after-attack-embassy-compound-n1109196.

56. https://twitter.com/Khamenei_fa/status/1212299106321870848.

57. Falih Hassan and Alissa J. Rubin, "Pro-Iranian Protesters End Siege of U.S. Embassy in Baghdad," *New York Times*, January 1, 2020, https://www.nytimes.com/2020/01/01/world/ middleeast/us-embassy-baghdad-iraq.html.

58. Eric Schmitt, Edward Wong, and Julian E. Barnes, "U.S. Unsuccessfully Tried Killing a Second Iranian Military Official," *New York Times*, January 10, 2020, https://www.nytimes.com/ 2020/01/10/world/middleeast/trump-iran-yemen.html.

59. Carol E. Lee and Courtney Kube, "Trump Authorized Soleimani's Killing 7 Months Ago, with Conditions," *NBC News*, January 13, 2020, https://www.nbcnews.com/politics/national-security/trump-authorized-soleimani-s-killing-7-months-ago-conditions-n1113271; and "Ex-Israeli Intel Chief Admits Role in Assassination of Iran's Qassem Soleimani," Haaretz, December 20, 2020, https://www.haaretz.com/israel-news/israeli-intel-chief-takes-respons ibility-for-assassination-of-iran-s-soleimani-1.10481220.

60. Jack Murphy and Zach Dorfman, "'Conspiracy Is Hard': Inside the Trump Administration's Secret Plan to Kill Qassem Soleimani," *Yahoo News*, May 8, 2021, https://news.yahoo.com/ conspiracy-is-hard-inside-the-trump-administrations-secret-plan-to-kill-qassem-soleimani-090058817.html; and Peter Baker, Ronen Bergman, David D. Kirkpatrick, Julian E. Barnes, and Alissa J. Rubin, "Seven Days in January: How Trump Pushed U.S. and Iran to the Brink of War," *New York Times*, January 11, 2020 (updated April 27, 2021), https://www.nytimes. com/2020/01/11/us/politics/iran-trump.html.

61. "Hajj Qasem Soleimani Had No Fear of Anyone or Anything in Performing His Duty for the Cause of God," *Khamenei.ir*, January 3, 2020, https://english.khamenei.ir/news/7274/Hajj-Qasem-Soleimani-had-no-fear-of-anyone-or-anything-in-performing.

62. Louisa Loveluck, "Iran Vows Revenge after U.S. Drone Strike Kills Elite Force Commander," *Washington Post*, January 3, 2020, https://www.washingtonpost.com/world/middle_east/ iran-vows-revenge-after-us-drone-strike-kills-elite-force-commander/2020/01/03/34512 7d6-2df4-11ea-bffe-020c88b3f120_story.html.

63. Baker, Bergman, Kirkpatrick, Barnes, and Rubin, "Seven Days in January: How Trump Pushed U.S. and Iran to the Brink of War"; and David Martin, "Inside the Attack That Almost Sent the U.S. to War with Iran," *CBS News*, August 8, 2021, https://www.cbsnews.com/news/iran-mis sle-strike-al-asad-airbase-60-minutes-2021-08-08/.

64. Michael Kaplan and Catherine Herridge, "Army to Award Purple Hearts to 50 Soldiers Injured in Iran Missile Attack Following CBS News Investigation," *CBS News*, December 20, 2021, https://www.cbsnews.com/news/purple-heart-iran-missile-attack-50-soldiers/.

65. "Yeksalegi-e amaliyat-e 'shahid-e solaymani': mushekbaran-e ayn'ul-assad keh jahan an ra tahsin kard" ["One year anniversary of Operation Martyr Soleimani: the missile attack admired by the world"], *Fars News*, January 8, 2021, https://www.farsnews.ir/news/1399101 9000321/.

66. "Iran Plane Crash: Tor-M1 Missiles Fired at Ukraine Jet," *BBC News*, January 21, 2020, https:// www.bbc.com/news/world-middle-east-51189779.

67. Libby Cathey, Lauren Lantry, and Morgan Winsor, "Trump Addresses Nation, De-escalates Crisis over Iran's Missile Attacks," *ABC News*, January 8, 2020, https://abcnews.go.com/ International/irans-supreme-leader-missile-attacks-slap-face-us/story?id=68138516.

68. Tara Sepehri Far, "Iran's Cover-up of Plane Crash Compounded Its Trouble in the Streets," *The Hill*, January 24, 2020, https://thehill.com/opinion/international/479324-irans-cover-up-of-plane-crash-compounded-its-trouble-in-the-streets.

69. Ashley Burke and Nahayat Tizhoosh, "Secret Recording Suggests Iranian Official Concedes Truth about Downing of Flight PS752 May Never Be Revealed," *CBC News*, February 10, 2021, https://www.cbc.ca/news/politics/audio-recording-iran-minister-foreign-affairs-fli ght-ps752-1.5906538.

70. Mark MacKinnon and Steven Chase, "Ukraine Now Says It Believes Iran Intentionally Shot Down Flight 752," *Globe and Mail*, April 15, 2021, https://www.theglobeandmail. com/world/article-ukraine-now-says-it-believes-iran-intentionally-shot-down-flight-752/; Ashley Burke and Nahayat Tizhoosh, "Iran Intentionally Shot Down Flight PS752 in 'an Act of Terrorism,' Ontario Court Rules," *CBC News*, May 20, 2021, https://www.cbc.ca/news/ politics/flightps752-private-lawsuit-against-iran-alleging-terrorist-activity-1.6034581; and Government of Canada, "The Downing of Ukraine International Airlines Flight 752: Factual Analysis," June 24, 2021, https://www.international.gc.ca/gac-amc/publications/flight-vol-ps752/factual_analysis-analyse_faits.aspx?lang=eng.

71. "Sardar hajizadeh: eqtedar va ta'sir-e shahid-e haj qasem soleimani dar montaqeh-ye emrooz bish az gozashteh ast" ["Sardar Hajizadeh: the power and influence of the martyr Haj Qassem Soleimani is greater today in the region than ever"], *IRNA*, December 31, 2021, https://www. irna.ir/news/84597250/.

Chapter 14

1. "Senior Official: Israel Is Weakening Iran at Home," *Times of Israel*, February 7, 2022, https://www.timesofisrael.com/liveblog_entry/senior-official-israel-is-weakening-iran-at-home/.
2. "Gas Explosion at Iran Medical Clinic Kills 19," *The Guardian*, June 30, 2020, https://www.theguardian.com/world/2020/jul/01/tehran-gas-explosion-at-iran-medical-clinic-kills-19.
3. David E. Sanger, Ronen Bergman, and Farnaz Fassihi, "After Iranian Missile Facility Blows Up, Conspiracy Theories Abound in Tehran," *New York Times*, June 29, 2020, https://www.nytimes.com/2020/06/29/world/middleeast/iran-missile-explosion.html.
4. Farnaz Fassihi, Richard Pérez-Peña, and Ronen Bergman, "Iran Admits Serious Damage to Natanz Nuclear Site, Setting Back Program," *New York Times*, July 5, 2020, https://www.nytimes.com/2020/07/05/world/middleeast/iran-Natanz-nuclear-damage.html.
5. Jake Wallis Simons, "Exclusive: Mossad Recruited Top Iranian Scientists to Blow Up Key Nuclear Facility," *Jewish Chronicle*, December 2, 2021, https://www.thejc.com/news/world/exclusive-mossad-recruited-top-iranian-scientists-to-blow-up-key-nuclear-facility-1.523163.
6. "Iran Natanz Nuclear Site Suffered Major Damage, Official Says," *BBC News*, April 13, 2021, https://www.bbc.com/news/world-middle-east-56734657.
7. Ronen Bergman and Farnaz Fassihi, "The Scientist and the A.I.-Assisted, Remote-Control Killing Machine," *New York Times*, September 18, 2021, https://www.nytimes.com/2021/09/18/world/middleeast/iran-nuclear-fakhrizadeh-assassination-israel.html.
8. Golnaz Esfandiari, "Remote-Control Killing: Iran Says Top Nuclear Scientist Assassinated by Machine Gun Guided via Satellite," *RFERL*, December 7, 2020, https://www.rferl.org/a/iran-nuclear-scientist-remote-control-killing-fakhrizadeh/30988770.html.
9. Jake Wallis Simons, "Truth behind Killing of Iran Scientist," *Jewish Chronicle*, February 10, 2021, https://www.thejc.com/news/world/world-exclusive-truth-behind-killing-of-iran-nuclear-scientist-mohsen-fakhrizadeh-revealed-1.511653.
10. Bergman and Fassihi, "The Scientist and the A.I.-Assisted, Remote-Control Killing Machine."
11. Simons, "Truth behind Killing of Iran Scientist."
12. "Iran Launches Advanced Uranium Enriching Machines to Mark Nuclear Day," *Reuters*, April 10, 2021, https://www.reuters.com/world/middle-east/iran-launches-advanced-uranium-enriching-machines-mark-nuclear-day-2021-04-10/.
13. Francois Murphy, John Irish, Arshad Mohammed, and Humeyra Pamuk, "U.S., Iran Clash on Sanctions; U.S. Sees Possible 'Impasse,'" *Reuters*, April 9, 2021, https://www.reuters.com/world/middle-east/chinese-envoy-says-iran-talks-resume-next-week-2021-04-09/.
14. "Iran Natanz Nuclear Site Suffered Major Damage, Official Says."
15. Patrick Kingsley, David E. Sanger, and Farnaz Fassihi, "After Nuclear Site Blackout, Thunder from Iran, and Silence from U.S.," *New York Times*, April 12, 2021 (updated April 27, 2021), https://www.nytimes.com/2021/04/12/world/middleeast/iran-israel-nuclear-site.html.
16. Simons, "Exclusive: Mossad Recruited Top Iranian Scientists to Blow Up Key Nuclear Facility."
17. Gordon Lubold, Benoit Faucon, and Felicia Schwartz, "Israeli Strikes Target Iranian Oil Bound for Syria," *Wall Street Journal*, March 11, 2021, https://www.wsj.com/articles/israel-strikes-target-iranian-oil-bound-for-syria-11615492789; and "Iranian Investigator Claims Israel behind Attack on Cargo Ship in Mediterranean," *Times of Israel*, March 13, 2021, https://www.timesofisrael.com/iranian-investigator-claims-israel-behind-attack-on-cargo-ship-in-mediterranean/.
18. Farnaz Fassihi, Eric Schmitt, and Ronen Bergman, "Israel-Iran Sea Skirmishes Escalate as Mine Damages Iranian Military Ship," *New York Times*, April 6, 2021, https://www.nytimes.com/2021/04/06/world/middleeast/israel-iran-ship-mine-attack.html.
19. Scott Neuman, "Explosion Damages Israeli-Owned Ship in Gulf of Oman," *NPR*, February 26, 2021, https://www.npr.org/2021/02/26/971854484/explosion-damages-israeli-owned-ship-in-gulf-of-oman.
20. Lazar Berman, "Iran Blamed as Israeli-Owned Ship Said Hit by Missile Near Oman," *Times of Israel*, March 25, 2021, https://www.timesofisrael.com/israeli-owned-ship-said-hit-by-missile-near-oman-iran-blamed/; and Emanuel Fabian, "UAE-Bound Vessel, Previously Israeli-Owned, Attacked in Indian Ocean," *Times of Israel*, July 3, 2021, https://www.timesofisrael.com/israeli-owned-vessel-bound-for-uae-said-struck-in-indian-ocean/.

21. Anna Ahronheim, "Iran Blamed as Two Killed in Strike on Israeli-Managed Ship," *Jerusalem Post*, July 31, 2021, https://www.jpost.com/breaking-news/israeli-ship-attacked-in-gulf-of-oman-report-675389; and Tzvi Joffre, "Hezbollah, Iranian Militia Commanders Killed in Syria," *Jerusalem Post*, July 25, 2021, https://www.jpost.com/middle-east/hezbollah-iranian-militia-commanders-killed-in-syria-674808.

22. Mona El-Naggar, "Gaza's Rockets: A Replenished Arsenal That Vexes Israel," *New York Times*, May 13, 2021, https://www.nytimes.com/2021/05/13/world/middleeast/gaza-rockets-hamas-israel.html; and "Rockets Target Tel Aviv after Gaza Tower Destroyed," *BBC News*, May 11, 2021, https://www.bbc.com/news/world-middle-east-57066275.

23. Seth J. Frantzman, "Iron Dome Intercepts Drone during Combat for First Time, Says Israeli Military," *Defense News*, May 17, 2021, https://www.defensenews.com/unmanned/2021/05/17/iron-dome-intercepts-drone-during-combat-for-first-time-says-israeli-military/.

24. Judah Ari Gross, "Netanyahu: Drone Downed by IDF This Week Was Armed, Launched by Iran," *Times of Israel*, May 20, 2021, https://www.timesofisrael.com/netanyahu-drone-downed-by-idf-this-week-was-armed-launched-by-iran/.

25. Patrick Wintour, "Blast at Iranian Complex Housing Drone Factory Injures Nine," *The Guardian*, May 23, 2021, https://www.theguardian.com/world/2021/may/23/blast-at-iran-factory-as-israel-accuses-state-of-providing-drones-to-hamas.

26. Erin Cunningham and Antonia Noori Farzan, "Why Both Israel and Hamas Are Claiming Victory," *Washington Post*, May 21, 2021, https://www.washingtonpost.com/world/2021/05/21/hamas-israel-gaza-war-victory/; Fares Akram and Joseph Krauss, "Gaza War Has Ended for Now, but Who Really Won This Round?," *Christian Science Monitor*, May 21, 2021, https://www.csmonitor.com/World/Middle-East/2021/0521/Gaza-war-has-ended-for-now-but-who-really-won-this-round; and Efraim Inbar, "Who Won the 2021 Gaza War?," Jerusalem Institute for Security and Strategy, May 21, 2021, https://jiss.org.il/en/inbar-who-won-the-2021-gaza-war/.

27. "Israeli Strikes on Gaza in May Killed up to Ten Times as Many Civilians as Lengthy Syria Campaign," *Airwars*, December 9, 2021, https://airwars.org/news-and-investigations/gaza-israel-syria-ewipa-report/.

28. "U.N. Agency Says 52,000 Displaced in Gaza, Amnesty Wants War Crimes Investigation," *Reuters*, May 18, 2021, https://www.reuters.com/world/middle-east/more-than-52000-palestinians-displaced-gaza-un-aid-agency-2021-05-18/

29. Fabian Hinz, "Missile Multinational: Iran's New Approach to Missile Proliferation," International Institute for Strategic Studies, April 2021, pp. 3–5; and Dion Nissenbaum, Sune Engel Rasmussen, and Benoit Faucon, "With Iranian Help, Hamas Builds 'Made in Gaza' Rockets and Drones to Target Israel," *Wall Street Journal*, May 20, 2021, https://www.wsj.com/articles/with-iranian-help-hamas-builds-made-in-gaza-rockets-and-drones-to-target-israel-11621535346.

30. Nidal Al-Mughrabi and Dan Williams, "Silos and Saturation Salvoes: Gaza Rockets Bedevil Israel," *Reuters*, May 19, 2021, https://www.reuters.com/world/middle-east/silos-saturation-salvoes-gaza-rockets-bedevil-israel-2021-05-19/; see also Fabian Hinz, "Iran Transfers Rockets to Palestinian Groups," Wilson Center, May 19, 2021, https://www.wilsoncenter.org/article/irans-rockets-palestinian-groups.

Chapter 15

1. Trump later claimed that he had felt used by Netanyahu in the Soleimani operation, and had "expected Israel to play a more active role in the attack." See Barak Ravid, "Trump Felt Used on Soleimani Strike: 'Israel Did Not Do the Right Thing,'" *Axios*, December 15, 2021, https://www.axios.com/2021/12/15/trump-soleimani-strike-netanyahu-israel.

2. Raphael Ahren, "In First-Ever Op-Ed for Israeli Paper, UAE Diplomat Warns against Annexation," *Times of Israel*, June 12, 2020, https://www.timesofisrael.com/in-first-ever-op-ed-for-israeli-paper-uae-diplomat-warns-against-annexation/.

3. David M. Halbfinger, "Netanyahu Drops Troubled Annexation Plan for Diplomatic Gain," *New York Times*, August 13, 2020, https://www.nytimes.com/2020/08/13/world/middleeast/israel-uae-annexation.html.

4. Anne Gearan and Steve Hendrix, "Sudan and Israel Agree to Normalize Ties, the Third Such Accord since August," *Washington Post*, October 23, 2020, https://www.washingtonpost.com/world/middle_east/israel-sudan-peace-normalization-terrorism/2020/10/23/285f53e4-1548-11eb-a258-614acf2b906d_story.html; and "Sudan Signs Deal Normalising Ties with Israel, Agrees Aid Deal," *France24*, June 1, 2021, https://www.france24.com/en/live-news/20210106-sudan-signs-deal-normalising-ties-with-israel-agrees-aid-deal.

5. Steve Holland, "Morocco Joins Other Arab Nations Agreeing to Normalize Israel Ties," *Reuters*, December 10, 2020, https://www.reuters.com/article/israel-usa-morocco-int/morocco-joins-other-arab-nations-agreeing-to-normalize-israel-ties-idUSKBN28K2CW.

6. Felicia Schwartz and Summer Said, "Israel's Netanyahu, Saudi Crown Prince Hold First Known Meeting," *Wall Street Journal*, November 23, 2020, https://www.wsj.com/articles/israels-netanyahu-meets-saudi-crown-prince-hebrew-media-says-11606120497.

7. Barak Ravid and Alayna Treene, "The Only Trump Foreign Policy Biden Wants to Keep," *Axios*, December 6, 2020, https://www.axios.com/biden-trump-abraham-accords-israel-bahrain-uae-8d3d3658-0561-4faf-b11a-09cad13c6d5d.html.

8. Kareem Fahim and John Hudson, "Key U.S. Allies Ease Years-Long Feud as Saudi Arabia Lifts Blockade of Qatar," *Washington Post*, January 4, 2021, https://www.washingtonpost.com/world/middle_east/saudi-arabia-qatar-gcc-feud/2021/01/04/709dda8a-4ebf-11eb-a1f5-fdaf28cfca90_story.html.

9. Mohammed Alsulami, "Where to Now for Saudi-Iranian Dialogue?," Middle East Institute, October 21, 2021, https://www.mei.edu/publications/where-now-saudi-iranian-dialogue; and "Iran Suspends Scheduled Round of Talks with Saudi Arabia—Report," *The Guardian*, March 13, 2022, https://www.theguardian.com/world/2022/mar/12/iraq-to-host-new-round-of-talks-between-iran-and-saudi-arabia.

10. Liz Sly and Sarah Dadouch, "Arab Outreach to Assad Raises Syrian Hopes of a Return to the Fold," *Washington Post*, November 18, 2021, https://www.washingtonpost.com/world/middle_east/syria-assad-uae-arab-relations/2021/11/17/0c837d9a-4624-11ec-beca-3cc7103bd814_story.html.

11. Eric Schmitt and Helene Cooper, "Lone ISIS Bomber Carried Out Attack at Kabul Airport, Pentagon Says," *New York Times*, February 4, 2022, https://www.nytimes.com/2022/02/04/us/politics/kabul-airport-attack-report.html.

12. Matthieu Aikins, Christoph Koettl, Evan Hill, Eric Schmitt, Ainara Tiefenthäler, and Drew Jordan, "Times Investigation: In U.S. Drone Strike, Evidence Suggests No ISIS Bomb," *New York Times*, September 10, 2021, https://www.nytimes.com/2021/09/10/world/asia/us-air-strike-drone-kabul-afghanistan-isis.html.

13. "Turkey, UAE Sign Agreements on Trade, Industry during Erdoğan Visit," *Reuters*, February 14, 2022, https://www.reuters.com/world/middle-east/turkeys-erdogan-visits-uae-first-time-decade-2022-02-14/.

14. Isabel Kershner and Safak Timur, "Israel's President Visits Turkey in Sign of Thawing Relations," *New York Times*, March 9, 2022, https://www.nytimes.com/2022/03/09/world/middleeast/israel-isaac-herzog-turkey-visit.html.

15. Cora Engelbrecht and Safak Timur, "Saudi Leader Visits Turkey, Moving to Mend Rift over Journalist's Murder," *New York Times*, June 22, 2022, https://www.nytimes.com/2022/06/22/world/middleeast/saudi-prince-mbs-erdogan-turkey.html.

16. Farnaz Fassihi and Steven Lee Myers, "China, with $400 Billion Iran Deal, Could Deepen Influence in Mideast," *New York Times*, March 27, 2021, https://www.nytimes.com/2021/03/27/world/middleeast/china-iran-deal.html.

17. Camille Lons (project editor), Jonathan Fulton, Degang Sun, and Naser Al-Tamimi, "China's Great Game in the Middle East," European Council on Foreign Relations, October 21, 2019, https://ecfr.eu/publication/china_great_game_middle_east/.

18. Nicole Bayat Grajewski, "Iran and the SCO: The Quest for Legitimacy and Regime Preservation," *Middle East Policy* 30, no. 2 (June 2023): 38–61.

19. William Figueroa, "China and Iran since the 25-Year Agreement: The Limits of Cooperation," *The Diplomat*, January 17, 2022, https://thediplomat.com/2022/01/china-and-iran-since-the-25-year-agreement-the-limits-of-cooperation/.

20. "Time Running Out to Revive Iran Nuclear Deal," *MSNBC*, February 4, 2022, https://www.msnbc.com/ayman-peacock/watch/time-running-out-to-revive-iran-nuclear-deal-132486725650.

21. Ian Talley, "Clandestine Finance System Helped Iran Withstand Sanctions Crush, Documents Show," *Wall Street Journal*, March 18, 2022, https://www.wsj.com/articles/clandestine-finance-system-helped-iran-withstand-sanctions-crush-documents-show-11647609741.

22. Bill Chappell and Colin Dwyer, "Trump Administration Moves to Brand Houthis in Yemen a Terrorist Group," *NPR*, January 11, 2021, https://www.npr.org/2021/01/11/936627548/trump-administration-moves-to-brand-houthis-in-yemen-a-terrorist-group.

23. John Hudson and Missy Ryan, "Biden Administration to Remove Yemen's Houthi Rebels from Terrorism List in Reversal of Trump-Era Policy," *Washington Post*, February 6, 2021, https://www.washingtonpost.com/national-security/biden-yemen-rebels-terrorist-list/2021/02/05/e65e55c8-5b40-11eb-aaad-93988621dd28_story.html.

24. "Houthi Projectile Kills Two in Saudi City of Jazan—Saudi State Media," *Reuters*, December 25, 2021, https://www.reuters.com/world/middle-east/saudi-led-coalition-says-hostile-projectile-hits-jazan-state-media-2021-12-24/; and "Yemen Houthis Attack Saudi Energy Facilities, Refinery Output Hit," *Reuters*, March 20, 2022, https://www.reuters.com/world/middle-east/saudi-led-coalition-says-four-houthi-attacks-hit-targets-kingdom-no-casualties-2022-03-19/.

25. Phil Stewart, "Exclusive: U.S. to Help UAE Replenish Missile Defense Interceptors after Houthi Attacks," *Reuters*, February 10, 2022, https://www.reuters.com/world/middle-east/exclusive-us-help-uae-replenish-missile-defense-interceptors-after-houthi-2022-02-10/; and Anthony Capaccio, "Lockheed's Thaad Anti-Missile System Makes Combat Debut in UAE," *Bloomberg*, February 3, 2022, https://www.bloomberg.com/news/articles/2022-02-03/lockheed-s-thaad-systems-gets-first-combat-use-in-uae-attack.

26. Karoun Demirjian, "U.S. Looks to Build on Security Guarantees to UAE after Houthi Missile Attacks," *Washington Post*, February 6, 2022, https://www.washingtonpost.com/national-security/2022/02/06/houthi-attacks-uae-pentagon/.

27. Farnaz Fassihi, Ronen Bergman, and Eric Schmitt, "Iran's Attack Was Response to Secret Israeli Attack on Drone Site," *New York Times*, March 16, 2022, https://www.nytimes.com/2022/03/16/world/middleeast/iran-israel-attack-drone-site.html.

28. Michael R. Gordon and David S. Cloud, "U.S. Held Secret Meeting with Israeli, Arab Military Chiefs to Counter Iran Air Threat," *Wall Street Journal*, June 26, 2022, https://www.wsj.com/articles/u-s-held-secret-meeting-with-israeli-arab-military-chiefs-to-counter-iran-air-threat-11656235802.

29. Patrick Kingsley and Lara Jakes, "Israeli Summit Mixes Historic Symbolism with Sharp Disputes," *New York Times*, March 28, 2022, https://www.nytimes.com/2022/03/28/world/middleeast/arab-israeli-summit.html.

30. Julia Shapero, "Russia Surpasses Iran to Become World's Most Sanctioned Country," *Axios*, March 7, 2022, https://www.axios.com/2022/03/08/russia-most-sanctioned-country.

31. "General Assembly Resolution Demands End to Russian Offensive in Ukraine," *UN News*, March 2, 2022, https://news.un.org/en/story/2022/03/1113152; and "UN Resolution against Ukraine Invasion: Full Text," *Aljazeera*, March 3, 2022, https://www.aljazeera.com/news/2022/3/3/unga-resolution-against-ukraine-invasion-full-text.

32. Dion Nissenbaum, Stephen Kalin, and David S. Cloud, "Saudi, Emirati Leaders Decline Calls with Biden during Ukraine Crisis," *Wall Street Journal*, March 8, 2022, https://www.wsj.com/articles/saudi-emirati-leaders-decline-calls-with-biden-during-ukraine-crisis-11646779430.

33. Summer Said and Stephen Kalin, "Saudi Arabia Considers Accepting Yuan Instead of Dollars for Chinese Oil Sales," *Wall Street Journal*, March 15, 2022, https://www.wsj.com/articles/saudi-arabia-considers-accepting-yuan-instead-of-dollars-for-chinese-oil-sales-11647351541.

34. Daniel R. DePetris, "Biden's Visit to Saudi Arabia Is the Right Thing to Do, Even if It Feels Wrong," *NBC News*, July 15, 2022, https://www.nbcnews.com/think/opinion/joe-biden-visits-saudi-arabia-bow-reality-rcna38419; Alex Emmons, Aída Chávez, and Akela Lacy, "Joe Biden, in Departure from Obama Policy, Says He Would Make Saudi Arabia a 'Pariah,'" *The Intercept*, November 20, 2019, https://theintercept.com/2019/11/21/democratic-debate-joe-biden-saudi-arabia/.

35. "Assessing the Saudi Government's Role in the Killing of Jama Khashoggi," Office of the Director of National Intelligence, February 11, 2021 (declassified on February 25, 2021).

36. David E. Sanger, "Biden Won't Penalize Saudi Crown Prince over Khashoggi's Killing, Fearing Relations Breach," *New York Times*, February 26, 2021, https://www.nytimes.com/2021/02/26/us/politics/biden-mbs-khashoggi.html; and Julian E. Barnes and David E. Sanger, "Saudi Crown Prince Is Held Responsible for Khashoggi Killing in U.S. Report," *New York Times*, February 26, 2021, https://www.nytimes.com/2021/02/26/us/politics/jamal-khashoggi-killing-cia-report.html.

37. "Timeline on the Progress of the Truce Implementation," Office of the Special Envoy of the Secretary-General for Yemen, https://osesgy.unmissions.org/timeline-progress-truce-imp lementation; and Ben Hubbard, "Yemen's Warring Parties Begin First Cease-Fire in 6 Years," *New York Times*, April 2, 2022, https://www.nytimes.com/2022/04/02/world/middleeast/yemen-cease-fire.html.

38. Summer Said and Stephen Kalin, "Saudi Arabia Pushed Yemen's Elected President to Step Aside, Saudi and Yemeni Officials Say," *Wall Street Journal*, April 17, 2022, https://www.wsj.com/articles/saudi-arabia-pushed-yemens-elected-president-to-step-aside-saudi-and-yem eni-officials-say-11650224802; and Gregory D. Johnsen, "The Growing Battle for South Yemen," The Arab Gulf States Institute in Washington, July 18, 2023, https://agsiw.org/the-growing-battle-for-south-yemen/.

39. Cora Engelbrecht and Safak Timur, "Saudi Leader Visits Turkey, Moving to Mend Rift over Journalist's Murder," June 22, 2022, https://www.nytimes.com/2022/06/22/world/mid dleeast/saudi-prince-mbs-erdogan-turkey.html.

40. Peter Baker and David E. Sanger, "Biden's Fraught Saudi Visit Garners Scathing Criticism and Modest Accords," *New York Times*, July 15, 2022, https://www.nytimes.com/2022/07/15/world/middleeast/biden-mbs-saudi-visit.html; and "Fact Sheet: Results of Bilateral Meeting between the United States and the Kingdom of Saudi Arabia," The White House, July 15, 2022, https://www.whitehouse.gov/briefing-room/statements-releases/2022/07/15/fact-sheet-results-of-bilateral-meeting-between-the-united-states-and-the-kingdom-of-saudi-arabia/.

41. "Remarks by President Biden at the GCC + 3 Summit Meeting," The White House, July 16, 2022, https://www.whitehouse.gov/briefing-room/speeches-remarks/2022/07/16/rema rks-by-president-biden-at-the-gcc-3-summit-meeting/.

42. Ibid.; and "Fact Sheet: The United States Strengthens Cooperation with Middle East Partners to Address 21st Century Challenges," The White House, July 16, 2022, https://www.whiteho use.gov/briefing-room/statements-releases/2022/07/16/fact-sheet-the-united-states-stre ngthens-cooperation-with-middle-east-partners-to-address-21st-century-challenges/.

43. Jenny Gross, "OPEC Plus Members Agree to a Small Increase in Oil Production," *New York Times*, August 3, 2022, https://www.nytimes.com/2022/08/03/business/energy-environm ent/opec-plus-meeting.html.

44. Summer Said, Benoit Faucon, Dion Nissenbaum, and Stephen Kalin, "Saudi Arabia Defied U.S. Warnings Ahead of OPEC+ Production Cut," *Wall Street Journal*, October 11, 2022, https://www.wsj.com/articles/saudi-arabia-defied-u-s-warnings-ahead-of-opec-product ion-cut-11665504230.

45. Natasha Turak, "Biden Administration Asked Saudi Arabia to Postpone OPEC Decision by a Month, Saudis Say," *CNBC*, October 13, 2022, https://www.cnbc.com/2022/10/13/biden-admin-asked-saudi-arabia-to-postpone-opec-cut-by-a-month-saudis-say.html.

46. "Chairman Menendez Statement on the Future of the United States—Saudi Relationship." October 10, 2022, https://www.menendez.senate.gov/newsroom/press/chairman-menen dez-statement-on-the-future-of-the-united-states-saudi-relationship.

47. Chuck Schumer, Twitter, October 6, 2022, https://twitter.com/SenSchumer/status/1578 142595795939330.

48. Zoë Richards, "Democratic Senator Seeks 'Freeze' on U.S.-Saudi Cooperation after OPEC Cuts Production," *NBC News*, October 10, 2022, https://www.nbcnews.com/politics/congr ess/democratic-senator-seeks-freeze-us-saudi-cooperation-opec-cuts-product-rcna51583.

49. Kevin Liptak, "Biden Says Putin 'Totally Miscalculated' by Invading Ukraine but Is a 'Rational Actor,'" *CNN*, October 11, 2022, https://www.cnn.com/2022/10/11/politics/joe-biden-interview-cnntv/index.html.

50. Bernard Haykel, "Why the Saudis Won't Pump More Oil," *Project Syndicate*, March 16, 2022, https://www.project-syndicate.org/commentary/saudi-arabia-oil-production-will-not-off set-russia-sanctions-by-bernard-haykel-2022-03.

51. "Joint Statement at the Conclusion of the Saudi-Chinese Summit," Saudi Press Agency, December 9, 2022, https://www.spa.gov.sa/2407997.

52. Grant Rumley et al., "Assessing Xi Jinping's Middle East Trip," Washington Institute for Near East Policy, Policy Watch 3687, December 22, 2022, https://www.washingtoninstitute.org/policy-analysis/assessing-xi-jinpings-middle-east-trip.

53. "Riyadh Arab-China Summit for Cooperation and Development Issues Final Communique," Saudi Press Agency, December 9, 2022, https://www.spa.gov.sa/viewfullstory.php?lang=en&newsid=2408273.

54. Nadeen Ebrahim, "China's Xi Gets a Grand Welcome to Saudi Arabia and Promises a 'New Era' in Chinese-Arab Relations," *CNN*, December 8, 2022, https://www.cnn.com/2022/12/08/middleeast/china-xi-jinping-mbs-saudi-arabia-intl/index.html.

55. "Mossad Helped Foil 12 Attack Plots on Israelis in Turkey over Past 2 Years," *Times of Israel*, February 12, 2022, https://www.timesofisrael.com/liveblog_entry/mossad-helped-foil-12-attack-plots-on-israelis-in-turkey-over-past-2-years-tv/.

56. "Mossad Reportedly Interrogated IRGC Member in Iran over Triple Assassination Plot," *Times of Israel*, April 30, 2022, https://www.timesofisrael.com/mossad-agents-interrogated-irgc-member-in-iran-over-assassination-plot-reports/.

57. "Iranian Who Allegedly Confessed to Plotting Hit on Israeli Says He Was Coerced," *Times of Israel*, May 8, 2022, https://www.timesofisrael.com/iranian-who-allegedly-confessed-to-assassination-plot-says-he-was-coerced/.

58. "Shahid-e Hassan Sayyad Khoda'i, haya'ti va damad-e yek az pir-gholaman-e Hosayn bud" ["The martyr Hassan Sayyad Khoda'i was a representative and son-in-law of one of the most sincere servants of Imam Husayn"], *Fars News*, May 23, 2022, https://www.farsnews.ir/news/14010302000094/.

59. Farnaz Fassihi and Ronen Bergman, "Israel Tells U.S. It Killed Iranian Officer, Official Says," *New York Times*, May 25, 2022, https://www.nytimes.com/2022/05/25/world/middleeast/iran-israel-killing-khodayee.html; see also Dov Lieber, Dion Nissenbaum, and Benoit Faucon, "Iranian Officer Killed in Tehran Was Involved in Plot to Kill Israeli Diplomat, U.S. General," *Wall Street Journal*, May 26, 2022, https://www.wsj.com/articles/iranian-officer-killed-in-teh ran-was-involved-in-plot-to-kill-israeli-diplomat-u-s-general-people-familiar-with-matter-say-11653536259.

60. "Exclusive: IRGC Killed a Quds Force Colonel on Suspicion of Espionage—Sources," *Iran International*, June 3, 2022, https://www.iranintl.com/en/202206025112.

61. "Yeki az farmandehan-e speah-e qods dar karaj terur shod?" ["Was a Quds Force officer assassinated in Karaj?"], *Khabar Online*, June 3, 2022, https://www.khabaronline.ir/news/1637737; see also Golnaz Esfandiari, "Accident or Assassination? 'Suspicious' Death of Another IRGC Colonel Inside Iran Raises Eyebrows," *RFE/RL*, June 3, 2022, https://www.rferl.org/a/iran-death-irgc-colonel-raises-eyebrows/31882315.html.

62. Dion Nissenbaum, Dov Lieber, and Aresu Eqbali, "Israel Expands Operations against Iranian Nuclear, Military Assets," *Wall Street Journal*, June 20, 2022, https://www.wsj.com/articles/israel-expands-operations-against-iranian-nuclear-military-assets-11655726066.

63. Farnaz Fassihi and Ronen Bergman, "Sensitive Iranian Military Site Was Targeted in Attack," *New York Times*, May 27, 2022, https://www.nytimes.com/2022/05/27/world/middleeast/iran-drone-attack.html; and Isabel Debre, "Cyberattack Forces Iran Steel Company to Halt Production," *Associated Press*, June 27, 2022, https://apnews.com/article/technology-mid dle-east-iran-dubai-b0404963ae23e5008439a0b607952de1.

64. "Israel Tells Its Citizens to Avoid Istanbul, Warns Iran Not to Harm Them," *Reuters*, June 13, 2022, https://www.reuters.com/world/middle-east/israel-urges-its-citizens-istanbul-leave-heightening-travel-warning-2022-06-13/.

65. Suzan Fraser, "Israeli FM Thanks Turkey for Foiling Attacks on Israelis," *Associated Press*, June 23, 2022, https://apnews.com/article/middle-east-iran-israel-turkey-689b2558816292bbe c99c01655cbcb85.

66. Farnaz Fassihi and Ronen Bergman, "Israel's Spies Have Hit Iran Hard. In Tehran, Some Big Names Paid the Price," *New York Times*, June 29, 2022, https://www.nytimes.com/2022/06/29/world/middleeast/israel-iran-spy-chief.html.

67. "Sardar Mohammad Kazemi ra'is-e sazman-e ettela'at-e sepah shod" ["Sardar Mohammad Kazemi becomes IRGC intelligence chief"], *Tasnim News*, June 23, 2022, https://www.tasnimnews.com/fa/news/1401/04/02/2733202.

68. Sarah Dadouch, "U.S. Reports Drone Strikes on Tanf Base in Syria, No Casualties," *Washington Post*, August 15, 2022, https://www.washingtonpost.com/world/2022/08/15/syria-tanf-drone-strike-us-base/; and Kanishka Singh, "U.S. Says a Drone Attack Targeted Its Syria Base, No Casualties," *Reuters*, August 15, 2022, https://www.reuters.com/world/middle-east/us-says-drone-attack-targeted-its-syria-base-no-casualties-2022-08-15/.

69. Michael Knights, "Kataib Hezbollah's Role in the August 15 al-Tanf Attack," Washington Institute for Near East Policy, August 25, 2022, https://www.washingtoninstitute.org/policy-analysis/kataib-hezbollahs-role-august-15-al-tanf-attack; and Shelly Kittleson, "Iran-Linked Attacks on US Forces in Syria Rekindle Iraq Border Concerns," *Al-Monitor*, August 26, 2022, https://www.al-monitor.com/originals/2022/08/iran-linked-attacks-us-forces-syria-rekindle-iraq-border-concerns.

70. Lara Seligman and Andrew Desiderio, "U.S. Strikes Back at Iran-Backed Groups in Syria as Skirmishes Intensify," *Politico*, August 24, 2022, https://www.politico.com/news/2022/08/24/iran-syria-rocket-irgc-00053663.

71. Jared Malsin, "U.S. Helicopter Gunships Hit Iran-Backed Militia in Syria," *Wall Street Journal*, August 25, 2022, https://www.wsj.com/articles/u-s-helicopter-gunships-hit-iran-backed-militia-in-syria-11661433894.

72. Karen DeYoung, "U.S. Responds to Iran's Latest Demands on Reviving Nuclear Deal," *Washington Post*, August 24, 2022, https://www.washingtonpost.com/national-security/2022/08/24/iran-nuclear-deal-biden-administration/.

73. Lahav Harkov, "Iran Deal Only Good for Israel if It Comes with Credible US Military Threat—Lapid," *Jerusalem Post*, August 28, 2022, https://www.jpost.com/middle-east/iran-news/article-715764.

74. "Gantz to Sullivan: US Needs Iran Strike Option on the Table Even if There Is a Deal," *Jerusalem Post*, August 27, 2022, https://www.jpost.com/middle-east/iran-news/article-715671.

75. Dov Lieber and Laurence Norman, "U.S., Iran Edge toward Nuclear Deal as Israel Warns It Cedes Too Much to Tehran," *Wall Street Journal*, August 24, 2022, https://www.wsj.com/articles/u-s-iran-edge-toward-nuclear-deal-as-israel-warns-it-cedes-too-much-to-tehran-11661352794.

76. Dion Nissenbaum, "Iran Has Begun Training Russia to Use Its Advanced Drones, U.S. Says," *Wall Street Journal*, August 10, 2022, https://www.wsj.com/articles/iran-has-begun-training-russia-to-use-its-advanced-drones-u-s-says-11660135921.

77. "Iran Acknowledges Sending Drones to Russia for First Time," *Associated Press*, November 5, 2022, https://www.yahoo.com/news/iran-acknowledges-sending-drones-russia-082803338.html.

78. Natasha Bertrand, "Exclusive: Iranian Drones Appear to Contain Modified Explosives Designed for Maximum Damage to Ukrainian Infrastructure, Report Finds," *CNN*, February 9, 2023, https://www.cnn.com/2023/02/09/politics/iranian-drones-modified-explosives-ukraine-infrastructure/index.html.

79. "On-the-Record Press Gaggle by NSC Coordinator for Strategic Communications John Kirby," The White House, October 20, 2022, https://www.whitehouse.gov/briefing-room/speeches-remarks/2022/10/20/on-the-record-press-gaggle-by-nsc-coordinator-for-strategic-communications-john-kirby/.

80. Julian Borger, "Iranian Advisers Killed Aiding Russians in Crimea, Says Kyiv," *The Guardian*, November 24, 2022, https://www.theguardian.com/world/2022/nov/24/iranian-military-advisers-killed-aiding-moscow-in-crimea-kyiv.

81. "Russia Signs Military Cooperation Deal with Iran," *Agence France-Presse*, January 20, 2015, https://www.defensenews.com/home/2015/01/20/russia-signs-military-cooperation-deal-with-iran/; and Aref Bijan, "20-Year Cooperation Treaty between Iran and Russia: Bilateral

Strategic Partnership or Disappointing Agreement," Russian International Affairs Council, July 22, 2021, https://russiancouncil.ru/en/blogs/abijan/20year-cooperation-treaty-betw een-iran-and-russia-bilateral-strategic-/.

82. "Iran to Purchase Sukhoi Su-35 from Russia: Report," *Tehran Times*, September 4, 2022, https://www.tehrantimes.com/news/476406/Iran-to-purchase-Sukhoi-Su-35-from-Rus sia-report; and "Iran to Receive Russian Sukhoi Su-35 Jets in Spring: MP," *Tasnim News Agency*, January 15, 2023, https://www.tasnimnews.com/en/news/2023/01/15/2837209/ iran-to-receive-russian-sukhoi-su-35-jets-in-spring-mp.

83. Christoph Koettl, "In Satellite Images and Video, Hidden Clues about an Iranian Air Force Upgrade," *New York Times*, February 17, 2023, https://www.nytimes.com/2023/02/17/ world/iran-air-force-base-jets.html.

84. Dion Nissenbaum and Warren P. Strobel, "Moscow, Tehran Advance Plans for Iranian-Designed Drone Facility in Russia," *Wall Street Journal*, February 5, 2023, https://www.wsj. com/articles/moscow-tehran-advance-plans-for-iranian-designed-drone-facility-in-russia-11675609087.

85. Akhtar Safi, "Security Forces in Violent Crackdown as Protests Grow across Kurdistan," *Iran Wire*, October 13, 2022, https://iranwire.com/en/politics/108558-security-forces-in-viol ent-crackdown-as-protests-grow-across-kurdistan/; "Iran: 'Bloody Friday' Crackdown This Year's Deadliest," Human Rights Watch, December 22, 2022, https://www.hrw.org/news/ 2022/12/22/iran-bloody-friday-crackdown-years-deadliest; and Golnaz Esfandiari, Elahe Ravanshad, Rasool Mohammadi, and Roozbeh Bolhari, "Iran's Kurdish Region Becomes Epicenter of Protests, Deadly Government Crackdown," *RFE/RL*, October 13, 2022, https:// www.rferl.org/a/iran-protests-kurdish-crackdown/32081052.html.

86. Sune Engel Rasmussen, "Iran's Deadly Street Protests Are Replaced by Quiet Acts of Rebellion," *Wall Street Journal*, January 31, 2023, https://www.wsj.com/articles/iran-prote sts-hijab-11675177547.

87. "Iran: EU Imposes Further Restrictive Measures against 32 Individuals and Two Entities Responsible for Human Rights Violations," Council of the European Union, Press Release, February 20, 2023, https://www.consilium.europa.eu/en/press/press-releases/2023/02/ 20/iran-eu-imposes-further-restrictive-measures-against-32-individuals-and-two-entities-responsible-for-human-rights-violations/; and Andrew England, George Parker, and Jasmine Cameron-Chileshe, "UK Weighs Designating Iran's Revolutionary Guards a Terrorist Organization," *Financial Times*, January 16, 2022, https://www.ft.com/content/f9710887-131e-423f-bf9f-c125a756b353.

88. Barak Ravid, "U.S. 'Not Going to Waste Time' on Iran Deal Right Now, Official Says," *Axios*, October 31, 2022, https://www.axios.com/2022/10/31/iran-nuclear-deal-talks-biden.

89. Barak Ravid and Hans Nichols, "Biden in Newly Surfaced Video: Iran Nuclear Deal Is 'Dead,'" *Axios*, December 20, 2022, https://www.axios.com/2022/12/20/biden-iran-nucl ear-deal-dead-video.

90. Stephanie Liechtenstein, "UN Report: Uranium Particles Enriched to 83.7% Found in Iran," *Washington Post*, February 28, 2023, https://www.washingtonpost.com/world/alleged-hig her-iran-enrichment-worries-germany-israel/2023/02/28/1b2bc93c-b771-11ed-b0df-8ca 14de679ad_story.html.

Chapter 16

1. See the official statement released by Saudi Arabia, Iran, and China marking the successful conclusion of talks: "Joint Trilateral Statement by the People's Republic of China, the Kingdom of Saudi Arabia, and the Islamic Republic of Iran," Ministry of Foreign Affairs of the People's Republic of China, March 10, 2023, https://www.fmprc.gov.cn/eng/wjdt_665 385/2649_665393/202303/t20230311_11039241.html; see also Peter Baker, "Chinese-Brokered Deal Upends Mideast Diplomacy and Challenges U.S.," *New York Times*, March 11, 2023, https://www.nytimes.com/2023/03/11/us/politics/saudi-arabia-iran-china-biden. html.

2. Summer Said, Stephen Kalin, and Benoit Faucon, "China Plans New Middle East Summit as Diplomatic Role Takes Shape," *Wall Street Journal*, March 12, 2023, https://www.wsj.com/

articles/china-plans-summit-of-persian-gulf-arab-and-iranian-leaders-as-new-middle-east-role-takes-shape-357cfd7e.

3. "Joz'iyyat-e goftogu-ye iran va 'arabestan az zaban-e amir 'abdollahian" ["Details of the discussion between Iran and Saudi Arabia in the words of Amir-Abdollahian"], *Tasnim*, April 17, 2023, https://www.tasnimnews.com/fa/news/1402/01/17/2876181; and Rachna Uppal and Aziz El Yaakoubi, "Saudi Arabia Could Invest in Iran 'Very Quickly' after Agreement—Minister," *Reuters*, March 15, 2023, https://www.reuters.com/world/middle-east/saudi-inv estment-iran-could-happen-very-quickly-after-agreement-minister-2023-03-15/.

4. "United Arab Emirates Reinstates Ambassador to Iran after Six-Year Absence," *Agence France-Presse*, August 21, 2022, https://www.theguardian.com/world/2022/aug/22/united-arab-emirates-reinstates-ambassador-to-iran-after-six-year-absence.

5. Edward Yeranian, "Iran Resumes Diplomatic Relations with UAE and Kuwait, Talks Continue with Saudi Arabia," *Voice of America*, August 23, 2022, https://www.voanews.com/a/iran-resumes-diplomatic-relations-with-uae-and-kuwait-talks-continue-with-saudi-arabia/6713 647.html; and "Bahrain, Iran Likely to Restore Diplomatic Ties Soon, US Diplomat Says," *Reuters*, June 13, 2023, https://www.reuters.com/world/middle-east/bahrain-iran-likely-restore-diplomatic-ties-soon-us-diplomat-2023-06-13/.

6. "Goftogu ba safir-e mo 'in-e iran dar 'arabestan: tavafoq-e iran va 'arabestan moqaddameh-e nazm-e jadid-e montaqeh-e khalij-e fars ast, niru-haye khraji bayad beravand" ["An interview with the ambassador-designate of Iran in Saudi Arabia: the agreement between Iran and Saudi Arabia presages a new order in the Persian Gulf / foreign forces must depart"], *Tasnim*, July 31, 2023, https://www.tasnimnews.com/fa/news/1402/05/09/2928823.

7. Benoit Faucon, "Iran Tried to Seize Two Oil Tankers Near Strait of Hormuz, U.S. Navy Says," *Wall Street Journal*, July 6, 2023, https://www.wsj.com/articles/iran-tried-to-seize-two-oil-tankers-near-strait-of-hormuz-u-s-navy-says-4be301e1.

8. Benoit Faucon and Dion Nissenbaum, "U.S. Pressured to Secure Persian Gulf after Iran Seizes Tankers," *Wall Street Journal*, May 30, 2023, https://www.wsj.com/articles/u-s-pressured-to-secure-persian-gulf-after-iran-seizes-tankers-7bab70cb.

9. Benoit Faucon and Dion Nissenbaum, "U.A.E. Says It Exited U.S.-Led Naval Force," *Wall Street Journal*, May 31, 2023, https://www.wsj.com/articles/u-a-e-says-it-exited-u-s-led-naval-force-fdbe23c9.

10. Sam LaGrone, "U.S. Sending Marines, More Warships to Middle East over Iranian Threats," *USNI News*, July 20, 2023, https://news.usni.org/2023/07/20/u-s-sending-marines-more-warships-to-middle-east-over-iranian-threats; and Chris Gordon, "F-16s Join A-10s to Deter Iran from Seizing Oil Tankers," *Air & Space Forces Magazine*, July 16, 2023, https://www.airandspaceforces.com/f-16s-a-10s-deter-iranian-sezuires-oil-tankers/.

11. Ruth Margalit, "Itamar Ben-Gvir, Israel's Minister of Chaos," *The New Yorker*, February 20, 2023, https://www.newyorker.com/magazine/2023/02/27/itamar-ben-gvir-israels-minis ter-of-chaos.

12. For example, see the press release from Virginian Democrat Gerry Connolly: "Connolly Statement on House Passage of H. Res. 31," April 25, 2023, https://connolly.house.gov/news/documentsingle.aspx?DocumentID=4745.

13. Gianluca Mezzofiore, Celine Alkhaldi, Abeer Salman, and Nima Elbagir, "Israel's Military Called the Settler Attack on This Palestinian Town a 'Pogrom.' Videos Show Soldiers Did Little to Stop It," *CNN*, June 15, 2023, https://www.cnn.com/2023/06/15/middleeast/huw ara-west-bank-settler-attack-cmd-intl/index.html.

14. Tovah Lazaroff, "US: Smotrich's Comment about Wiping Out Huwara Is Disgusting," *Jerusalem Post*, March 1, 2023, https://www.jpost.com/arab-israeli-conflict/article-733091.

15. Yonah Jeremy Bob, "Two Rockets Fired at Israel from West Bank for First Time in 18 Years," *Jerusalem Post*, June 26, 2023, https://www.jpost.com/breaking-news/article-747738.

16. Barak Ravid, "Israeli Defense Minister Calls on Bibi to Stop Judicial Overhaul Legislation," *Axios*, March 25, 2023, https://www.axios.com/2023/03/25/israel-judicial-overhaul-gall ant-national-security-threat.

17. Patrick Kingsley and Isabel Kershner, "Huge Protest March Reaches Jerusalem after 5-Day Trek from Tel Aviv," *New York Times*, July 22, 2023, https://www.nytimes.com/2023/07/22/world/middleeast/jerusalem-protest-march-israel.html.

18. "Readout of President Joe Biden's Call with Prime Minister Benjamin Netanyahu of Israel," The White House, July 17, 2023, https://www.whitehouse.gov/briefing-room/statements-releases/2023/07/17/readout-of-president-joe-bidens-call-with-prime-minister-benjamin-netanyahu-of-israel-2/.

19. Isabel Kershner, Aaron Boxerman, and Richard Pérez-Peña, "Protests Intensify Despite Offer to Delay Broader Judicial Overhaul," New York Times, July 24, 2023, https://www.nytimes.com/live/2023/07/24/world/israel-protests-vote#israel-judiciary-reasonableness-netanyahu.

20. "Esra'il va tars-e nadidan-e hashtadsalegi" ["Israel and the Fear of Not Reaching 80 Years"], Khamenei.ir, July 9, 2023, https://farsi.khamenei.ir/speech-content?id=53319; see also "Ezterab-e shahrakneshinan-e sahyunisti az shelik-e mushak-haye moqavemat" ["Zionist settlers panic as the resistance's rockets fire"], Tasnim, July 13, 2023, https://www.tasnimnews.com/fa/news/1402/04/22/2925241.

21. Sune Engel Rasmussen and Benoit Faucon, "Weapons Flood West Bank, Fueling Fears of New War Front with Israel," Wall Street Journal, October 25, 2023, https://www.wsj.com/world/middle-east/iran-weapons-west-bank-israel-war-8bf12d1f.

22. Peter Baker and Ronen Bergman, "Biden Presses Ahead with Effort to Broker Israeli-Saudi Rapprochement," New York Times, July 29, 2023, https://www.nytimes.com/2023/07/29/us/politics/biden-israel-saudi-arabia-negotiations.html.

23. "Statement of the Riyadh Summit for Cooperation and Development between the GCC and the People's Republic of China," The General Secretariat of the Cooperation Council for the Arab States of the Gulf, December 9, 2022, https://www.gcc-sg.org/ar-sa/MediaCenter/NewsCooperation/News/Pages/news2022-12-9-4.aspx.

24. Maziar Motemedi, "Iran Summons China Envoy over Islands Dispute Statement with UAE," Aljazeera, December 11, 2022, https://www.aljazeera.com/news/2022/12/11/iran-summons-china-envoy-over-disputed-islands-with.

25. Maziar Motemedi, "How Will Raisi's Beijing Visit Affect Iran-China Ties?," Aljazeera, February 18, 2023, https://www.aljazeera.com/news/2023/2/18/how-will-raisis-beijing-visit-impact-iran-china-ties.

26. "Joint Statement of the 6th Russia–GCC Joint Ministerial Meeting for Strategic Dialogue," The Ministry of Foreign Affairs of the Russian Federation, July 12, 2023, https://mid.ru/en/foreign_policy/rso/1896567/.

27. "Iran Summons Russian Envoy over Persian Gulf Islands," Tehran Times, July 12, 2023, https://www.tehrantimes.com/news/486796/Iran-summons-Russian-envoy-over-Persian-Gulf-islands.

28. "Vahedi: beh Sukhoi-haye jadid niyaz darim" ["Vahedi: We need the new Sukhois"], Tasnim, June 14, 2023, https://www.tasnimnews.com/fa/news/1402/03/12/2905134; see also Saeed Azimi, "Iran Paid for Su-35 Jets, but Russia Won't Deliver Them," Bourse & Bazaar, July 13, 2023, https://www.bourseandbazaar.com/articles/2023/7/13/iran-paid-for-su-35-jets-but-russia-wont-deliver-them.

29. "Duri-ye 'arabestan-e sa'udi az amrika ta koja edameh darad?" ["How long will Saudi Arabia's distancing from America continue?"], Tasnim, July 14, 2023, https://www.tasnimnews.com/fa/news/1402/04/23/2925308.

30. Shira Rubin and Loveday Morris, "How Hamas Broke through Israel's Border Defenses during Oct. 7 Attack," Washington Post, October 27, 2023, https://www.washingtonpost.com/world/2023/10/27/hamas-attack-israel-october-7-hostages/.

31. Ibid.; David Browne, Nancy Dillon, and Kory Grow, "'They Wanted to Dance in Peace. And They Got Slaughtered,'" Rolling Stone, October 15, 2023, https://www.rollingstone.com/music/music-features/hamas-israel-nova-music-festival-massacre-1234854306/; and Isabel Derbe and Michael Biesecker, "Israeli Survivors Recount Terror at Music Festival, Where Hamas Militants Killed at Least 260," Associated Press, October 9, 2023, https://apnews.com/article/israel-palestinians-gaza-hamas-music-festival-6a55aae2375944f10ecc4c52d05f2ffe.

32. Rubin and Morris, "How Hamas Broke through Israel's Border Defenses during Oct. 7 Attack."

33. Lauren Leatherby et al., "The Long Wait for Help as Massacres Unfolded in Israel," *New York Times*, October 11, 2023, https://www.nytimes.com/interactive/2023/10/11/world/middleeast/israel-gaza-hamas-attack-timeline.html.
34. "Resistance to Definitely Win in Al-Aqsa Storm Operation," *Mehr News Agency*, October 8, 2023, https://en.mehrnews.com/news/206890/Resistance-to-definitely-win-in-Al-Aqsa-Storm-operation; "Iran's Official Terms 'Al-Aqsa Storm' as Onset of Zionist Regime's Collapse," *IRNA*, October 8, 2023, https://en.irna.ir/news/85251463/Iran-s-official-terms-Al-Aqsa-Storm-as-onset-of-Zionist-regime-s; and Sayyid Mostafa Khoshcheshm, "Al-Aqsa Storm Operation: Zionist's Humiliating Defeat on All Levels," *Khamenei.ir*, October 23, 2023, https://english.khamenei.ir/news/10208/Al-Aqsa-Storm-Operation-Zionist-s-humiliating-defeat-on-all.
35. Summer Said, Benoit Faucon, and Stephen Kalin, "Iran Helped Plot Attack on Israel over Several Weeks," *Wall Street Journal*, October 28, 023, https://www.wsj.com/world/middle-east/iran-israel-hamas-strike-planning-bbe07b25; Farnaz Fassihi and Ronen Bergman, "Hamas Attack on Israel Brings New Scrutiny of Group's Ties to Iran," *New York Times*, October 13, 2023, https://www.nytimes.com/2023/10/13/world/middleeast/hamas-iran-israel-attack.html; Summer Said, Dov Lieber, and Benoit Faucon, "Hamas Fighters Trained in Iran before Oct. 7 Attacks," *Wall Street Journal*, October 25, 2023, https://www.wsj.com/world/middle-east/hamas-fighters-trained-in-iran-before-oct-7-attacks-e2a8dbb9; Paul Kirkby, "Israel Faces 'Long, Difficult War' after Hamas Attack from Gaza," *BBC News*, October 8, 2023, https://www.bbc.com/news/world-middle-east-67044182; Zachary Cohen, Katie Bo Lillis, Natasha Bertrand, and Jeremy Herb, "Initial US Intelligence Suggests Iran Was Surprised by the Hamas Attack on Israel," *CNN*, October 11, 2023, https://www.cnn.com/2023/10/11/politics/us-intelligence-iran-hamas-doubt/index.html; Dan De Luce and Ken Dilanian, "U.S. Intelligence Indicates Iranian Leaders Were Surprised by Hamas Attack," *NBC News*, October 11, 2023, https://www.nbcnews.com/news/investigations/us-intelligence-indicates-iranian-leaders-surprised-hamas-attack-rcna119946; Adam Entous, Julian E. Barnes, and Jonathan Swan, "Early Intelligence Shows Hamas Attack Surprised Iranian Leaders, U.S. Says," *New York Times*, October 11, 2023, https://www.nytimes.com/2023/10/11/us/politics/iran-israel-gaza-hamas-us-intelligence.html.
36. "Netanyahu: Can't Say for Certain if Iran Was Involved in Planning October 7 Attacks," *Times of Israel*, October 28, 2023, https://www.timesofisrael.com/liveblog_entry/netanyahu-cant-say-for-certain-if-iran-was-involved-in-planning-october-7-attacks/.
37. Steven Erlanger, "Israel Says It Will Destroy Hamas. But Who Will Govern Gaza?," *New York Times*, October 24, 2023, https://www.nytimes.com/2023/10/24/world/europe/israel-hamas-gaza-war.html.
38. "World Reaction to Surprise Attack by Palestinian Hamas on Israel," *Aljazeera*, October 7, 2023, https://www.aljazeera.com/news/2023/10/7/we-are-at-war-reactions-to-palestinian-hamas-surprise-attack-in-israel.
39. Sinan Ciddi, "Erdogan's Damning Response to the Hamas Attacks," *FDD*, October 22, 2023, https://www.fdd.org/analysis/2023/10/22/erdogans-damning-response-to-the-hamas-attacks/.
40. Barak Ravid and Laurin-Whitney Gottbrath, "Biden Warns Israel's Enemies against Taking Advantage of Fighting in Israel, Gaza," *Axios*, October 7, 2023, https://www.axios.com/2023/10/07/israel-gaza-hamas-war-biden-saudi-iran-qatar-reaction.
41. "Mapping Israel's War in Gaza," *The Economist*, October 17, 2023 (updated October 29, 2023), https://www.economist.com/interactive/briefing/2023/10/17/israel-gaza-map-hamas-war/.
42. Yaroslav Trofimov, Margherita Stancati, and Abu Bakr Bashir, "Palestinian Death Statistics, Doubted by the U.S., Remain a Subject of Controversy," *Wall Street Journal*, October 28, 2023, https://www.wsj.com/world/middle-east/palestinian-death-statistics-doubted-by-the-u-s-remain-a-subject-of-controversy-90ead302.
43. "Israeli Delegation Attends UNESCO Gathering in Saudi Arabia," *Reuters*, September 11, 2023, https://www.reuters.com/world/middle-east/israeli-delegation-attends-unesco-gathering-saudi-arabia-2023-09-11/.

44. "HRH Crown Prince Receives Phone Call from Iranian President," *Saudi Press Agency*, October 12, 2023, https://spa.gov.sa/en/N1978598.
45. Barak Ravid, "Scoop: Iran Warns Israel through UN against Ground Offensive in Gaza," *Axios*, October 14, 2023, https://www.axios.com/2023/10/14/iran-warning-israel-hezbol lah-hamas-war-gaza; and "Deep Dive: Armed Groups in Iraq, Yemen Warn US of Multi-Front Response to Gaza War," *Amwaj*, October 11, 2023, https://amwaj.media/article/deep-dive-armed-groups-in-iraq-yemen-warn-us-of-multi-front-response-to-gaza-war.
46. Maziar Motamedi, "Iran Warns Israel of Regional Escalation if Gaza Ground Offensive Launched," *Aljazeera*, October 15, 2023, https://www.aljazeera.com/news/2023/10/15/iran-warns-israel-of-regional-escalation-if-gaza-ground-offensive-launched.
47. Oren Liebermann, "Incident Involving US Warship Intercepting Missiles Near Yemen Lasted 9 Hours," *CNN*, October 20, 2023, https://www.cnn.com/2023/10/20/politics/us-wars hip-intercept-missiles-near-yemen/index.html.
48. Eric Bazail-Eimil, "Biden Warns of Response if Iran Attacks U.S. Troops," *Politico*, October 25, 2023, https://www.politico.com/news/2023/10/25/biden-iran-troops-attacks-00123 561; and Eleanor Watson, "U.S. Strikes Iranian-Backed Militias in Eastern Syria to Retaliate for Attacks on U.S. Troops," *CBS News*, October 26, 2023, https://www.cbsnews.com/news/u-s-strikes-iranian-backed-militias-eastern-syria-retaliation-attacks-on-u-s-troops/.
49. "Statement from Secretary of Defense Lloyd J. Austin III on Steps to Increase Force Posture," U.S. Department of Defense, October 21, 2023, https://www.defense.gov/News/Releases/Release/Article/3564874/statement-from-secretary-of-defense-lloyd-j-austin-iii-on-steps-to-increase-for/.
50. Bazail-Eimil, "Biden Warns of Response if Iran Attacks U.S. Troops."
51. "Secretary of Defense Lloyd J. Austin III's Statement on U.S. Military Strikes in Eastern Syria," U.S. Department of Defense, October 26, 2023, https://www.defense.gov/News/Releases/Release/Article/3570798/secretary-of-defense-lloyd-j-austin-iiis-statement-on-us-military-strikes-in-ea/.
52. Eric Schmitt and Helene Cooper, "Iran's Proxies Fire Back after U.S. Airstrikes," *New York Times*, October 27, 2023, https://www.nytimes.com/2023/10/27/us/politics/us-airstrikes-iran.html.
53. "Full Text of Iranian Foreign Minister Hossein Amirabdollahian's Speech at the UN General Assembly Meeting, New York," Islamic Republic of Iran Ministry of Foreign Affairs, October 26, 2023, https://en.mfa.ir/portal/newsview/732605/Full-text-of-Iranian-Foreign-Minis ter-Hossein-Amirabdollahians-speech-at-the-UN-General-Assembly-meeting-New-York.
54. Schmitt and Cooper, "Iran's Proxies Fire Back after U.S. Airstrikes."

INDEX

For the benefit of digital users, indexed terms that span two pages (e.g., 52–53) may, on occasion, appear on only one of those pages.

Figures are indicated by *f* following the page number